Core HTML5
2D Game Programming

Core HTML5
2D Game Programming

David Geary

PRENTICE
HALL

Upper Saddle River, NJ • Boston • Indianapolis • San Francisco
New York • Toronto • Montreal • London • Munich • Paris • Madrid
Capetown • Sydney • Tokyo • Singapore • Mexico City

Many of the designations used by manufacturers and sellers to distinguish their products are claimed as trademarks. Where those designations appear in this book, and the publisher was aware of a trademark claim, the designations have been printed with initial capital letters or in all capitals.

The author and publisher have taken care in the preparation of this book, but make no expressed or implied warranty of any kind and assume no responsibility for errors or omissions. No liability is assumed for incidental or consequential damages in connection with or arising out of the use of the information or programs contained herein.

For information about buying this title in bulk quantities, or for special sales opportunities (which may include electronic versions; custom cover designs; and content particular to your business, training goals, marketing focus, or branding interests), please contact our corporate sales department at corpsales@pearsoned.com or (800) 382–3419.

For government sales inquiries, please contact governmentsales@pearsoned.com.

For questions about sales outside the United States, please contact international@pearsoned.com.

Visit us on the Web: informit.com/ph

Library of Congress Cataloging-in-Publication Data

Geary, David M. (David Mark), 1957- author.
  Core HTML5 2D game programming / David Geary.
      pages   cm
  Includes index.
  ISBN 978-0-13-356424-2 (pbk. : alk. paper) — ISBN 0-13-356424-X (pbk. : alk. paper)
  1. HTML (Document markup language) 2. Computer games—Programming. 3.
Computer animation. I. Title.
  QA76.76.H94G43 2015
  006.7'4—dc23

                                                                        2014014836

ISBN-13: 978-0-13-356424-2
ISBN-10: 0-13-356424-X
Text printed in the United States on recycled paper at RR Donnelley in Crawfordsville, Indiana.
First printing, July 2014

Contents

Preface

This book is for experienced JavaScript developers who want to implement 2D games with HTML5. In this book, I chronicle the development of a sophisticated side-scroller platform video game, named Snail Bait, from scratch. I do not use any third-party graphics or game frameworks, so that you can learn to implement everything from smooth animations and exploding sprites to developer backdoors and in-game metrics, entirely on your own. If you do use a game framework, this book provides valuable insights into how they work.

Because it's meant for instructional purposes, Snail Bait has only a single level, but in all other respects it's a full-fledged, arcade-style game. Snail Bait simultaneously manipulates dozens of animated objects, known as *sprites*, on top of a scrolling background and simultaneously plays multiple sound effects layered over the game's soundtrack. The sprites run, jump, fly, sparkle, bounce, pace, explode, collide, shoot, land on platforms, and fall through the bottom of the game.

Snail Bait also implements many other features, such as a time system that can slow the game's overall time or speed it up; an animated loading screen; special effects, such as shaking the game when the main character loses a life; and particle systems that simulate smoke and fire. Snail Bait pauses the game when the game's window loses focus; and when the window regains focus, Snail Bait resumes with an animated countdown to give the user time to regain the controls.

Although it doesn't use game or graphics frameworks, Snail Bait uses Node.js and socket.io to send in-game metrics to a server, and to store and retrieve high scores, which the game displays with a heads-up display. Snail Bait shows a warning when the game runs too slowly, and if you type CTRL-d as the game runs, Snail Bait reveals a developer backdoor that gives you special powers, such as modifying the flow of time or displaying sprite collision rectangles, among other things.

Snail Bait detects when it runs on a mobile device and reconfigures itself by installing touch event handlers and resizing the game to fit snugly on the mobile device's screen.

In this book I show you how to implement all of Snail Bait's features step by step, so that you can implement similar features in your own games.

A Brief History of This Book

In 2010, I downloaded the graphics and sound from a popular open source Android game named *Replica Island*, and used them to implement a primitive version of Snail Bait on Android.

At that time, I became interested in HTML5 Canvas and I started working on my previous book, *Core HTML5 Canvas*. As I wrote the Canvas book, I continued to work on Snail Bait, converting it from Android's Java to the browser's JavaScript and the HTML5 canvas element. By the time that book was finished in 2012, I had a still primitive, but close to feature-complete, version of the game.

Later in 2012, I started writing a 10-article series for IBM developerWorks on game programming, based on Snail Bait. Over the course of the next ten months, I continued to work on the game as I wrote the articles. (See "Online Resources" below for a link to those articles.)

By summer 2013, Snail Bait had matured a great deal, so I put together a presentation covering Snail Bait's development and traveled to Sebastopol, California to shoot a 15-hour O'Reilly video titled "HTML5 2D Game Development." In some respects that video is the film version of this book. Although the video wasn't released until September, it was one of the top 10 bestselling O'Reilly videos for 2013. (The "Online Resources" below has a link to that video.)

When I returned home from Sebastopol in July 2013, I started writing this book full time. I started with the ten articles from the IBM developerWorks series, rewrote them as book chapters, and ultimately added ten more chapters. As I was writing, I constantly iterated over Snail Bait's code to make it as readable as possible.

In December 2013, with Chapters 1–19 written, I decided to add a final chapter on using the techniques in the book to implement a simpler video game. That game is Bodega's Revenge, and it's the subject of Chapter 20.

How to Use This Book

This book's premise is simple: It shows you how to implement a sophisticated video game so that you can implement one of your own.

There are several ways you can use this book. First, I've gone to great lengths to make it as skim-friendly as possible. The book contains lots of screenshots, code listings, and diagrams.

I make liberal use of Notes, Tips, Cautions, and Best Practices. Encapsulating those topics in callouts streamlines the book's main discussion, and since each Note, Tip, Caution, and Best Practice has a title (excluding callouts with a single line), you can decide at a glance whether those ancillary topics are pertinent to your situation. In general, the book's main discussion shows you how things work, whereas the callouts delve into why things work as they do. If you're in a hurry, you can quickly get to the bottom of how things work by sticking to the main discussion, skimming the callouts to make sure you're not missing anything important.

Chapters 1–19 of the book chronicle the development of Snail Bait, starting with a version of the game that simply displays graphics and ending with a full-featured HTML5 video game. Chapter 20 is the Epilogue, which uses much of what the book covered in the previous 19 chapters to implement a second video game.

If you plan to read the book, as opposed to using it solely as reference, you will most likely want to start reading at either Chapter 1 or Chapter 20. If you start at the beginning, Chapter 20 will be a recap and review of what you learned previously, in addition to providing new insights such as using polar coordinates and rotating coordinate systems.

If you start reading at Chapter 20, perhaps even just skimming the chapter, you can get an idea for what lies behind in the previous 19 chapters. If you start at Chapter 20, don't expect to understand a lot of what you read in that chapter the first time around.

I assume that many readers will want to use this book as a reference, so I've included references to section headings at the start of each chapter, in addition to a short discussion at the beginning of each chapter about what the chapter entails. That will help you locate topics. I've also included many step-by-step instructions on how to implement features so that you can follow those steps to implement similar features of your own.

The Book's Exercises

Passively reading a book won't turn anyone into a game programmer. You've got to get down in the trenches and sling some code to really learn how to implement games. To that end, each chapter in this book concludes with a set of exercises.

To perform the exercises, download the final version of Snail Bait and modify that code. In some cases, the exercises will instruct you to modify code for a chapter-specific version of the game. See the next section for more information about chapter-specific versions of Snail Bait.

Source Code and Chapter-specific Versions of Snail Bait

This book comes with the source to two video games. See "Online Resources" below for URLs to the games and their source code.

You will undoubtedly find it beneficial to refer to Snail Bait's source code as you read this book. You will find it more beneficial, however, to refer to the version of the game that corresponds to the chapter you are reading. For example, in the first chapter we implement a nascent version of Snail Bait that simply draws the background and the game's main character. That version of the game bears little resemblance to the final version, so referring to the final version of the game is of little use at that point. Instead, you can access the version of Snail Bait corresponding to the end of Chapter 1 at corehtml5games.com/book/code/ch01. URLs for each of the book's chapters follow the format corehtml5games.com/book/code/ch??, where ?? represents two digits corresponding to chapter numbers from 01 to 20, excluding Chapter 2.

As mentioned above, exercises at the end of each chapter correspond to the final version of Snail Bait, unless otherwise stated.

Prerequisites

No one would think of taking a creative writing class in a language they couldn't speak or write. Likewise, you must know JavaScript to implement sophisticated games with HTML5. JavaScript is a nonnegotiable prerequisite for this book.

Nearly all the code listings in this book are JavaScript, but you still need to know your way around HTML and CSS. You should also be familiar with computer graphics and have a good grasp of basic mathematics.

Your Game

Finally, let's talk about why we're here. I assume you're reading this book because you want to implement a game of your own.

The chapters of this book discuss individual aspects of game programming, such as implementing sprites or detecting collisions. Although they pertain to Snail Bait, you will be able to easily translate those aspects to your own game.

The order of the chapters, however, is also significant because it shows you how to implement a game from start to finish. In the beginning of the book, we gather raw materials, set up our development environment, and then start development by drawing the game's basic graphics. Subsequent chapters add animation, sprites, sprite behaviors, and so on. If you're starting a game from scratch, you may want to follow that same outline, so you can alternate between reading about features and implementing them on your own.

Before you get started coding in earnest, you should take the time to set up your development environment and become as familiar as you can with the browser's developer tools. You should also make sure you shorten your development cycle as discussed at the end of Chapter 2. The time you initially spend preparing will make you more productive later on.

Finally, thank you for buying this book. I can't wait to see the games you create!

David Geary
Fort Collins, Colorado
2014

Online Resources

Core HTML5 2D Game Programming's companion website: corehtml5games.com

Play Snail Bait: corehtml5games.com/snailbait

Play Bodega's Revenge: corehtml5games.com/bodegas-revenge

Download Snail Bait: corehtml5games.com/book/downloads/snailbait

Download Bodega's Revenge: corehtml5games.com/book/downloads/bodegas-revenge

David's "HTML5 2D Game Development" video from O'Reilly: shop.oreilly.com/product/0636920030737.do.

David's "HTML5 2D Game Development" series on IBM developerWorks: www.ibm.com/developerworks/java/library/j-html5-game1/index.html

A video of David speaking about HTML5 game programming at the Atlanta HTML5 Users Group in 2013: youtube.com/watch?v=S256vAqGY6c

Core HTML5 Canvas at http://amzn.to/1jfuf0C. Take a deep dive into Canvas with David's book.

Acknowledgments

I am fortunate to have a great editor—the only editor I've had in nearly twenty years of writing books—who is always receptive to my ideas for my next book and who guides my books from conception to completion. This book was no different. Greg Doench helped shepherd this book through the process from an idea to a finished book.

I'm also fortunate to have a wonderful copyeditor, Mary Lou Nohr. She has copyedited every one of my previous books, and she graciously agreed to smooth out my rough edges once again.

This is the second book that I've done with Alina Kirsanova, who's a wizardess at taking my PDFs and making them look super. Once again, Julie Nahil oversaw the production of the book and kept everything on track as we headed to the printer.

For every book I write, I select reviewers who I think will make the book much better than I ever could have alone. For this book, I had four excellent reviewers: Jim O'Hara, Timothy Harrington, Simon Sarris, and Willam Malone. Gintas Sanders also gave me permission to use his coins in Snail Bait and gave me some great critiques of the game.

When I shot the "HTML5 2D Game Development" video for O'Reilly, I taught a class in front of a live audience. One of the audience members asked great questions and came up with several insights. Jim O'Hara was one of my most conscientious reviewers and, as he did in class, provided lots of great questions and insights.

My editor, Greg Doench, put me in touch with Tim Harrington, who is a Senior Academic Applications Analyst at Devry University with a background in game development. Like Jim, Tim came up with lots of insights that made me rethink how I presented material.

I wanted to find a graphics expert for this book who knew a lot about game programming, and I found one. Simon Sarris, who, much to my delight, is not only both of those things, but is also an excellent writer. He made this book better in several different ways.

Finally, I was fortunate to have William Malone review this book. William is a professional game developer who's implemented games for *Sesame Street* (see Cookie Kart Racing at http://bit.ly/1nlSY3N). William made a tremendous difference in this book by pointing out many subtleties that would've escaped me, especially concerning mobile devices.

About the Author

David is the author of *Core HTML5 Canvas* and coauthor of *Core JavaServer Faces*. David has written several other bestselling books on client- and server-side Java, including one of the bestselling Java books of all time, *Graphic Java*.

CHAPTER **1**

Introduction

Topics in This Chapter

The great thing about software development is that you can make nearly anything you can imagine come to life on screen. Unencumbered by physical constraints that hamper engineers in other disciplines, software developers have long used graphics APIs and UI toolkits to implement creative and compelling applications. Arguably, the most creative genre of software development is game programming; few endeavors are more rewarding from a creative standpoint than making the vision you have for a game become a reality.

The great thing about game programming is that it's never been more accessible. With the advent of open source graphics, sound, and music, you no longer need to be an artist and a musician to implement games. And the development environments built into modern browsers are not only free, they contain all the tools you need to create the most sophisticated games. You need only supply programming prowess, a good understanding of basic math (mostly trigonometry), and a little physics.

In this book we implement two full-fledged HTML5 video games so that you can learn how to create one of your own. Here are some of the things you will learn to do:

- Use the browser's development tools to implement sophisticated games
- Create smooth, flicker-free animations
- Scroll backgrounds and use parallax to create a 3D effect
- Implement graphical objects, known as *sprites*, that you can draw and manipulate in a canvas
- Detect collisions between sprites
- Animate sprites to make them explode
- Implement a time system that controls the rate at which time flows through your game
- Use nonlinear motion to create realistic jumping
- Simulate gravity
- Pause and freeze your game
- Warn players when your game runs slowly
- Display scoreboards, controls, and high scores
- Create a developer's backdoor with special features
- Implement particle systems to simulate natural phenomenon, such as smoke and fire
- Store high scores and in-game metrics on a server with Node.js and socket.io
- Configure games to run on mobile devices

 NOTE: HTML5 technologies used in Snail Bait

This book discusses the implementation of an HTML5 video game, named Snail Bait, using the following HTML5 APIs, the most predominant of which is the Canvas 2D API:

- Canvas 2D API
- Timing Control for Script-based Animations
- Audio
- CSS3 Transitions

In this book we develop Snail Bait entirely from scratch, without any third-party game frameworks, so you can learn how to implement all the common aspects of a video game from the ground up. That knowledge will be invaluable whether you implement a game by using a framework or not.

The book's epilogue discusses the implementation of a second video game—Bodega's Revenge—that shows how to combine the concepts discussed in the book to implement a simpler video game.

NOTE: Play Snail Bait and Bodega's Revenge online

To get the most out of this book, you should play Snail Bait and Bodega's Revenge so you're familiar with the games. You can play Snail Bait online at corehtml5games.com/snailbait, and you can find Bodega's Revenge at corehtml5games.com/bodegas-revenge.

NOTE: Particle systems

A particle system uses many small particles that combine to simulate natural phenomena that do not have well-defined boundaries and edges. Snail Bait implements a particle system to simulate smoke, as you can see in Figure 1.1. We discuss particle systems in detail in Chapter 16.

1.1 Snail Bait

Snail Bait is a classic platform game. The game's main character, known as the runner, runs along and jumps between floating platforms that move horizontally. The runner's ultimate goal is to land on a gold button that paces back and forth on top of a pulsating platform at the end of the game. That button is guarded by two bees and a bomb-shooting snail. The runner, pulsating platform, gold button, bees, bomb, and snail are all shown in Figure 1.1.

The player controls the game with the keyboard:

- *d* or ← turns the runner to the left and scrolls the background from left to right.
- *k* or → turns the runner to the right and scrolls the background from right to left.
- *j* makes the runner jump.
- *p* pauses the game.

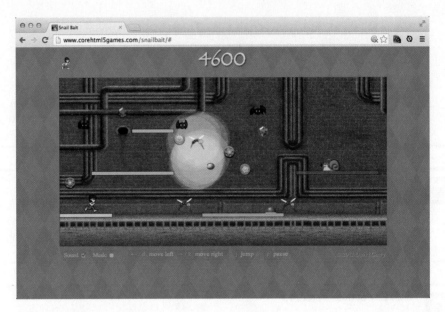

Figure 1.1 Snail Bait

When the game begins, the player has three lives. Icons representing the number of remaining lives are displayed above and to the left of the game's canvas, as you can see in Figure 1.1. In the runner's quest to make it to the end of the level, she must avoid bad guys—bees and bats—while trying to capture valuable items such as coins, rubies, and sapphires. If the runner collides with bad guys, she blows up, the player loses a life, and the runner goes back to the beginning of the level. When she collides with valuable items, the valuable item disappears, the score increases, and the game plays a pleasant sound effect.

The snail periodically shoots snail bombs (the gray ball shown near the center of Figure 1.1). The bombs, like bees and bats, blow up the runner when they hit her.

The game ends in one of two ways: the player loses all three lives, or the player lands on the gold button. If the player lands on the gold button, the player wins the game and Snail Bait shows the animation depicted in Figure 1.2.

Snail Bait maintains high scores on a server. If the player beats the existing high score, Snail Bait lets the player enter their name with a heads-up display (HUD), as shown in Figure 1.3.

Figure 1.2 Snail Bait's winning animation

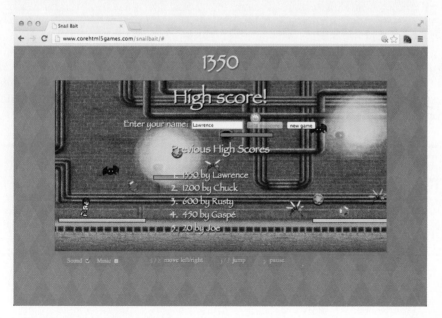

Figure 1.3 Snail Bait's high scores

If the player doesn't win the game or beat the existing high score, Snail Bait displays game credits, as shown in Figure 1.4.

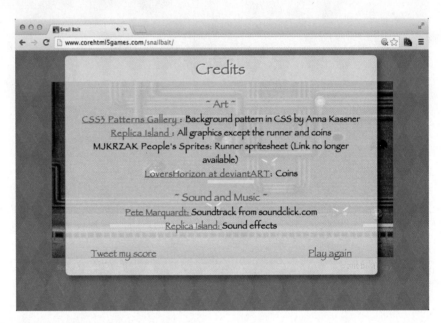

Figure 1.4 Snail Bait's credits

With the exception of the runner, everything in Snail Bait scrolls continuously in the horizontal direction. That scrolling further categorizes Snail Bait as a *side-scroller* platform game. However, that's not the only motion in the game, which leads us to sprites and their behaviors.

 NOTE: Platform video games

Donkey Kong, Mario Bros., Sonic the Hedgehog, and Braid are all well-known, best-selling games where players navigate 2D platforms, a genre known as platformers. At one time, platformers represented up to one-third of all video game sales. Today, their market share is drastically lower, but there are still many successful platform games.

CAUTION: Snail Bait performance

Hardware acceleration for Canvas makes a huge difference in performance and has been implemented by most browsers since the middle of 2012. Should you run Snail Bait in a browser that does not have hardware-accelerated Canvas, performance will be terrible and the game probably won't work correctly. When you play the game, make sure your browser has hardware-accelerated Canvas. Here is a list of browser versions that have hardware-accelerated Canvas:

- Chrome 13
- Firefox 4
- Internet Explorer 9
- Opera 11
- Safari 5

WASD?

By convention, computer games often use the w, a, s, and d keys to control play. That convention evolved primarily because it lets right-handed players use the mouse and keyboard simultaneously. It also leaves the right hand free to press the spacebar or modifier keys such as CTRL or ALT. Snail Bait doesn't use WASD because it doesn't receive input from the mouse or modifier keys. But you can easily modify the game's code to use any combination of keys.

1.1.1 Sprites: The Cast of Characters

With the exception of the background, everything in Snail Bait is a sprite. A sprite is a visual representation of an object in a game that you draw on the game's canvas. Sprites are not a part of the HTML5 Canvas API, but they are simple to implement. Following are the game's sprites:

- Platforms (inanimate objects)
- Runner (main character)
- Buttons (good)
- Coins (good)

- Rubies and sapphires (good)
- Bees and bats (bad)
- Snail (bad)
- Snail bombs (bad)

Besides scrolling horizontally, nearly all the game's sprites move independently of one another. For example, rubies and sapphires bounce up and down at varying rates of speed, and the buttons and the snail pace back and forth along the length of the platform on which they reside.

That independent motion is one of many sprite behaviors. Sprites can have other behaviors that have nothing to do with motion; for example, besides bouncing up and down, the rubies and sapphires sparkle.

Each sprite has an array of behaviors. A behavior is just a JavaScript object with an execute() method. Every animation frame, the game iterates over all its visible sprites and, for each sprite, iterates over the sprite's behaviors, invoking each behavior's execute() method and passing the method a reference to the sprite in question. In that method, behaviors manipulate their associated sprite according to game conditions. For example, when you press j to make the runner jump, the runner's jump behavior subsequently moves the runner through the jump sequence, one animation frame at a time.

Table 1.1 lists the game's sprites and their respective behaviors.

Table 1.1 Snail Bait sprites

Sprites	Behaviors
Platforms	Pulsate (only one platform)
Runner	Run; jump; fall; collide with other sprites; explode
Bees and bats	Explode; flap their wings
Buttons	Pace; collapse; make bad guys explode
Coins, rubies, and sapphires	Sparkle; bounce up and down
Snail	Pace; shoot bombs
Snail bombs	Move from right to left; collide with runner

Behaviors are simple JavaScript objects, as illustrated by Example 1.1, which shows how Snail Bait instantiates the runner sprite.

Example 1.1 Creating sprites

```
runBehavior = {  // Just a JavaScript object with an execute method

   execute: function (sprite, // Sprite associated with the behavior
                      now,     // The current game time
                      fps,     // The current frame rate
                      context, // The context for the game's canvas
                      lastAnimationFrameTime) { // Time of last frame

      // Update the sprite's attributes, based on the current time
      // (now), frame rate (fps), and the time at which Snail Bait
      // drew the last animation frame (lastAnimationFrameTime),
      // to make it look like the runner is running.

      // The canvas context is provided as a convenience for things
      // like hit detection, but it should not be used for drawing
      // because that's the responsibility of the sprite's artist.

      // Method implementation omitted. See Section 7.3 on p. 187
      // for a discussion of this behavior.
   }

};

var runner = new Sprite('runner',        // name
                        runnerArtist,     // artist
                        [ runBehavior, ... ]); // behaviors
```

Snail Bait defines a runBehavior object, which it passes—in an array with other behaviors—to the runner sprite's constructor, along with the sprite's type (runner) and its artist (runnerArtist). For every animation frame in which the runner is visible, the game invokes the runBehavior object's execute() method. That execute() method makes it appear as though the runner is running by advancing through the set of images that depict the runner in various run poses.

 NOTE: Replica Island

The idea for sprite behaviors, which are an example of the Strategy design pattern, comes from Replica Island, a popular open source (Apache 2 license) Android platform game. Additionally, most of Snail Bait's graphics are from Replica Island. You can find out more about Replica Island at replicaisland.net, and you can read about the Strategy design pattern at http://en.wikipedia.org/wiki/Strategy_design_pattern.

NOTE: Sprite artists

Besides encapsulating behaviors in separate objects—which makes it easy to add and remove behaviors at runtime—sprites also delegate how they are drawn to another JavaScript object, known as a sprite artist. That makes it possible to plug in a different artist at runtime.

NOTE: Freely available resources

Most game developers need help with graphics, sound effects, and music. Fortunately, an abundance of assets are freely available under various licensing arrangements. Snail Bait uses the following:

- Graphics and sound effects from Replica Island
- Soundtrack from soundclick.com
- Coins from LoversHorizon at deviantART

See Chapter 2 for more information on obtaining game resources and setting up a development environment.

1.2 HTML5 Game Development Best Practices

We discuss game development best practices throughout this book, starting here with seven that are specific to HTML5.

1. Pause the game when the window loses focus.
2. Implement a countdown when the window regains focus.
3. Use CSS for user interface (UI) effects.
4. Detect and react to slowly running games.
5. Incorporate social features.
6. Put all the game's images in a single sprite sheet.
7. Store high scores and realtime in-game metrics on a server.

We examine the preceding best practices in detail later in the book; for now, a quick look at each of them introduces more of Snail Bait's features.

1.2.1 Pause the Game When the Window Loses Focus

If an HTML5 game is running in a browser and you change focus to another tab or browser window, most browsers severely clamp the frame rate at which the game's animation runs so as to save resources such as CPU and battery power; after all, why waste resources on a window or tab that's not visible?

Frame-rate clamping wreaks havoc with most collision detection algorithms because those algorithms check for collisions every time the game draws an animation frame; if it takes too long between animation frames, sprites can move past one another without detection. To avoid collision detection meltdowns resulting from frame-rate clamping, *you must automatically pause the game when the window loses focus.*

When Snail Bait pauses the game, it displays a toast to let the player know the game is paused, as shown in Figure 1.5.

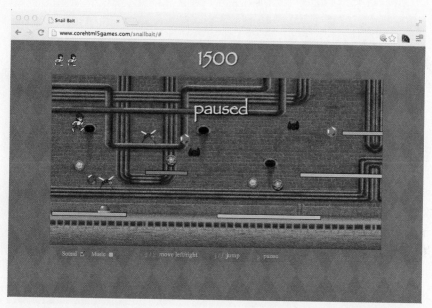

Figure 1.5 Snail Bait paused

 NOTE: Pausing is more than stopping the game

When a paused game resumes, everything must be in exactly the same state as it was when the game was paused; for example, in Figure 1.5, when play resumes, the runner must continue her jump from exactly where she was when the game was paused.

In addition to pausing and unpausing the game, therefore, you must also freeze and thaw the game to ensure a smooth transition when the game resumes. We discuss pausing and freezing the game in more detail in Chapter 4.

NOTE: Toasts

A toast—as in raising a glass to one's health—is information that a game displays to a player for a short time. A toast can be simple text, as in Figure 1.5, or it can represent a more traditional dialog box, as in Figure 1.8 on p. 14.

1.2.2 Implement a Countdown When the Window Regains Focus

When your window regains focus, you should give the player a few seconds to prepare for the game to restart. Snail Bait uses a three-second countdown when the window regains focus, as shown in Figure 1.6.

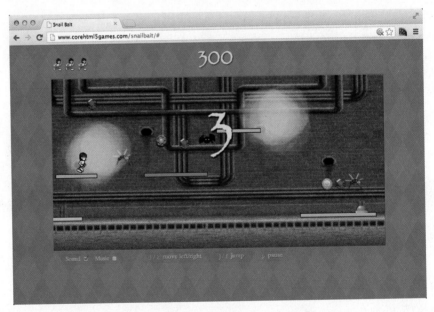

Figure 1.6 Snail Bait's countdown after the window regains focus

1.2.3 Use CSS for UI Effects

Figure 1.7 shows a screenshot taken a short time after the game loads.

Note especially two things about Figure 1.7. First, a toast containing simple instructions is visible. That toast fades in when the game loads, and after five seconds, it fades out.

Second, when the game starts, the checkboxes (for sound and music) and instructions (telling which keystrokes perform which functions) below the game's canvas

Figure 1.7 Snail Bait's toasts

are fully opaque, whereas the lives indicators and scoreboard at the top of the game are partially transparent, as shown in Figure 1.7. As the game's instructions toast fades, that transparency reverses; the lives indicator and scoreboard become fully opaque, while the checkboxes and instructions become nearly transparent, as they are in Figure 1.6.

Snail Bait dims elements and fades toasts with CSS3 transitions.

 NOTE: Focus on what's currently important

When Snail Bait starts, the instructions below the game's canvas are fully opaque, whereas the lives indicator and score above the game's canvas are partially transparent. Shortly thereafter, they switch opacities; the elements above the canvas become fully opaque and the elements below become partially transparent.

Snail Bait goes to all that trouble to focus attention on what's currently important. Initially, players should pay attention to the instructions below the game's canvas; once the game is underway, players will be more focused on their score and how many lives are remaining.

1.2.4 Detect and React to Slowly Running Games

Unlike console games, which run in a tightly controlled environment, HTML5 games run in a highly variable, unpredictable, and chaotic one. Players can do things directly that significantly affect system performance, for example, running YouTube videos in another browser tab or window. Other performance killers, such as system backup software running in the background unbeknown to game players, can easily make an HTML5 game run so slowly that it becomes unplayable. And there's always the possibility that your players will use a browser that can't keep up.

As an HTML5 game developer, you must monitor frame rate and react when it dips below an unplayable threshold. When Snail Bait detects that an average of the last 10 frame rates falls below 40 frames per second (fps), it displays the running slowly toast shown in Figure 1.8.

Figure 1.8 Snail Bait's running slowly toast

1.2.5 Incorporate Social Features

Many modern games incorporate social aspects, such as posting scores on Twitter or Facebook. When a Snail Bait player clicks on the Tweet my score link that appears at the end of the game (see Figure 1.4 on p. 6), Snail Bait creates a tweet announcing the score in a separate browser tab, as shown in Figure 1.9.

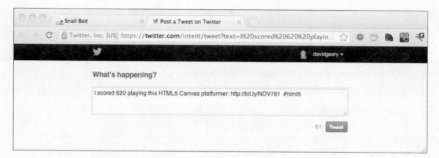

Figure 1.9   Snail Bait's Twitter integration

1.2.6   Put All the Game's Images in a Single Sprite Sheet

You can do several things to make your HTML5 game (or any HTML5 application) load more quickly, but the single most effective thing is to decrease the number of HTTP requests you make to the server. One way to do that is to put all your game's images in a single image, known as a sprite sheet. Figure 1.10 shows Snail Bait's sprite sheet.

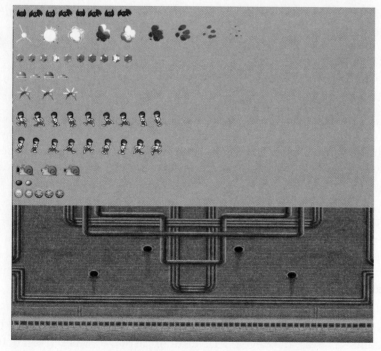

Figure 1.10   Snail Bait's sprite sheet (the gray background is transparent)

When Snail Bait draws the game's sprites, it copies rectangles from the sprite sheet into the canvas.

 NOTE: Sprite sheets on mobile devices

Some mobile devices place limits on the size of image files, so if your sprite sheet is too large, you may have to split it into multiple files. Your game will load more slowly as a result, but that's better than not loading at all.

1.2.7 Store High Scores and Send Realtime, In-game Metrics to the Server

Most games interact with a server for a variety of reasons. Snail Bait stores high scores on a server in addition to sending game metrics during gameplay. Snail Bait does not use any third-party graphics frameworks; however, it does use two JavaScript frameworks—Node.js and socket.io—to communicate between the player's computer and a server. See Chapter 19 for more details.

1.3 Special Features

Snail Bait has three noteworthy features that add polish to the game and make playtesting more productive:

- Developer backdoor
- Time system
- Particle systems

Snail Bait reveals the developer backdoor, shown in Figure 1.11, when you press CTRL-d. With the backdoor visible, you can control the rate at which time flows through the game, making it easy to run the game in slow motion to see how game events such as collision detection take place. Conversely, you can run the game faster than normal to determine the best pace for the game.

You can turn collision rectangles on for a better look at exactly how collisions occur; if the smoking holes obscure your view, you can turn the smoke off by deselecting the Smoke checkbox. You can also fine-tune the threshold at which Snail Bait displays the game's running slowly warning, shown in Figure 1.8, or you can turn it off entirely, which lets you playtest slow frame rates without Snail Bait intervening at all.

When you playtest a particular section of the game, you can avoid playing through the preceding sections every time you test: In addition to the controls at the top of the game's canvas, the developer backdoor displays a ruler at the bottom of the canvas that shows how far the background has scrolled horizontally in pixels.

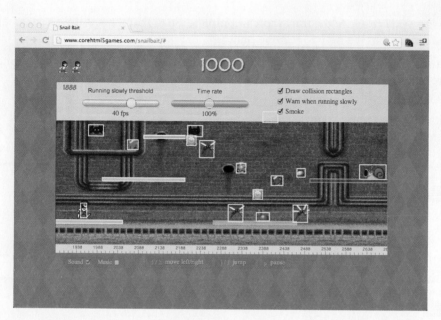

Figure 1.11 Snail Bait's developer backdoor

You use those values to restart the game at a particular horizontal location, thereby avoiding the preceding sections of the game. For convenience, when the developer backdoor is visible you can also simply drag the game, including the background and all the sprites, horizontally to reposition the runner.

The developer backdoor lets you control the rate at which time flows through the game by virtue of Snail Bait's time system. Everything that happens in Snail Bait depends on the current game time, which is the elapsed time since the game started; for example, when the runner begins a jump, the game records the current game time, and thereafter moves the runner through the jump sequence frame by frame, depending on how much time has elapsed since the runner began the jump.

By representing the current game time as the real time, which is Snail Bait's default mode, the game runs at its intended rate. However, Snail Bait's time system can *mis*represent the current game time as something other than the real time; for example, the time system can consistently report that the current game time is half of the actual time, causing the game to run at half speed.

Besides letting you control the rate at which time flows through the game, Snail Bait's time system is also the source of special effects. When the runner collides with a bad guy and explodes, Snail Bait slows time to a crawl while transitioning to the next life. Once the transition is complete, Snail Bait returns time to normal, indicating that it's time to resume play.

Finally, Snail Bait uses two particle systems to create the illusion of smoke and fire in the background. In Chapter 16, we take a close look at those particle systems so you can create similar effects of your own.

Now that you have a high-level understanding of the game, let's take a look at some code.

NOTE: Snail Bait's code statistics (lines of code)

- JavaScript: 5,230
- CSS: 690
- HTML: 350

NOTE: A closer look at Snail Bait's code

- snailbait.js: 3,740
- Supporting JavaScript code: 1,500
- Initializing data for sprites: 500
- Creating sprites: 400
- Sprite behavior implementations: 730
- Event handling: 300
- User interface: 225
- Sound: 130

1.4 Snail Bait's HTML and CSS

Snail Bait is implemented with HTML, CSS, and JavaScript, the majority of which is JavaScript. In fact, the rest of this book is primarily concerned with JavaScript, with only occasional forays into HTML and CSS.

Figure 1.12 shows the HTML elements, outlined in white, and their corresponding CSS for the top half of the game proper.

Everything in Snail Bait takes place in the arena, which is an HTML DIV element. The arena's margin attribute is 0, auto, which means the browser centers the arena and everything inside it horizontally, as shown in Figure 1.13.

```
                                                    #snailbait-game-canvas {
                                                      border: 1px solid blue;

                           #snailbait-score {
                             font: 46px fantasy;        width: 100%;
                             text-align: center;
  #snailbait-lives {         color: yellow;           -webkit-transition: opacity 5s;
    position: absolute;      text-shadow: 2px 2px 4px  -moz-transition: opacity 5s;
    margin-top: 20px;                rgba(0,0,80,1.0);  -o-transition: opacity 5s;
    margin-left: 5px;                                   transition: opacity 5s;

    -webkit-transition: opacity 5s;  -webkit-transition: opacity 5s;  display: none;
    -moz-transition: opacity 5s;     -moz-transition: opacity 5s;     opacity: 0;
    -o-transition: opacity 5s;       -o-transition: opacity 5s;     }
    transition: opacity 5s;          transition: opacity 5s;
                                                             #snailbait-arena {
                                                               margin: 0 auto;
    display: none;                   display: none;             width: 802px;
    opacity: 0;                      opacity: 0;                height: 520px;
  }                                }                          }
```

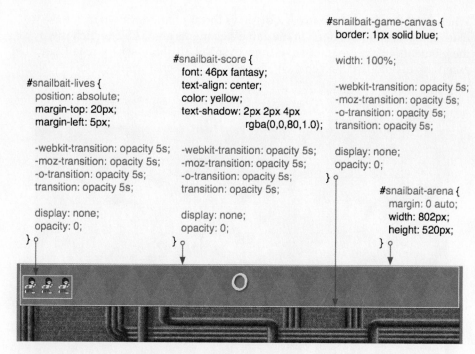

Figure 1.12 Snail Bait's CSS for the top half of the game

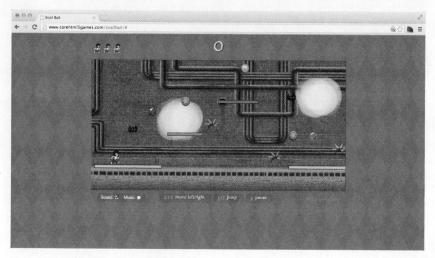

Figure 1.13 Snail Bait stays centered horizontally in the window

When Snail Bait loads resources, it displays the animation shown in Figure 1.14. During that animation, none of the game's elements are visible, which is why all the elements in Figure 1.12 have their display attribute set to none (with the exception of snailbait-arena, which has no visible characteristics of its own).

Figure 1.14 Snail Bait at startup

After the game loads resources, it fades in the game's elements by setting their display attribute to block and subsequently setting their opacity to 1.0 (fully opaque). Elements that have a transition associated with their opacity property, like snailbait-lives, snailbait-score, and snailbait-game-canvas, transition into view over a specified period of time.

The snailbait-lives element has an absolute position; otherwise, with its default position of static, it will expand to fit the width of its enclosing DIV, forcing the score beneath it.

The game canvas, which is an HTML5 canvas element, is where all the game's action takes place; it's the only element in Figure 1.12 that's not a DIV.

Figure 1.15 shows the HTML elements in the lower half of the game.

Like the lives and score elements in the upper half of the game, the browser does not display the elements at the bottom during the game's loading animation, so those elements are initially invisible and have an opacity transition of five seconds,

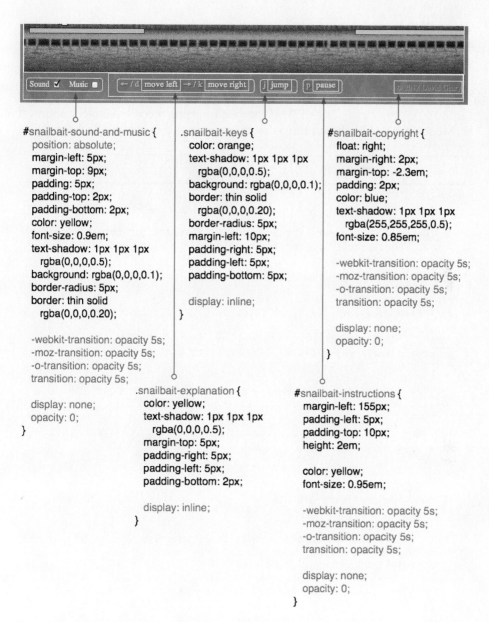

```
#snailbait-sound-and-music {
   position: absolute;
   margin-left: 5px;
   margin-top: 9px;
   padding: 5px;
   padding-top: 2px;
   padding-bottom: 2px;
   color: yellow;
   font-size: 0.9em;
   text-shadow: 1px 1px 1px
      rgba(0,0,0,0.5);
   background: rgba(0,0,0,0.1);
   border-radius: 5px;
   border: thin solid
      rgba(0,0,0,0.20);

   -webkit-transition: opacity 5s;
   -moz-transition: opacity 5s;
   -o-transition: opacity 5s;
   transition: opacity 5s;

   display: none;
   opacity: 0;
}
```

```
.snailbait-keys {
   color: orange;
   text-shadow: 1px 1px 1px
      rgba(0,0,0,0.5);
   background: rgba(0,0,0,0.1);
   border: thin solid
      rgba(0,0,0,0.20);
   border-radius: 5px;
   margin-left: 10px;
   padding-right: 5px;
   padding-left: 5px;
   padding-bottom: 5px;

   display: inline;
}
```

```
.snailbait-explanation {
   color: yellow;
   text-shadow: 1px 1px 1px
      rgba(0,0,0,0.5);
   margin-top: 5px;
   padding-right: 5px;
   padding-left: 5px;
   padding-bottom: 2px;

   display: inline;
}
```

```
#snailbait-copyright {
   float: right;
   margin-right: 2px;
   margin-top: -2.3em;
   padding: 2px;
   color: blue;
   text-shadow: 1px 1px 1px
      rgba(255,255,255,0.5);
   font-size: 0.85em;

   -webkit-transition: opacity 5s;
   -moz-transition: opacity 5s;
   -o-transition: opacity 5s;
   transition: opacity 5s;

   display: none;
   opacity: 0;
}
```

```
#snailbait-instructions {
   margin-left: 155px;
   padding-left: 5px;
   padding-top: 10px;
   height: 2em;

   color: yellow;
   font-size: 0.95em;

   -webkit-transition: opacity 5s;
   -moz-transition: opacity 5s;
   -o-transition: opacity 5s;
   transition: opacity 5s;

   display: none;
   opacity: 0;
}
```

Figure 1.15 Snail Bait's CSS for the bottom of the game

which Snail Bait uses to fade them and all their contained elements in along with the score and lives elements at the beginning of the game.

The snailbait-sound-and-music element, like the snailbait-lives element, has an absolute position to prevent its width from expanding. The snailbait-keys and snailbait-explanation DIVs have display attributes of inline so they appear horizontally inline with the other elements in their enclosing DIV, instead of being stacked vertically.

Example 1.2 lists Snail Bait's HTML proper, omitting a considerable amount of HTML for things like the running slowly warning and developer backdoor.

Example 1.2 index.html (excerpt)

```
<!DOCTYPE html>

    <!--
        Basic HTML elements for Snail Bait. Elements for things such
        as sounds, credits, toasts, developer backdoor, etc. are
        omitted for brevity.
    -->

<html>
    <!-- Head.................................................-->

    <head>
        <title>Snail Bait</title>
        ...

      <link rel='stylesheet' href='snailbait.css'>
    </head>

    <!-- Body.................................................-->

    <body>
        <!-- Arena.............................................-->

        <div id='snailbait-arena'>
            ...

            <!-- Lives indicator...............................-->

            <div id='snailbait-lives'>
                <img id='snailbait-life-icon-left'
                    src='images/runner-small.png'/>

                <img id='snailbait-life-icon-middle'
                    src='images/runner-small.png'/>

                <img id='snailbait-life-icon-right'
                    src='images/runner-small.png'/>
            </div>
```

```
<!-- Score .............................................-->

<div id='snailbait-score'>0</div>
...

<!-- The game canvas.....................................-->

<canvas id='snailbait-game-canvas' width='800' height='400'>
    Your browser does not support HTML5 Canvas.
</canvas>
...

<!-- Sound and music.....................................-->

<div id='snailbait-sound-and-music'>
    <div id='snailbait-sound-checkbox-div'
      class='snailbait-checkbox-div'>

        Sound <input id='snailbait-sound-checkbox'
                    type='checkbox' checked/>

    </div>

    <div class='snailbait-checkbox-div'>
        Music <input id='snailbait-music-checkbox'
                    type='checkbox' checked/>
    </div>
</div>

<!-- Instructions........................................-->

<div id='snailbait-instructions'>
    <div class='snailbait-keys'>
        &larr; / d
        <div class='snailbait-explanation'>move left</div>
        &rarr; / k
        <div class='snailbait-explanation'>move right</div>
    </div>

    <div class='snailbait-keys'>
      j <div class='snailbait-explanation'>jump</div>
    </div>

    <div class='snailbait-keys'>
      p <div class='snailbait-explanation'>pause</div>
    </div>
</div>

<div id='snailbait-mobile-instructions'>
```

(Continues)

Example 1.2 *(Continued)*

```
            <div class='snailbait-keys'>
                Left
                <div class='snailbait-explanation'>
                    Run left or jump
                </div>
            </div>

            <div class='snailbait-keys'>
                Right
                <div class='snailbait-explanation'>
                    Run right or jump
                </div>
            </div>
        </div>

        <!-- Copyright....................................................-->

        <div id='snailbait-copyright'> &copy; 2012 David Geary</div>
    </div>

    <!-- JavaScript...................................................-->

    <!-- Other script tags for the game's other JavaScript files are
         omitted for brevity. The final version of the game puts all
         the game's JavaScript into a single file. See Chapter 19
         for more details about how Snail Bait is deployed. -->

    <script src='snailbait.js'></script>
</body>
</html>
```

The canvas element is where all the action takes place. The canvas comes with a 2D context with a powerful API for implementing 2D games, among other things, as you will see in Section 3.1, "Draw Graphics and Images with the HTML5 canvas Element," on p. 64. The text inside the canvas element is fallback text that the browser displays only if it does not support HTML5 canvas element.

One final note about the game's HTML and CSS: Notice that the width and height of the canvas is set with canvas element attributes in the preceding listing. Those attributes *pertain to both the size of the canvas element and the size of the drawing surface contained within that element.*

On the other hand, using CSS to set the width and height of the canvas element *sets only the size of the element.* The drawing surface remains at its default width and height of 300 × 150 pixels, respectively. That means you will have a mismatch between the canvas element size and the size of its drawing surface when you set the element's size to something other than the default 300 × 150 pixels, and in that case *the browser scales the drawing surface to fit the element*. Most of the time that effect is unwanted, so it's a good idea to set the size of the canvas element with its width and height attributes, and not with CSS.

At this point, you've already seen the end of the Snail Bait story. Now let's go back to the beginning.

Draw into a small canvas and let CSS scale it?

Some games purposely draw into a small canvas and use CSS to scale the canvas to a playable size. That way, the canvas is not manipulating as many pixels, and so increases performance. You will take a performance hit for scaling the canvas, of course, but scaling with CSS is typically hardware accelerated, so the cost of the scaling can be minimal. Today, however, nearly all the latest versions of modern browsers come equipped with hardware-accelerated Canvas, so it's just as fast to draw into a full-sized canvas in the first place.

NOTE: Namespacing HTML elements and CSS classes

To avoid naming collisions with other HTML elements, Snail Bait starts each HTML element and CSS classname with snailbait-.

1.5 Snail Bait's Humble Beginning

Figure 1.16 shows Snail Bait's initial set of files. Throughout this book we add many more files, but for now all we need is an HTML file to define the structure of the game's HTML elements, a CSS file to define the visual properties for those elements, a JavaScript file for the game's logic, and two images, one for the background and another for the runner.

Name	Size	Kind
▼ ⬜ images	--	Folder
⚊ background.png	1.2 MB	Portable Network Graphics image
⬤ runner.png	845 bytes	Portable Network Graphics image
⬤ index.html	442 bytes	HTML document
▣ snailbait.css	127 bytes	CSS
▣ snailbait.js	668 bytes	JavaScript

Figure 1.16 Snail Bait's initial files

Figure 1.17 shows the starting point for the game, which simply draws the background and the runner. To start, the runner is not a sprite; instead, the game draws her directly.

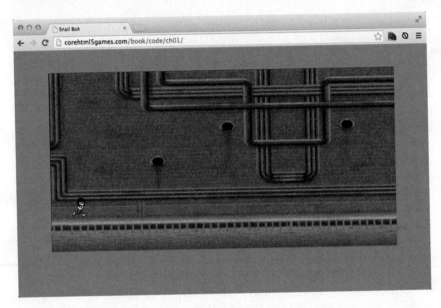

Figure 1.17 Drawing the background and runner

Example 1.3 lists the starting point for the game's HTML, which is just a distilled version of the HTML in Example 1.2.

Example 1.3 The starting point for Snail Bait's HTML

```html
<!DOCTYPE html>
<html>
    <head>
        <title>Snail Bait</title>
        <link rel='stylesheet' href='snailbait.css'/>
    </head>

    <body>
        <div id='snailbait-arena'>
            <canvas id='snailbait-game-canvas' width='800' height='400'>
                Your browser does not support HTML5 Canvas.
            </canvas>
        </div>
```

```
    <!-- JavaScript......................................................-->

    <script src='snailbait.js'></script>
  </body>
</html>
```

Initially, the arena contains only the game's canvas, which is 800 pixels wide by 400 pixels high and has a thin blue border. Example 1.4 shows the starting point for Snail Bait's CSS.

Example 1.4 The starting point for Snail Bait's CSS

```
body {
    background: cornflowerblue;
}

#snailbait-arena {
    margin: 0 auto;
    margin-top: 50px;
    width: 800px;
    height: 400px;
}

#snailbait-game-canvas {
    border: 1.5px solid blue;
}
```

Example 1.5 shows the starting point for Snail Bait's JavaScript.

Example 1.5 The starting point for Snail Bait's JavaScript

```
var canvas = document.getElementById('snailbait-game-canvas'),
    context = canvas.getContext('2d'),

    background  = new Image(),
    runnerImage = new Image();

function initializeImages() {
    background.src = 'images/background.png';
    runnerImage.src = 'images/runner.png';

    background.onload = function (e) {
        startGame();
    };
}
```

(Continues)

Example 1.5   *(Continued)*

```
function startGame() {
    draw();
}

function draw() {
    drawBackground();
    drawRunner();
}

function drawBackground() {
    context.drawImage(background, 0, 0);
}

function drawRunner() {
    context.drawImage(runnerImage, 50, 280);
}

// Launch game.....................................................

initializeImages();
```

The preceding JavaScript accesses the canvas element and subsequently obtains a reference to the canvas's 2D context. The code then draws the background and runner by using the three-argument variant of drawImage() to draw images at a particular location in the canvas.

The game starts when the background image loads. For now, starting the game entails simply drawing the background and the runner.

1.6 The Use of JavaScript in This Book

Proficiency in JavaScript is an absolute prerequisite for this book, as discussed in the Preface. JavaScript, however, is a flexible and dynamic language, so there are many ways to use it. The purpose of this section is to show you how this book uses JavaScript; the intent is not to teach you anything at all about the language. To get the most out of this book, you must already know everything that you are about to read, or preferably skim, in this section.

This book defines several JavaScript objects that in more traditional languages such as C++ or Java would be implemented with classes. Those objects range from the games themselves (Snail Bait and Bodega's Revenge) to objects they contain, such as sprites and sprite behaviors. JavaScript objects are defined with a constructor function and a prototype, as shown in Example 1.6, a severely truncated listing of the SnailBait object.

Example 1.6 Defining JavaScript objects

```javascript
var SnailBait = function () {
   // Constants and variables are declared here

   this.LEFT = 1;
   ...
};

SnailBait.prototype = {
   // Methods are defined here

   draw: function(now) { // The draw method takes a single parameter
      ...
   },
   ...
};
```

JavaScript objects are instantiated in this book with JavaScript's new operator, as shown in Example 1.7.

Example 1.7 Creating JavaScript objects

```javascript
SnailBait.prototype = {
   ...

   createSnailSprites: function () {
      var snail,
          snailArtist = new SpriteSheetArtist(this.spritesheet,
                                              this.snailCells);

      for (var i = 0; i < this.snailData.length; ++i) {
         snail = new Sprite('snail',
                            snailArtist,

                            [
                               this.paceBehavior,
                               this.snailShootBehavior,

                               new CycleBehavior(
                                       300,   // 300ms per image
                                       5000) // 1.5 seconds interlude
                            ]);

         snail.width  = this.SNAIL_CELLS_WIDTH;
         snail.height = this.SNAIL_CELLS_HEIGHT;
```

(Continues)

Example 1.7   *(Continued)*

```
        snail.velocityX = snailBait.SNAIL_PACE_VELOCITY;

        this.snails.push(snail);
    }
  },
  ...
};
```

The createSnailSprites() function, which we refer to as a method because it resides in an object, creates a sprite sheet artist, a sprite, and an instance of CycleBehavior. That cycle behavior resides in an array of behaviors that createSnailSprites() passes to the Sprite constructor.

This book also defines objects using JSON (JavaScript Object Notation), as shown in Example 1.8.

Example 1.8 Defining JavaScript objects with JSON

```
var SnailBait = function () {
   ...

   // A single object with three properties

   this.fallingWhistleSound = {
      position: 0.03, // seconds
      duration: 1464, // milliseconds
      volume: 0.1
   };

   // An array containing three objects, each of which has two properties

   this.audioChannels = [
      { playing: false, audio: null, },
      { playing: false, audio: null, },
      { playing: false, audio: null, }
   ];
   ...
};
```

Finally, the JavaScript code in this book adheres closely to the subset of JavaScript discussed in Douglas Crockford's book *JavaScript: The Good Parts.* The code in this book also follows the coding conventions discussed in that book.

NOTE: The use of ellipses in this book

Most of the code listings in this book omit irrelevant sections of code. Those irrelevant sections are identified with ellipses (...) so that you can distinguish partial from full listings.

1.7 Conclusion

Snail Bait is an HTML5 platform game implemented with the canvas element's 2D API. As you'll see throughout the rest of this book, that API provides a powerful and intuitive set of functions that let you implement nearly any 2D game you can imagine.

In this chapter, we looked at Snail Bait from a high level to get a feel for its features and to understand some of the best practices it implements. Although you can get a good grasp of its gameplay from reading this chapter, you will have a much better understanding of the game if you play it, which you can do at corehtml5games.com.

At the end of this chapter, we looked at a starting point for Snail Bait that simply draws the background and the runner. Before we build on that starting point and begin coding in earnest, however, we'll take a brief detour in the next chapter to become familiar with the browser development environment and to see how to access freely available graphics, sound, and music. If you're already up to speed on HTML5 development in general and you know how to access open source assets online, feel free to skip ahead to Chapter 3.

1.8 Exercises

1. Use a different image for the background.
2. Draw the runner at different locations in the canvas.
3. Draw the background at different locations in the canvas.
4. In the draw() function, draw the runner first and then the background.
5. Remove the width and height attributes from the snailbait-game-canvas element in index.html and add width and height properties—with the same values of 800px and 400px, respectively—to the snailbait-game-canvas element in the CSS file. When you restart the game, does it look the same as before? Can you explain the result?

Raw Materials and Development Environment

Topics in This Chapter

In this book we build a game. Like all builders, we must gather raw materials and become competent with our tools before we begin. For most games, the following raw materials are standard fare:

- Graphics
- Sound effects
- Music

The following, which add some polish to your HTML5 game, are optional:

- A favicon
- A webpage background
- An animated GIF

Favicons are small images that browsers display either in the address bar or in a tab. Webpage backgrounds can be images or, as is the case with Snail Bait, they can be drawn with CSS. Snail Bait also displays an animated GIF while it loads its resources.

Fortunately, all the necessary materials, from game graphics to animated GIFs, are readily available. Not only that, but you can easily find high-quality graphics, sound effects, and music on the Internet under permissive open source licenses, such as Creative Commons.

The following developer tools will help us turn the preceding materials into a compelling video game:

- Text editor
- Console
- Debugger
- Profiler
- Timelines

Additionally, game developers must have:

- An image editor
- A sound editor

Browser development environments, which typically contain all the preceding development tools and more, are also free. And you can also use high quality, freely available image and sound editors, such as GIMP and Audacity.

This chapter briefly describes the Chrome developer tools and shows you how to access freely available graphics, sound effects, and music on the Internet. You will also see how to edit sounds and images and how to create animated GIFs, favicons, and CSS backgrounds.

 NOTE: Game development wasn't always this accessible

Before the advent of open source resources and freely available development environments, game development was much more difficult. Developers had to pay steep prices for development environments in addition to typically paying artists and musicians to create graphics, sound, and music for their games.

NOTE: Money-making games use open source resources

Nowadays there are many types of open source licenses, and some of them, like Creative Comments, pretty much let you do anything you want with open source resources, as long as you attribute works to the original artists. In fact, quite a few for-sale games are based entirely on open source graphics.

2.1 Use Developer Tools

You will undoubtedly use developer tools as you implement HTML5 games, and your familiarity with those tools will help determine how quickly and easily you can implement a game.

As this book was written, all major browser vendors—Chrome, Safari, Firefox, Opera, and Internet Explorer—provided powerful developer tools for free. Although the specifics of those tools vary, the fundamentals are similar. Developers log information to the console, debug with a debugger, locate performance bottlenecks with a profiler, and monitor events with timelines.

A comprehensive discussion of browser developer tools is beyond the scope of this book; however, this section exemplifies the use of Chrome's developer tools to implement games.

 CAUTION: Chrome is a moving target

Over the course of the development of this book, Chrome's look-and-feel changed considerably. Some of the screenshots you see in this book may not correspond exactly to the current version of Chrome, but the functionality should be the same.

2.1.1 The Console

Video games are predicated upon time. Games tirelessly create one animation frame after another to create the illusion of motion. When a game draws an animation frame, it uses the elapsed time since the last animation frame to determine where to move its graphical objects, known as sprites.

If you set a breakpoint in the debugger at a line of code that's called for every animation frame, you will greatly increase the amount of time between frames, no matter how quickly you click the debugger's resume button. More importantly, values that depend on the amount of time between animation frames, such as the frame rate itself, will be enormously out of whack, as Figure 2.1 depicts in the top screenshot, which shows a nonsensical frame rate of less than one frame per second in the debugger.

On the other hand, logging to the console does not cause the game's code to stop running, so you can monitor values such as frame rate, as illustrated in the bottom screenshot in Figure 2.1.

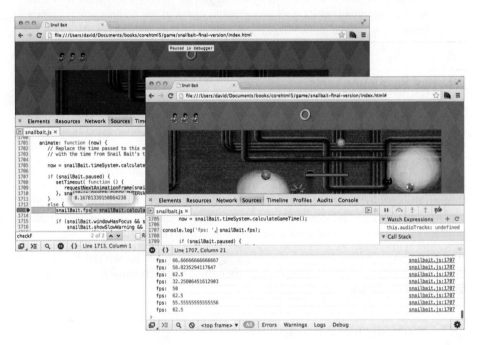

Figure 2.1 Debugger vs. console

In the bottom screenshot in Figure 2.1, Snail Bait uses the console.log() method to display the game's frame rate. Chrome's console comes with several other methods that, like console.log(), log messages to the console: debug(), error(), info(), and warn(). Those methods are identical to log(), but the browser categorizes them so you can filter out particular types of messages. Example 2.1 shows how Snail Bait uses the error() and warn() methods.

The JavaScript in Example 2.1 shows two of Snail Bait's sound methods, which we discuss in much greater detail in Chapter 14. It's an error if we cannot move to a particular position in a sound file (known as seeking) because by the time seekAudio() is invoked, all sounds are loaded and we should therefore be able to seek anytime we want.

On the other hand, if by some chance Snail Bait tries to simultaneously play more sounds than it can support, no audio channels will be available and Snail Bait won't be able to play the sound. However, not being able to play a sound when multiple sounds are already playing is not an error, so Snail Bait emits a warning to the console instead.

Example 2.1 Using the console to report warnings and errors

```
SnailBait.prototype = { // An object containing the game's methods
  ...

  seekAudio: function (sound, audio) {
    try {
      audio.pause();
      audio.currentTime = sound.position;
    }
    catch (e) {
      console.error('Cannot seek audio');
    }
  },

  playSound: function (sound) {
    var channel,
        audio;

    if (this.soundOn) {
      channel = this.getFirstAvailableAudioChannel();

      if (!channel) {
        if (console) {
          console.warn('All audio channels are busy. ' +
                       'Cannot play sound');
        }
      }
      else {
        ...
      }
    }
  },
  ...
};
```

Browsers graphically depict errors and warnings with red and yellow icons, respectively, and they also group them under error and warning categories so that you can view one or the other. The bottom screenshot in Figure 2.1 shows buttons in the browser's status bar for filtering log messages by error, warning, log, or debug.

Chrome's console is full featured, as Table 2.1 illustrates.

Table 2.1 The Chrome Console API

Method	Description
assert(expression, errormsg)	If expression is false, the browser appends errormsg to "Assertion failed: " and shows the resulting string in the console as an error.
clear()	Erases all content from the console.
count(label)	Appends the number of times count() has been called (at that location in the code, and with the same label) to the label and displays the resulting string; for example, console.count('Drawing') results in output such as Drawing: X, where X is the number of times that line of code has executed with the label Drawing.
debug(object [, object,...])	The same as log() except messages are grouped under debug messages.
dir(object)	Displays a JavaScript representation of object.
dirxml(object)	Displays an XML JavaScript representation of object (as it would appear in the Elements panel).
error(object, [, object,...])	Identical to log() except that it emits an error message with a red icon and stack trace.
group(object, [, object,...])	Begins a new logging group that persists until the first call to groupEnd(). The browser visually groups all console output between those two calls.
groupCollapsed(object, [, object,...])	The same as group() except that the browser displays the group initially collapsed, instead of open (the default).
groupEnd()	Ends a group. See group() and groupCollapsed().
info(object, [, object,...])	Identical to log().

(Continues)

Table 2.1   *(Continued)*

Method	Description
`log(object, [, object,...])`	Displays each of the objects it is passed, concatenated into a space-delimited string. The first object can be a string with formatting characters, similar to `printf()` from the C language. Those formatting characters are: • %s (string) • %d or %i (integer) • %f (floating point) • %o (expandable DOM element) • %O (expandable JavaScript object) • %c (format with CSS you provide)
`profile(label)`	Starts a profile and assigns it the specified label. The profile runs until you call `profileEnd()`.
`profileEnd(label)`	Ends the profiler with the specified label.
`time(label)`	Starts a timer with a specified label. The timer runs until you call `timeEnd()`.
`timeEnd(label)`	Stops the timer with the specified label and displays the elapsed time in the console.
`timeline(label)`	Starts a timeline with a specified label. The timeline runs until you call `timelineEnd()`.
`timelineEnd(label)`	Stops the timeline with a specified label.
`timeStamp(label)`	Adds a timestamp event to a timeline when you are recording.
`trace()`	Prints a stacktrace.
`warn(object, [, object,...])`	The same as `log()` except that it emits a warning, complete with a yellow icon.

Several methods listed in Table 2.1 take arguments which are depicted in the table like this: (`object, [, object,...]`). The first argument is a string that can have formatting characters as enumerated in the description of the log(object, [, object,...]) method. The browser substitutes the formatting characters in the string with the remaining arguments, similar to C's printf(). For example, you could add a log statement in Snail Bait's loseLife() method, like this:

```
console.log('Life lost while playing %s. %d lives remain.', 'Snail
Bait', snailBait.lives);
```

Snail Bait keeps track of the number of remaining lives with a lives property. The preceding call to console.log() substitutes that value, along with the string Snail Bait, for the formatting characters in the order in which they appear.

Some of the console methods, however, have nothing to do with formatting messages and two of them are quite valuable to game developers: profile() and profileEnd(). Those methods let you start and stop profiling, respectively, which gives you much more fine-grained control over profiling than the brute force method of clicking a button in the browser's status bar.

NOTE: Online Console API reference

You can find an online reference to Chrome's Console API at https://developers. google.com/chrome-developer-tools/docs/console-api.

CAUTION: Undocumented methods

As this book went to press, the timeline() and timelineEnd() console methods, which were added to the console late in 2013, were undocumented. See Section 2.1.4, "Timelines," on p. 44 to learn how to use those methods.

2.1.2 Chrome Canary's Frame Rate Counter

Section 2.1.1, "The Console," on p. 35 demonstrated how the console can sometimes be more effective than the debugger for monitoring frame rate. In practice, neither the debugger nor the console is an effective way to monitor frame rate. The former can give nonsensical results, whereas the latter can degrade performance, which in turn affects your game's frame rate.

Instead of using the console or debugger to monitor frame rate, you can use Chrome Canary's frame rate counter, shown in Figure 2.2.

The frame rate counter is not enabled by default. To enable it, type chrome://flags in Chrome Canary's address bar and enable the FPS counter, as shown in Figure 2.3.

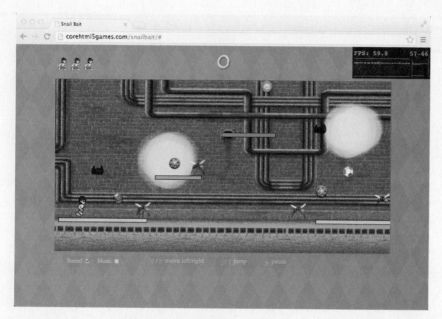

Figure 2.2 Chrome Canary's frame rate counter

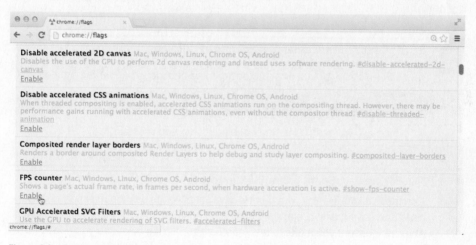

Figure 2.3 Enabling Chrome Canary's frame rate counter

 NOTE: We implement a frame rate counter in the next chapter.

NOTE: Chrome Canary

A reference to canaries in coal mines, Chrome Canary contains cutting edge features, some of which will eventually be incorporated into Chrome. The download link for Chrome Canary depends on your type of hardware and language. Type "Chrome Canary" in Google to find an appropriate link.

2.1.3 Debugging

It's hard to imagine writing any software, let alone games, without a proper debugger. All the major browser vendors provide debuggers that are instantly recognizable as such, with a gutter in which you can click to set breakpoints and buttons for resuming execution, and for stepping in, around, and out of functions. You can also watch expressions and view the call stack, as you can see from the bottom screenshot in Figure 2.4.

Your productivity in the debugger will increase if you take advantage of conditional breakpoints, a feature that's supported by all major browsers. Instead of looping over a collection of objects looking for a specific condition, you can set a breakpoint that's tripped by that condition. For example, Figure 2.4 shows a conditional breakpoint that acts as a breakpoint only when a sprite's type is runner.

NOTE: Setting conditional breakpoints in Chrome

1. Right-click in the gutter at the desired line of code to pop up the breakpoint menu.

2. Select Add Conditional Breakpoint from the popup menu.

3. Type an expression into the ensuing dialog and press Enter.

NOTE: Live JavaScript editing in Chrome

Chrome lets you live-edit your game's JavaScript. In the debugger, simply change code and save it with a standard save keystroke such as CTRL-s on Windows. Any changes that you make to the code persist until the next time you reload the page. As this book was written, Chrome was the only major browser that let you live-edit JavaScript; however, add-ons for other browsers, such as Firefox, let you do the same thing.

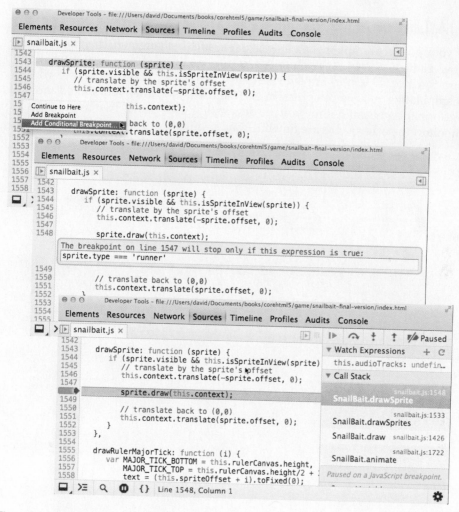

Figure 2.4 Conditional breakpoints in Chrome

 NOTE: The debugger; statement

Besides clicking in the gutter, you can also set breakpoints in Chrome's debugger by adding the following statement to your code: `debugger;`

2.1.4 Timelines

If your goal is to implement a simple game such as hangman, then not only are you reading the wrong book, but you also don't need to worry much about performance. If you're implementing a video game, however, where you are manipulating dozens of sprites in each animation frame, you should monitor performance the entire time you are developing your game. Two useful tools for monitoring performance are timelines and profiles.

Timelines let you monitor events, frame rates, and memory usage in real time. Figure 2.5 shows frame rates for the finished version of Snail Bait.

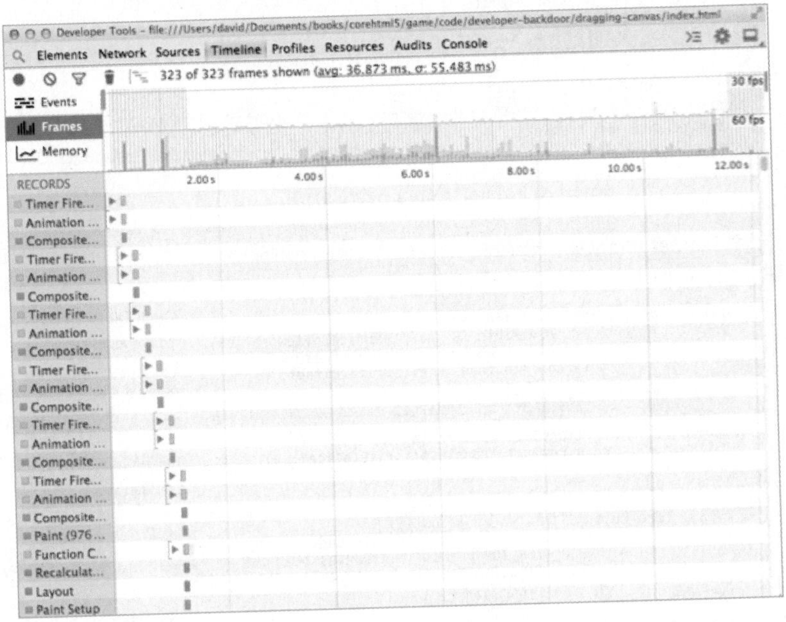

Figure 2.5 Timeline showing frame rates

To begin a timeline, you click the filled circle at the top-left in Figure 2.5, and the circle turns red. To stop the timeline, you click the red circle, which returns to its original color.

Starting and stopping timelines by clicking the mouse is appropriate when you want to get a general idea of your game's performance. For example, in Figure 2.6 players can observe the timeline as they are playing, which is quite useful when the player is also the game's developer, because the developer can see, in real time, when performance bottlenecks arise.

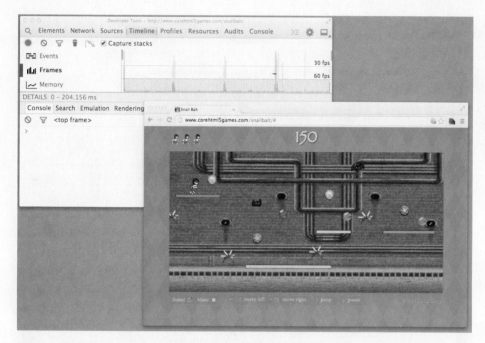

Figure 2.6 A running timeline

Clicking the mouse to start and stop a timeline is a rather coarse-grained, unwieldy approach. It's often better to start and stop timelines programmatically, which you can do with the Chrome console's timeline() and timelineEnd() methods, as shown in Figure 2.7.

Chrome lets you live-edit JavaScript, as illustrated in Figure 2.7. The highlighted line of code in the top screenshot was added to Chrome's editor after the game started running. The asterisk next to the file name indicates that the source has been temporarily modified.

The newly added line of code starts a timeline with the identifier countdown --> explosion. Chrome uses that identifier in the messages it prints to the console when the timeline starts or stops.

The bottom screenshot in Figure 2.7 shows a second line of code added to Chrome's editor to end the countdown --> explosion timeline. That screenshot also shows the effect of saving the changes in the editor; Chrome prints a message to the console, changes the editor's background color, and adds an information icon next to the file, thus signaling the presence of the new message in the console.

The calls to timeline() and timelineEnd() shown in Figure 2.7 are strategically placed. The timeline starts after the three-second countdown when a paused

Figure 2.7 Starting and stopping a timeline programmatically

game resumes and ends when a sprite (who is almost always the runner) explodes. The results of that timeline for a short run of three seconds is shown in Figure 2.10 on p. 49.

Chrome displays the timeline at the top of the window as shown in the top screenshot in Figure 2.8. Underneath the timeline is a list of events that occurred during the timeline's selected range (the entire timeline is selected in the top screenshot). You can change the selected range by dragging the range handles or clicking in the timeline, as shown in bottom screenshot in Figure 2.8. When you modify the range, the list of events updates to display only events within that range.

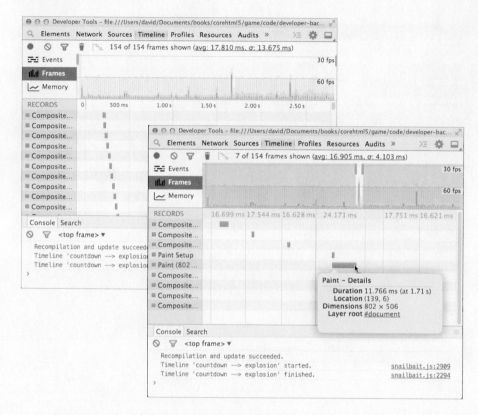

Figure 2.8 Changing the range within the bar graph

If you hover the mouse over a rectangle representing an event, as shown in the bottom screenshot in Figure 2.8, Chrome displays a tooltip with information about the event.

You can filter events in two ways, as shown in the top screenshot in Figure 2.9. You select the types of events you want to see by checking the appropriate checkboxes for Loading, Scripting, Rendering, and Painting events; you filter events by their duration with the drop-down menu shown in the top screenshot in Figure 2.9. Filtering events does not affect the timeline itself.

Filtering events that took longer than 15 ms is especially pertinent to game developers because at 60 frames per second, one frame takes 16.66 seconds. If no events take longer than 15 ms, as is the case in Figure 2.9, your game is performing well.

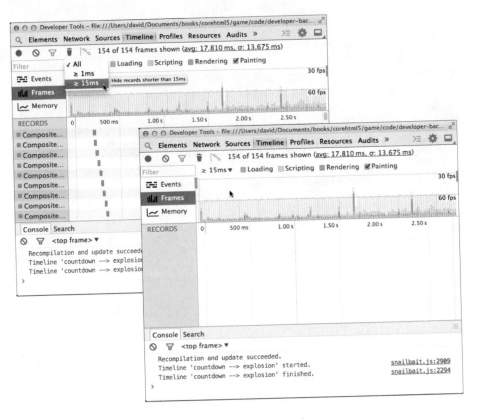

Figure 2.9 Filtering events according to how long they took

Now that you know how to start and stop timelines, how to correlate frames with events, and how to filter events, let's take a look at the timeline itself, shown in Figure 2.10.

The bars in the timeline represent individual frames, and the size of the bar represents how long the frame took. Longer times, meaning taller bars, correlate to slower frame rates, which is why 30 fps is above 60 fps in Figure 2.10.

Each bar is colored according to how much time Loading, Scripting, Rendering, and Painting events took during a frame. Clear regions represent idle time. Figure 2.10 is a timeline of the final version of Snail Bait, revealing that the game spends the majority of its time doing nothing. We'll see exactly how much time Snail Bait spends idling in the next section.

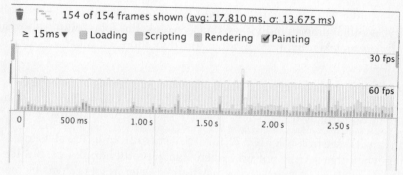

Figure 2.10 A closeup look at a timeline

 BEST PRACTICE: Constantly monitor performance from the outset

The ease with which you locate and fix performance bottlenecks is inversely proportional to how long it takes to start monitoring performance in the first place.

2.1.5 Profiling

JavaScript profiling is another feature that's supported by all major browsers. It lets you see exactly where your game spends its time. Figure 2.11 shows the

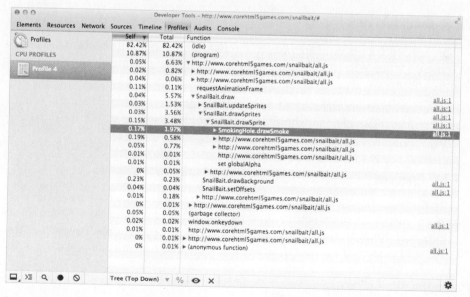

Figure 2.11 Profiling in Chrome

Chrome profiler running against the final version of Snail Bait. The Self column shows how much time an individual function took; the Total column shows how much time was taken by an individual function and each function called from within that function.

As you can see from Figure 2.11, Snail Bait's most performance-intensive endeavor is drawing smoking holes. Each smoking hole contains 20 sprites, whose artists draw them as partially transparent, filled circles that slowly dissipate.

As you can also see from Figure 2.11, Snail Bait spent around 80% of its time doing nothing when that screenshot was taken. That's pretty impressive, but it's only possible due to the fact that Chrome hardware accelerates its canvas element.

Now that you have a high-level understanding of browser developer tools, let's see how to access freely available assets, such as graphics, sound, and music.

 NOTE: Starting and stopping profiling in Chrome

In Chrome, you can start and stop profiling by clicking the filled circle on the left side of the browser's status bar. For more precise accounting, however, you can start and stop profiling at specific locations in your code with `console.profile()` and `console.profileEnd()`, which were discussed in Section 2.1.1, "The Console," on p. 35.

2.2 Obtain Assets

Software developers who are not accomplished artists or musicians can still implement games with high-quality graphics, sound, and music by using open source resources.

This section takes a brief look at open source resources used by Snail Bait. With a browser and Google, you should have no trouble locating similar resources of your own.

2.2.1 Graphics

With the exception of the runner and coins, all Snail Bait's graphics come from Replica Island, an open source Android game, whose homepage is shown in Figure 2.12. Replica Island's graphics and code are open source, covered by the Apache 2.0 license. That license lets you modify and redistribute works covered by the license as long as you follow some simple rules, such as providing a copy of the license and any original NOTICE files (containing attributions).

Figure 2.12 Replica Island

NOTE: Accessing Replica Island's graphics

To access Replica Island's graphics, go to replicaisland.net and download the game. Under the game's top-level directory you will find a directory named res/drawable that contains the game's graphics.

NOTE: The Apache 2 license

You can find the Apache 2 license online at apache.org/licenses/LICENSE-2.0.

2.2.2 Image Manipulation

Once you have graphics for your game, you'll want to manipulate images. A graphics editor, such as GIMP, shown in Figure 2.13, will help you do that. You may not actually have much image manipulation to do, but at the very least you should put all your images in a single sprite sheet, to reduce the number of

HTTP requests, making your game load much faster. See Chapter 6 for more details about sprite sheets (and for a caveat about mobile devices).

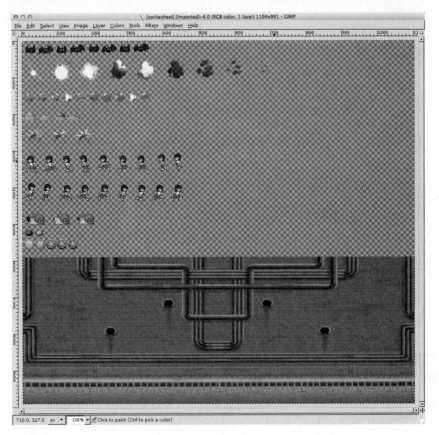

Figure 2.13 Snail Bait's sprite sheet in GIMP

2.2.3 Sound and Music

Plenty of sites on the Internet let you download freely available sound and music. Snail Bait uses sound effects from Replica Island, and its soundtrack comes from soundclick.com.

Just like you need an image editor for your open source graphics, you'll also need a sound editor for your sound effects and music. And like graphics, at the very least you will need to put all your game's sound effects in a single sound file, known as an audio sprite sheet. We discuss how to do that in Section 14.6.1, "Create Audio Sprites," on p. 350.

Audacity, an open source sound editor, shown in Figure 2.14, should suffice for all your sound editing needs.

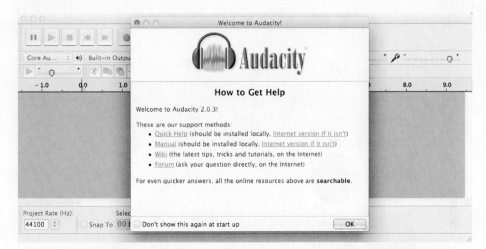

Figure 2.14 Using Audacity to create audio sprites

2.2.4 Animations

Most games display an animation as they load—typically, a spinning wheel or a progress bar. Snail Bait displays an animation of the game's snail attempting to shoot snail bombs without ammunition, as shown in Figure 2.15.

Figure 2.15 Snail Bait's loading animation

Lots of people seem to be intent on implementing websites that let you create animated GIFs from a series of images. One such website is shown in Figure 2.16.

Figure 2.16 Creating animated GIFs online

2.3 Use CSS Backgrounds

HTML5 games run in a web browser, so in addition to a game's background for its playing surface, such as Snail Bait's red-brick background, you must also consider the webpage background.

Figure 2.17 shows Snail Bait's webpage background, which is drawn with CSS gradients. CSS backgrounds do not incur the overhead associated with an image, and it's easy to make CSS backgrounds infinitely repeatable in both horizontal and vertical directions so that the background always looks the same regardless of the size of the window.

The CSS for the webpage background shown in Figure 2.17 is listed in Example 2.2. It uses repeating linear gradients to create an argyle effect. That code was copied from the CSS3 Patterns Gallery website, shown in Figure 2.18.

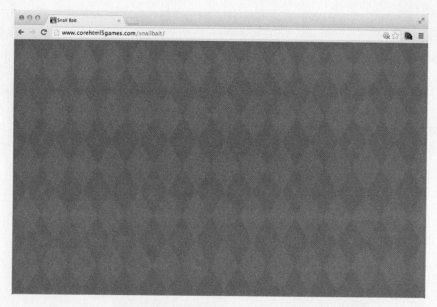

Figure 2.17 Snail Bait's webpage background

Example 2.2 Snail Bait's background (excerpt from snailbait.css)

```
body {
    /* Background from CSS3 Patterns Gallery by Anna Kassner */

    background-color: #6d6aff;

    background-image:
        repeating-linear-gradient(
            120deg, rgba(255,255,255,.1), rgba(255,255,255,.1) 1px,
            transparent 1px, transparent 60px),

        repeating-linear-gradient(
            60deg, rgba(255,255,255,.1), rgba(255,255,255,.1) 1px,
            transparent 1px, transparent 60px),

        linear-gradient(
            60deg, rgba(0,0,0,.1) 25%, transparent 25%, transparent 75%,
            rgba(0,0,0,.1) 75%, rgba(0,0,0,.1)),
```

(Continues)

Example 2.2   *(Continued)*

```
linear-gradient(
    120deg, rgba(0,0,0,.1) 25%, transparent 25%, transparent 75%,
    rgba(0,0,0,.1) 75%, rgba(0,0,0,.1));

background-size: 70px 120px;
}
```

Figure 2.18   The CSS3 Patterns Gallery

The CSS3 Patterns Gallery lets you select CSS code to create the backgrounds displayed on the website. All you have to do is click the background you want, copy the ensuing CSS code, and put it into your own CSS.

2.4 Generate Favicons

Favicons (short for favorite icons) add a little polish to your game. Snail Bait's favicon is shown in the browser tab in Figure 2.19.

Figure 2.19 Snail Bait's favicon

Lots of websites let you create favicons; Figure 2.20 shows one such site.

Figure 2.20 Creating favicons online

After you've created a favicon, you can display it by adding a link element in the head section of your HTML, as shown in Example 2.3.

Example 2.3 Specifying Snail Bait's favicon in HTML

```
<!DOCTYPE html>
<html>
    <head>
        <title>Snail Bait</title>
        ...

        <link rel="icon" href="/favicon.ico" type="image/x-icon">
    </head>

    <body>
        ...
    </body>
</html>
```

2.5 Shorten the Coding Cycle

JavaScript is an interpreted language, so you need not compile when you change your code. That means you can change your code and simply refresh the browser to immediately restart your game with the most up-to-date changes.

However, refreshing the browser after you change code in your editor means you must switch applications from the editor to the browser and refresh the page, typically with a keystroke or click of the mouse. And then, assuming you're not finished for the day, you must switch back to your editor.

That switching between applications and refreshing the browser may not seem like a big deal until you do it dozens of times a day. Automating browser refreshing when you change code in your editor will significantly turbocharge your coding cycle, in turn letting you implement games faster.

To automate browser refreshing when you save changes in your editor, you can use the Ruby script shown in Figure 2.21 that monitors files in a directory. When any of those files change, the Ruby script automatically updates a specific browser window. You indicate the directory and (a regular expression of) the text in the browser window's address bar, and the Ruby script takes care of the rest.

With the Ruby script shown in Figure 2.21 (or something similar) in place, you no longer have to leave your editor as you edit your code. Every time you save your changes in the editor, the Ruby script automatically refreshes the browser window you specified.

Figure 2.21 A Ruby script for monitoring files

NOTE: The benefits of shortening the coding cycle

If you're modifying gameplay, the benefits of automatically refreshing the browser when you save files in your editor are minimal because you still must switch from your editor to the browser to test your modifications; the only thing you save by automatically refreshing the browser is the keystroke to reload the page.

If you're modifying other aspects of the game, for example, the game's loading screen, you may not have to leave the editor to see changes in your browser after your game automatically reloads.

You'll get the most out of automatically refreshing the browser when you're experimenting with CSS. You can change CSS and immediately see the results in the browser without ever leaving your editor, making it easy to make many small adjustments to your game's CSS in rapid succession.

NOTE: The LiveReload Chrome extension

Chrome has a free extension named LiveReload that also monitors files and refreshes a browser window. You can find it at http://bit.ly/1ojCxVq.

2.6 Conclusion

Browser developer tools are essential for implementing HTML5 games, and at the time this book was written all major browsers provided capable toolsets. This chapter briefly described the Chrome developer tools, with some guidance about making the most of those tools when you're implementing games. And browser vendors implement similar enough toolsets that most of what you learned about Chrome developer tools in this chapter is applicable to other browsers.

It's rare to find skilled video game developers who are also accomplished artists and musicians, so most game developers rely on other resources for graphics, sound, and music. In this chapter, you've seen how to access open source resources and how to incorporate some of them, such as CSS backgrounds and favicons, into your games.

Now that we have all our tools and materials in order, we can start implementing Snail Bait in earnest in the next chapter.

2.7 Exercises

1. Run the final version of Snail Bait in the debugger. Set some breakpoints and step through some code.

2. Run the profiler while Snail Bait is running and evaluate game performance with your particular browser and operating system.

3. The final version of Snail Bait has a showSmokingHoles attribute, which is set to true. Change the line of code that initializes showSmokingHoles so that its value is false instead of true and restart Snail Bait. You should not see smoking holes. Run the profiler without the smoking holes and compare performance with that of the game run with smoking holes turned on.

4. Start Snail Bait in Chrome and open the developer tools in another window. As shown in Figure 2.6 on p. 45, position the windows so that you can see the developer tools as you play the game. Start a timeline, and keep an eye on performance out of the corner of your eye as you play the game.

5. Install the Ruby script described in Section 2.5, "Shorten the Coding Cycle," on p. 58. Position your editor and browser windows so that you can see the game as you work in your editor. Perform Exercise 5 from Chapter 1 and subsequently undo the changes required by that exercise. Did the Ruby script make the exercise from Chapter 1 any easier?

CHAPTER 3

Graphics and Animation

Topics in This Chapter

Graphics and animation are the most fundamental aspects of any video game. The ability to draw images and shapes and to create smooth, flicker-free animations are the most important skills a game developer must possess.

Animations continuously draw animation frames, typically between 30 and 60 times per second. That rate is known as the animation's *frame rate*. Each animation frame is much like a page in a flip book; frames look almost identical to the last, with minor differences from the preceding frame to create the illusion of motion as the game rapidly displays animation frames. See Section 3.2, "Implement Smooth HTML5 Animations," on p. 70 for more about flip books.

Figure 3.1 shows a screenshot of a single animation frame. That version of the game, which is where the game stands at the end of this chapter, also displays the animation's frame rate as it scrolls the background and platforms from right to left.

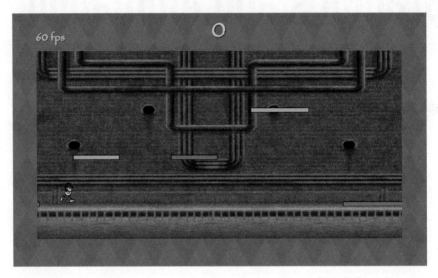

Figure 3.1 Scrolling the background and monitoring frame rate

The platforms are in the foreground, so they move noticeably faster than the background, creating the illusion of depth. That illusion is known as the parallax effect.

At this stage of development, the runner does not move. Also, the game has no collision detection yet, so the runner floats in mid-air when no platforms are underneath her.

Eventually, icons above and to the left of the game's canvas will indicate the number of remaining lives. For now, the game displays the current animation rate in frames per second at that location.

This chapter starts with a brief overview of the Canvas 2D API, followed by a discussion of the implementation of Snail Bait's central animation. In this chapter, you will learn how to do the following:

- Draw images and graphics primitives into a canvas (Section 3.1 on p. 64)
- Create smooth, flicker-free animations (Section 3.2 on p. 70)
- Implement a game loop (Section 3.3 on p. 75)
- Calculate frame rate in frames per second (Section 3.4 on p. 77)
- Scroll the game's background (Section 3.5 on p. 78)
- Implement motion that's unaffected by the underlying animation frame rate (Section 3.6 on p. 85)
- Reverse scroll direction (Section 3.7 on p. 86)
- Draw individual animation frames (Section 3.8 on p. 86)
- Use the parallax effect to simulate three dimensions (Section 3.9 on p. 87)

Before continuing, you might want to try the version of the game for this chapter as shown in Figure 3.1; the code will be easier to understand if you do.

 NOTE: Immediate-mode graphics

Canvas is an immediate-mode graphics system, meaning it immediately draws what you specify and then immediately forgets. Other graphics systems, such as Scalable Vector Graphics (SVG), implement retained-mode graphics, which means they retain a list of objects to draw. Without the overhead of maintaining a display list, Canvas is faster than SVG; however, if you want to maintain a list of objects that users can manipulate, you must implement that functionality on your own in Canvas.

 NOTE: Canvas double buffering

The preceding note indicated that the canvas element immediately draws whatever you specify. That claim needs further clarification.

When the browser invokes Snail Bait's animate() method to draw the current animation frame, the canvas element does indeed immediately draw whatever you specify; however, it draws to an off-screen canvas instead of the canvas on-screen. After the call to animate() returns, the browser copies the entire contents of the off-screen canvas to the on-screen canvas in one graphics operation. That technique, known as double buffering, results in smoother animations than if the browser draws directly into the on-screen canvas in the first place.

NOTE: Path-based graphics

Like Apple's Cocoa and Adobe's Illustrator, the Canvas API is path based, meaning you draw graphics primitives in a canvas by creating a path and then subsequently stroking or filling that path. The `strokeRect()` and `fillRect()` methods are convenience methods that stroke or fill a rectangle, respectively.

NOTE: HTML5 Canvas was introduced by Apple

Apple included what would eventually become HTML5 Canvas in WebKit in 2004. You can read more at http://en.wikipedia.org/wiki/Html5_canvas.

3.1 Draw Graphics and Images with the HTML5 `canvas` Element

The Canvas 2D context provides an extensive graphics API that lets you implement everything from text editors to platform video games. At the time this book was written, that API contained more than 30 methods; Snail Bait uses about one-third of them, listed in Table 3.1.

Table 3.1 Canvas 2D context methods

Method	Description
`arc(x,y,radius, startAngle,endAngle, counterClockwise)`	Adds an arc to the current path. You also use the `arc()` method to add circular paths to the current path by specifying a start angle of 0° and an end angle of 2π (360°).
`beginPath()`	Ends the current path and starts a new one.
`drawImage(image,sx,sy, sw,sh,dx,dy, dw,dh)`	Draws all or part of an image (*source*) at a specific location in a canvas (*destination*); The s and d in the arguments stand for *source* and *destination*, respectively, that is, sx means *source x*, and dh means *destination height*, and so on. In addition to an image, the source can also be a video or another canvas. The destination is always the canvas associated with the context.

(Continues)

Table 3.1 *(Continued)*

Method	Description
	You can call drawImage() with all nine arguments as listed to the left, or you can call it with three or five arguments, like this: drawImage(image, dx, dy) or drawImage(image, dx, dy, dw, dh). Both the three- and five-argument versions of the method draw the entire image at the specified location in the canvas. The five-argument version lets you scale the image by specifying the destination width and height.
	The nine-argument version of drawImage() lets you draw all or part of the image and scale it at the same time.
fill()	Fills a path's interior with the current fill style, which can be a color, pattern, or gradient.
fillRect(x,y,w,h)	Fills a rectangle with the current fill style.
isPointInPath()	Determines whether a point lies inside the current path, which can be an irregular shape.
rect(x,y,w,h)	Adds a rectangle to the current path.
restore()	Restores the state of the context to what it was the last time you called save().
save()	Saves the state of the context. You restore that state with the restore() method. Between calls to save() and restore(), all changes you make to context attributes are temporary.
stroke()	Strokes a path's outline with the current stroke style, which can be a color, pattern, or gradient.
strokeRect(x,y,w,h)	Draws an unfilled rectangle with the current stroke style.
translate(x,y)	Translates the coordinate system. This is a powerful method that is useful in many different scenarios. All horizontal scrolling in Snail Bait is implemented with this one method call.

The Canvas 2D context also has more than 30 attributes, but only the handful listed in Table 3.2 are used by Snail Bait.

Table 3.2 Canvas 2D context attributes

Method	Description
lineWidth	The width of lines and the thickness of outlines for circles, rectangles, arcs, and curves.
fillStyle	Any valid CSS color, such as rgb(0,0,0), #ffffff, or skyblue, that the context subsequently uses when it fills shapes. Besides colors, you can specify a gradient or a pattern for the fill style.
strokeStyle	Any valid CSS color string that the context subsequently uses when it strokes shape outlines or lines. You can specify a gradient or a pattern for the stroke style, as you can for the fill style.
globalAlpha	The opacity of all graphics operations, such as stroke(), fill(), and drawImage(), except for getImageData() and putImageData(), which you use to directly manipulate canvas pixels.

Everything in Snail Bait, with the exception of the platforms, is an image. The background, the runner, and all the good guys and bad guys are images that the game draws with the drawImage() method.

Ultimately Snail Bait uses a sprite sheet—a single image containing all the game's graphics—but for now we use separate images for the background and the runner.

3.1.1 Draw the Background

Snail Bait draws its background with the game's drawBackground() function. The initial version of that function is shown in Example 3.1.

Example 3.1 Drawing the background (initial version of drawBackground())

```
function drawBackground() {
   context.drawImage(background, 0, 0);
}
```

The drawBackground() function in Example 3.1 draws the background image at (0,0) in the canvas. That location places the upper-left corner of the image exactly at the upper-left corner of the canvas's drawing surface. Later, in Section 3.5, "Scroll the Background," on p. 78, we modify that function to scroll the background horizontally.

3.1.2 Draw the Runner

Until we get to sprites in Chapter 6, Snail Bait draws the runner with a drawRunner() function, listed in Example 3.2.

Example 3.2 Drawing the runner

```
var RUNNER_LEFT = 50;

function drawRunner() {
   context.drawImage(
      runnerImage,                                              // image
      RUNNER_LEFT,                                              // left
      calculatePlatformTop(runnerTrack) - runnerImage.height); // top
}
```

The drawRunner() function passes three arguments to drawImage(): an image and the left and top coordinates at which to draw that image in the canvas. The left coordinate is a constant, RUNNER_LEFT; the drawRunner() function calculates the runner's top coordinate by subtracting the runner's height from the top of the platform on which the runner resides. The function subtracts the runner's height to place the runner's feet on the platform. You might think it should add the runner's height instead of subtracting, but the canvas coordinate system increases from top to bottom, so to move something up in a canvas, you decrease its Y coordinate.

3.1.3 Draw Platforms

Snail Bait's platforms are not images, so drawing them requires a more extensive use of the Canvas API than merely invoking drawImage(), as shown in Example 3.3.

Example 3.3 The drawPlatforms() function

```
// An array of JavaScript objects that describe platforms

var platformData = [ // An array of JavaScript objects

   // A JavaScript object with properties that describe a platform

   {
      left:      10,
      width:     230,
      height:    PLATFORM_HEIGHT,
```

(Continues)

Example 3.3 *(Continued)*

```
        fillStyle:  'rgb(250,250,0)',
        opacity:    0.5,
        track:      1,
        pulsate:    false
    },

    // Other platform data definitions omitted for brevity.
],

// Track baselines.................................................

TRACK_1_BASELINE = 323, // pixels in the vertical direction from (0,0)
TRACK_2_BASELINE = 223, // pixels in the vertical direction from (0,0)
TRACK_3_BASELINE = 123; // pixels in the vertical direction from (0,0)
...

// Functions.......................................................

function calculatePlatformTop(track) {
    if      (track === 1) { return TRACK_1_BASELINE; } // 323 pixels
    else if (track === 2) { return TRACK_2_BASELINE; } // 223 pixels
    else if (track === 3) { return TRACK_3_BASELINE; } // 123 pixels
}

function drawPlatform(data) {
    var platformTop = calculatePlatformTop(data.track);

    context.lineWidth   = PLATFORM_STROKE_WIDTH;
    context.strokeStyle = PLATFORM_STROKE_STYLE;
    context.fillStyle   = data.fillStyle;
    context.globalAlpha = data.opacity;

    context.strokeRect(data.left, platformTop, data.width, data.height);
    context.fillRect  (data.left, platformTop, data.width, data.height);
}

function drawPlatforms() {
    var index;

    for (index = 0; index < platformData.length; ++index) {
        drawPlatform(platformData[index]);
    }
}
```

The JavaScript in Example 3.3 defines an array named platformData. Each object in that array describes an individual platform. Those platforms have properties such as left, width, height, track, and so on, that describe the platform's position and what it looks like.

Platforms move on horizontal tracks, as illustrated in Figure 3.2.

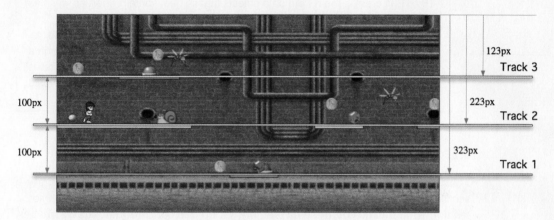

Figure 3.2 Platform tracks

The drawPlatforms() function iterates over the platformData array, in turn passing each object in the array to the drawPlatform() function, which calculates the top of the platform, sets context variables, and draws the platform's rectangle.

The drawPlatform() function uses the Canvas context's strokeRect() and fillRect() methods to draw platform rectangles. It uses the characteristics of those rectangles, which are stored in the objects in the platformData array, to set the context's line width, stroke style, fill style, and it uses the globalAlpha attribute to set the opacity of the platform.

At this point, you know almost everything you need to know about the 2D canvas context to implement Snail Bait. The rest of this book focuses on other aspects of HTML5 game development, starting with animation.

NOTE: Saving and restoring canvas context properties

When you set properties of a canvas context, such as lineWidth or fillStyle, those settings are permanent, meaning they affect all subsequent graphics operations you perform with the canvas context. To make settings temporary, you enclose them within calls to the context's save() and restore() methods, which save and restore all the context's properties.

BEST PRACTICE: Keep sprite data separate from the code that creates sprites

All Snail Bait's graphical objects (known as sprites) are *data driven*, meaning Snail Bait creates them from data objects that contain sprite properties, such as `left`, `top`, and so on, similar to the objects in the `platformData` array. That sprite metadata provides an important separation of concerns; for example, although Snail Bait stores sprite metadata in static arrays, the same metadata could come from, for example, a sophisticated level generator that generates game levels at runtime based on game conditions. Such a level generator would require no changes to Snail Bait's code that creates sprites.

3.2 Implement Smooth HTML5 Animations

Fundamentally, implementing animations is simple: You continuously draw a sequence of images that make it appear as though objects are animating in some fashion. That means you must implement a loop that continuously draws images.

Traditionally, animation loops were implemented in JavaScript with `setTimeout()` or, as illustrated in Example 3.4, `setInterval()`.

If you implement a `draw()` function that draws your next animation frame, the code in Example 3.4 will undoubtedly produce an animation by continuously invoking that function. However, you may not be satisfied with the results, because `setInterval()` and `setTimeout()` *know nothing about animation and are* not *millisecond precise.*

Example 3.4 Implementing animations with `setInterval()`

```
// DO NOT USE setInterval() for time-critical animations

setInterval( function (e) {
   draw();                       // A function that draws the current frame
}, 1000 / 60);                   // Approximately 60 frames/second (fps)
```

The code in Example 3.4 invokes a function named `draw()` every 1000/60 milliseconds, which equates to 60 frames per second. That rate is an estimate of an optimal frame rate, and since it's an estimate, it might not be accurate.

We must estimate the optimal time to draw the next animation frame because `setInterval()` and `setTimeout()` don't know anything about animation, leaving it up to developers to specify the frame rate. *It would be much better if the browser, which assuredly knows better than the developer when to draw the next animation frame, specified the frame rate instead.*

There is an even more serious drawback to using `setTimeout()` and `setInterval()`. Although you pass those methods time intervals specified in milliseconds, the methods are not millisecond precise; in fact, according to the HTML specification, *those methods, in an effort to conserve resources, can generously pad the interval you specify.*

To ensure smooth animations, you should never use `setTimeout()` and `setInterval()` for time-critical animations; instead, you should use `requestAnimationFrame()`, which we discuss in the next section.

NOTE: Flip books

Before animation and film, there were flip books. The pages of a flip book contain drawings that gradually change as you flip through the book, creating the illusion of motion. Flip books were popularized by Cracker Jack (a sweet mix of popcorn and nuts), which included them as a prize in each box of the snack.

The techniques we use today to implement animations in video games is similar to a flip book. Instead of a finite number of pages in a book, video games have a never-ending stream of animation frames, and like the pages of a flip book, a game's animation frames display a static picture that, at the millisecond level, gradually changes over time.

BEST PRACTICE: Always use **requestAnimationFrame()** instead of **setTimeout()** or **setInterval()** for time-critical animations.

3.2.1 The `requestAnimationFrame()` Method

A W3C specification titled "Timing Control for Script-based Animations" defines a method on the `window` object named `requestAnimationFrame()`. Unlike `setTimeout()` or `setInterval()`, `requestAnimationFrame()` is specifically meant for implementing animations. It therefore suffers from none of the drawbacks discussed above associated with `setTimeout()` and `setInterval()`. It's also simple to use, as Example 3.5 illustrates.

You pass `requestAnimationFrame()` a reference to a callback function, and when the browser is ready to draw the next animation frame, it calls back (thus, the name) to the callback. To sustain the animation, the callback also invokes `requestAnimationFrame()`, identifying itself as the function to invoke when it's time to draw the next animation frame.

Example 3.5 Implementing animations with requestAnimationFrame()

```
function animate(now) {          // Animation loop
    draw(now);                   // Draws the current animation frame
    requestAnimationFrame(animate); // Keep the animation going
}
...

requestAnimationFrame(animate);  // Start the animation
```

As you can see from Example 3.5, the browser passes a parameter referred to as now to the callback function. You may wonder exactly what that now parameter means. Is it a string representing the current time, a number representing how many seconds have elapsed since Jan. 1, 1970, or something else?

Surprisingly, there is no set definition of that time. The only thing you can be sure of is that for any given browser, it always represents the same thing; therefore, you can use it to calculate the elapsed time between animation frames, as illustrated in Section 3.4, "Calculate Frame Rates," on p. 77.

3.2.2 A requestAnimationFrame() Polyfill

In many ways, HTML5 is a programmer's utopia. Free from proprietary APIs, developers use HTML5 to implement applications that run across platforms and devices in the ubiquitous browser. The specifications progress rapidly, constantly incorporating new technology and refining existing functionality.

New technology, however, often makes its way into the specification through existing browser-specific functionality. Browser vendors often prefix such functionality so that it doesn't interfere with another browser's implementation; requestAnimationFrame(), for example, was originally implemented by Mozilla as mozRequestAnimationFrame(). Then it was implemented by other browser vendors such as WebKit, who named their function webkitRequest-AnimationFrame(). Finally, the W3C standardized it as requestAnimationFrame().

Vendor-prefixed implementations and varying support for standard implementations make new functionality tricky to use, so the HTML5 community invented something known as a polyfill. Polyfills, which also go by the names *shim* and *shiv*, determine the browser's level of support for a particular feature. They give you either direct access to it if the browser implements it or access to a stopgap implementation that does its best to mimic the standard functionality.

Polyfills are simple to use but can be complicated to implement. Example 3.6 shows the implementation of a polyfill for requestAnimationFrame().

Example 3.6 A requestAnimationFrame() polyfill

```javascript
window.requestNextAnimationFrame =
    (function () {
        var originalWebkitRequestAnimationFrame = undefined,
            wrapper      = undefined,
            callback     = undefined,
            geckoVersion = 0,
            userAgent    = navigator.userAgent,
            index        = 0,
            self         = this;

        // Workaround for Chrome 10 bug where Chrome
        // does not pass the time to the animation function.

        if (window.webkitRequestAnimationFrame) {
            // Define the wrapper

            wrapper = function (time) {
                if (time === undefined) {
                    time = +new Date();
                }
                self.callback(time);
            };

            // Make the switch

            originalWebkitRequestAnimationFrame =
                window.webkitRequestAnimationFrame;

            window.webkitRequestAnimationFrame =
                function (callback, element) {
                    self.callback = callback;

                    // Browser calls the wrapper and
                    // wrapper calls the callback.

                    originalWebkitRequestAnimationFrame(wrapper, element);
                };
        }


        // Workaround for Gecko 2.0, which has a bug in
        // mozRequestAnimationFrame() that restricts animations
        // to 30-40 fps.

        if (window.mozRequestAnimationFrame) {
            // Check the Gecko version. Gecko is used by browsers
            // other than Firefox. Gecko 2.0 corresponds to
            // Firefox 4.0.
```

(Continues)

Example 3.6 *(Continued)*

```
        index = userAgent.indexOf('rv:');

      if (userAgent.indexOf('Gecko') != -1) {
        geckoVersion = userAgent.substr(index + 3, 3);

        if (geckoVersion === '2.0') {
          // Forces the return statement to fall through
          // to the setTimeout() function.

          window.mozRequestAnimationFrame = undefined;
        }
      }
    }

    return window.requestAnimationFrame       ||
       window.webkitRequestAnimationFrame  ||
       window.mozRequestAnimationFrame     ||
       window.oRequestAnimationFrame       ||
       window.msRequestAnimationFrame      ||

       function (callback, element) {
         var start,
             finish;

         window.setTimeout( function () {
           start = +new Date();
           callback(start);
           finish = +new Date();

           self.timeout = 1000 / 60 - (finish - start);

         }, self.timeout);
       };
    }
  )
();
```

The polyfill implemented in **Example 3.6** attaches a function named requestNextAnimationFrame() to the window object. The inclusion of Next in the function name differentiates it from the underlying requestAnimationFrame() function.

The function that the polyfill assigns to requestNextAnimationFrame() is either requestAnimationFrame() or a vendor-prefixed implementation. If the browser does not support any of those functions, the function is an ad-hoc implementation that uses setTimeout() to mimic requestAnimationFrame() the best it can.

Nearly all the polyfill's complexity involves working around two bugs and constitutes the code before the `return` statement at the end of Example 3.6. The first bug involves Chrome 10, which passes an undefined value for the time. The second bug involves Firefox 4.0, which restricts frame rates to 35–40 frames per second.

Although the `requestNextAnimationFrame()` polyfill's implementation is interesting, it's not necessary that you understand the implementation; all you need to know is how to use it, as the next section illustrates.

NOTE: Programming for the future with polyfills

In the past, cross-platform software was implemented for the lowest common denominator. Polyfills turn that notion on its head by giving you access to advanced features if they are available and falling back to a less capable implementation when necessary.

NOTE: +new `Date()`

+new `Date()` is one of several ways to access the current time in JavaScript. The plus sign coerces the date created by new `Date()` into a number.

NOTE: `requestAnimationFrame()` vs. `requestNextAnimationFrame()`

Throughout this book we use the `requestNextAnimationFrame()` polyfill discussed above, which uses the underlying `requestAnimationFrame()` if it's available; otherwise, the polyfill works as a fallback solution.

3.3 Implement a Game Loop

Now that we've covered graphics and animation prerequisites, it's time to put Snail Bait in motion. To start, we include the JavaScript for `requestNextAnimationFrame()` in the game's HTML, as shown in Example 3.7.

Example 3.7 The HTML

```
<!DOCTYPE html>
<html>
...

   <body>
      ...
```

(Continues)

Example 3.7 *(Continued)*

```
        <!-- The final version of Snail Bait has only
             one JavaScript file. -->

        <script src='js/requestNextAnimationFrame.js'></script>
        <script src='game.js'></script>
    </body>
</html>
```

Example 3.8 shows the starting point for the game's animation loop, commonly referred to as the game loop.

Example 3.8 The game loop

```
var fps,
    background  = new Image(),
    runnerImage = new Image();

function draw(now) {
   drawBackground();
   drawPlatforms();
   drawRunner();
}

function animate(now) {
   fps = calculateFps(now);
   draw(now); // Draw an animation frame
   requestNextAnimationFrame(animate); // Call animate() again
}

function startGame() {
   requestNextAnimationFrame(animate);
}

function initializeImages() {
   background.src  = 'images/background.png';
   runnerImage.src = 'images/runner.png';

   background.onload = function (e) {
      startGame();
   };
}

// Launch game................................................

initializeImages();
```

The startGame() function, which is invoked by the onload event handler for the background image, starts the game by calling the requestNextAnimationFrame() polyfill for the first time. Subsequently, when it's time to draw the game's first animation frame, the browser invokes the animate() function.

The animate() function invokes the calculateFps() function to calculate the animation's frame rate, given the current time. (See Section 3.2.1 on p. 71 for more about that time value.) After calculating the frame rate, animate() invokes a draw() function that draws the next animation frame. Subsequently, animate() calls requestNextAnimationFrame() to sustain the animation.

3.4 Calculate Frame Rates

Example 3.9 shows the implementation of Snail Bait's calculateFps() function, which calculates the frame rate.

Example 3.9 Calculating frame rate

```
var lastAnimationFrameTime = 0;

function calculateFps(now) {
   var fps = 1 / (now - lastAnimationFrameTime) * 1000;

   lastAnimationFrameTime = now;
   ...

   return fps;
}
```

The frame rate, expressed in frames/second, is one frame divided by the amount of time, in seconds, since the last animation frame.

A small modification to the preceding function results in updates to the frame rate readout shown in Example 3.10.

Example 3.10 Updating the snailbaits-fps element

```
var lastAnimationFrameTime = 0,
    lastFpsUpdateTime = 0,
    fpsElement = document.getElementById('snailbait-fps');
```

(Continues)

Example 3.10 *(Continued)*

```
function calculateFps(now) {
   var fps = 1 / (now - lastAnimationFrameTime) * 1000;

   if (now - lastFpsUpdateTime > 1000) { // Once per second
      lastFpsUpdateTime = now;
      fpsElement.innerHTML = fps.toFixed(0) + ' fps';
   }

   lastAnimationFrameTime = now;

   return fps;
}
```

Example 3.10 also illustrates an important animation technique: performing a task at a rate other than the animation rate. If you update the frames/second readout every animation frame, it will be unreadable because it will always be in flux; instead, the preceding code updates the readout once per second.

With the game loop in place and frame rate in hand, we are now ready to scroll the background.

 NOTE: Keep the game loop in mind

It's important to keep in mind that Snail Bait invokes many of its methods continuously, typically around 60 frames/second.

If you lose sight of the fact that Snail Bait invokes methods continuously, code will be hard to understand. For example, in Example 3.9 the declaration of the lastAnimationFrameTime variable and its assignment to zero only happens once. But Snail Bait invokes the calculateFps() function every animation frame, meaning that the first time Snail Bait calls calculateFps(), the value of lastAnimationFrameTime is zero, but on subsequent calls, it is not (because of the assignment to lastAnimationFrameTime in calculateFps()).

3.5 Scroll the Background

Everything in Snail Bait, with the exception of the runner, continuously scrolls in the horizontal direction while the game is in play. This section discusses the implementation of that scrolling.

3.5.1 Translate the Coordinate System

Every canvas element consists of two things: its HTML element and a drawing surface, which are depicted in Figure 3.3 as a picture frame and a sheet of graph paper, respectively.

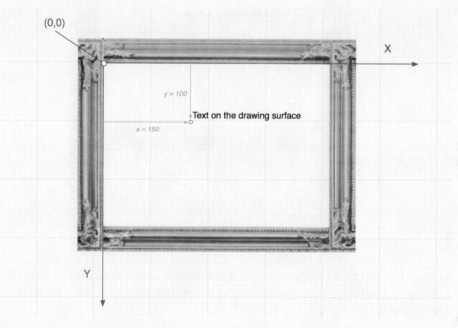

Figure 3.3 A canvas element (picture frame) and its drawing surface (graph paper)

The drawing surface has a coordinate system so that you can draw at specific locations, such as the text in Figure 3.3, which is located at (150,100). You draw that text with the canvas context as shown in Example 3.11.

Example 3.11 Drawing text on the drawing surface

```
context.drawText("Text on the drawing surface", 100, 150);
```

By default the origin of the coordinate system—meaning the location of (0,0)—is at the upper-left corner of the canvas. X coordinates increase from left to right, and Y coordinates increase from top to bottom, as you can see from Figure 3.3. The direction in which X and Y coordinates increase is nonnegotiable, but the origin of the coordinate system is not fixed. You can move it, as shown in Figure 3.4, like moving the graph paper underneath the picture frame.

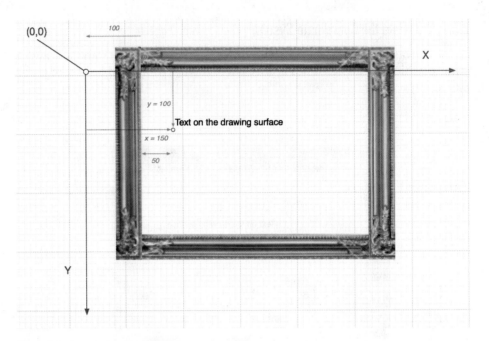

Figure 3.4 Translating the coordinate system

In Figure 3.4, the coordinate system is translated to the left by 100 pixels. The code for translating the coordinate system and drawing the text is shown in Example 3.12.

Example 3.12 Setting the background offset

```
context.translate(-100, 0); // Translate drawing surface to the left
context.drawText("Text on the drawing surface", 100, 150);
```

The two arguments you pass to context.translate() represent how far, in pixels, to translate the coordinate system in the horizontal and vertical directions. In this example, we are only translating horizontally, but context.translate() can translate in both directions.

Notice that the text in Figure 3.4 appears to move to the left relative to the canvas compared with its original location in Figure 3.3, even though it's drawn at the same coordinates. Conversely, the canvas appears to move to the right in relation to the text. *That apparent motion comes from translating the coordinate system.*

You can draw anywhere you want on the drawing surface, but anything you draw outside the canvas cannot be seen, as illustrated by Figure 3.5.

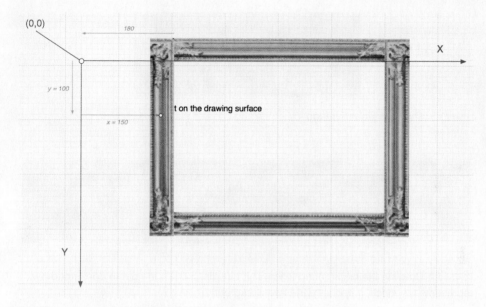

Figure 3.5 Drawing outside the picture frame (canvas) has no effect.

The code for translating the coordinate system as shown in Figure 3.5 is listed in Example 3.13.

Example 3.13 Setting the background offset

```
context.translate(-180, 0);
context.drawText('Text on the drawing surface', 100, 150);
```

The preceding code translates the coordinate system far enough to the left so that only part of the text is visible in the canvas.

As the previous discussion illustrates, *you can create apparent motion by continuously translating the coordinate system and redrawing everything at the same coordinates.* That's how Snail Bait scrolls the background and everything else.

3.5.2 Scroll Snail Bait's Background

Snail Bait's background image is shown in Figure 3.6.

Snail Bait draws the background twice, end to end, to accommodate scrolling, as shown in Figure 3.7.

Figure 3.6 The background image

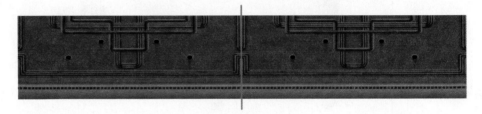

Figure 3.7 Drawing the background twice. The blue line, which the game does not draw, represents the junction between the two backgrounds.

The drawBackground() function is shown in Example 3.14.

Example 3.14 Drawing the background

```
var backgroundOffset = 0; // Constantly updated as the game runs

function drawBackground() {
    context.translate(-backgroundOffset, 0);

    context.drawImage(background, 0, 0);
    context.drawImage(background, background.width, 0);

    context.translate(backgroundOffset, 0);
}
```

The drawBackground() function is invoked by draw(), which Snail Bait calls for every animation frame. drawBackground() translates the coordinate system to the left by backgroundOffset pixels, draws the background twice end to end, and then translates the coordinate system back to where it was before drawBackground() was called. To scroll the background, therefore, Snail Bait continuously increases the value of backgroundOffset. The effect of increasing that value is shown in Figure 3.8.

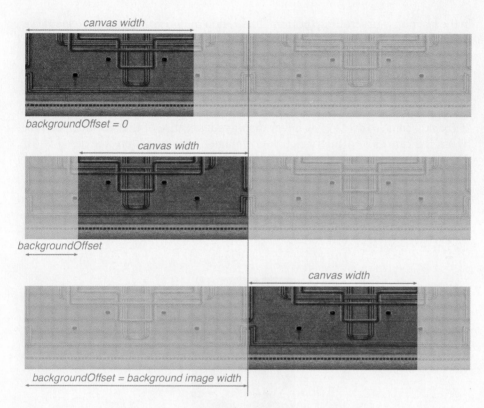

canvas width

backgroundOffset = 0

canvas width

backgroundOffset

canvas width

backgroundOffset = background image width

Figure 3.8 Scrolling right to left: Translucent areas represent the offscreen parts of the images. The canvas coordinate system moves from right to left.

Continuously translating the coordinate system to the left makes the game's background appear to scroll to the left in the canvas, as you can see in Figure 3.8.

The background image, whose width is 1103 pixels, is wider than the game's canvas, which is 800 pixels wide. When the game begins, backgroundOffset is zero, and the only visible part of the two backgrounds is approximately the first three-quarters of the image drawn at (0,0), as shown in the top illustration in Figure 3.8. The final quarter of that image and the entire image drawn at (background.width,0) are initially not visible because they lie outside the bounds of the canvas.

A short time after the game starts, backgroundOffset is no longer zero, and the coordinate system is translated to the left by a significant amount, as shown in the middle illustration in Figure 3.8. The background drawn at (background.width,0), however, is still not visible.

In the last phase of scrolling (bottom illustration in Figure 3.8), backgroundOffset is equal to the width of the background image; more importantly, *the visible part of the background is exactly the same as the visible part of the background when scrolling begins*. At that point, Snail Bait resets backgroundOffset to zero, taking us back to the top illustration in Figure 3.8.

It's interesting to note that the final quarter or so of the background image drawn at (background.width, 0) is never displayed, because of the size mismatch between the canvas and the background image. If the two were the same width, that final quarter of the background image drawn at (background.width, 0) would be visible at some point.

It may not be readily apparent from the preceding figures, but the background image has a special quality that makes it well suited to game backgrounds: The vertical rows of pixels on the left and right edges of the image are identical, as shown in Figure 3.9.

Figure 3.9 Identical edges make smooth transitions (left: right edge; right: left edge).

Without identical edges, the background would have a noticeable discontinuity where the two backgrounds meet, meaning the blue lines in Figure 3.7 and Figure 3.8.

There is one unanswered question concerning the scrolling of Snail Bait's background: How does the game adjust the backgroundOffset variable that controls background scrolling? That question is answered in the next section, where we scroll the background at a constant rate regardless of the underlying animation frame rate.

 BEST PRACTICE: Make sure your background image has identical edges for smooth scrolling.

3.6 Create Time-Based Motion

Your animation's frame rate will vary, but you cannot let that varying frame rate affect the speed of objects in your game, including the background. You must unfurl smooth continuous action regardless of any chaos that's disrupting the game's underlying animation. For example, Snail Bait scrolls the background at 25 pixels/second regardless of the animation's underlying frame rate. Motion must be *time based*, meaning it depends only on time (e.g., pixels/second) and not the animation's frame rate.

Using time-based motion to calculate the number of pixels to move an object for any given animation frame is simple: *Multiply the object's velocity by the elapsed time, in seconds, since the last animation frame.* When you multiply velocity (pixels/second) by the elapsed time since the previous animation frame (seconds/frame), the seconds cancel out and you get pixels/frame, meaning *the number of pixels you need to move something for the current frame.*

Example 3.15 shows how Snail Bait uses time-based motion to calculate the background's offset.

To calculate the number of pixels to move the background for the current frame, the setBackgroundOffset() function multiplies the background velocity by the time it took, in seconds, to complete the previous animation frame. The function then adds that value to the background offset.

To continuously scroll the background, setBackgroundOffset() resets the background offset to zero when it becomes less than zero or greater than the width of the background.

Example 3.15 Setting the background offset

```
var BACKGROUND_VELOCITY = 25, // pixels / second
    bgVelocity = BACKGROUND_VELOCITY;

function setBackgroundOffset(now) {
   backgroundOffset +=
      bgVelocity * (now - lastAnimationFrameTime) / 1000;

   if (backgroundOffset < 0 || backgroundOffset > background.width) {
      backgroundOffset = 0;
   }
}
```

 NOTE: Snail Bait uses time-based motion to move everything in the game, not just the background.

3.7 Reverse Scroll Direction

Recall that all horizontal motion in Snail Bait is the result of continuously translating the coordinate system of the game's drawing surface and continually redrawing everything at the same horizontal location. That method of creating apparent horizontal motion results in several simplifications in the game's code. First, the game never has to calculate horizontal locations for any of its sprites, because their horizontal location never changes; instead, one sprite offset controls their horizontal motion, just as the background offset controls the background's horizontal motion. Second, changing direction so that everything scrolls horizontally in the opposite direction merely involves setting the game's background velocity, as in Example 3.16.

Example 3.16 Turning left and right

```
function turnLeft() {
   bgVelocity = -BACKGROUND_VELOCITY;
}

function turnRight() {
   bgVelocity = BACKGROUND_VELOCITY;
}
```

Once again, keep in mind that Snail Bait's animation loop is continuous. Setting the bgVelocity variable has an effect the next time Snail Bait draws an animation frame.

Now that you've seen how to scroll the background at a constant rate regardless of the underlying animation frame rate, let's see how the setBackgroundOffset() and drawBackground() functions discussed above are used by Snail Bait.

3.8 Draw Animation Frames

Recall Section 3.3, "Implement a Game Loop," on p. 75, which lists Snail Bait's game loop. That loop consists of an animate() function that the browser invokes when it's time to draw the game's next animation frame. That animate() function, in turn, invokes a draw() function that draws the next animation frame. The code for the draw() function at this stage of development is shown in Example 3.17.

The draw() function sets the background offset and then draws the background, runner, and platforms. All the methods invoked by the draw() function have already been discussed in this chapter.

Example 3.17 The draw() function

```
function draw(now) {
   setBackgroundOffset(now);

   drawBackground();
   drawRunner();
   drawPlatforms();
}
```

Now that you've seen how Snail Bait scrolls its background with time-based motion, let's see how it scrolls the game's platforms.

3.9 Use Parallax to Create the Illusion of Depth

If you've ever sat in the passenger seat of a moving car and watched your hand race against telephone poles at high speed, you know that things close to you appear to move faster than things that are farther away. That's known as parallax.

Snail Bait is a 2D platformer, but it uses a mild parallax effect to make it appear as though the platforms are closer to the player than the background. The game implements that parallax by scrolling the platforms noticeably faster than the background, as illustrated in Figure 3.10. The top screenshot shows the background at a particular point in time, and the bottom screenshot shows the background a few animation frames later. From those two screenshots you can see that the platforms have moved much farther than the background in the same amount of time.

To implement parallax, the first thing we do is revise the drawPlatforms() function, as in Example 3.18.

The original version of drawPlatforms() simply iterated over the platform data and invoked drawPlatform() for each data instance as listed in Example 3.3 on p. 67. The revised version of drawPlatforms() translates the game canvas's coordinate system to the left by platformOffset pixels, iterates over the data, and then translates the coordinate system back to where it was before drawPlatforms() was invoked.

Realize that the revised implementation of drawPlatforms() scrolls platforms similarly to how drawBackground() scrolls the background, as listed in Example 3.14 on p. 82. Snail Bait uses two offsets to scroll the background and platforms: one for the background and another for the platforms.

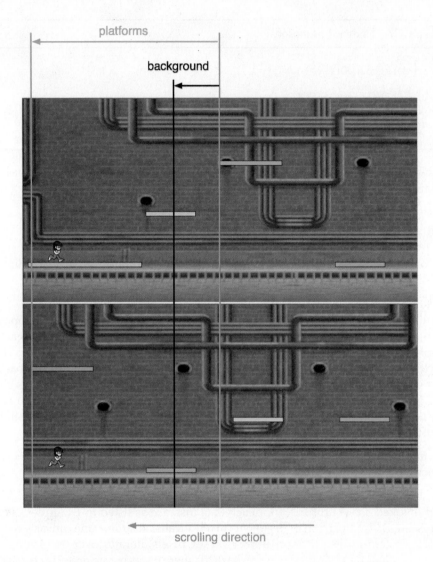

Figure 3.10 Parallax: The platforms (near) scroll faster than the background (far)

Example 3.18 The drawPlatforms() function, revised

```
function drawPlatforms() {
   var index;

   context.translate(-platformOffset, 0);
```

```
for (index = 0; index < platformData.length; ++index) {
    drawPlatform(platformData[index]);
}

context.translate(platformOffset, 0);
}
```

Now that we're using a platform offset to scroll the platforms, we must calculate that value. Example 3.19 shows the implementation of Snail Bait's setPlatformOffset() function, which calculates the platform offset similarly to how setBackgroundOffset() calculates the background offset, as listed in Example 3.15 on p. 85.

Example 3.19 Setting platform velocities and offsets

```
var platformOffset = 0,
    PLATFORM_VELOCITY_MULTIPLIER = 4.35;

function setPlatformVelocity() {
    // Platforms move 4.35 times as fast as the background
    platformVelocity = bgVelocity * PLATFORM_VELOCITY_MULTIPLIER;
}

function setPlatformOffset(now) {
    platformOffset +=
        platformVelocity * (now - lastAnimationFrameTime) / 1000;
}
```

The final piece to the parallax puzzle is to update the draw() function to account for scrolling the platforms. That revised version of draw() is listed in Example 3.20.

Example 3.20 The draw() function, revised

```
function setOffsets(now) {
    setBackgroundOffset(now);
    setPlatformOffset(now);
}

function draw(now) {
    setPlatformVelocity();
    setOffsets(now);

    drawBackground();
```

(Continues)

Example 3.20 *(Continued)*

```
    drawRunner();
    drawPlatforms();
}
```

For every animation frame, the draw() function sets the platform velocity with setPlatformVelocity(), sets offsets, and then draws the background, runner, and platforms.

3.10 Conclusion

The most salient aspects of any video game are its graphics and animation. In this chapter you learned the fundamentals of drawing shapes and images with the HTML5 canvas element, and you saw the correct way to implement time-critical animations with requestAnimationFrame()—wrapped in a requestNextAnimationFrame() polyfill—instead of the traditional setTimeout() and setInterval(), which are poorly suited for animation.

This chapter also showed you how to continuously translate the coordinate system for a canvas's drawing surface to create apparent motion. Although the discussion of translating coordinate systems in this chapter focused on horizontal scrolling, you can easily extrapolate the code in this chapter to scroll vertically or even in both directions at once.

Objects in video games should not slow down or speed up simply because the underlying animation frame rate changed, so this chapter showed you how to implement time-based motion, meaning motion that is strictly based on time and does not depend on the current frame rate.

Finally, this chapter covered how you can create the illusion of depth by making objects in the foreground move faster than objects in the background.

3.11 Exercises

1. The canvas 2D context has four attributes for drawing shadows:

    • shadowColor: A CSS color string, gradient, or pattern with which to draw the shadow

    • shadowOffsetX: The shadow's offset, in pixels, in the X direction

    • shadowOffsetY: The shadow's offset, in pixels, in the Y direction

- shadowBlur: A Gaussian blur applied to the shadow; the higher the number, the blurrier the shadow.

In the drawPlatform() function in this chapter's version of the game, set all four of the preceding values in addition to lineWidth, fillStyle, strokeStyle, and globalAlpha, to create shadows underneath the platforms. Do those shadows affect the frame rate?

2. Notice that setting context shadow attributes in Exercise 1 not only adds shadows to the platforms but also adds a shadow to the runner's image. That's because setting shadow attributes affects all further graphics operations in the canvas (except for getImage() and putImage(), which are not discussed in this book).

   To add shadows to the platforms but not the runner, save the graphics context at the beginning of drawPlatform() and restore it at the end of the function, with context.save() and context.restore(), respectively. Any settings you make to the graphics context between context.save() and context.restore() are only in effect between those two calls. As a result, you will see shadows underneath the platforms, but not the runner.

3. Use a different background for this chapter's version of the game. Make sure the new background does *not* have identical rows of vertical pixels on the right and left edges of the left and right sides of the image, respectively, as discussed in Section 3.5, "Scroll the Background," on p. 78. Is the discontinuity between the two background images obvious as the animation progresses?

4. Run this chapter's version of the game and see if you can slow the frame rate by doing other things on your computer. Good candidates for slowing the game are playing YouTube videos in another browser window; running system backup software; opening semitransparent windows.

CHAPTER

4

Infrastructure

Topics in This Chapter

Many aspects of game programming have nothing to do with gameplay. Displaying instructions, pausing games, transitioning between levels, and displaying game credits are just some features that game developers implement besides gameplay. Those features, however, contribute a great deal to the overall impression your game makes on players, so it's important to implement them well and add some polish.

In the last chapter, we discussed graphics and animation, which are fundamental to Snail Bait's gameplay. In this chapter, we implement some of the game's infrastructure, starting by encapsulating Snail Bait's code in a JavaScript object.

You will also see how to pause and freeze Snail Bait and subsequently how to thaw and restart the game with an animated countdown. And you'll see how to handle keyboard events to control the runner and how to display temporary messages—known as toasts—to players. In Figure 4.1, Snail Bait reveals a toast that's part of the three-second countdown that gives players time to regain the controls after the game's window regains focus.

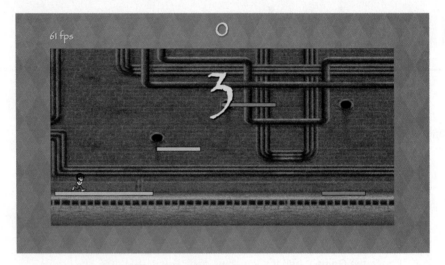

Figure 4.1 Counting down after regaining focus

In this chapter, you'll learn how to do the following:

- Encapsulate game functions in a JavaScript object (Section 4.1 on p. 95)
- Understand JavaScript's persnickety this reference (Section 4.2 on p. 100)
- Handle keyboard input (Section 4.3 on p. 103)
- Pause or resume the game when the player presses the p key (Section 4.4 on p. 105)
- Freeze the game to ensure it resumes exactly where it left off (Section 4.5 on p. 107)
- Pause the game when the window loses focus (Section 4.6 on p. 108)
- Resume a paused game with an animated countdown (Section 4.7 on p. 110)
- Display toasts (brief messages) to players (Section 4.7.1 on p. 111)

Along the way, you'll learn how to implement and instantiate JavaScript objects, how to combine CSS and JavaScript to make HTML elements appear and disappear, and how to use `setTimeout()` to display a countdown when a paused game resumes.

BEST PRACTICE: Implement infrastructure up front

When inspiration for a game strikes, it usually doesn't include ingenious ways to resume a paused game, for example, so it's natural to dive into implementing game mechanics without giving much thought to the game's infrastructure. But as in most projects, bolting on infrastructure as an afterthought is more work than if you incorporate it from the beginning.

4.1 Encapsulate Game Functions in a JavaScript Object

Up to now, we've implemented all Snail Bait functions, along with several of its variables, as global variables. That, of course, will never do. Fundamentally, global variables are a bad idea because it's too easy to inadvertently overwrite them.

Instead of using global variables, from now on we encapsulate all Snail Bait functions and variables in a single JavaScript object. By doing so, we reduce to nearly zero the odds of some other JavaScript code overwriting Snail Bait functions. For example, consider the game's `startGame()` function. As a global function, it's easy to inadvertently overwrite simply by implementing another function with the same name. However, if the same function resides in an object named `SnailBait`, the odds of someone unintentionally overwriting it—by assigning a function to `SnailBait.startGame`—are next to nil.

The `SnailBait` object, like all JavaScript objects, is composed of two parts: a constructor function and a prototype object. Let's look at the constructor function first.

4.1.1 Snail Bait's Constructor

Example 4.1 partially lists the game's constructor.

The `SnailBait` variable is a function that the JavaScript interpreter invokes when you create a new instance of `SnailBait`, like this: `new SnailBait()`. That function is known as a *constructor* function because it constructs the `SnailBait` JavaScript object, which you access in the constructor with the `this` variable. Constructor functions typically assign properties—such as `this.LEFT` or `this.canvas`—that are subsequently used by the object's methods.

Example 4.1 Snail Bait's constructor (partial listing)

```
var SnailBait = function () {
   // Variables......................................................

   this.canvas  = document.getElementById('game-canvas');
   this.context = this.canvas.getContext('2d');
   ...

   // HTML elements..................................................

   this.toast = document.getElementById('snailbait-toast');
   this.fpsElement = document.getElementById('snailbait-fps');
   ...

   // Constants

   this.LEFT = 1;
   this.RIGHT = 2;
   this.PLATFORM_HEIGHT = 8;
   ...

   this.platformData = [
      // Screen 1
      {
          left:      10,
          width:     230,
          height:    this.PLATFORM_HEIGHT,
          fillStyle: 'rgb(150,190,255)',
          opacity:   1.0,
          track:     1,
          pulsate:   false
      },

      // More data objects defining platforms are omitted for brevity
   ];
   ...

   // Many more properties are omitted for brevity
};
```

Snail Bait's constructor is much longer than the listing in Example 4.1; the final
version is more than 1400 lines, with substantial sections for variables, references
to HTML elements, constants, and the definition of game objects, such as the
platformData array listed in Example 4.1, which defines properties of the game's
platforms.

Now that you've seen how Snail Bait's constructor is implemented, let's look at the `SnailBait` object's associated prototype.

4.1.2 Snail Bait's Prototype

The functions associated with a JavaScript object are known as the object's *methods*. They reside in a separate JavaScript object known as the *prototype*, as shown in Figure 4.2, which depicts the `SnailBait` JavaScript object and its prototype.

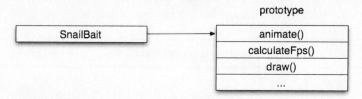

Figure 4.2 Snail Bait's prototype

Example 4.2 partially lists the `SnailBait` object's prototype, which at approximately 2300 lines of code is considerably longer than `SnailBait`'s constructor function.

Example 4.2 The game's prototype (partial listing)

```
SnailBait.prototype = {
  ...

  draw: function (now) {
    this.setPlatformVelocity();
    this.setOffsets(now);

    this.drawBackground();
    this.drawRunner();
    this.drawPlatforms();
  },
  ...

  // Many more methods are defined in the rest of this prototype object
};
```

Example 4.2 lists only the game's `draw()` method. Throughout the rest of this chapter, we convert the other functions discussed in the last chapter into `SnailBait` methods. In those methods you access the `SnailBait` JavaScript object with the this reference, just like you do in the object's constructor, which is listed in Example 4.1. A substantial caveat comes with the this reference, however, as discussed in Section 4.2, "Understand JavaScript's Persnickety this Reference," on p. 100.

Now that we've implemented the SnailBait constructor function and its prototype, we can create an instance of SnailBait and invoke its initializeImages() method, whose implementation we discuss in the next section, to start the game as shown in Example 4.3. The initializeImages() method assigns an onload event handler to the background image. That event handler, which the browser calls when the background image is fully loaded, starts the game.

Example 4.3 Creating the snailBait JavaScript object

```
var snailBait = new SnailBait();

snailBait.initializeImages(); // Initially discussed in
                              //   Section 3.3 on p. 75
```

As we incorporate new features throughout this book, we will add and remove methods and also modify some method implementations. Table 4.1 lists the game's methods as they exist as of the end of this chapter.

Table 4.1 Snail Bait methods at the end of this chapter (listed in invocation order)

Method	Description
initializeImages()	Initializes the game's images and defines an onload event handler for the background image that invokes startGame().
startGame()	Starts the game by invoking the requestNextAnimationFrame() polyfill, which is either a reference to the browser's underlying requestAnimationFrame() if it exists, or a reference to a fallback implementation that does its best to mimic requestAnimationFrame(). Either way, the polyfill calls the game's animate() method when it's time to draw the first animation frame. See Chapter 3 for more details about the requestNextAnimationFrame() polyfill.
revealToast(text, duration)	Displays the specified text for the specified duration (in milliseconds). The duration is optional; the default duration is 1000 ms (one second).

(Continues)

Table 4.1 *(Continued)*

Method	Description
animate(now)	If the game is not paused, draws the next animation frame and invokes requestNextAnimationFrame() to schedule another call to animate(). If the game is paused, animate() waits 200 ms before invoking requestNextAnimationFrame(). The now variable represents the current time.
calculateFps(now)	Calculates the frame rate based on the elapsed time since the last animation frame by dividing one frame by the elapsed time in seconds (1 / elapsed). One frame divided by a certain number of seconds yields a value whose units are frames/second.
draw(now)	Draws the next animation frame based on the current time (now).
setOffsets(now)	Sets translation offsets for the background and platforms. Those offsets control horizontal scrolling.
setBackgroundOffset(now)	Sets the background translation offset.
setPlatformOffset(now)	Sets the platform translation offset.
setPlatformVelocity()	Sets platform velocity to 4.35 times the background velocity to produce a mild parallax effect, which makes it seem as though the platforms are closer to the player than to the background. The value 4.35 was determined empirically.
drawBackground()	Translates the coordinate system for the game's canvas to create apparent horizontal motion, draws the background twice end to end, and translates the coordinate system back to its original position.
drawRunner()	Draws the runner with the 2D context's drawImage() method.
drawPlatforms()	Draws rectangular platforms with the 2D context's strokeRect() and fillRect().
calculatePlatformTop(track)	Calculates the Y coordinate of the top of a platform, given a track (recall that platforms move on one of three horizontal tracks). Valid values for the track parameter are the numbers 1–3, inclusive.

(Continues)

Table 4.1 *(Continued)*

Method	Description
turnLeft()	Scrolls the background and platforms to the right, making the runner appear to move to the left.
turnRight()	Scrolls the background and platforms to the left, making the runner appear to move to the right.
togglePaused()	Toggles the paused state of the game.

NOTE: Functions vs. methods

Functions that are members of a JavaScript object are referred to as methods, whereas standalone functions are simply called functions.

4.2 Understand JavaScript's Persnickety `this` Reference

In Section 4.1, "Encapsulate Game Functions in a JavaScript Object," on p. 95 you saw how to access the SnailBait JavaScript object with the this operator in its constructor function and methods. Unlike the this reference in other computer languages, however, JavaScript's this reference *sometimes refers to a different JavaScript object, depending on who called the enclosing method.*

For example, consider the animate() function discussed in Chapter 3, and relisted in Example 4.4.

Example 4.4 The `animate()` function

```
function animate(now) {
    fps = calculateFps(now);
    draw(now);
    lastAnimationFrameTime = now;
    requestNextAnimationFrame(animate);
}
```

The preceding animate() function makes assignments to two global variables and invokes three global functions. You might easily be misled by Example 4.2 on p. 97, which lists Snail Bait's draw() method, into thinking that you can turn those variables and functions into SnailBait properties and methods, as shown in Example 4.5.

Example 4.5 A naive implementation of Snail Bait's `animate()` method

```
// WARNING: DO NOT DO THIS, IT DOES NOT WORK...

SnailBait.prototype = {
   ...

   // Implementations of calculateFps() and
   // requestNextAnimationFrame() are  omitted for brevity.

   animate: function (now) {
      this.fps = snailBait.calculateFps(now); // This is not Snail Bait!
      this.draw(now);                          // It's the window object.
      this.lastAnimationFrameTime = now;
      requestNextAnimationFrame(this.animate);
   },
   ...
};
```

The preceding implementation of the `animate()` method does not work because the `this` reference in the `animate()` method refers to the `window` object, not the `SnailBait` object. That's because the browser calls the `animate()` method (when the underlying `requestAnimationFrame()` method is available; see Chapter 3 for details).

Because the `this` reference in Snail Bait's `animate()` method refers to the `window` object and not the `SnailBait` object, the `animate()` method references the `SnailBait` object directly, as shown in Example 4.6.

Example 4.6 The `animate()` method

```
SnailBait.prototype = {
   ...

   // ...DO THIS INSTEAD OF THE PREVIOUS EXAMPLE.

   animate: function (now) {
      snailBait.fps = snailBait.calculateFps(now);
      snailBait.draw(now);
      snailBait.lastAnimationFrameTime = now;
      requestNextAnimationFrame(snailBait.animate);
   },
   ...
};

var snailBait = new SnailBait();
```

The fact that JavaScript's this reference can change depending on who invokes a particular method is frustrating enough; however, this JavaScript oddity is even more insidious than it first appears because sometimes *the this operator can change in the middle of a method*. Consider the initializeImages() function listed in Example 4.7.

Example 4.7 The initializeImages() function

```
function initializeImages() {
    background.src  = 'images/background.png';
    runnerImage.src = 'images/runner.png';

    background.onload = function (e) {
        startGame();
    };
}
```

Example 4.8 shows the initializeImages() function converted into a SnailBait method.

Example 4.8 The initializeImages() method

```
SnailBait.prototype = {
    ...

    // Snail Bait calls the initializeImages() method directly

    initializeImages: function() {
        this.background.src  = 'images/background.png';
        this.runnerImage.src = 'images/runner.png';

        // The browser calls the onload event handler

        background.onload = function (e) {
            snailBait.startGame();
        };
    }
    ...
};
```

Because Snail Bait calls the initializeImages() method directly, the this reference in that method refers to the SnailBait JavaScript object, and we can access its background and runnerImage properties. However, *the browser* invokes the background image's onload event handler, and therefore the this reference within that event handler is once again the window object, so we access the snailBait object directly inside that event handler.

> **NOTE: Be skeptical of your interpretation of the this reference.**
>
> If you've used classic object-oriented programming languages such as C++ or Java, you will undoubtedly find that a high percentage of the bugs you run into involve your misinterpretation of the this reference. That interpretation should be the first thing you examine when debugging troublesome code.

> **NOTE: Other strategies for dealing with JavaScript's this reference**
>
> Snail Bait deals with the chameleon-like nature of JavaScript's this reference by directly using the snailBait reference when the this reference does not refer to the game. There are other strategies, however, for dealing with the this reference, such as the popular Module pattern in JavaScript. (See www.adequatelygood.com/JavaScript-Module-Pattern-In-Depth.html for an excellent explanation of the Module pattern.)
>
> Another option when the this reference changes in the middle of a method, as illustrated above, is to create a variable—typically named self—in the method and assign it to the this reference. Subsequently, when the this reference does not refer to the game, you can use the self reference instead.
>
> You can also simply use the snailBait reference everywhere throughout the game. That may be the simplest and most effective strategy; however, Snail Bait uses both this and snailBait, so you can see places in the code where the this reference changes.

4.3 Handle Keyboard Input

When Snail Bait begins, its background is stationary. The background starts to scroll when the player presses either the d or left arrow keys to make it appear as though the runner is moving to the left, or the k or right arrow keys to make it appear as though the runner is moving to the right.

You can attach key event handlers only to focusable HTML elements, such as text fields and windows, and Snail Bait takes place in a canvas element, which is not a focusable element. Therefore, because we cannot attach a key event handler to Snail Bait's canvas, we attach it to the game's window, as shown in Example 4.9.

Example 4.9 Mapping keys to change direction

```
window.addEventListener(
   'keydown',

   function (e) {
      var key = e.keyCode;

      if (key === 68 || key === 37) { // 'd' or left arrow
         snailBait.turnLeft();
      }
      else if (key === 75 || key === 39) { // 'k' or right arrow
         snailBait.turnRight();
      }
});
```

The preceding event handler invokes Snail Bait's `turnLeft()` method or `turnRight()` method depending on the key the player pressed. Those methods are listed in Example 4.10.

Example 4.10 Snail Bait's `turnLeft()` and `turnRight()` methods

```
SnailBait.prototype = {
   ...

   turnLeft: function () {
      this.bgVelocity = -this.BACKGROUND_VELOCITY; // pixels/second
      ...
   },

   turnRight: function () {
      this.bgVelocity = this.BACKGROUND_VELOCITY; // pixels/second
      ...
   },
   ...
};
```

Once again it's interesting to note that Snail Bait implements horizontal motion by translating the coordinate system for the game's drawing surface, which makes the implementations of `turnLeft()` and `turnRight()` as simple as possible by merely reversing the background's direction.

 NOTE: JavaScript key codes

You can find out the JavaScript key codes for Latin-based languages at www.cambiaresearch.com/articles/15/javascript-char-codes-key-codes.

NOTE: addEventListener() vs. onkeydown

You can add event handlers to HTML elements in one of two ways. One way is to assign a function to a property of the element's corresponding JavaScript object, such as the onblur property of the window object. Another way is to call JavaScript's addEventListener() method to add a handler to a list of functions that the browser invokes for a particular event. For example, instead of assigning the function to the window object's onblur property, you can add a blur event handler with the addEventListener() method.

All other things being equal, you should prefer addEventListener() to properties such as onblur. The reasoning behind that preference is that it's easy to inadvertently override properties such as onblur.

4.4 Pause or Resume the Game When the Player Presses the p Key

HTML5 games and especially video games must be able to pause. Example 4.11 shows a first cut at pausing and resuming Snail Bait.

Example 4.11 Pause and resume

```
var SnailBait = function () {
   ...

   this.paused = false,
   this.PAUSED_CHECK_INTERVAL = 200; // milliseconds
   ...
};

SnailBait.prototype = {
   ...

   togglePaused: function () {
      this.paused = !this.paused;
   },

   animate: function (now) {
      if (snailBait.paused) {
         // Try again later

         setTimeout( function () {
            requestNextAnimationFrame(snailBait.animate);
         }, snailBait.PAUSED_CHECK_INTERVAL);
      }
      else {
```

(Continues)

Example 4.11   *(Continued)*

```
    // Game loop

    snailBait.fps = snailBait.calculateFps(now);
    snailBait.draw(now);
    snailBait.lastAnimationFrameTime = now;
    requestNextAnimationFrame(snailBait.animate);
    }
  },
  ...
};
```

The `togglePaused()` method simply toggles the game's paused variable. When that variable's value is `true`, it means that the game is paused so the `animate()` method does not execute the game loop.

It's neither necessary nor efficient to check 60 times per second (assuming a frame rate of 60 fps) to see if it's time to resume a paused game; therefore, the `animate()` method in **Example 4.11** waits 200 ms before invoking the `requestNextAnimationFrame()` polyfill, which schedules another call to `animate()` when it's time to draw the next animation frame.

NOTE: The 200 ms threshold and user interface latency

When Snail Bait is paused, it waits 200 ms between checks to see if the game has resumed. The 200 ms number is widely regarded as the threshold at which applications feel sluggish, so Snail Bait ensures that players never have to wait longer than that threshold when the game's window regains focus. See http://ajaxian.com/archives/craftmanship-and-ui-latency to read more about user interface latency.

NOTE: `setTimeout()` and `setInterval()` are useful functions

As you saw in Chapter 3, you should never use `setTimeout()` and `setInterval()` for time-critical animations; however, those methods are indispensable for timing things like user interface effects.

BEST PRACTICE: Don't do everything at full speed

Games do many things that should not be done every animation frame. For example, in addition to checking for the resumption of a paused game, Snail Bait also updates the game's frames per second display once per second.

4.5 Freeze the Game to Ensure It Resumes Exactly Where It Left Off

Pausing a game involves more than simply halting its animation. *Games must resume exactly where they left off.* The code in Example 4.11 may appear to fill that requirement; after all, while the game is paused, nothing happens, so it seems as though the game should resume exactly as it was before it was paused. However, that's not the case, because the primary currency for all animations—Snail Bait's included—is time.

As you saw in Chapter 3, after you call `requestAnimationFrame()`, the browser invokes a callback function you specify, passing that function the current time. In Snail Bait's case, that callback is the `animate()` method, which in turn passes the time to the `draw()` method. See Chapter 3 for more information about `requestAnimationFrame()` and the time that the browser passes to the `animate()` method.

Even though the animation does not run while the game is paused, time still marches on unabated. And because Snail Bait's `draw()` method draws the next animation frame based on the time it receives from `animate()`, the previous implementation of `togglePaused()` in Example 4.11 causes the game to lurch ahead in time when the paused game resumes.

Example 4.12 shows a revised implementation of `togglePaused()` that avoids an abrupt time shift when the paused game resumes.

Example 4.12 Freezing the game (`togglePaused()` revisited)

```
var SnailBait = function () {
   ...

   this.paused = false,
   this.pauseStartTime = 0,
   this.lastAnimationFrameTime = 0,
   ...
};

SnailBait.prototype = {
   ...

   togglePaused: function () {
      var now = +new Date();

      this.paused = !this.paused;

      if (this.paused) {
         this.pauseStartTime = now;
```

(Continues)

Example 4.12   (Continued)

```
      }
      else {
         this.lastAnimationFrameTime += (now - this.pauseStartTime);
      }
   },
};
```

When the player pauses the game, the preceding implementation of togglePaused() toggles the paused property and stores the current time in the pauseStartTime property.

When the game resumes, togglePaused() again toggles the paused property and calculates the amount of time the game was paused. The togglePaused() method then moves the time of last animation frame ahead by the amount of time the game was paused, which erases the pause. Subsequently, the game resumes exactly where it left off when the pause began.

CAUTION: Snail Bait doesn't always tell the truth

Snail Bait stores the time of the last animation frame in its lastAnimationFrameTime property. Until the game is paused for the first time, that property's value reflects the actual time of the last animation frame. However, as you saw in the last section, when a player resumes a paused game, that value deviates from reality.

In Chapter 10 we discuss the implementation of Snail Bait's time system, which is also less than truthful about how long the game has been running to slow time or to speed it up.

4.6 Pause the Game When the Window Loses Focus

If your game is running in a window or tab that's not visible and you're using requestAnimationFrame(), then according to the W3C specification:

> If the page is not currently visible, animations on that page can be throttled heavily so that they do not update often and thus consume little CPU power.

The term *throttled heavily* means the browser invokes your animation callback at an abysmal frame rate, usually somewhere between 1 and 10 fps, as illustrated by Figure 4.3, which shows a frame rate of 6 fps immediately after the window has regained focus.

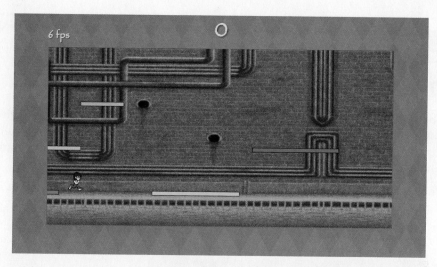

Figure 4.3 Browsers heavily throttle frame rate when a tab is not visible

Heavily throttled frame rates can wreak havoc on collision detection algorithms, because a sudden increase in the amount of time between animation frames can cause sprites to pass one another without colliding, as is the case when the browser heavily throttles the frame rate.

You can avoid collision detection meltdowns resulting from heavily throttled frame rates by pausing the game when the game's window loses focus and restarting it when the window regains focus. You can see how to do that in Example 4.13.

Example 4.13 Autopause

```
window.addEventListener('blur', function (e) {
   if (!snailBait.paused) {      // If the game is not paused,
      snailBait.togglePaused(); // pause
   }
});

window.addEventListener('focus', function (e) {
   if (snailBait.paused) {       // If the game is paused,
      snailBait.togglePaused(); // resume
   }
});
```

✅ **BEST PRACTICE:** Pause the game when the window loses focus and resume when it regains focus.

4.7 Resume a Paused Game with an Animated Countdown

When your game resumes after its window receives focus, you should give players a few seconds to regain the controls. During that time, it's a good idea to provide feedback concerning the amount of time remaining before the game resumes.

When Snail Bait's window regains focus, it displays a three-second countdown to give players time to get ready, as shown in Figure 4.4.

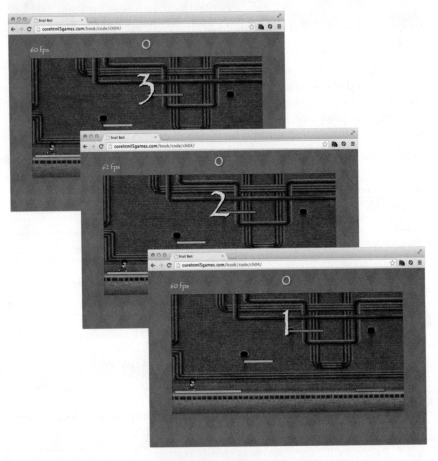

Figure 4.4 Snail Bait after losing and regaining focus

Snail Bait implements its countdown with a toast, so we begin this discussion of that countdown with toasts.

4.7.1 Display Toasts (Brief Messages) to Players

The numerals that Snail Bait displays during the countdown—along with other briefly displayed messages throughout the game—are text in an HTML DIV element, known as the game's toast. That DIV is declared in the game's HTML file with a `snailbait-toast` ID, as shown in Example 4.14.

Example 4.14 Toast: HTML

```
<!DOCTYPE html>
<html>
   <head>
      ...
   </head>

   <body>
      <div id='snailbait-arena'>
         <!-- Toast.................................................-->

         <!-- Initially empty and invisible -->
         <div id='snailbait-toast'></div>
         ...

      </div>
   </body>
</html>
```

The browser displays the `snailbait-toast` element on top of the canvas by virtue of its `z-index` CSS attribute whose value, as you can see from Example 4.15, is 1. By default, the `snailbait-canvas` element's `z-index` is zero, and therefore the browser displays the DIV on top of the canvas. The DIV, however, is not initially visible because its `display` attribute's value is none.

Example 4.15 Toast: CSS

```
#snailbait-toast {
   position: absolute;
   margin-left: 100px;
   margin-top: 20px;
   ...
   z-index: 1;
   display: none;
}
```

Snail Bait reveals the toast DIV with its revealToast() method, whose initial implementation is listed in **Example 4.16**.

Example 4.16 Revealing toasts in JavaScript

```
var SnailBait = function () {
   ...

   this.DEFAULT_TOAST_TIME = 3000; // 3 seconds
   this.toast = document.getElementById('snailbait-toast');
   ...
};

SnailBait.prototype = {
   ...

   revealToast: function (text, duration) {
      var DEFAULT_TOAST_DISPLAY_DURATION = 1000;

      duration = duration || DEFAULT_TOAST_DISPLAY_DURATION;

      this.toast.style.display = 'block'; // Show the toast DIV
      this.toast.innerHTML = text;        // with the specified text

      setTimeout( function (e) {
         if (snailBait.windowHasFocus) {
            snailBait.toast.style.display = 'none'; // Hide the toast DIV
         }
      }, duration);
   },
   ...
}
```

The revealToast() method displays a string in the toast DIV for a particular duration. You can specify that duration with revealToast()'s optional second argument. If you call revealToast() with only the first argument, the duration defaults to one second.

4.7.2 Snail Bait's Countdown

When Snail Bait's window regains focus, it starts the countdown, displaying each numeral for one second. Once the countdown reaches zero, the focus event handler calls togglePaused() to resume the game, as shown in **Example 4.17**.

Example 4.17 Countdown JavaScript

```javascript
var SnailBait = function () {
    ...

    this.toast = document.getElementById('snailbait-toast'),
    ...
};

window.addEventListener('blur', function (e) {
    if (!snailBait.paused) {
        snailBait.togglePaused(); // Pause if not paused
    }
});

window.addEventListener('focus', function (e) {
    var originalFont = snailBait.toast.style.fontSize, // Restore later
        DIGIT_DISPLAY_DURATION = 1000; // milliseconds

    if (snailBait.paused) {
        snailBait.toast.style.font = '128px fantasy'; // Large font

        snailBait.revealToast('3', 1000); // Display 3 for 1.0 sec

        setTimeout(function (e) {
            snailBait.revealToast('2', 1000); // Display 2 for 1.0 sec

            setTimeout(function (e) {
                snailBait.revealToast('1', 1000); // Display 1 for 1.0 sec

                setTimeout(function (e) {
                    snailBait.togglePaused();
                    snailBait.toast.style.fontSize = originalFont;

                }, DIGIT_DISPLAY_DURATION); // End of '1'

            }, DIGIT_DISPLAY_DURATION); // End of '2'

        }, DIGIT_DISPLAY_DURATION); // End of '3'
    }
});
```

The code in Example 4.17 does not work properly, however, if a player activates another window or tab during the countdown, because the game will restart at the end of the countdown whether the window has focus or not. That's easy to fix with `windowHasFocus` and `countdownInProgress` flags, as shown in Example 4.18.

Example 4.18 Accounting for lost focus during the countdown

```
window.addEventListener(
    'blur',

    function (e) {
        snailBait.windowHasFocus = false;

        if ( ! snailBait.paused) {
            snailBait.togglePaused(); // Pause if not paused
        }
    }
);

window.addEventListener(
    'focus',

    function (e) {
        var DIGIT_DISPLAY_DURATION = 1000, // milliseconds
            takeAction = function () {
                return snailBait.windowHasFocus &&
                    snailBait.countdownInProgress;
            };

        snailBait.windowHasFocus = true;

        if (!snailBait.playing) {
            snailBait.togglePaused();
        }
        else if (snailBait.paused) {
            snailBait.countdownInProgress = true;
            snailBait.toastElement.style.font = '128px fantasy';

            if (takeAction()) {
                snailBait.revealToast('3', 500);

                setTimeout(function (e) {
                    if (takeAction()) {
                        snailBait.revealToast('2', 500);
                    }

                    setTimeout(function (e) {
                        if (takeAction()) {
                            snailBait.revealToast('1', 500);
                        }

                        setTimeout(function (e) {
```

```
        if (takeAction()) {
            snailBait.togglePaused();
            snailBait.toastElement.style.font =
                snailBait.originalFont;
        }

        snailBait.countdownInProgress = false;

        }, DIGIT_DISPLAY_DURATION);
        }, DIGIT_DISPLAY_DURATION);
        }, DIGIT_DISPLAY_DURATION);
    }
  }
 }
);
```

When the window loses focus, it sets the windowHasFocus attribute to false. When it regains focus, it sets the attribute to true, begins the countdown, and sets the countdownInProgress attribute to true. Subsequently, the focus event handler only executes the steps of the countdown if the window still has focus and a countdown is in progress.

 BEST PRACTICE: Give players time to regain the controls when the game's window regains focus.

4.8 Conclusion

This chapter sets the stage for the rest of the book by encapsulating Snail Bait's code in a single global JavaScript object named SnailBait and by implementing fundamental infrastructure such as pausing and resuming the game when the window loses and regains focus, respectively.

When you pause your game, it's not enough to merely disengage the game's animation. That's because time marches on and when players resume the game, you must account for the time the game was paused to avoid a noticeable time discontinuity.

It's also a good idea to give players a few seconds to regain the controls when your game regains focus. You saw how to do that in this chapter, and you also saw how to implement a three-second countdown that gives players visual feedback as the countdown progresses.

In the next chapter, we continue implementing Snail Bait's basic infrastructure with the game's loading screen.

4.9 Exercises

1. In the final version of Snail Bait, comment out the line of code in
    togglePaused() that adjusts the value of lastAnimationFrameTime, as in
    Example 4.12. Start the game, pause, and wait a few seconds before resuming.
    Notice the lurch forward in time when the game resumes. Now uncomment
    the line of code in togglePaused() and restart the game. Notice that the game
    now resumes exactly where it left off.

2. Change the JavaScript in this chapter's version of Snail Bait to use snailBait
    everywhere instead of this in Snail Bait's constructor and methods.

3. Change the initializeImages() method to use the self technique described
    in Section 4.2, "Understand JavaScript's Persnickety this Reference," on
    p. 100.

CHAPTER

5

Loading Screens

Topics in This Chapter

The first thing players do when they play your game is watch it load. First impressions are important, so it's worthwhile to implement a memorable loading screen. Besides making a good first impression, an interesting loading screen also makes the inevitable delay before players get to the fun part of your game pass more quickly. Players will appreciate that.

As it currently stands, Snail Bait simply shows its webpage background as the game's background image loads. In this chapter, we implement a loading screen and subsequently reveal the game, as shown in Figure 5.1.

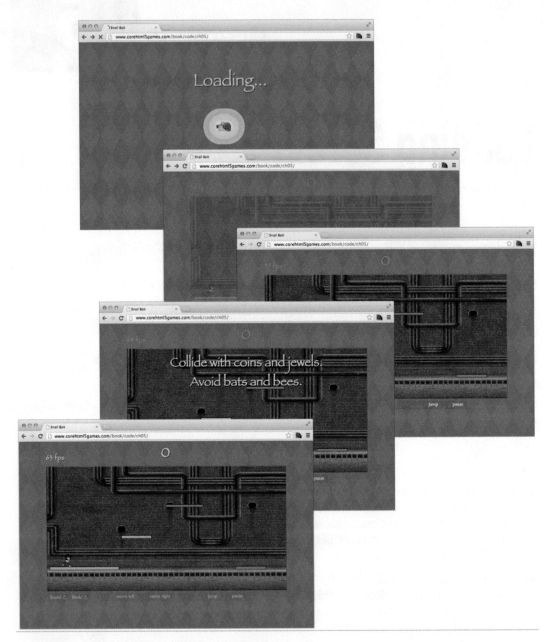

Figure 5.1 Snail Bait's loading sequence

As it starts to load resources, Snail Bait fades in the *Loading…* text and the animated GIF shown in the top screenshot in **Figure 5.1**. The animated GIF shows the snail shooting snail bombs without any ammunition. The game displays the *Loading…* text and the animated GIF until it finishes loading resources.

When Snail Bait is done loading resources, it simultaneously fades out the *Loading…* text and the animated GIF and fades in the game's *chrome*—the HTML elements above and below the canvas—along with the canvas itself. The second screenshot from the top in **Figure 5.1** shows the canvas and chrome fading into view.

Once they fade into view, the canvas and the bottom chrome are fully opaque, but the opacity of the top chrome, containing the fps indicator and score, is only 0.25. The top chrome is initially barely visible so the player focuses on the instructions at the bottom of the game. You can see the partially transparent top chrome and the fully opaque bottom chrome in the third and fourth screenshots from the top in **Figure 5.1**.

Shortly after Snail Bait starts to fade in the canvas and chrome, it starts fading in the *Collide with…* text shown in the fourth screenshot from the top in **Figure 5.1**. Once that text is fully opaque, Snail Bait displays it for three seconds, before fading it from view.

After the *Collide with…* text fades from view, Snail Bait reverses the opacity of the top and bottom chrome, so the top chrome becomes fully opaque and the bottom chrome is barely visible, as shown in the bottom screenshot in **Figure 5.1**. That reversal of opacity triggers CSS transitions that smoothly animate the chrome elements to their final state of opacity. The reduced visibility of the bottom chrome focuses the player's attention on the canvas and the top chrome.

As we implement various facets of the loading sequence in this chapter, you will learn how to do the following:

- Define a game's chrome, meaning HTML elements outside the game's canvas (Section 5.1 on p. 120)
- Fade the game's chrome elements in and out with CSS transitions (Section 5.2 on p. 123)
- Fade any HTML element that has a CSS transition associated with its opacity property in or out (Section 5.3 on p. 132)
- Implement the loading screen (**Figure 5.4** on p. 135)
- Reveal the game (Section 5.5 on p. 140)

Let's start by defining Snail Bait's chrome.

5.1 Define Snail Bait's Chrome

Most games have elements besides their canvas that let players manipulate game settings for things such as sound and music. Those elements are commonly referred to as chrome. Snail Bait's chrome, at this stage of development, is shown in **Figure 5.2**.

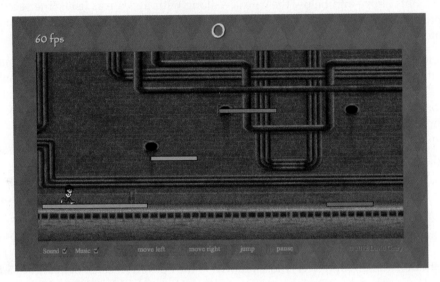

Figure 5.2 Snail Bait's chrome

Snail Bait's top chrome, meaning the chrome above the game's canvas, contains a frame rate (fps) indicator and the score. In Section 17.2 on p. 442, we replace the fps indicator with a lives indicator that shows how many lives the player has left. Until then we'll leave the fps indicator in place so we can keep an eye on performance. Also, for the time being, the scoreboard registers zero no matter what, but in Chapter 17 we monitor the score and update it accordingly.

Snail Bait's bottom chrome contains Sound and Music checkboxes that ultimately will control whether the game plays sound effects or music, respectively. The bottom chrome also contains instructions for controlling the game with the keyboard, along with a copyright notice.

Example 5.1 shows the HTML for Snail Bait's chrome.

Example 5.1 HTML elements for Snail Bait's chrome

```html
<!DOCTYPE html>
<html>
  ...

  <body>
    ...

    <div id='snailbait-arena'>
      ...

      <!--.....................TOP CHROME.........................-->

      <!-- Score and fps.........................................-->

      <div id='snailbait-fps'></div>
      <div id='snailbait-score'>0</div>

      <!--.....................BOTTOM CHROME......................-->

      <!-- Sound and music.......................................-->

      <div id='snailbait-sound-and-music'>
        <div id='snailbait-sound-checkbox-div'
             class='snailbait-checkbox-div'>
          Sound <input id='snailbait-sound-checkbox'
                       type='checkbox' checked />
        </div>

        <div class='snailbait-checkbox-div'>
          Music <input id='snailbait-music-checkbox'
                       type='checkbox' checked />
        </div>
      </div>

      <!-- Instructions.........................................-->

      <div id='snailbait-instructions'>
        <div class='snailbait-keys'>
          &larr; / d
          <div class='snailbait-explanation'>move left</div>
          &rarr; / k
          <div class='snailbait-explanation'>move right</div>
        </div>

        <div class='snailbait-keys'>
          j <div class='snailbait-explanation'>jump</div>
        </div>
```

(Continues)

Example 5.1   *(Continued)*

```
        <div class='snailbait-keys'>
            p <div class='snailbait-explanation'>pause</div>
        </div>
    </div>

    <!-- Copyright.........................................-->

        <div id='snailbait-copyright'>&copy; 2012 David Geary</div>
    </div>
    ...
</body>
</html>
```

The preceding HTML, which defines the elements for Snail Bait's chrome, is a simple hierarchy of DIV elements with a couple of checkboxes. Most of the complexity surrounding those elements concerns how they look and behave and is encapsulated in CSS and JavaScript, respectively.

Snail Bait uses three symbols, which are listed in Table 5.1, in the preceding HTML5.

Table 5.1 HTML symbols used by Snail Bait

Symbol	Meaning	Result
←	left arrow	←
→	right arrow	→
©	copyright	©

 NOTE: Styling Snail Bait's chrome with CSS
See Chapter 1 for a discussion of the CSS for Snail Bait's chrome.

5.1.1 Accessing Chrome Elements in JavaScript

Snail Bait's JavaScript accesses the HTML elements in its chrome as shown in Example 5.2.

As is the case for all of Snail Bait's elements, the preceding code uses the JavaScript function getElementById() to access the elements in the game's chrome.

Example 5.2 Accessing chrome elements in Snail Bait's constructor

```
var SnailBait = function () { // Snail Bait's constructor function
   ...

   // Top chrome.........................................................

   this.fpsElement   =
      document.getElementById('snailbait-fps');

   this.scoreElement =
      document.getElementById('snailbait-score');

   // Bottom chrome.......................................................

   this.soundAndMusicElement =
      document.getElementById('snailbait-sound-and-music');

   // The soundCheckboxElement and musicCheckboxElement references
   // are not discussed in this chapter. Snail Bait's use of those
   // references is discussed in Chapter 14.

   this.soundCheckboxElement =
      document.getElementById('snailbait-sound-checkbox');

   this.musicCheckboxElement =
      document.getElementById('snailbait-music-checkbox');

   this.instructionsElement =
      document.getElementById('snailbait-instructions');

   this.copyrightElement =
      document.getElementById('snailbait-copyright');
   ...
};
```

With references to the elements at hand, we are ready to fade them in and out at appropriate times during the game's loading sequence.

5.2 Fade Elements In and Out with CSS Transitions

Several of Snail Bait's HTML elements fade in and out at certain times. Examples are: the loading sequence, the credits screen, and the countdown digits. Figure 5.3 shows a countdown digit fading from view.

To fade elements, Snail Bait manipulates their opacity and display CSS properties. It also defines a CSS transition for the opacity property, so when Snail Bait

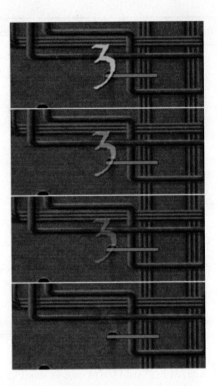

Figure 5.3 Fading Snail Bait's countdown digits when a paused game resumes

subsequently changes the opacity property, the browser invokes an animation that smoothly *transitions* from the current opacity to the new setting. Snail Bait specifies the duration of those animations with the CSS transition property.

Initially, Snail Bait sets the opacity property of elements it fades in and out to zero so that the elements are not visible when the game begins (the only element that's initially visible is the loading screen, shown in the top screenshot in Figure 5.1 on p. 118). The game also sets their display property to none so that the browser does not initially render them. Elements that the browser does not render do not take up space; more importantly for Snail Bait, which displays elements on top of each other, such elements do not prevent events from reaching elements underneath.

The initial settings for HTML elements that Snail Bait fades in and out are summarized as follows:

- `display: none`
- `opacity: 0`
- `transition: opacity Xs`

The Xs for the `transition` property specifies the duration, in seconds, for the transition's associated animation.

Now that we've discussed initial settings for an element's CSS properties that make the element initially invisible and incapable of trapping events, let's see how Snail Bait fades those elements into view.

5.2.1 Fade Elements Into View

Snail Bait fades elements into view in two steps. The first step sets the element's `display` property to `block`. That setting causes the browser to insert the element into the DOM tree so that it takes up space and captures events; however, because its `opacity` is still zero, the element remains invisible.

The second step is to change the element's opacity so the CSS transition starts and the element fades into view. However, to start the transition associated with the `opacity` property, *you cannot set the `opacity` property immediately after you set the `display` property, because the browser will not start any transitions associated with the element*, as shown in Example 5.3.

Example 5.3 A failed attempt to animate an element's opacity setting

```
element.style.display = 'block'; // The element is added to the DOM tree
element.style.opacity = 1.0; // The browser will not start the transition
```

To ensure that the transition starts, *you must set the `opacity` property after the current JavaScript is done executing and the single thread upon which everything runs returns to the browser*. To do that, you can use `setTimeout()`, as shown in Example 5.4.

Example 5.4 Successfully animating an element's opacity setting

```
element.style.display = 'block'; // The element is added to the DOM tree

setTimeout ( function () {
   element.style.opacity = 1.0; // The browser starts the transition
}, 50); // milliseconds - any value will work
```

Why does setting an element's `opacity` immediately after `display` cancel any transitions associated with the element?

To understand why the call to `setTimeout()` in Example 5.4 is necessary to start the element's CSS transition, you have to understand three things.

First, when you set CSS style properties in JavaScript—for example, setting the `display` property to `block`—the browser queues those property settings and *sets them all simultaneously later on* in what's known as a *style change event*.

Second, setting an element's `display` property to none removes the element from the DOM tree. That's why an element does not take up space or trap events when its `display` property is set to none. If you set an element's property from none to `block`, the browser inserts the element into the DOM tree in the subsequent style change event.

Third, before you insert an element into the DOM tree, the element does not have a computed style. After you insert the element, the browser computes a style for the element, so it has a computed style.

Finally, according to the CSS Transitions specification (www.w3.org/TR/css3-transitions) when this book went to press:

> If an element does not have a computed style either before or after the style change event, then transitions are not started for that element in that style change event.

The preceding statement means that when Snail Bait adds elements to the DOM tree by setting the element's `display` property to `block`, the browser will not start any transitions associated with those elements in the ensuing style change event.

 CAUTION: Using `setTimeout()` to force transitions is not guaranteed to work

HTML5 has its sharp edges; here's one of them. According to the same CSS specification cited above as this book went to press:

> *Since this specification does not define when a style change event occurs, and thus what changes to computed values are considered simultaneous, authors should be aware that changing any of the transition properties a small amount of time after making a change that might transition can result in behavior that varies between implementations, since the changes might be considered simultaneous in some implementations but not others.*

If an implementation of the specification (most likely a browser) considers *changing transition properties a small amount of time after making a change* to be *simultaneous*, then the trick, if you will, of using `setTimeout()` to get transitions to occur when adding elements to the DOM tree will not work. Note also that the specification does not further elaborate on the specific meaning of *a small amount of time*.

As this book went to press, using `setTimeout()` as described above does indeed work in browsers that support HTML5, but if you find that it has stopped working, you'll know why.

CAUTION: HTML5 specifications are living documents

Keep in mind that HTML5 specifications are constantly under revision, so you might want to look at the current version of the CSS Transitions specification cited above to see what changes have been made to the specification since this book went to press.

5.2.2 Fade Elements Out of View

Snail Bait fades elements out of view with nearly the inverse of the procedure it uses to fade them into view.

The first step to fade an element out of view is to set its opacity property to zero. That setting triggers the animation associated with the element's CSS transition.

After waiting for the element to fully fade out of view, Snail Bait sets the element's display property to none so that the element does not take up space or capture events. Example 5.5 shows the JavaScript for fading an element out of view.

Example 5.5 Fading out

```
var TRANSITION_DURATION = 2000; // 2 seconds

element.style.opacity = 0; // The browser starts the transition

setTimeout ( function () {
   element.style.display = 'none'; // Removes element from the DOM tree
}, TRANSITION_DURATION);
```

Now that you've seen how to fade elements in and out, let's see how Snail Bait applies that formula for its toast.

NOTE: A key difference between fading in and fading out

When Snail Bait fades elements in, it doesn't need to know the transition's duration because there's nothing to do after the element fades in. When the game fades elements out, on the other hand, it must know the transition's duration because after the transition, the game sets the element's display property to none to remove it from the tree so that the element doesn't capture events.

NOTE: Other ways to fade elements in and out

There are other ways to fade HTML elements in and out with CSS; for example, you can manipulate an element's visibility property. If you set visibility to hidden, the corresponding element will not be visible, but it will still be rendered by the browser, meaning it will take up space and capture events. Because Snail Bait displays HTML elements on top of each other (for example, the high score elements are directly above the game's canvas), we do not want invisible elements inadvertently capturing events; therefore, the game manipulates both the opacity and display properties instead of simply manipulating the visibility property.

5.2.3 The snailbait-toast Element's CSS

Snail Bait's snailbait-toast element, first discussed in Section 4.7.1 on p. 111 and shown in **Figure 5.3** on p. 124, is a DIV the game uses to briefly display messages to players. **Example 5.6** shows that element's CSS.

Example 5.6 Specifying a CSS transition for the snailbait-toast element

```
#snailbait-toast {
   position: absolute;
   margin-left: 100px;
   margin-top: 20px;
   width: 600px;
   font: 40px fantasy;
   text-align: center;
   color: #ff6;
   text-shadow: 2px 2px 4px rgb(0,0,0);

   /* The duration of the following transition is
      tightly coupled to Snail Bait's
      JavaScript. See SnailBait.hideToast(). */

   -webkit-transition: opacity 0.5s;
   -moz-transition: opacity 0.5s;
```

```
-o-transition: opacity 0.5s;
transition: opacity 0.5s;

opacity: 0;
display: none;
z-index: 1;
}
```

The properties near the top of Example 5.6 set the toast's position, size, margins, font, and color. The most interesting part of the preceding CSS is the transition along with settings for the element's `opacity` and `display` properties. That transition and those settings coincide to the CSS discussed in Section 5.3 on p. 132 and indicate that Snail Bait fades the toast in and out.

NOTE: Four versions of the CSS `transition` property

To ensure that its CSS transitions work across browsers that support HTML5, Snail Bait defines four versions of the transition, the first three of which have a browser-specific prefix. The version without a prefix corresponds to the W3C standard. See Chapter 3 for more information about using standard and browser-specific functionality.

NOTE: Another way to specify CSS transitions

Snail Bait uses a single CSS attribute for transitions, but you can specify each aspect of a transition with separate attributes: `transition-property`, `transition-duration`, `transition-timing-function`, and `transition-delay`.

NOTE: CSS transitions vs. CSS animations

Snail Bait opts for the simpler and less capable CSS transitions instead of CSS animations. Animations can be triggered by something other than a change in a CSS property. Animations also give you more fine-grained control of the animation itself. See www.kirupa.com/html5/css3_animations_vs_transitions.htm for a discussion of the differences between CSS transitions and animations.

5.2.4 Revealing and Hiding Toasts

Snail Bait's `revealToast()` method, originally discussed in Section 4.7.1, "Display Toasts (Brief Messages) to Players," on p. 111, is reimplemented in Example 5.7

to fade the toast in and out instead of merely displaying and hiding it as was the case in Chapter 4.

Example 5.7 Revealing toast, revisited

```
SnailBait.prototype = {
   ...

   revealToast: function (text, duration) {
      var DEFAULT_TOAST_DURATION = 1000;

      duration = duration || DEFAULT_TOAST_DURATION;

      this.startToastTransition(text, duration); // Start CSS transition

      setTimeout( function (e) {
         snailBait.hideToast();
      }, duration);
   },
   ...
};
```

The revealToast() method takes two arguments: the text that Snail Bait displays in the toast, and the duration, in milliseconds, that the toast is visible. The duration is optional; it defaults to one second if you don't specify it.

revealToast() invokes Snail Bait's startToastTransition() method, which is listed in Example 5.8.

Example 5.8 Starting the toast transition

```
var SnailBait = function () {
   ...

   this.OPAQUE = 1.0;      // opacity
   this.SHORT_DELAY = 50; // milliseconds
   ...
};

SnailBait.prototype = {
   ...

   startToastTransition: function (text) {
      this.toastElement.innerHTML = text;
      this.toastElement.style.display = 'block';
```

```
  setTimeout( function () {
      snailBait.toastElement.style.opacity = snailBait.OPAQUE;
  }, this.SHORT_DELAY);
},
...
};
```

The `startToastTransition()` method uses `setTimeout()` to fade in the snailbait-toast element by setting the element's `display` CSS property to `block` and subsequently, after a short delay, setting the element's opacity property to 1.0.

After the toast has been displayed for the specified duration, the `revealToast()` method hides it with the `hideToast()` method, listed in Example 5.9.

Example 5.9 Hiding the toast

```
var SnailBait = function () {
   ...

   this.TRANSPARENT = 0; // opacity
   ...
};

SnailBait.prototype = {
   ...

   hideToast: function () {
      var TOAST_TRANSITION_DURATION = 500; // Tightly coupled to CSS

      this.toastElement.style.opacity = this.TRANSPARENT;

      setTimeout( function (e) {
         snailBait.toastElement.style.display = 'none';
      }, TOAST_TRANSITION_DURATION);
   },
   ...
};
```

The `hideToast()` method fades the snailbait-toast element out of view by setting the element's `opacity` CSS property to zero and subsequently, when the transition has completed, setting the `display` property to none.

Now that you've seen how to fade elements in and out, let's implement Snail Bait methods that let the game fade any element in or out.

NOTE: Snail Bait's constants

To increase code readability, Snail Bait defines constant variables, such as the TOAST_TRANSITION_DURATION and snailBait.TRANSPARENT variables used in Example 5.9. Notice that the former variable is a local function variable, whereas the latter is a property of the SnailBait object.

Snail Bait uses local constants when those constants are only used by a single method. Snail Bait defines constants that are used by multiple methods as properties of the SnailBait object.

NOTE: Snail Bait's transition durations are tightly coupled to the game's JavaScript

Snail Bait's fadeOutElements() method sets an element's CSS display property to none to make the element disappear at the end of the element's opacity transition, so fadeOutElements() must know the duration of that transition, thereby creating a dependency between Snail Bait's CSS and its JavaScript.

That dependency means, for example, that you must change the TOAST_TRANSITION_DURATION constant in Snail Bait's hideToast() method if you change the duration of the toast's transition in CSS.

Admittedly, such a dependency is far from ideal; in fact, the dependency could be removed by programmatically determining the transition duration in the fadeOutElements() method. It's not trivial, however, to reliably determine transition durations in JavaScript across browsers, so Snail Bait lives with the dependency.

5.3 Fade Any Element In or Out That Has a CSS Transition Associated with Its Opacity

Snail Bait has several HTML elements besides the snailbait-toast DIV that it fades in and out over the course of the game, so it's worth the effort to implement more general methods that fade HTML elements in or out.

Snail Bait fades multiple elements simultaneously at certain points in the game, so in this section we implement two methods—fadeInElements() and fadeOutElements()—that can fade any number of elements simultaneously *as long as those elements have a CSS transition associated with their opacity property*. Example 5.10 shows how to use those methods to fade elements in and out.

Example 5.10 Using `fadeInElements()` and `fadeOutElements()`

```
snailBait.fadeInElements(snailBait.fpsElement,
                         snailBait.scoreElement);
...

snailBait.fadeOutElements(snailBait.fpsElement,
                          snailBait.scoreElement,
                          3000); // Fade duration in milliseconds
```

The preceding code fades the frames/second indicator and the score element into view and subsequently fades them out of view over a three-second duration.

The `fadeInElements()` method is listed in Example 5.11.

Example 5.11 `fadeInElements()`

```
SnailBait.prototype = {
  ...

  fadeInElements: function () { // Variable-length argument list
    var args = arguments;

    for (var i=0; i < args.length; ++i) {
      args[i].style.display = 'block';
    }

    setTimeout( function () {
      for (var i=0; i < args.length; ++i) {
        args[i].style.opacity = snailBait.OPAQUE; // OPAQUE is 1.0
      }
    }, this.SHORT_DELAY);
  },
  ...
};
```

Both `fadeInElements()` and `fadeOutElements()` take advantage of JavaScript's support for variable-length argument lists. Every JavaScript function has a local variable named arguments, which is an array-like object that lets you access the function's arguments. For example, you access the first argument to a function with arguments[0] and the last argument with arguments[arguments.length-1].

You pass `fadeInElements()` a variable-length list of elements to fade; the method uses the arguments variable to iterate over the elements, setting each element's CSS display property to block. Subsequently, after a short delay of approximately 50 ms, `fadeInElements()` sets the opacity of each element to 1.0 (fully opaque), which triggers any CSS transitions associated with the element's opacity property, fading those elements into view.

The fadeOutElements() method is listed in Example 5.12.

Example 5.12 fadeOutElements()

```
SnailBait.prototype = {
   ...

   fadeOutElements: function () { // Variable-length argument list
      var args = arguments,
          fadeDuration = args[args.length-1]; // Last argument

      for (var i=0; i < args.length-1; ++i) {
         args[i].style.opacity = snailBait.TRANSPARENT; // zero
      }

      setTimeout(function() {
         for (var i=0; i < args.length-1; ++i) {
            args[i].style.display = 'none';
         }
      }, fadeDuration);
   },
   ...
};
```

Like fadeInElements(), fadeOutElements() takes a variable number of arguments. Unlike fadeInElements(), however, the last argument to fadeOutElements() is the fade's duration and not an element. fadeOutElements() iterates over the elements you pass it, setting each element's CSS opacity property to zero, which kicks in any transitions associated with that property. Subsequently, after the elements have faded, fadeOutElements() sets each element's CSS display property to none so that the elements do not take up space or intercept events.

Now that we have more general methods for fading elements in and out, we use those methods to reimplement Snail Bait's startToastTransition() and hideToast() methods, as shown in Example 5.13.

Example 5.13 Using fadeInElements() and fadeOutElements() for showing toasts

```
SnailBait.prototype = {
   ...
   hideToast: function () {
      var TOAST_TRANSITION_DURATION = 500;
```

```
            this.fadeOutElements(this.toastElement,
                                 TOAST_TRANSITION_DURATION);
         },

         startToastTransition: function (text) {
            this.toastElement.innerHTML = text;
            this.fadeInElements(this.toastElement);
         },
         ...
};
```

You've seen how to define Snail Bait's chrome and how to fade elements in and out, so let's see how to implement the game's loading screen.

5.4 Implement the Loading Screen

As it loads resources, Snail Bait reveals the loading screen, which consists of the text *Loading…* and an animated GIF as illustrated in Figure 5.4.

Figure 5.4 The loading screen

The HTML for the loading screen is shown in Example 5.14.

The img element for the animated GIF does not have a src attribute because Snail Bait assigns a value to that attribute in the game's JavaScript.

Example 5.14 HTML elements for Snail Bait's loading screen

```html
<!DOCTYPE html>
<html>
   ...

   <body>
      ...

      <div id='snailbait-arena'>
         ...

         <!-- Loading screen.......................................-->

         <div id='snailbait-loading'>
            <div id='snailbait-loading-title'>Loading...</div>
            <img id='snailbait-loading-animated-gif'/> <!-- no src -->
         </div>
         ...
      </div>
      ...
   </body>
</html>
```

The CSS for Snail Bait's loading screen is shown in Example 5.15.

Example 5.15 CSS for the loading screen

```css
#snailbait-loading {
    position: absolute;
    margin-top: 80px;
    width: 790px;
    font: 55px fantasy;
    text-align: center;

    -webkit-transition: opacity 2.0s;
    -moz-transition: opacity 2.0s;
    -o-transition: opacity 2.0s;
    transition: opacity  2.0s;
}

#snailbait-loading-title {
    padding-left: 40px;
    padding-bottom: 30px;
    color: #ff6;
    text-shadow: 2px 2px 4px rgb(0,0,0);

    -webkit-transition: opacity 2.0s;
    -moz-transition: opacity 2.0s;
```

```
  -o-transition: opacity 2.0s;
  transition: opacity  2.0s;

  opacity: 0;
  display: none;
}

#snailbait-loading-animated-gif {
  margin: 0 auto;
  border: thin solid rgba(0, 0, 255, 0.7);
  border-radius: 60px 60px 60px;
  padding: 40px;
  margin-top: 10px;

  /* Radial gradient from www.colorzilla.com/gradient-editor */

  background: -moz-radial-gradient(center, ellipse cover, #f2f6f8 0%,
              #d8e1e7 50%, #b5c6d0 51%, #e0eff9 100%);

  background: -webkit-gradient(radial, center center, 0px,
              center center, 100%,
              color-stop(0%,#f2f6f8),
              color-stop(50%,#d8e1e7),
              color-stop(51%,#b5c6d0),
              color-stop(100%,#e0eff9));

  background: -webkit-radial-gradient(center, ellipse cover,
              #f2f6f8 0%,
              #d8e1e7 50%,
              #b5c6d0 51%,
              #e0eff9 100%);

  background: -o-radial-gradient(center, ellipse cover, #f2f6f8 0%,
              #d8e1e7 50%,#b5c6d0 51%,#e0eff9 100%);

  background: -ms-radial-gradient(center, ellipse cover, #f2f6f8 0%,
              #d8e1e7 50%,#b5c6d0 51%,#e0eff9 100%);

  background: radial-gradient(ellipse at center, #f2f6f8 0%,
              #d8e1e7 50%,#b5c6d0 51%,#e0eff9 100%);

  filter: progid:DXImageTransform.Microsoft.gradient(
          startColorstr='#f2f6f8', endColorstr='#e0eff9',
          GradientType=1 );

  -webkit-transition: opacity 2.0s;
  -moz-transition: opacity 2.0s;
  -o-transition: opacity 2.0s;
  transition: opacity  2.0s;
```

(Continues)

Example 5.15 *(Continued)*

```
    opacity: 0;
    display: none;
}
```

A good deal of the preceding CSS defines the radial gradient around the snail in the loading screen's animated GIF. The CSS for that gradient was generated by an online tool found at www.colorzilla.com/gradient-editor.

The snailbait-loading DIV, which has no visible aspects of its own, is initially displayed by the browser, but the DIV's contents—the snailbait-loading-title and snailbait-loading-animated-gif elements—are not displayed. The opacity and display property values for the snailbait-loading-title and snailbait-loading-animated-gif elements, along with their transitions, are an indication that Snail Bait uses the formula discussed in Section 5.3 on p. 132 to fade those elements in and out.

With the HTML and CSS for the loading screen out of the way, we turn our attention to the associated JavaScript for the loading screen. First, Snail Bait defines a Boolean value gameStarted, which is initially false. Subsequently, Snail Bait obtains references to the three elements that constitute the loading screen, as shown in Example 5.16.

Example 5.16 Accessing loading-screen elements

```
var SnailBait = function () {
   ...

   this.gameStarted = false;

   // Loading screen elements........................................

   this.loadingElement =
      document.getElementById('snailbait-loading');

   this.loadingTitleElement =
      document.getElementById('snailbait-loading-title');

   this.loadingAnimatedGIFElement =
      document.getElementById('snailbait-loading-animated-gif');
   ...
};
```

Example 5.17 lists a revised implementation of Snail Bait's initializeImages() method, which was originally discussed in Chapter 3. As in the original implementation, the method sets the src attributes for the background and runner images besides adding an onload event handler to the background image that starts the game. Additionally, the revised version of initializeImages() sets the src attribute of the animated GIF and adds an onload event handler to that image, which fades in the animated GIF and its associated title.

Example 5.17 Starting the game, revisited

```
SnailBait.prototype = {
  ...

  backgroundLoaded: function () {
    var LOADING_SCREEN_TRANSITION_DURATION = 2000;

    this.fadeOutElements(this.loadingElement,
                    LOADING_SCREEN_TRANSITION_DURATION);

    setTimeout ( function () {
      snailBait.startGame();
      snailBait.gameStarted = true;
    }, LOADING_SCREEN_TRANSITION_DURATION);
  },

  loadingAnimationLoaded: function () {
    if (!this.gameStarted) {
      this.fadeInElements(this.loadingAnimatedGIFElement,
                      this.loadingTitleElement);
    }
  },

  initializeImages: function () {
    this.background.src = 'images/background.png';
    this.runnerImage.src = 'images/runner.png';
    this.loadingAnimatedGIFElement.src = 'images/snail.gif';

    this.background.onload = function (e) {
      snailBait.backgroundLoaded();
    };

    this.loadingAnimatedGIFElement.onload = function () {
      snailBait.loadingAnimationLoaded();
    };
  },
  ...
};
```

The difference in byte size between Snail Bait's background image and the animated GIF it displays on its loading screen is enormous; 11MB for the background versus only 8K for the animated GIF. That difference in size virtually ensures that the animated GIF will load more quickly than the background image; in that case, Snail Bait starts the game after the background loads.

The gameStarted property serves as a guard in the unlikely event that it takes longer for the animated GIF to load than the background image. If that happens, Snail Bait starts the game after the animated GIF loads.

Now that you've seen how Snail Bait implements its loading screen, let's look at the next step: revealing the game.

5.5 Reveal the Game

Once Snail Bait loads all its resources and the loading screen has faded out, Snail Bait reveals the game itself, as discussed at the beginning of this chapter and as shown in Figure 5.5.

Here's how Snail Bait reveals the game:

1. For a duration of 5 seconds, the game fades in the top chrome at 0.25 opacity, and fades in the canvas and bottom chrome at 1.0 opacity (the top two screenshots in Figure 5.5).

2. For a duration of 0.5 seconds, the game fades in the initial toast, subsequently displays it for 3 seconds, then fades it out for 0.5 seconds. (The third screenshot from the top in Figure 5.5)

3. Finally, the game changes the top chrome's opacity to 1.0 and the bottom chrome's opacity to 0.5 (The bottom screenshot in Figure 5.5). The browser smoothly animates both changes in opacity over a period of 5 seconds thanks to CSS transitions on the elements.

Snail Bait's startGame() method is shown in Example 5.18.

Example 5.18 Starting the game

```
SnailBait.prototype = {
   ...

   startGame: function () {
      this.revealGame();
      this.revealInitialToast();
      requestNextAnimationFrame(this.animate);
   },
   ...
};
```

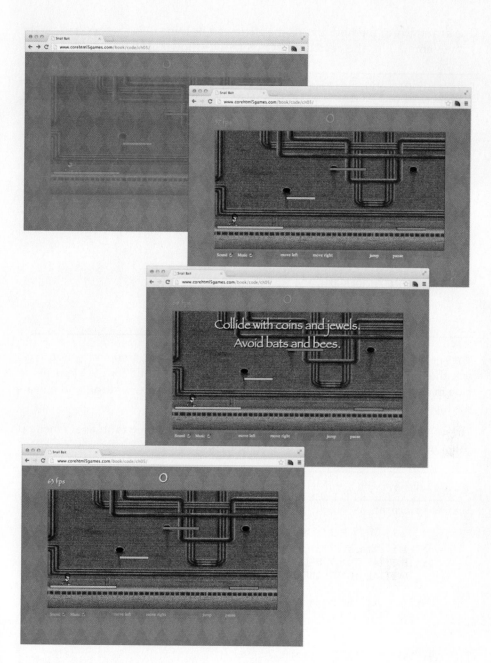

Figure 5.5   Revealing Snail Bait

The startGame() method reveals the game and its initial toast before starting the game's animation. The revealGame() method is shown in Example 5.19.

Example 5.19 Revealing the game

```
SnailBait.prototype = {
   ...

   revealGame: function () {
      var DIM_CONTROLS_DELAY = 5000; // Tightly coupled to CSS

      this.revealTopChromeDimmed();
      this.revealCanvas();
      this.revealBottomChrome();

      setTimeout( function () {
         snailBait.dimControls();
         snailBait.revealTopChrome();
      }, DIM_CONTROLS_DELAY);
   },
   ...
};
```

The revealGame() method reveals the top chrome dimmed, along with the canvas and the bottom chrome at full opacity. It takes five seconds for the elements to fade in, and after that length of time, revealGame() dims the controls and reveals the top chrome at full opacity.

The revealInitialToast() method, which is invoked by the startGame() method listed in Example 5.18, is listed in Example 5.20.

Example 5.20 Revealing the initial toast

```
SnailBait.prototype = {
   ...

   revealInitialToast: function () {
      var INITIAL_TOAST_DELAY = 1500,
          INITIAL_TOAST_DURATION = 3000;

      setTimeout( function () {
         snailBait.revealToast('Collide with coins and jewels. ' +
                               'Avoid bats and bees.',
                               INITIAL_TOAST_DURATION);
      }, INITIAL_TOAST_DELAY);
   },
   ...
};
```

The revealInitialToast() delays 1.5 seconds before calling the revealToast() method to actually reveal the initial toast. That delay lets the game fade into view briefly before the message appears.

The revealCanvas(), revealTopChrome(), and revealBottomChrome() methods are listed in Example 5.21. Those methods use the more general fadeInElements() method, discussed in Section 5.3 on p. 132.

Example 5.21 Revealing the canvas and chrome

```
SnailBait.prototype = {
   ...

   revealCanvas: function () {
      this.fadeInElements(this.canvas);
   },

   revealTopChrome: function () {
      this.fadeInElements(this.fpsElement,
                          this.scoreElement);
   },

   revealBottomChrome: function () {
      this.fadeInElements(this.soundAndMusicElement,
                          this.instructionsElement,
                          this.copyrightElement);
   },
   ...
};
```

When the game starts, the top chrome is nearly transparent and the bottom chrome is fully opaque. Subsequently, the bottom controls fade to nearly transparent while the top chrome becomes fully opaque. The revealTopChromeDimmed() and dimControls() methods dim those elements. They are listed in Example 5.22.

Example 5.22 Dimming controls and the top chrome

```
SnailBait.prototype = {
   ...

   dimControls: function () {
      var FINAL_OPACITY = 0.5;

      snailBait.instructionsElement.style.opacity = FINAL_OPACITY;
      snailBait.soundAndMusicElement.style.opacity = FINAL_OPACITY;
   },
```

(Continues)

Example 5.22   *(Continued)*

```
...

revealTopChromeDimmed: function () {
   var DIM = 0.25;

   this.scoreElement.style.display = 'block';
   this.fpsElement.style.display = 'block';

   setTimeout( function () {
      snailBait.scoreElement.style.opacity = DIM;
      snailBait.fpsElement.style.opacity = DIM;
   }, this.SHORT_DELAY);
},
...
};
```

5.6 Conclusion

Smooth transitions between states, such as returning to the beginning of a level when a player loses a life, add polish to a game. In this chapter you saw how to implement a fundamental operation: defining CSS transitions for a particular CSS property (such as `opacity`) and subsequently manipulating that property with JavaScript to initiate the transition's animation.

Snail Bait fades HTML elements in and out with CSS transitions on the elements' `opacity` properties as described above, but it also goes to the trouble of manipulating the `display` property to make sure that invisible elements are not rendered by the browser so that they do not take up space and, more importantly, do not capture events meant for elements underneath them.

You can combine fading elements in and out with the `setTimeout()` method to produce sophisticated effects, as you saw in this chapter's coverage of Snail Bait's loading sequence.

In the next chapter, we discuss how to implement graphical objects known as sprites.

5.7 Exercises

1. Create a different animated GIF for Snail Bait's loading screen and integrate it into the game. See Chapter 2 for a discussion of online resources for creating animated GIFs.

2. If you only briefly see the loading screen, clear your browser's cache and reload the game. You should see the loading screen for a much longer period of time.

3. Modify the `fadeInElements()` and `fadeOutElements()` methods so that they do *not* manipulate the `display` CSS property. Change the CSS for the canvas, chrome, and toast so those elements' `display` property is `block` instead of `none`. Does everything work the same as it did before?

6

Sprites

Topics in This Chapter

Like other art forms, such as film, theatre, and novels, games have a cast of characters, each of which plays a particular role. For example, Snail Bait has the runner (the game's central character), coins, rubies, sapphires, bees, bats, buttons, and a snail, all of which are shown in Figure 6.1. See Chapter 1 for a discussion of those characters and their roles in the game.

Each character in Snail Bait is a sprite, which are animated characters you endow with behaviors; for example, the runner can run, jump, fall, and collide with other sprites in the game, whereas rubies and sapphires sparkle, bob up and down, and disappear when they collide with the runner.

Because sprites are one of the most fundamental aspects of any game, and because games typically have many of them, it makes sense to encapsulate their

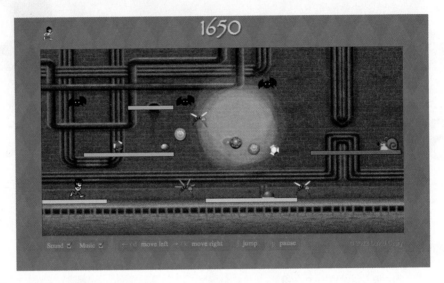

Figure 6.1 Snail Bait's sprites

functionality in reusable JavaScript objects. In this chapter you will learn how to do the following:

- Implement a `Sprite` JavaScript object you can reuse in any game (Section 6.1 on p. 149)
- Decouple sprites from the objects that draw them (referred to as sprite artists) (Section 6.1 on p. 149)
- Decouple sprites from the objects that manipulate them (referred to as sprite behaviors) (Section 6.1 on p. 149)
- Incorporate sprites into a game loop (Section 6.2 on p. 156)
- Implement sprite artists (Section 6.3 on p. 160)
- Use sprite sheets to reduce startup time and memory requirements (Section 6.3.3 on p. 162)
- Create and initialize a game's sprites (Section 6.4 on p. 167)
- Define sprites with metadata to separate sprite definition from sprite creation (Section 6.5 on p. 171)
- Scroll sprites horizontally (Section 6.6 on p. 174)

NOTE: The term sprite

One of the implementers of the Texas Instruments 9918A video-display processor was the first to use the term sprite for animated characters. (In standard English, the word—derived from the Latin spiritus—means elf or fairy.) Sprites have been implemented in both software and hardware; the Commodore Amiga in 1985 supported up to eight hardware sprites.

NOTE: The first animated character

Before Mickey Mouse, and even before Gertie the dinosaur, there was Little Nemo by Winsor McCay who was a pioneer among animators. Little Nemo made his appearance in the silent short film titled *Winsor McCay, the Famous Cartoonist of the N.Y. Herald and His Moving Comics*. You can watch the silent film on YouTube at http://bit.ly/1gzsWWr.

NOTE: Game engines

In this chapter you will see how to implement reusable JavaScript objects known as sprites that you can customize, mostly through the sprite's artist and its behaviors, in any fashion you desire.

Reusable code is important for rapid development of sophisticated games; in fact, many games are implemented with an underlying game engine, which encapsulates many other aspects of game development in addition to sprites. One of the most popular game engines is the Unreal Engine, which has been used to create hundreds of games on different platforms. You can read more about the Unreal Engine on Wikipedia at http://en.wikipedia.org/wiki/Unreal_Engine.

6.1 Sprite Objects

You can create and manipulate sprites in any game, not just Snail Bait, so the sprite implementation resides in a file of its own in the game's js directory. Snail Bait includes that file in its HTML, shown in Example 6.1.

The snailbait.js file depends on js/sprites.js, so Snail Bait includes the former first.

Example 6.1 Including the sprite JavaScript

```
<!DOCTYPE html>
<html>
    ...

    <body>
        ...

        <!-- The final version of Snail Bait puts all the
             game's JavaScript into a single file. See
             Chapter 19 for more details about how
             Snail Bait is deployed. -->

        <script src='js/sprites.js'></script>
        <script src='snailbait.js'></script>
    </body>
</html>
```

To create a sprite in JavaScript, you invoke the Sprite constructor, as shown in Example 6.2.

Example 6.2 Initially creating the runner sprite

```
var SnailBait = function () {
    ...

    this.runner = new Sprite(
        'runner', // type

        new SpriteSheetArtist(this.spritesheet, // artist
                              this.runnerCellsRight)
    );
    ...
};
```

Snail Bait initially creates the runner sprite without any behaviors, so the preceding instantiation of the runner specifies the minimum amount of information required to create a sprite: its type and its artist.

A sprite's type is a string and its artist is an object with a draw() method that draws the sprite. The runner's artist is a sprite sheet artist, which copies images from a sprite sheet—a single image containing all the game's images—into the game's canvas. Section 6.3, "Implement Sprite Artists," on p. 160 takes a closer look at implementing sprite artists.

Example 6.3 shows the runner's instantiation in the final version of the game, complete with behaviors.

Example 6.3 Creating the runner sprite with behaviors

```
var SnailBait = function () {
   ...

   this.runner = new Sprite(
      'runner', // type

      new SpriteSheetArtist(this.spritesheet, // artist
                            this.runnerCellsRight),

      [ this.runBehavior, // an array of behaviors
        this.jumpBehavior,
        this.fallBehavior,
        this.collideBehavior,
        this.runnerExplodeBehavior
      ]
   );
   ...
};
```

Like artists, behaviors are also objects, but instead of a draw() method, behaviors implement an execute() method that manipulates the sprite so it exhibits some sort of behavior. Section 6.1.3, "Sprite Methods," on p. 154 shows how sprites invoke their behaviors' execute() method.

You've seen how to create sprites. Next, we look at their properties.

NOTE: The benefits of artists and behaviors

Sprites don't do much on their own. Much of what constitutes a sprite—such as what it looks like and how it behaves—is implemented by separate objects, known as artists and behaviors, respectively. That separation of concerns results in a simple implementation for sprites themselves and the ability to plug in different artists and behaviors at runtime.

NOTE: Including separate JavaScript files

Throughout this book we add JavaScript files to Snail Bait for other functionality besides sprites, such as the game's time system. Ultimately, however, Snail Bait includes only one JavaScript file that contains all of the game's minified JavaScript. See Chapter 19 for details.

6.1.1 Sprite Properties

Sprites are JavaScript objects with properties and methods. Those properties are listed in Table 6.1.

Table 6.1 Sprite properties

Property	Description
artist	An object whose draw() method draws the artist's associated sprite.
behaviors	An array of objects, each of which has an execute() method. That method manipulates the behavior's associated sprite to implement a behavior over time.
left	The X coordinate of the sprite's upper-left corner.
top	The Y coordinate of the sprite's upper-left corner.
width	The sprite's width in pixels.
height	The sprite's height in pixels.
hOffset	The sprite's horizontal offset. See Section 6.6 for more information.
opacity	A number that determines whether a sprite is opaque, transparent, or somewhere in between. Valid values are between 0.0 (invisible) and 1.0 (fully opaque), inclusive.
type	A string representing the sprite's type, such as bat, bee, or runner.
velocityX	The sprite's horizontal velocity, specified in pixels/second.
velocityY	The sprite's vertical velocity, specified in pixels/second.
visible	The sprite's visibility. If the value is false, Snail Bait does not update or draw the sprite.

Sprites maintain their location and size, velocity, and visibility. They also have a type to distinguish one sprite from another, and an opacity, so that sprites can be partially transparent.

Like the background, Snail Bait's sprites scroll horizontally. And also like the background, sprites keep track of a horizontal offset (hOffset) that determines where they appear in the game's canvas. See Chapter 3 for more information about scrolling the background and Section 6.6, "Scroll Sprites," on p. 174 to see how Snail Bait uses the hOffset property.

NOTE: Sprites have only horizontal offsets

The sprites implemented in this book have a horizontal offset stored in their hOffset property, but not a vertical offset because Snail Bait scrolls sprites only in the horizontal direction. It would be a simple matter, however, to add support for vertical scrolling with an analogous vOffset property.

NOTE: A sprite's horizontal position never changes

Recall from Chapter 3 that Snail Bait scrolls the background by continuously translating the coordinate system for the game's canvas. Snail Bait always draws the background at the same coordinates; it's the translation of the coordinate system that gives the background its apparent horizontal motion.

Snail Bait moves sprites in the horizontal direction in exactly the same manner as the background. A sprite's horizontal position, stored in the sprite's left property, never changes; instead, the game changes the sprite's horizontal offset, stored in the sprite's hOffset property. When Snail Bait draws sprites, it translates the coordinate system by the sprite's horizontal offset (hOffset), draws the sprite at its never-changing horizontal location (left), and translates the coordinate system back to where it was in first place. See Section 6.2, "Incorporate Sprites into a Game Loop," on p. 156 for more details.

6.1.2 The Sprite Constructor

Example 6.4 lists the Sprite constructor, which sets a sprite's properties to initial values.

Example 6.4 The Sprite constructor

```
var Sprite = function (type, artist, behaviors) {
   var DEFAULT_WIDTH = 10,
       DEFAULT_HEIGHT = 10,
       DEFAULT_OPACITY = 1.0;

   this.artist    = artist;
   this.type      = type;
   this.behaviors = behaviors || [];

   this.hOffset   = 0; // Horizontal offset
   this.left      = 0;
```

(Continues)

Example 6.4 *(Continued)*

```
    this.top      = 0;
    this.width    = DEFAULT_WIDTH;
    this.height   = DEFAULT_HEIGHT;
    this.velocityX = 0;
    this.velocityY = 0;
    this.opacity  = DEFAULT_OPACITY;
    this.visible  = true;
};
```

The Sprite constructor takes three arguments: a type, an artist, and an array of behaviors. If you don't specify behaviors, the constructor creates an empty array. If you don't specify a type or an artist, they are undefined.

6.1.3 Sprite Methods

Sprites initially have only two methods, listed in Table 6.2.

Table 6.2 ■ Snail Bait sprite methods

Method	Description
draw(context)	Calls the draw() method of the sprite's artist if the sprite is visible and has an artist.
update(now, fps, context, lastAnimationFrameTime)	Invokes the execute() method for each of the sprite's behaviors.

Every animation frame, Snail Bait invokes each visible sprite's update() method followed by a call to its draw() method; see Section 6.2, "Incorporate Sprites into a Game Loop," on p. 156 for details. The update() method delegates to the sprite's behaviors to update the sprite's properties, and the draw() method subsequently delegates to the sprite's artist to draw the sprite.

When we implement collision detection in Chapter 11, we add a couple of methods and properties to the Sprite object, but for now the draw() and update() methods listed in Example 6.5 will suffice.

Example 6.5 Sprite method implementations

```
Sprite.prototype = {  // An object containing Sprite methods
    draw: function (context) {
        context.save();
```

```
    context.globalAlpha = this.opacity;

    if (this.visible && this.artist) {
        this.artist.draw(this, context);
    }

    // Restore globalAlpha and any other changes
    // the artist may have made to the context
    // in the artist's draw() method.

    context.restore();
  },

  update: function (now, fps, context, lastAnimationFrameTime) {
    for (var i = 0; i < this.behaviors.length; ++i) {
        this.behaviors[i].execute(this,
                                  now,
                                  fps,
                                  context,
                                  lastAnimationFrameTime);
    }
  }
};
```

As you can see from Examples 6.4 and 6.5, sprites are not complicated. Much of a sprite's complexity is encapsulated in its artist and behaviors.

If a sprite is visible and has an artist, the sprite's draw() method invokes the artist's draw() method. The calls to the context's save() and restore() methods ensure that the context.globalAlpha property's value, along with any other changes to context properties made by the artist's draw() method, are restored after the sprite is drawn. See Chapter 3 for more information on saving and restoring the context.

A sprite's update() method iterates over the sprite's behaviors, invoking each behavior's execute() method in turn. Those execute() methods typically update their associated sprite by modifying the sprite's properties or invoking its methods.

Because sprites are decoupled from their artists and behaviors, you can change artists and behaviors at runtime. In fact, it's possible, and often highly desirable, to implement general behaviors that can be used with multiple sprites, as you will see in Chapter 7.

Now that you've seen how sprites are implemented, you're set to see how Snail Bait incorporates them into its game loop.

NOTE: Implementing sprites

This book illustrates one way to implement sprites, but there are many ways to do it. Depending on the game you are implementing, you may wish to use the book's implementation or perhaps some variation thereof. Or you may want to implement your own sprites from scratch, perhaps using some of the ideas from this chapter and the next.

6.2 Incorporate Sprites into a Game Loop

Snail Bait maintains an array of sprite objects, as you can see in Example 6.6. The game populates that array when it creates sprites at the beginning of the game, as you will see in Section 6.4, "Create and Initialize a Game's Sprites," on p. 167.

Example 6.6 Snail Bait's `sprites` array

```
var SnailBait = function () {
   ...

   this.sprites = [];
   ...
};
```

Snail Bait's `draw()` method, as discussed in Chapter 4, invoked separate methods, `drawRunner()` and `drawPlatforms()`, for drawing the runner and platforms. Now that the runner and platforms are sprites, we remove `drawRunner()` and `drawPlatforms()` from the game and modify the `draw()` method, as shown in Example 6.7.

Example 6.7 Updating and drawing sprites every animation frame

```
SnailBait.prototype = {
   ...

   draw: function (now) { // Called by animate() every animation frame
      ...

      this.updateSprites(now);
      this.drawSprites();
   },
   ...
};
```

For every animation frame, Snail Bait's `animate()` method invokes the preceding `draw()` method, which updates and draws the game's sprites. The `updateSprites()` method is listed in Example 6.8.

Example 6.8 Updating sprites

```
SnailBait.prototype = {
  ...

  updateSprites: function (now) {
    var sprite;

    for (var i=0; i < this.sprites.length; ++i) {
      sprite = this.sprites[i];

      if (sprite.visible && this.isSpriteInView(sprite)) {
        sprite.update(now,
                      this.fps,
                      this.context,
                      this.lastAnimationFrameTime);
      }
    }
  },
  ...
};
```

Snail Bait's `updateSprites()` method iterates over the game's sprites, and for every visible sprite that's currently in view, `updateSprites()` invokes the sprite's `update()` method, which we discussed in Section 6.1.3, "Sprite Methods," on p. 154. The `isSpriteInView()` method returns `true` when the sprite lies within the visible canvas, as shown in Example 6.9.

Example 6.9 Determining whether a sprite is in view

```
SnailBait.prototype = {
  ...

  isSpriteInView: function (sprite) {
    return sprite.left + sprite.width > sprite.hOffset &&
           sprite.left < sprite.hOffset + this.canvas.width;
  },
  ...
};
```

The preceding method takes into account the sprite's horizontal offset, stored in the hOffset property. We discuss that offset and how Snail Bait sets it in Section 6.6, "Scroll Sprites," on p. 174.

Example 6.10 shows the implementation of Snail Bait's drawSprites() method.

Example 6.10 Drawing sprites

```
SnailBait.prototype = {
   ...

   drawSprites: function () {
      var sprite;

      for (var i=0; i < this.sprites.length; ++i) {
         sprite = this.sprites[i];

         if (sprite.visible && this.isSpriteInView(sprite)) {

            this.context.translate(-sprite.hOffset, 0);

            sprite.draw(this.context);

            this.context.translate(sprite.hOffset, 0);

         }
      }
   },
   ...
};
```

Like updateSprites(), drawSprites() also iterates over Snail Bait's sprites. For every sprite that's visible and in view, the drawSprites() method *translates the coordinate system to the left by* sprite.hOffset *pixels*, invokes the sprite's draw() method, and *translates the coordinate system back to where it was initially*. That temporary translation of the coordinate system gives sprites their apparent horizontal motion.

Now that you've seen how to implement sprites and incorporate them into Snail Bait, let's look at sprite artists.

NOTE: A sprite's `update()` method receives important information

Snail Bait's `animate()` method invokes the game's `draw()` method, which in turn iterates over all visible sprites, invoking each sprite's `update()` method. That `update()` method in turn iterates over all of the sprite's behaviors, invoking each behavior's `execute()` method.

Valuable information, along with the graphics context, is passed from the `animate()` method to the `execute()` method of a sprite's behaviors, namely:

- The current time
- The current frame rate
- The time at which the game drew the last animation frame

Behaviors use that information to determine how to manipulate their sprite at a particular point in time.

NOTE: Updating sprites based on the current time

Snail Bait enforces a subtle separation of concerns when it updates and draws its sprites: The game's `draw()` method, listed in Example 6.7 on p. 156, passes the current time to the game's `updateSprites()` method, whereas it does not pass the current time to the game's `drawSprites()` method.

That difference exists because sprite artists should simply draw their sprites. Manipulating sprites, which is typically dependent on the current time, is the sole purview of sprite behaviors.

BEST PRACTICE: Update all sprites in one pass and draw them in another

Every animation frame, Snail Bait iterates over its sprites twice, once to update them and a second time to draw them. You might wonder why Snail Bait doesn't just iterate once, updating and drawing each sprite in turn, which would admittedly result in ever-so-slightly better performance.

The reason Snail Bait updates sprites in one pass and draws them in another is that updating a sprite may affect another sprite's position or the way it looks; for example, when Snail Bait's snail shoots a snail bomb, the snail's shoot behavior makes the bomb visible. If the bomb were updated and drawn before the snail, the bomb would make a belated appearance.

In your own games you should also update and draw your sprites in two passes to avoid timing issues related to sprite interdependencies.

6.3 Implement Sprite Artists

Recall that sprites do not draw themselves; instead, they delegate that responsibility to another object, known as the sprite's artist.

Also, recall the chain of events that result in a sprite artist drawing its sprite. Every animation frame, Snail Bait's `animate()` method invokes the game's `draw()` method, which iterates over the game's sprites, invoking every visible sprite's `draw()` method. The sprite's `draw()` method invokes the `draw()` method of its artist.

Generally, there are three types of sprite artist:

- *Stroke and fill artist:* Draws graphics primitives, such as lines, arcs, and curves
- *Image artist:* Draws an image with the 2D context's `drawImage()` method
- *Sprite sheet artist:* Draws an image from a sprite sheet, also with `drawImage()`

Regardless of an artist's type, all sprite artists must fulfill only one requirement: Implement a `draw()` method that takes a sprite and a Canvas 2D context as arguments and use the context to draw the sprite.

6.3.1 Stroke and Fill Artists

Stroke and fill artists do not have a canonical implementation; instead, you implement them ad hoc with the graphics capabilities of the Canvas 2D context. Example 6.11 shows the implementation of the stroke and fill artist that draws Snail Bait's platform sprites.

Example 6.11 Drawing platform sprites

```
var SnailBait = function () {
   ...

   this.platformArtist = {
      draw: function (sprite, context) {
         var PLATFORM_STROKE_WIDTH = 1.0,
             PLATFORM_STROKE_STYLE = 'black',
             top;

         top = snailBait.calculatePlatformTop(sprite.track);

         context.lineWidth = PLATFORM_STROKE_WIDTH;
```

```
      context.strokeStyle = PLATFORM_STROKE_STYLE;
      context.fillStyle   = sprite.fillStyle;

      context.strokeRect(sprite.left, top,
                         sprite.width, sprite.height);

      context.fillRect  (sprite.left, top,
                         sprite.width, sprite.height);
   }
};
   ...
};
```

The platform artist's draw() method is similar to the standalone draw() function discussed in Chapter 3. Like that function, the platform artist draws its platform as a filled rectangle.

6.3.2 Image Artists

Image artists draw an image; for example, Example 6.12 shows how the runner's artist *could* draw the runner's image (but does not).

Example 6.12 Drawing the runner with an image artist

```
var SnailBait = function () {
   ...

   // Snail Bait does NOT use the following artist. It is listed
   // merely to illustrate image artists, which Snail Bait does
   // not use. Instead, Snail Bait uses sprite sheet artists
   // to draw its sprites.

   this.runnerArtist = {
      draw: function (sprite, context) {
         snailBait.context.drawImage(
            snailBait.runnerImage, sprite.left, sprite.top);
      }
   };
   ...
};
```

Snail Bait however does not implement the runner's artist as shown in Example 6.12; instead, the game implements the runner's artist as a sprite sheet artist.

6.3.3 Sprite Sheet Artists

One of the most effective ways to ensure that your game loads quickly is to reduce the number of HTTP requests you make to a minimum. Most games use lots of images, and your startup time will suffer significantly if you make separate HTTP requests for each of them. For that reason, HTML5 game developers typically create a single large image containing all of the game's images. That single image is known as a sprite sheet. Figure 6.2 shows Snail Bait's sprite sheet.

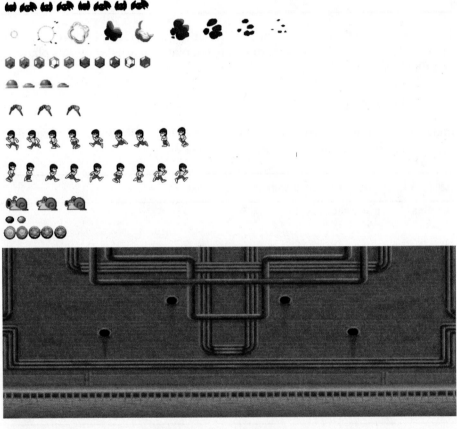

Figure 6.2 Snail Bait's sprite sheet

To draw sprites from a sprite sheet, you copy rectangles from the sprite sheet onto a canvas. You can easily do that with the Canvas 2D context's drawImage() method, as shown in Example 6.13, which lists the implementation of the SpriteSheetArtist object.

Example 6.13 Sprite sheet artists

```
SpriteSheetArtist = function (spritesheet, cells) {
   this.cells = cells;
   this.spritesheet = spritesheet;
   this.cellIndex = 0;
};

SpriteSheetArtist.prototype = {
   draw: function (sprite, context) {
      var cell = this.cells[this.cellIndex];

      context.drawImage(this.spritesheet, cell.left,   cell.top,
                                          cell.width,  cell.height,
                                          sprite.left, sprite.top,
                                          cell.width,  cell.height);
   },

   advance: function () {
      if (this.cellIndex === this.cells.length-1) {
         this.cellIndex = 0;
      }
      else {
         this.cellIndex++;
      }
   }
};
```

The 2D graphics context's drawImage() method used in the preceding listing is the same method used in Example 6.12; however, the preceding listing uses the nine-argument version of the method to draw from a cell in a sprite sheet to the sprite's location in the canvas.

Sprites in sprite sheets are often aligned in strips, as is the case for Snail Bait's sprite sheet, as you can see from Figure 6.2. Typically, each strip contains multiple images of a single sprite in different poses. Sprite sheet artists can advance through those images, drawing each in turn, thereby animating the sprite.

You instantiate sprite sheet artists with a reference to a sprite sheet and an array of bounding boxes, called cells. Those cells represent rectangular areas within the sprite sheet. Each cell encloses a single sprite image.

Sprite sheet artists also maintain an index into their cells. The sprite sheet artist's draw() method uses that index to access the current cell and then uses the nine-argument version of the Canvas 2D context's drawImage() to draw the contents of that cell into a canvas at the sprite's location.

The sprite sheet artist's `advance()` method advances the cell index to the next cell, wrapping around to the beginning when the index points to the last cell. A subsequent call to the sprite sheet artist's `draw()` method draws the corresponding image. By repeatedly advancing the index and drawing, sprite sheet artists can draw a set of images sequentially from a sprite sheet.

Sprite sheet artists are easy to implement. They are also easy to use; you just instantiate the artist with a sprite sheet and cells, and subsequently invoke the `advance()` and `draw()` methods as desired.

Now that we've seen how sprite sheet artists draw cells from a sprite sheet, let's see how Snail Bait defines those cells in the first place.

 NOTE: Sprite sheets on mobile devices

Memory on mobile devices is much more limited than available memory on the desktop, so large images, such as a game's sprite sheet, can fail to load on mobile devices.

iOS sets specific limits on image size. Apple discusses those limits at http://bit.ly/17h7baT under the heading "Known iOS Resource Limits." Here's an online calculator that tells you whether your image will load on different versions of iOS: http://bit.ly/PJqEXy.

Android does not have any fixed limits on image size; however, if you exceed the amount of available memory when loading an image, you will get the dreaded `java.lang.OutofMemoryError: bitmapsize exceeds VM budget` error. The Android Developers Guide at http://developer.android.com/training/displaying-bitmaps/index.html shows you how to deal with that scenario.

6.3.4 Define Sprite Sheet Cells

Example 6.14 shows cell definitions within Snail Bait's sprite sheet for the game's bats, bees, and snail.

Example 6.14 Some sprite sheet cell definitions

```
var SnailBait = function () {
   ...

   this.BAT_CELLS_HEIGHT = 34; // Bat cell width varies; not constant

   this.BEE_CELLS_HEIGHT = 50;
```

```
this.BEE_CELLS_WIDTH  = 50;
...

this.SNAIL_CELLS_HEIGHT = 34;
this.SNAIL_CELLS_WIDTH  = 64;
...

this.batCells = [
   { left: 3,   top: 0, width: 36, height: this.BAT_CELLS_HEIGHT },
   { left: 41,  top: 0, width: 46, height: this.BAT_CELLS_HEIGHT },
   { left: 93,  top: 0, width: 36, height: this.BAT_CELLS_HEIGHT },
   { left: 132, top: 0, width: 46, height: this.BAT_CELLS_HEIGHT }
];

this.beeCells = [
   { left: 5,   top: 234, width: this.BEE_CELLS_WIDTH,
                          height: this.BEE_CELLS_HEIGHT },

   { left: 75,  top: 234, width: this.BEE_CELLS_WIDTH,
                          height: this.BEE_CELLS_HEIGHT },

   { left: 145, top: 234, width: this.BEE_CELLS_WIDTH,
                          height: this.BEE_CELLS_HEIGHT }
];

this.snailCells = [
   { left: 142, top: 466, width: this.SNAIL_CELLS_WIDTH,
                          height: this.SNAIL_CELLS_HEIGHT },

   { left: 75,  top: 466, width: this.SNAIL_CELLS_WIDTH,
                          height: this.SNAIL_CELLS_HEIGHT },

   { left: 2,   top: 466, width: this.SNAIL_CELLS_WIDTH,
                          height: this.SNAIL_CELLS_HEIGHT }
];
...
};
```

Determining cell bounding boxes is a tedious task, so it's worth the time to implement a tool that can do it for you, such as the one shown in Figure 6.3.

The application shown in Figure 6.3 displays an image and tracks mouse movement within that image. As you move the mouse, the application draws guidelines and displays the current mouse location in a readout in they upper-left corner of the application. The tool makes it easy to determine bounding boxes for each image in the sprite sheet. You can access the tool at corehtml5games.com/spritesheet-tool.

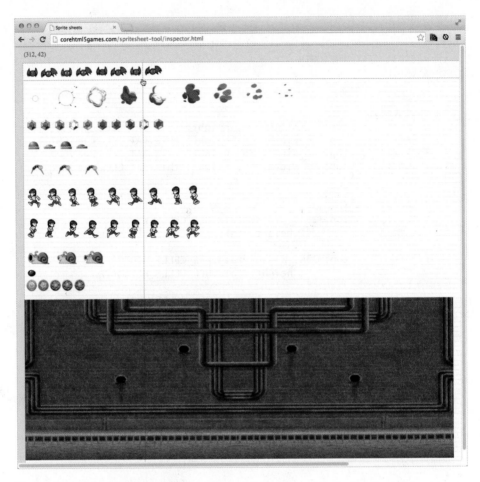

Figure 6.3 A sprite sheet inspector

Now that you have a good idea how to implement sprites and their artists, it's time to look at how Snail Bait creates and initializes its sprites.

 NOTE: The game developer's tool chest

A game developer's work is pretty much all fun and games. But occasionally, game developers must perform tedious tasks such as determining sprite sheet cells. Most game developers, therefore, spend a fair amount of time implementing tools, such as the one shown in Figure 6.3, to assist them with those tasks. Creating those tools can be fun too, so make sure you heed the following note.

NOTE: Every developer tool has a sweet spot

The sprite sheet inspector shown in Figure 6.3 is a simple tool that leaves a considerable amount of work to the developer, who must manually record the coordinates of every corner of every image in the sprite sheet. A more industrial strength sprite sheet inspector could automatically detect images in the sprite sheet and record the coordinates of their bounding boxes, but that would be a lot more work to implement.

Developer tools that you implement are a trade-off between the amount of time you invest in them versus their ultimate influence on your productivity. It's easy to get carried away developing tools, so it's a good idea to keep that trade-off in mind as you develop them.

6.4 Create and Initialize a Game's Sprites

As we discussed in Section 6.2, "Incorporate Sprites into a Game Loop," on p. 156, Snail Bait maintains a single array named `sprites` in which it stores references to all its sprites. For convenience, Snail Bait also maintains separate arrays for different types of sprites, as you can see in Example 6.15.

Example 6.15 Defining sprite arrays in the game constructor

```
var SnailBait = function () { // constructor
   ...

   this.bats      = [];
   this.bees      = [];
   this.buttons   = [];
   this.coins     = [];
   this.platforms = [];
   this.rubies    = [];
   this.sapphires = [];
   this.snails    = [];

   this.sprites = []; // Contains references to all the sprites
                      // in the preceding arrays
   ...
};
```

The individual arrays for bees, bats, and so on are not strictly necessary. In fact, they are redundant—but they facilitate performance. For example, when the game checks to see if the runner has landed on a platform, it's more efficient to iterate over the `platforms` array than to iterate over the `sprites` array looking for platforms.

When the game starts, Snail Bait invokes its `createSprites()` method, which is listed in **Example 6.16**.

Example 6.16 Creating sprites

```
SnailBait.prototype = {
   ...

   createSprites: function () {
      this.createPlatformSprites();

      this.createBatSprites();
      this.createBeeSprites();
      this.createButtonSprites();
      this.createCoinSprites();
      this.createRunnerSprite();
      this.createRubySprites();
      this.createSapphireSprites();
      this.createSnailSprites();

      this.initializeSprites();

      // All sprites are also stored in a single array

      this.addSpritesToSpriteArray();
   },
};
```

The `createSprites()` method creates the game's sprites with helper methods such as `createBatSprites()` and `createSnailSprites()`. Three of those methods are listed in **Example 6.17**.

Example 6.17 Some of Snail Bait's sprite creation methods

```
SnailBait.prototype = {
   ...

   // In the interest of brevity, not all Snail Bait's sprite
   // creation methods are listed here.

   createBatSprites: function () {
      var bat,
          BAT_FLAP_DURATION = 200,
          BAT_FLAP_INTERVAL = 50;

      for (var i = 0; i < this.batData.length; ++i) {
```

```
          bat = new Sprite('bat',
                          new SpriteSheetArtist(this.spritesheet,
                                                this.batCells),

                          [ new CycleBehavior(BAT_FLAP_DURATION)
                                              BAT_FLAP_INTERVAL ]);

          // Bat cell width varies; batCells[1] is widest

          bat.width = this.batCells[1].width;
          bat.height = this.BAT_CELLS_HEIGHT;

          bat.collisionMargin = {
             left: 6, top: 11, right: 4, bottom: 8
          };

          this.bats.push(bat);
       }
   },

   createPlatformSprites: function () {
      var sprite, pd,  // Sprite, Platform data
          PULSE_DURATION = 800,
          PULSE_OPACITY_THRESHOLD = 0.1;

      for (var i=0; i < this.platformData.length; ++i) {
         pd = this.platformData[i];

         sprite = new Sprite('platform', this.platformArtist);

         sprite.left = pd.left;
         sprite.width = pd.width;
         sprite.height = pd.height;
         sprite.fillStyle = pd.fillStyle;
         sprite.opacity = pd.opacity;
         sprite.track = pd.track;
         sprite.button = pd.button;
         sprite.pulsate = pd.pulsate;

         sprite.top = this.calculatePlatformTop(pd.track);

         if (sprite.pulsate) {
            sprite.behaviors =
               [ new PulseBehavior(PULSE_DURATION,
                                   PULSE_OPACITY_THRESHOLD) ];
         }

         this.platforms.push(sprite);
      }
   },
```

(Continues)

Example 6.17   *(Continued)*

```
createRunnerSprite: function () {
   var RUNNER_LEFT = 50,
       RUNNER_HEIGHT = 53,
       STARTING_RUNNER_TRACK = 1,
       STARTING_RUN_ANIMATION_RATE = this.RUN_ANIMATION_RATE;

   this.runner = new Sprite('runner',
                  new SpriteSheetArtist(this.spritesheet,
                                        this.runnerCellsRight),
                  [ this.runBehavior,
                    this.jumpBehavior,
                    this.collideBehavior,
                    this.runnerExplodeBehavior,
                    this.fallBehavior ]);

   this.runner.runAnimationRate = STARTING_RUN_ANIMATION_RATE;

   this.runner.track = STARTING_RUNNER_TRACK;

   this.runner.left = RUNNER_LEFT;
   this.runner.width = this.RUNNER_CELLS_WIDTH;
   this.runner.height = this.RUNNER_CELLS_HEIGHT;

   this.putSpriteOnTrack(this.runner, STARTING_RUNNER_TRACK);

   this.runner.collisionMargin = {
      left: 15,
      top: 10,
      right: 10,
      bottom: 10,
   };

   this.sprites.push(this.runner);
},
...
};
```

The preceding listing shows sprite creation methods for bats, platforms, and the
runner, leaving out methods that create coins, bees, buttons, rubies, sapphires,
snails, and snail bombs in the interest of brevity. The methods that are not listed
in the preceding listing are similar to `createBatSprites()`, which creates several
sprites of a certain type, outfits those sprites with a sprite sheet artist and
behaviors, and initializes the sprite's properties.

The methods that create the runner and the platforms are included in the preceding
listing because they are special cases. Platforms do not have sprite sheet artists
like the rest of Snail Bait's sprites; the platform artist, as you saw in Example 6.11

on p. 160, draws a filled rectangle instead of an image. The runner, on the other hand, is unique because it's one of a kind, so the `createRunnerSprite()` method adds the runner directly to the game's `sprites` array.

The most interesting aspect of Snail Bait's sprite creation methods, however, is that, except for the runner, they all create sprites from arrays of sprite metadata. Let's look at that metadata next.

6.5 Define Sprites with Metadata

Snail Bait draws all its sprites, except for platforms, from a single sprite sheet. As you saw in Section 6.3.4, "Define Sprite Sheet Cells," on p. 164, Snail Bait defines data objects that specify the location and size of the game's images in the sprite sheet.

Besides data objects that specify where a sprite's images reside in the game's sprite sheet, Snail Bait also defines objects for other sprite properties, for example, their location or whether they pulsate or not. Example 6.18 lists some of that metadata.

Example 6.18 Sprite metadata

```
var SnailBait = function () {
  ...
  // Sprite data.......................................................

  this.batData = [
    { left: 85,
      top: this.TRACK_2_BASELINE - 1.5*this.BAT_CELLS_HEIGHT },

    { left: 620,
      top: this.TRACK_3_BASELINE },

    { left: 904,
      top: this.TRACK_3_BASELINE - 3*this.BAT_CELLS_HEIGHT },

    { left: 1150,
      top: this.TRACK_2_BASELINE - 3*this.BAT_CELLS_HEIGHT },

    { left: 1720,
      top: this.TRACK_2_BASELINE - 2*this.BAT_CELLS_HEIGHT },

    { left: 1960,
      top: this.TRACK_3_BASELINE - this.BAT_CELLS_HEIGHT },
```

(Continues)

Example 6.18   *(Continued)*

```
      { left: 2200,
         top: this.TRACK_3_BASELINE - this.BAT_CELLS_HEIGHT },

      { left: 2380,
         top: this.TRACK_3_BASELINE - 2*this.BAT_CELLS_HEIGHT }

   ];

   this.beeData = [
      { left: 200,
         top: this.TRACK_1_BASELINE - this.BEE_CELLS_HEIGHT*1.5 },

      { left: 350,
         top: this.TRACK_2_BASELINE - this.BEE_CELLS_HEIGHT*1.5 },

      { left: 550,
         top: this.TRACK_1_BASELINE - this.BEE_CELLS_HEIGHT },

      { left: 750,
         top: this.TRACK_1_BASELINE - this.BEE_CELLS_HEIGHT*1.5 },

      { left: 924,
         top: this.TRACK_2_BASELINE - this.BEE_CELLS_HEIGHT*1.75 },

      { left: 1500, top: 225 },
      { left: 1600, top: 115 },
      { left: 2225, top: 125 },
      { left: 2295, top: 275 },
      { left: 2450, top: 275 }
   ];

   this.buttonData = [
      { platformIndex: 7 },
      { platformIndex: 12 }
   ];
   ...
};
```

Creating sprites from metadata is a good idea because of the following:

- Sprite metadata is located in one place, instead of spread throughout the code.
- Methods that create sprites are simpler when they are decoupled from the metadata.
- Metadata can come from anywhere.

Because sprite metadata is located in one place in the code, it's easy to find and modify. Also, because metadata is defined apart from methods that create sprites, those methods are simpler, and therefore easier to understand and modify. Finally, although the metadata for Snail Bait is embedded directly in the code, sprite metadata can come from anywhere—including, for example, a level editor that might create metadata at runtime. Metadata is easier to modify, and it's more flexible than specifying sprite data directly within methods that create sprites.

Recall from Example 6.16 on p. 168 that after creating the game's sprites, Snail Bait's createSprites() method invokes two methods: initializeSprites() and addSpritesToSpriteArray(). Example 6.19 shows the implementation of the initializeSprites() method and its positionSprites() helper method.

Example 6.19 Initializing Snail Bait's sprites

```
SnailBait.prototype = {
   ...

   initializeSprites: function() {
      this.positionSprites(this.bats,      this.batData);
      this.positionSprites(this.bees,      this.beeData);
      this.positionSprites(this.buttons,   this.buttonData);
      this.positionSprites(this.coins,     this.coinData);
      this.positionSprites(this.rubies,    this.rubyData);
      this.positionSprites(this.sapphires, this.sapphireData);
      this.positionSprites(this.snails,    this.snailData);

      this.setSpriteValues();

      this.armSnails();
      this.equipRunner();
   },

   positionSprites: function (sprites, spriteData) {
      var sprite;

      for (var i = 0; i < sprites.length; ++i) {
         sprite = sprites[i];

         if (spriteData[i].platformIndex) {
            this.putSpriteOnPlatform(sprite,
               this.platforms[spriteData[i].platformIndex]);
         }
         else {
            sprite.top  = spriteData[i].top;
            sprite.left = spriteData[i].left;
         }
      }
   },
   ...
};
```

The initializeSprites() method invokes positionSprites() for each of the game's sprite arrays. That method, in turn, positions sprites at locations specified by the sprite's metadata. Some sprites, such as buttons and snails, reside on platforms, so Snail Bait's putSpriteOnPlatform() method puts those sprites on their platforms, as shown in Example 6.20.

Example 6.20 Putting sprites on platforms

```
SnailBait.prototype = {
   ...

   putSpriteOnPlatform: function (sprite, platformSprite) {
      sprite.top  = platformSprite.top - sprite.height;
      sprite.left = platformSprite.left;

      sprite.platform = platformSprite;
   },
   ...
};
```

The putSpriteOnPlatform() method positions a sprite on top of a platform on the platform's left side. For future use, the method also adds a platform reference to the sprite that points to the platform.

6.6 Scroll Sprites

Recall from Chapter 3 that Snail Bait scrolls the background and platforms horizontally by translating the 2D graphics context. Now that platforms are sprites, Snail Bait scrolls the platform sprites and of all the game's other sprites, with the exception of the runner, in the horizontal direction. To implement sprite scrolling, we begin by adding a spriteOffset property to Snail Bait, in addition to the backgroundOffset property, as shown in Example 6.21.

Example 6.21 Snail Bait's offsets

```
var SnailBait = function () {
   ...

   this.STARTING_BACKGROUND_OFFSET = 0;
   this.STARTING_SPRITE_OFFSET = 0;

   // Translation offsets.......................................
```

```
   this.backgroundOffset = this.STARTING_BACKGROUND_OFFSET;
   this.spriteOffset = this.STARTING_SPRITE_OFFSET;
   ...
};
```

Next we modify Snail Bait's `setOffsets()` method, first discussed in Section 4.1.2 on p. 97, to set sprite offsets in addition to the offset for the background. The `setOffsets()` method is listed in Example 6.22.

Example 6.22 Setting offsets

```
SnailBait.prototype = {
   ...

   setOffsets: function (now) {
      this.setBackgroundOffset(now);
      this.setSpriteOffsets(now);
   },
   ...
};
```

The `setOffsets()` method sets the background offset, followed by the sprite offset. The `setBackgroundOffset()` method was discussed in Section 3.6 on p. 85, but because it's a short listing and because it's pertinent to setting sprite offsets, it's listed again here in Example 6.23.

Example 6.23 Setting the background offset

```
SnailBait.prototype = {
   ...

   setBackgroundOffset: function (now) {
      this.backgroundOffset +=
         this.bgVelocity * (now - this.lastAnimationFrameTime) / 1000;

      if (this.backgroundOffset < 0 ||
            this.backgroundOffset > this.BACKGROUND_WIDTH) {
         this.backgroundOffset = 0;
      }
   },
   ...
};
```

The `setSpriteOffsets()` method is listed in Example 6.24.

Example 6.24 Setting sprite offsets

```
SnailBait.prototype = {
   ...

   setSpriteOffsets: function (now) { // In step with platforms
      var sprite;

      this.spriteOffset +=
         this.platformVelocity *
         (now - this.lastAnimationFrameTime) / 1000;

      for (var i=0; i < this.sprites.length; ++i) {
         sprite = this.sprites[i];

         if ('runner' !== sprite.type) {
            sprite.hOffset = this.spriteOffset;
         }
      }
   },
   ...
};
```

Both setBackgroundOffset() and setSpriteOffsets() increment their respective offset properties by using time-based motion, as discussed in Section 3.6. The setSpriteOffsets() iterates over all of the game's sprites, setting each sprite's hOffset property to the current sprite offset. Ultimately, Snail Bait uses those offsets when drawing sprites, as discussed in Section 6.2, "Incorporate Sprites into a Game Loop," on p. 156.

6.7 Conclusion

Animated characters known as sprites are fundamental to all video games, and in this chapter you saw one way to implement them. The sprite implementation in this chapter separates drawing sprites and sprite behaviors from the actual sprites themselves, resulting in more flexibility than if sprites drew themselves and implemented their own behaviors.

Reducing the number of HTTP requests you make to load your game's resources will increase the speed with which your game initially loads, so it's a good idea to put all your images into one large image known as a sprite sheet. Fortunately, the 2D graphics context makes it easy to copy rectangles from a sprite sheet into the context's associated canvas, which is how we implemented sprite sheet artists in this chapter. Recall, however, that you may have to resort to multiple sprite sheets on mobile devices because of image file size limitations.

Besides decoupling sprites from the objects that draw them and endowing them with behaviors, the sprites implemented in this chapter are also decoupled from the data that defines them. Defining sprite data outside the methods that create sprites results in simpler sprite creation methods and more flexibility because you can change the source of the metadata without changing sprite creation methods.

Finally, in this chapter, you saw how to scroll sprites horizontally in the same manner that Snail Bait scrolls the background.

6.8 Exercises

1. Change Snail Bait's sprite metadata to move sprites to different initial locations.
2. Add another sprite of your choosing to the game. Here's what you need to do:
   a) Find images for your sprite and add them to Snail Bait's sprite sheet.
   b) Calculate the bounding boxes for each image and add that data to your sprite's metadata.
   c) Instantiate the sprite and add it to the game.
3. Add a `zIndex` property to the `Sprite` object and modify the `Sprite.draw()` method to draw sprites with higher z-indexes on top of sprites with lower z-indexes.

Sprite Behaviors

Topics in This Chapter

Great stories have great characters. And like books and movies, video games also need characters with interesting behaviors. For example, the protagonist in Braid—one of the most popular platform games of all time—can manipulate time. That ingenious behavior set the game apart from its contemporaries.

Behaviors are the soul of any video game, and adding behaviors to Snail Bait's inert sprites immediately makes the game more interesting, as shown in Figure 7.1.

Recall that Snail Bait's sprites do not implement their own activities such as running, jumping, or exploding. Instead, sprites rely on other objects, known as behaviors, to control how they act.

Figure 7.1 shows the snail shooting a snail bomb. Other behaviors that are not evident from the static image in Figure 7.1 are

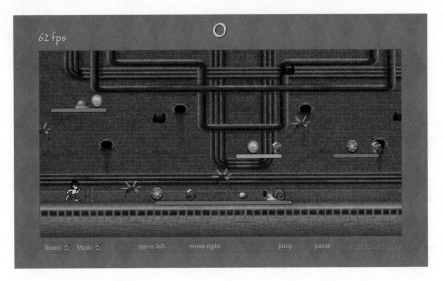

Figure 7.1 Sprites with behaviors

- Bats and bees flapping their wings
- Buttons and the snail pacing back and forth on their platforms
- Coins throbbing
- Rubies and sapphires sparkling
- The runner running
- The snail bomb moving from right to left

Table 7.1 summarizes the behaviors discussed in this chapter.

The behaviors listed in Table 7.1 represent less than half of Snail Bait's behaviors. They are also the game's most basic behaviors; jumping, for example, is considerably more complex, as discussed in forthcoming chapters. Nonetheless, there's a lot to learn from the implementation of the simpler behaviors in this chapter, including how to do the following:

- Implement behaviors and assign them to sprites (Section 7.1 on p. 182)
- Cycle a sprite through a sequence of images (Section 7.3 on p. 187)

- Create flyweight behaviors to save on memory usage (Section 7.4 on p. 190)
- Implement behaviors that can be used in any game (Section 7.5 on p. 193)
- Combine behaviors to shoot projectiles (Section 7.6 on p. 199)

Table 7.1 Sprite behaviors discussed in this chapter

Sprites	Type of behavior	Description
Bats and bees	Cycle	Cycles through the sprite's images to make it look as though it's flapping its wings.
Buttons and snails	Pace	Paces back and forth along a platform.
Coins	Cycle	Cycles through a coin's images to make it look as though the coin is throbbing.
Rubies and sapphires	Cycle	Cycles through the sprite's images to make it look as though they are sparkling.
Runner	Run	Cycles through the runner's images to make it appear as though she is running.
Snail	Cycle	Cycles through the snail's images to make it look as though the snail is opening and closing its mouth.
Snail	Shoot	Makes the snail bomb visible just in front of the snail's mouth.
Snail bomb	Move bomb	Moves the snail bomb horizontally to the left while it's visible in the canvas.

NOTE: Manipulating time

In Braid, the main character manipulates time, but every game developer is also a master at manipulating time. In this chapter, you will see the undercurrent of time flowing through behaviors; in the next two chapters, you'll see how to bend time itself to implement nonlinear motion, which is the basis for realistic motion such as jumping and falling.

NOTE: Types of behaviors

In this chapter we discuss three types of behaviors:

- Sprite-specific
- Flyweights (stateless)
- Game-independent

Some behaviors, such as the runner's run behavior, are sprite specific, meaning the behavior can be used only with a certain sprite.

Behaviors that do not maintain state are flyweights. Because they are stateless, a single flyweight behavior can be used with multiple sprites simultaneously. Flyweights can drastically reduce memory usage, especially for things like particle systems, which can consist of hundreds of sprites.

A third category of behaviors are game-independent behaviors, meaning general behaviors that work with any sprite. For example, in this chapter we discuss the implementation of a cycle behavior that cycles through a sprite's images. You can use a cycle behavior with any sprite whose artist is a sprite sheet artist, regardless of the game in which the sprite resides. See Chapter 6 for more information about sprites and their artists.

7.1 Behavior Fundamentals

Any JavaScript object can be a behavior as long as it has an execute() method. Example 7.1 shows how to implement a behavior.

Example 7.1 Implementing a behavior

```
var aBehavior = { // A JavaScript object with an execute() method
   ...

   execute: function (sprite, now, context,
                      fps, lastAnimationFrameTime) {

      // Manipulate the sprite depending on game conditions

   }
};
```

A behavior's `execute()` method takes five arguments, in the following order:

- The sprite to which the behavior is attached (`sprite`)
- The current time (`now`)
- The game's 2D graphics context (`context`)
- The game's current frame rate (`fps`)
- The time of the last animation frame (`lastAnimationFrameTime`)

The preceding arguments determine how a behavior's `execute()` method manipulates the sprite associated with the behavior for a given animation frame. For example, the behavior that moves the snail bomb from right to left calculates, from the bomb's speed and the elapsed time since the last animation frame (`now - lastAnimationFrameTime`), how far to move the bomb for a given animation frame. See Example 7.17 on p. 204 to see the implementation of that behavior.

Behaviors are powerful for the following reasons:

- They enforce a separation of concerns between sprites and sprite behaviors, making both the code for sprites and the code for behaviors easier to read and maintain than if sprites directly implemented their behaviors.
- You can change a sprite's behaviors at runtime.
- Stateless behaviors can be used as flyweights, meaning one behavior can be used with multiple sprites simultaneously, resulting in substantial reductions in memory usage.
- You can implement behaviors that work with any sprite and therefore can be used in multiple games.
- You can combine behaviors to create interesting personalities for your sprites.

Before we discuss the implementation details of the behaviors listed in Table 7.1, let's have a high-level look at how to create behaviors and associate them with sprites. To that end, we'll look at the runner's collective behaviors.

NOTE: Replica Island's game components

The idea for behaviors (originally called game components) comes from the popular open source Android game named Replica Island. See replicaisland. blogspot.com/2009/09/aggregate-objects-via-components.html for a blog post by Replica Island's main developer about the benefits of game components (behaviors).

NOTE: Use the graphics context with care

Behaviors should not use the graphics context the game passes to their `execute()` method to draw, because drawing sprites is the responsibility of the sprite's artist. Instead, behaviors should, as Snail Bait's behaviors do, restrict their use of the graphics context to nongraphical functionality, such as determining whether a point lies within the current path. See Chapter 3 for more information about the graphics context.

7.2 Runner Behaviors

Snail Bait's runner has five behaviors, listed in Table 7.2.

Table 7.2 The runner's behaviors

Behavior	Description
`runBehavior`	Cycles through the runner's cells from the sprite sheet to make it appear as though the runner is running.
`jumpBehavior`	Controls all aspects of jumping: ascent, descent, and landing.
`fallBehavior`	Controls the vertical movement of the runner as she falls.
`collideBehavior`	Detects and reacts to collisions between the runner and the other sprites.
`runnerExplodeBehavior`	Makes the runner explode.

Snail Bait ultimately instantiates the runner with an array of behaviors, as shown in Example 7.2.

Example 7.2 Creating Snail Bait's runner

```
var SnailBait = function () {
    ...

  this.runner = new Sprite(
    'runner', // Type

    new SpriteSheetArtist(this.spritesheet,   // Artist
                          this.runnerCellsRight),
```

```
      [ this.runBehavior, // Behaviors
        this.jumpBehavior,
        this.fallBehavior,
        this.collideBehavior
        this.runnerExplodeBehavior
      ]
   );
   ...
};
```

The runner's behaviors are shown in **Example 7.3**, with implementation details removed.

Example 7.3 Runner behavior objects

```
var SnailBait = function () {
   ...

   this.runBehavior = {
      execute: function(sprite, now, context, fps,
                        lastAnimationFrameTime) {
         ...
      }
   };

   this.jumpBehavior = {
      execute: function(sprite, now, context, fps,
                        lastAnimationFrameTime) {
         ...
      }
   };

   this.fallBehavior = {
      execute: function(sprite, now, context, fps,
                        lastAnimationFrameTime) {
         ...
      }
   };

   this.runnerExplodeBehavior = {
      execute: function(sprite, now, context, fps,
                        lastAnimationFrameTime) {
         ...
      }
   };
```

(Continues)

Example 7.3 *(Continued)*

```
    this.collideBehavior = {
        execute: function(sprite, now, context, fps,
                          lastAnimationFrameTime) {
            ...
        }
    };
    ...
};
```

Because the runner's behaviors are associated only with the runner, the sprite that `Sprite.update()`, listed in Example 7.4, passes to each behavior is always the runner.

Example 7.4 Updating sprites

```
Sprite.prototype = {
    update: function (now, fps, context, lastAnimationFrameTime) {
        for (var i=0; i < this.behaviors.length; ++i) {
            this.behaviors[i].execute(this, now, fps,
                                      lastAnimationFrameTime);
        }
    }
    ...
};
```

Recall that Snail Bait continuously—once per animation frame—iterates over all visible sprites, invoking each sprite's `update()` method. As you can see in Example 7.4, the `Sprite.update()` method iterates over a sprite's behaviors, invoking each behavior's `execute()` method.

A behavior's `execute()` method, therefore, is not like the methods of ordinary JavaScript objects whose methods are invoked relatively infrequently; instead, each behavior's `execute()` method is like a little motor that's constantly running while the behavior's associated sprite is visible.

Now that you understand how sprites and behaviors fit together, let's see how to implement behaviors.

NOTE: Behaviors are implemented in Snail Bait's constructor

A behavior's execute() method is not a SnailBait method, so it's not defined in Snail Bait's prototype object. Instead, Snail Bait defines behavior objects, and their execute() methods, in the game's constructor function, as you can see in Example 7.3.

NOTE: The Strategy design pattern

Behaviors are an example of the Strategy design pattern, which encapsulates algorithms into objects. At runtime, you can mix and match those algorithms. Behaviors give you more flexibility than would hard-coding their algorithms directly into individual sprites. You can read more about the Strategy design pattern at http://en.wikipedia.org/wiki/Strategy_pattern.

NOTE: Behaviors as machines

Behaviors are like little machines that are constantly running. As long as a behavior's associated sprite is visible, Snail Bait invokes the behavior's execute() method every animation frame. Some behaviors, such as the runner's run behavior, are constantly doing something meaningful nearly every animation frame; other behaviors, however, such as the runner's exploding behavior, are idle most of the time.

7.3 The Runner's Run Behavior

Snail Bait does two things that make it appear as though the runner is running. First, as you saw in Chapter 3, the game continuously scrolls the background, making it appear as though the runner is moving horizontally. Second, the runner's run behavior cycles the runner through a sequence of images from the game's sprite sheet, as shown in Figure 7.2.

The code in Example 7.5 implements the run behavior.

The run behavior's execute() method periodically advances the runner's artist to the next image in the runner's sequence from the game's sprite sheet.

The rate at which the run behavior advances the runner's image determines how quickly the runner runs. That rate is controlled with the runner's runAnimationRate property.

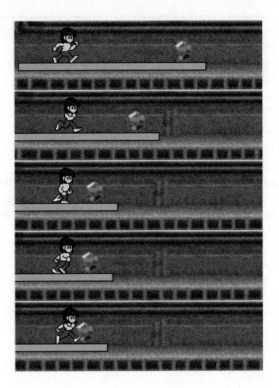

Figure 7.2 The run behavior. Notice the different poses for the runner.

Example 7.5 The runner's run behavior

```
var SnailBait = function () {
  ...

  this.runBehavior = {
    lastAdvanceTime: 0,

    execute: function (sprite,
                       now,
                       fps,
                       context,
                       lastAnimationFrameTime) {
      if (sprite.runAnimationRate === 0) {        // not running
        return;
      }

      if (this.lastAdvanceTime === 0) {           // skip first time
        this.lastAdvanceTime = now;
      }
```

```
        else if (now - this.lastAdvanceTime >
                1000 / sprite.runAnimationRate) { // time to advance
            sprite.artist.advance();
            this.lastAdvanceTime = now;
        }
    }
    };
    ...
};
```

The runner is not running when the game starts, so its runAnimationRate is initially zero. As you can see from **Example 7.5**, the run behavior does nothing when the runner's runAnimationRate is zero.

When the player turns left or right, Snail Bait sets the runAnimationRate to snailBait.RUN_ANIMATION_RATE (30 frames/second), the run behavior kicks in, and the runner starts to run. The final versions of the turnLeft() and turnRight() methods are listed in **Example 7.6**.

Example 7.6 Turning starts the run animation

```
var SnailBait = function () {
    ...

    this.RUN_ANIMATION_RATE = 30; // frames per second
    ...
};

SnailBait.prototype = {
    ...

    turnLeft: function () {
        this.bgVelocity = -this.BACKGROUND_VELOCITY;
        this.runner.runAnimationRate = this.RUN_ANIMATION_RATE;
        this.runnerArtist.cells = this.runnerCellsLeft;
        this.runner.direction = snailBait.LEFT;
    },

    turnRight: function () {
        this.bgVelocity = this.BACKGROUND_VELOCITY;
        this.runner.runAnimationRate = this.RUN_ANIMATION_RATE;
        this.runnerArtist.cells = this.runnerCellsRight;
        this.runner.direction = snailBait.RIGHT;
    },
    ...
};
```

The game's keyboard event handlers invoke the `turnLeft()` and `turnRight()` methods, to control the direction in which the runner appears to move. Those methods set Snail Bait's `bgVelocity` property, which is the rate at which the background scrolls.

The `turnLeft()` and `turnRight()` methods also set the appropriate cells (either left poses or right) from the game's sprite sheet for the runner's artist.

NOTE: The flow of time

Like the runner's run behavior, nearly all behaviors are predicated on time. And because a game's animation is constantly in effect, many functions that modify a game's behavior, such as `turnLeft()` and `turnRight()` in Example 7.6, do so by simply setting game properties. When the game draws the next animation frame, those properties influence the game's behavior.

7.4 Flyweight Behaviors

The runner's run behavior discussed in the preceding section maintains state, namely, the time at which the behavior last advanced the sprite's image. That state tightly couples the runner to the run behavior. So, for instance, if you wanted to make another sprite run, you would need another run behavior.

Behaviors that do not maintain state are known as flyweights. They are more flexible because they can be used by many sprites simultaneously. Example 7.7 illustrates a stateless pace behavior that makes sprites pace back and forth on a platform. A single instance of that behavior is used for the game's buttons and its snail, all of which pace back and forth on their platforms. Figure 7.3 shows a button pacing on a platform.

Example 7.7 shows Snail Bait's `createButtonSprites()` method, which adds the lone pace behavior to each button.

Example 7.7 Creating pacing buttons

```
SnailBait.prototype = {
   ...

   createButtonSprites: function () {
      var button;

      for (var i = 0; i < this.buttonData.length; ++i) {
         if (i !== this.buttonData.length - 1) {
            button = new Sprite('button',
```

```
                        new SpriteSheetArtist(this.spritesheet,
                                              this.blueButtonCells),
                        [ this.paceBehavior, ... ]);
        }
        else {
            button = new Sprite('button',
                        new SpriteSheetArtist(this.spritesheet,
                                              this.goldButtonCells),
                        [ this.paceBehavior, ... ]);
        }

        button.width = this.BUTTON_CELLS_WIDTH;
        button.height = this.BUTTON_CELLS_HEIGHT;
        button.velocityX = this.BUTTON_PACE_VELOCITY;

        this.buttons.push(button);
    }
  },
  ...
};
```

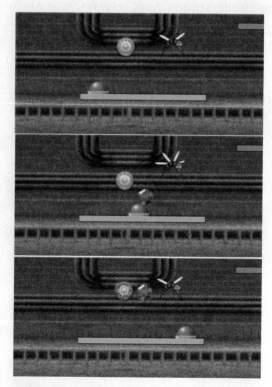

Figure 7.3 A pacing button

The createButtonSprites() method iterates over the metadata for the game's buttons, creating a button for every metadata object. All the buttons are blue except for the last button, which is gold.

Example 7.8 shows the implementation of the paceBehavior object.

Example 7.8 The pace behavior

```javascript
var SnailBait = function () {
   ...

   this.paceBehavior = {
      execute: function (sprite, now, fps, context,
                         lastAnimationFrameTime) {
         this.setDirection(sprite);
         this.setPosition(sprite, now, lastAnimationFrameTime);
      }

      setDirection: function (sprite) {
         var sRight = sprite.left + sprite.width,
             pRight = sprite.platform.left + sprite.platform.width;

         if (sprite.direction === undefined) {
            sprite.direction = snailBait.RIGHT;
         }

         if (sRight > pRight && sprite.direction === snailBait.RIGHT) {
            sprite.direction = snailBait.LEFT;
         }
         else if (sprite.left < sprite.platform.left &&
                  sprite.direction === snailBait.LEFT) {
            sprite.direction = snailBait.RIGHT;
         }
      },

      setPosition: function (sprite, now, lastAnimationFrameTime) {
         var pixelsToMove = sprite.velocityX *
                            (now - lastAnimationFrameTime) / 1000;

         if (sprite.direction === snailBait.RIGHT) {
            sprite.left += pixelsToMove;
         }
         else {
            sprite.left -= pixelsToMove;
         }
      },
   };
   ...
};
```

The pace behavior modifies a sprite's horizontal position. The behavior implements time-based motion to calculate how many pixels to move the sprite for the current animation frame by multiplying the sprite's velocity by the time it took to draw the last animation frame. See Chapter 3 for more information about time-based motion.

NOTE: Flyweights and state

The pace behavior can be used as a flyweight because it's stateless. It's stateless because it stores state—each sprite's position and direction—in the sprites themselves.

7.5 Game-Independent Behaviors

In Section 7.3, "The Runner's Run Behavior," on p. 187 of this chapter, we discussed the runner's run behavior, which is a stateful behavior that's tightly coupled to a single sprite. The paceBehavior, which we discussed in Section 7.4, "Flyweight Behaviors," on p. 190, is a stateless behavior, which decouples it from individual sprites so a single instance can be used by multiple sprites.

Behaviors can be generalized even further. You can decouple behaviors not only from individual sprites but also from the game itself. Snail Bait uses three behaviors that can be used in any game:

- bounceBehavior
- cycleBehavior
- pulseBehavior

The bounce behavior bounces a sprite up and down; the cycle behavior cycles a sprite through a set of images; and the pulse behavior manipulates a sprite's opacity to make it appear as though the sprite is pulsating.

The bounce and pulse behaviors both involve nonlinear animation, which we discuss in Chapter 9. The cycle behavior cycles through a sprite's images linearly, however, so we use the implementation of that behavior to illustrate implementing behaviors that can be used in any game.

7.5.1 The Cycle Behavior

The cycle behavior cycles through a sprite's images, showing each image for a specific duration. Example 7.9 shows the implementation of the cycle behavior.

Example 7.9 The cycle behavior

```
CycleBehavior = function (duration, interval) {
   this.duration = duration || 1000;  // milliseconds
   this.lastAdvance = 0;
   this.interval = interval;
};

CycleBehavior.prototype = {
   execute: function (sprite,
                      now,
                      fps,
                      context,
                      lastAnimationFrameTime) {
      if (this.lastAdvance === 0) { // First time only
         this.lastAdvance = now;
      }

      if (now - this.lastAdvance > this.duration) {
         sprite.artist.advance();
         this.lastAdvance = now;
      }
      else if (this.interval &&            // If there's a interval
         sprite.artist.cellIndex === 0) { // and the cycle is complete
         if (now - this.lastAdvance > this.interval) { // Time to advance
            sprite.artist.advance();
            this.lastAdvance = now;
         }
      }
   }
};
```

The cycle behavior endlessly cycles through its associated sprite's images from the game's sprite sheet. The duration you pass to the CycleBehavior constructor represents the amount of time each image is visible, and it's optional; if you don't specify the duration, it defaults to one second.

The interval, which is also optional, represents a time gap between cycles. For example, the snail cycles through its images and then waits for 1.5 seconds before starting the cycle again. That 1.5 second interval throttles the rate at which the snail fires snail bombs; without it, the snail would continuously fire snail bombs when the snail is in view. See Section 7.6, "Combine Behaviors," on p. 199 for more details.

The cycle behavior's simple implementation belies its significance because

• The cycle behavior is neither sprite- nor game-specific

- The cycle behavior is general enough that it can be used for many types of effects
- You can easily modify the cycle behavior to be a flyweight

The cycle behavior is not coupled to any sprite, so it can be reused in other games. In contrast, the sprite-specific run behavior in Example 7.5, even though it has a lot in common with the cycle behavior, stores the runner's animation rate, which is specific to the runner, and therefore, the run behavior cannot be reused.

The general nature of the cycle behavior is the source of its reusability, and it's also the reason that cycle behaviors can be used to implement different kinds of effects. Because it cycles through a sequence of images, a cycle behavior is similar to a flip book where you define what goes on each page. Snail Bait uses cycle behaviors for several effects, including

- Sparkling rubies and sapphires
- Bats and bees that flap their wings
- Throbbing coins

We discuss each of those effects in the following sections.

BEST PRACTICE: Generalize behaviors

It's a good idea to look for opportunities to generalize behaviors so that they can be used in a wider range of circumstances.

NOTE: Cycle behaviors as flyweights

It's only about 20 lines of code, but the cycle behavior is useful because it's the source of many types of effects and can be used in multiple games. Cycle behaviors, however, maintain state, so they are coupled to a particular sprite. If cycle behaviors instead stored that state in sprites themselves, the behaviors would be stateless and you could use one cycle behavior for many sprites.

7.5.1.1 Sparkling Rubies and Sapphires

Snail Bait's rubies and sapphires sparkle, as shown in Figure 7.4.

Snail Bait's sprite sheet contains sequences of images for both rubies and sapphires. Cycling through those images creates the sparkling illusion.

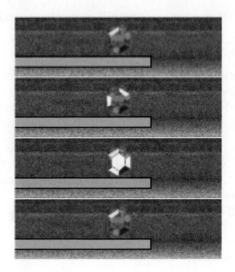

Figure 7.4 Sparkling rubies

Example 7.10 shows the Snail Bait method that creates rubies. A nearly identical method (not shown) creates sapphires. The createRubySprites() method also creates a cycle behavior that displays each image from the ruby-sparkling sequence for a duration of 100 ms. After cycling through the ruby-sparkling images, the behavior waits one half second before repeating the sequence.

Example 7.10 Creating rubies

```
SnailBait.prototype = {
  ...

  createRubySprites: function () {
    var RUBY_SPARKLE_DURATION = 100,
        RUBY_SPARKLE_INTERVAL = 500,
        ruby,
        rubyArtist = new SpriteSheetArtist(this.spritesheet,
                                           this.rubyCells);

    for (var i = 0; i < this.rubyData.length; ++i) {
      ruby = new Sprite('ruby',
                        rubyArtist,
                        [ new CycleBehavior(RUBY_SPARKLE_DURATION,
                                            RUBY_SPARKLE_INTERVAL) ]);

      ruby.width  = this.RUBY_CELLS_WIDTH;
      ruby.height = this.RUBY_CELLS_HEIGHT;
```

```
      this.rubies.push(ruby);
      ...
   }
},
...
};
```

7.5.1.2 Flapping Wings and Throbbing Coins

Snail Bait's bats and bees flap their wings with cycle behaviors that cycle through images and make it appear as though wings are flapping, as illustrated in **Figure 7.5**.

Figure 7.5 Bats flapping their wings

Example 7.11 shows how Snail Bait creates bats and bees with cycle behaviors.

Example 7.11 Creating bats and bees with cycle behaviors

```
SnailBait.prototype = {
   ...

   createBatSprites: function () {
      var bat,
          BAT_FLAP_DURATION = 200,
          BAT_FLAP_INTERVAL = 50;

      for (var i = 0; i < this.batData.length; ++i) {
         bat = new Sprite('bat',
                     new SpriteSheetArtist(this.spritesheet,
                                           this.batCells),

                     [ new CycleBehavior(BAT_FLAP_DURATION,
                                         BAT_FLAP_INTERVAL) ]);
         ...
      }
   },

   createBeeSprites: function () {
      var bee,
          beeArtist,
          BEE_FLAP_DURATION = 100,
          BEE_FLAP_INTERVAL = 30;
```

(Continues)

Example 7.11   *(Continued)*

```
    for (var i = 0; i < this.beeData.length; ++i) {
        bee = new Sprite('bee',
                        new SpriteSheetArtist(this.spritesheet,
                                              this.beeCells),

                        [ new CycleBehavior(BEE_FLAP_DURATION,
                                            BEE_FLAP_INTERVAL) ]);

        ...
    }
 },
 ...
};
```

Finally, Snail Bait uses cycle behaviors to make its coins throb. Those behaviors
cycle through the two images on the left in **Figure 7.6** for blue coins and the three
images on the right for orange coins.

Figure 7.6   Coin images from Snail Bait's sprite sheet

Snail Bait's `createCoinSprites()` method creates the cycle behaviors associated
with the coins, as shown in **Example 7.12**.

Example 7.12   Cycling through coin images

```
SnailBait.prototype = {
    ...

    createCoinSprites: function () {
        var BLUE_THROB_DURATION = 100,
            GOLD_THROB_DURATION = 500,
            ...
            coin;

        for (var i = 0; i < this.coinData.length; ++i) {
            if (i % 2 === 0) {
                coin = new Sprite('coin',
                    new SpriteSheetArtist(this.spritesheet,
                                          this.goldCoinCells),
```

```
        [ ...

            new CycleBehavior(GOLD_THROB_DURATION)
        ]
    );
}
else {
    coin = new Sprite('coin',
        new SpriteSheetArtist(this.spritesheet,
                              this.blueCoinCells),

        [ ...

            new CycleBehavior(BLUE_THROB_DURATION)
        ]);
}

coin.width = this.COIN_CELLS_WIDTH;
coin.height = this.COIN_CELLS_HEIGHT;
coin.value = 50;

...

this.coins.push(coin);
    }
 },
  ...
};
```

Like sapphires and rubies, Snail Bait's coins bounce up and down on platforms. In the preceding listing, the associated bounce behaviors have been omitted for brevity.

The createCoinSprites() method alternates between creating gold and blue coins before pushing the newly created coins onto the game's coin array.

Now that you've seen how to implement individual behaviors, let's see how to combine behaviors for interesting effects.

7.6 Combine Behaviors

Individual behaviors encapsulate specific actions such as running, pacing, or sparkling. You can also combine behaviors for more complicated effects; for example, as the snail paces back and forth on its platform, it periodically shoots snail bombs, as shown in Figure 7.7.

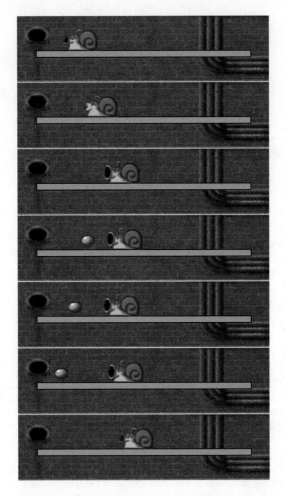

Figure 7.7 Snail Bait's shooting sequence

The snail shooting sequence is a combination of three behaviors:

- paceBehavior
- snailShootBehavior
- snailBombMoveBehavior

paceBehavior and snailShootBehavior are associated with the snail; snailBombMoveBehavior is associated with snail bombs.

Snail Bait creates the game's only snail in the `createSnailSprites()` method, as you can see in **Example 7.13**.

Example 7.13 Creating snails

```
var SnailBait = function () {
    ...
    this.SNAIL_CELLS_WIDTH   = 64;
    this.SNAIL_CELLS_HEIGHT  = 34;
    this.SNAIL_PACE_VELOCITY = 50;
    ...
};

SnailBait.prototype = {
    ...

    createSnailSprites: function () {
        var snail,
            snailArtist = new SpriteSheetArtist(this.spritesheet,
                                                this.snailCells),

            SNAIL_CYCLE_DURATION = 300,
            SNAIL_CYCLE_INTERVAL = 1500;

        for (var i = 0; i < this.snailData.length; ++i) {
            snail = new Sprite('snail',
                               snailArtist,
                               [ this.paceBehavior,
                                 this.snailShootBehavior,
                                 new CycleBehavior(SNAIL_CYCLE_DURATION,
                                                   SNAIL_CYCLE_INTERVAL)
                               ]);

            snail.width  = this.SNAIL_CELLS_WIDTH;
            snail.height = this.SNAIL_CELLS_HEIGHT;
            snail.velocityX = snailBait.SNAIL_PACE_VELOCITY;

            this.snails.push(snail);
        }
    },
    ...
};
```

Every 1.5 seconds, the snail's `CycleBehavior` cycles through the snail's images in the sprite sheet, shown in **Figure 7.8**, and displays each image for 300 ms, which makes it look as though the snail is periodically opening and closing its mouth. The snail's `paceBehavior` moves the snail back and forth on its platform.

Figure 7.8 Sprite sheet images for the snail shooting sequence

Snail Bait creates snail bombs with the armSnails() method, which is invoked by the game's initializeSprites() method, listed in Example 7.14.

Example 7.14 Initializing sprites, revised

```
SnailBait.prototype = {
   ...

   initializeSprites: function() {
      this.positionSprites(this.bats,      this.batData);
      this.positionSprites(this.bees,      this.beeData);
      this.positionSprites(this.buttons,   this.buttonData);
      this.positionSprites(this.coins,     this.coinData);
      this.positionSprites(this.rubies,    this.rubyData);
      this.positionSprites(this.sapphires, this.sapphireData);
      this.positionSprites(this.snails,    this.snailData);

      this.armSnails();
   },
   ...
};
```

The armSnails() method, listed in Example 7.15, iterates over the game's snails, creates a snail bomb for each snail, equips each bomb with a snailBombMoveBehavior, and stores a reference to the snail in the snail bomb.

Example 7.15 Arming snails

```
SnailBait.prototype = {
   ...

   armSnails: function () {
      var snail,
          snailBombArtist = new SpriteSheetArtist(this.spritesheet,
                                                  this.snailBombCells);

      for (var i=0; i < this.snails.length; ++i) {
         snail = this.snails[i];
```

```
snail.bomb = new Sprite('snail bomb',
                        snailBombArtist,
                        [ this.snailBombMoveBehavior ]);

snail.bomb.width  = snailBait.SNAIL_BOMB_CELLS_WIDTH;
snail.bomb.height = snailBait.SNAIL_BOMB_CELLS_HEIGHT;

snail.bomb.top = snail.top + snail.bomb.height/2;
snail.bomb.left = snail.left + snail.bomb.width/2;
snail.bomb.visible = false;

// Snail bombs maintain a reference to their snail

snail.bomb.snail = snail;

this.sprites.push(snail.bomb);
      }
   },
   ...
};
```

The snailShootBehavior shoots the snail bomb, as shown in Example 7.16.

Example 7.16 Shooting snail bombs

```
var SnailBait = function () {
   ...

   this.snailShootBehavior = { // sprite is the snail
      execute: function (sprite, now, fps, context,
                         lastAnimationFrameTime) {
         var bomb = sprite.bomb,
             MOUTH_OPEN_CELL = 2;

         if ( ! snailBait.isSpriteInView(sprite)) {
            return;
         }

         if ( ! bomb.visible &&
              sprite.artist.cellIndex === MOUTH_OPEN_CELL) {
            bomb.left = sprite.left;
            bomb.visible = true;
         }
      }
   };
   ...
};
```

Because the snailShootBehavior is associated with the snail, the sprite passed to the behavior's execute() method is always the snail.

The snail maintains a reference to its snail bomb, so the snailShootBehavior accesses the bomb through the snail. The snailShootBehavior then checks to see if the snail's current image is the one on the far right in Figure 7.8, meaning the snail is on the verge of opening its mouth; if that's the case, the behavior puts the bomb in the snail's mouth and makes it visible.

Shooting the snail bomb, therefore, involves positioning the bomb and making it visible under the right conditions. Subsequently moving the bomb is the responsibility of the snailBombMoveBehavior, shown in Example 7.17.

Example 7.17 Snail bomb move behavior

```
var SnailBait = function () {
   ...

   this.snailBombMoveBehavior = {
      execute: function (sprite, now, fps, context,
                         lastAnimationFrameTime) {
         var SNAIL_BOMB_VELOCITY = 550;

         if ( sprite.left + sprite.width > sprite.hOffset &&
             sprite.left + sprite.width < sprite.hOffset +
             sprite.width) {
            sprite.visible = false;
         }
         else {
            sprite.left -= SNAIL_BOMB_VELOCITY *
                        ((now - lastAnimationFrameTime) / 1000);
         }
      }
   };
   ...
};
```

If the bomb is about to disappear off the left edge of the canvas, the snail bomb move behavior makes the bomb invisible; otherwise, the behavior advances the bomb to the left at a constant rate of 550 pixels/second.

NOTE: Behavior-based games

With a behavior-based game, once you've got the basic infrastructure implemented, fleshing out the game is mostly a matter of implementing behaviors.
Freed from the concerns of the game's underlying mechanics, such as animation,
frame rates, scrolling backgrounds, and so forth, you can make your game come
to life by concentrating almost exclusively on implementing behaviors. And because behaviors can be mixed and matched at runtime, you can rapidly prototype
scenarios by combining behaviors.

7.7 Conclusion

Behaviors breathe life into sprites, making games come alive. In this chapter, we
went from static images of sprites to sprites that do interesting things. Crossing
that threshold is significant on two levels. First, at this stage of development, Snail
Bait begins to feel like an actual game as the game's characters reveal their personalities. Second, the introduction of behaviors into the mix results in a significant
shift in the actual implementation of the game.

In this chapter you saw how to implement behaviors and attach them to sprites.
Behaviors are sometimes tightly coupled to specific sprites such as the runner's
run behavior, whereas behaviors that don't maintain state can be used simultaneously by many sprites. Some behaviors, such as cycling sprites through a sequence
of images, can be used in multiple games.

Up to this chapter, we've been concerned with the fundamental aspects of implementing video games, such as creating smooth animations, scrolling backgrounds,
and drawing sprites. We've also discussed user interface aspects, such as fading
elements in and out and implementing a loading screen while the game initially
loads resources.

From here on, however, our focus in this book shifts primarily to implementing
behaviors when we discuss implementing Snail Bait's gameplay. Almost every
aspect of implementing gameplay will involve implementing a behavior and
attaching it to the appropriate sprite. In the next chapter, we discuss how to
implement a jump behavior for Snail Bait's runner.

7.8 Exercises

1. Modify the runner's run behavior so she runs only when she's on a platform.

2. Modify the snail shoot behavior so the snail shoots a snail bomb once every second.

3. Modify the cycle behavior so it maintains state in the sprites it manipulates instead of in the behavior itself. That change makes the cycle behavior a flyweight. Subsequently, modify Snail Bait so that it creates only one cycle behavior for all the game's bats. Are there negative consequences for converting the cycle behavior into a flyweight? Explain your answer.

CHAPTER

8

Time, Part I: Finite Behaviors and Linear Motion

Topics in This Chapter

The last chapter discussed how to encapsulate actions—such as running, falling, pacing, or sparkling—that sprites undertake in JavaScript objects known as behaviors. At runtime, you can configure a sprite's array of behaviors however you desire. Among its many benefits, that flexibility encourages exploration of game aspects that might otherwise lie dormant.

This chapter continues to discuss sprite behaviors, with a few twists. To start, this is the first of two consecutive chapters devoted to a single sprite behavior: the runner's jump behavior. By the end of the next chapter, Snail Bait will ultimately arrive at a natural jump sequence, which involves nonlinear motion. Figure 8.1 illustrates that sequence.

Figure 8.1 A natural jump sequence

First, though, in this chapter we implement the simpler case of linear motion during the jump.

Second, jumps last for a specific amount of time, unlike the behaviors discussed in the preceding chapter. Because of that simple difference, Snail Bait must track time as jumps progress. That requirement means we need something that lets us time jumps and other finite behaviors, so in this chapter we also implement a JavaScript stopwatch and use it to time the runner's ascent and descent as she jumps.

Third, we must be able to pause and resume finite behaviors that time themselves, so at the end of this chapter we implement that functionality.

In this chapter you will learn how to do the following:

• Encapsulate jumping in a sprite behavior (Section 8.2 on p. 210)

- Implement a JavaScript stopwatch (Section 8.4 on p. 214)
- Use stopwatches to time finite animations (Section 8.5 on p. 217)
- Implement linear motion (Section 8.6 on p. 220)
- Pause and resume a finite behavior such as jumping (Section 8.7 on p. 225)

8.1 Implement an Initial Jump Algorithm

We begin with a simple algorithm for jumping that we refine throughout this chapter and the next. Our first attempt at jumping is listed in Example 8.1.

Example 8.1 Keyboard handling for jumps

```
window.addEventListener(
   'keydown',

   function (e) {
      var key = e.keyCode;

      if (key === 74) { // 'j'
         if (snailBait.runner.track === 3) { // At the top; nowhere to go
            return;
         }

         snailBait.runner.track++;

         snailBait.runner.top =
            snailBait.calculatePlatformTop(snailBait.runner.track) -
                              snailBait.RUNNER_CELLS_HEIGHT;
      }
   }
);
```

When the player presses the j key, the preceding event handler immediately puts the runner's feet on the track above her if she is not already on the top track. Figure 8.2 illustrates instantaneous jumping.

The jumping implementation shown in Figure 8.2 has two serious drawbacks. First, the runner moves instantly from one level to another, which is far from the desired effect. Second, the jumping implementation is at the wrong level of abstraction. A window event handler has no business directly manipulating the runner's properties; instead, the runner herself should be responsible for jumping.

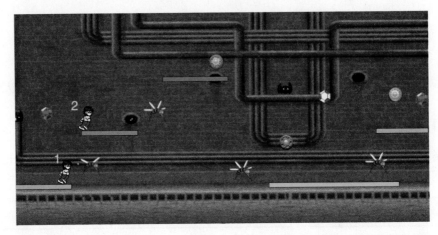

Figure 8.2 Instantaneous jumping: 1) Player presses the j key. 2) Runner instantly jumps to the next track.

8.2 Shift Responsibility for Jumping to the Runner

Example 8.2 shows a modified implementation of the window's keydown event handler. It's simpler than the implementation in Example 8.1, and it shifts responsibility for jumping from the event handler to the runner.

Example 8.2 The window's key handler, delegating to the runner

```
window.addEventListener(
   'keydown',

   function (e) {
      var key = e.keyCode;
      ...

      if (key === 74) { // 'j'
         snailBait.runner.jump();
      }
   }
);
```

Next we implement the runner's jump() method. We begin by modifying Snail Bait's initializeSprites() method, which Snail Bait calls at the beginning of the game. The updated version of initializeSprites() invokes a helper method named equipRunner(), as shown in Example 8.3.

Example 8.3 Equipping the runner at the start of the game

```
SnailBait.prototype = {
   ...

   initializeSprites: function() {
      ...

      this.equipRunner();
   },

   equipRunner: function () {
      ...

      this.equipRunnerForJumping(); // Equip the runner for falling later
   },
   ...
};
```

The `equipRunner()` method invokes a method named `equipRunnerFor-Jumping()`. In Chapter 12, we also equip the runner for falling with an `equipRunnerForFalling()` method, but for now we focus on jumping.

An initial implementation of the `equipRunnerForJumping()` method is listed in Example 8.4.

Example 8.4 Equipping the runner: The runner's `jump()` method

```
SnailBait.prototype = {
   ...

   equipRunnerForJumping: function () {
      var INITIAL_TRACK = 1;

      this.runner.jumping = false;
      this.runner.track   = INITIAL_TRACK;

      this.runner.jump = function () {
         if (this.jumping) // 'this' is the runner
            return;

         this.jumping = true;
      };
```

(Continues)

Example 8.4 *(Continued)*

```
    this.runner.stopJumping = function () {
        this.jumping = false;
    };
  },
  ...
};
```

The equipRunnerForJumping() method adds two methods to the runner JavaScript object: jump() and stopJumping().

If the runner is not already jumping, runner.jump() merely sets the value of the runner's jumping property to true, so the method doesn't really implement jumping at all, because, as it does for all sprite behaviors, Snail Bait implements the act of jumping in a separate behavior object. The runner's jumping property acts as a *trigger* for the runner's jump behavior, as you'll see in the next section.

The runner's stopJumping() method simply sets the runner's jumping property to false, which disengages the jump behavior.

When it creates the runner, Snail Bait adds the jump behavior to the runner's array of behaviors, as shown in Example 8.5.

Every animation frame, Snail Bait invokes the execute() method of the runner's jump behavior. That behavior does nothing until the player presses the j key (or taps the screen on mobile devices) to make the runner jump. When that happens, as you saw in Example 8.4, the runner's jump() method sets the runner's jumping property to true, which acts as a trigger that engages the jump behavior.

Example 8.5 Running and jumping

```
var SnailBait = function () {
  ...

  this.jumpBehavior = {
    execute: function(sprite, now, fps, context,
                      lastAnimationFrameTime) {

        // Implement jumping here

    },
    ...
  };
};
```

```
    this.runner = new Sprite(
        'runner',              // type

        new SpriteSheetArtist(this.spritesheet,
                              this.runnerCellsRight),  // artist

        [ // behaviors
          this.runBehavior,
          this.jumpBehavior,
          ...
        ]
    );
    ...
};
```

Now that the infrastructure is in place for initiating a jump, we can concentrate solely on the jump behavior.

8.3 Implement the Jump Behavior

Our first implementation of the runner's jump behavior, listed in Example 8.6, mimics the functionality of our original attempt at jumping.

Example 8.6 An instantaneous jump behavior

```
var SnailBait =  function () {
   ...

   this.jumpBehavior = {
      ...

      execute: function(sprite, now, fps, context,
                        lastAnimationFrameTime) {
         if ( ! sprite.jumping || sprite.track === 3) {
            return;
         }

         sprite.track++;

         sprite.top = snailBait.calculatePlatformTop(sprite.track) -
               snailBait.RUNNER_CELLS_HEIGHT;

         sprite.jumping = false;
      }
   };
   ...
};
```

Compared with many of Snail Bait's other sprite behaviors, jumping is a relatively infrequent occurrence. Most of the time the runner's jump behavior does nothing because the behavior's *trigger*—the runner's jumping property—is false. When the runner's jump() method sets that property to true, the behavior's trigger is tripped and the jump behavior takes action in the next animation frame, provided the runner has a track above her.

With the code for jumping encapsulated in a behavior, we're ready to refine that behavior to implement more realistic jumping, but first we must implement stopwatches so we can time jumps.

 NOTE: Invoking the jump behavior

Recall that every animation frame, Snail Bait iterates over all behaviors associated with each visible sprite, invoking each behavior's execute() method. The runner sprite is always visible, which means Snail Bait invokes the jump behavior in every animation frame.

 NOTE: Behavior triggers

Behaviors that last for a finite amount of time typically have some sort of trigger—such as the runner's jumping property—that causes the behavior to take action. When the behavior concludes, it resets the trigger and lies dormant until the next time the game trips the trigger.

8.4 Time Animations with Stopwatches

All the motion we've implemented so far in Snail Bait has been constant. For example, all the game's sprites, except for the runner, scroll continuously in the horizontal direction, and buttons and snails constantly pace back and forth on their platforms. Coins, sapphires, and rubies bob up and down without ever stopping to take a break.

Jumping, however, is not constant; it has a definite start and end. To implement jumping, therefore, we need a way to monitor how much time has elapsed since a jump began. What we need is a stopwatch.

Example 8.7 shows the implementation of a Stopwatch constructor function.

Stopwatches keep track of whether they are running, the time they started running, and the time that elapsed since they started running. Stopwatches also keep track of whether they are paused, the start time of the pause, and the total time the stopwatch has been paused.

Example 8.7 The Stopwatch constructor

```
var Stopwatch = function () {
   this.startTime = 0;
   this.running = false;
   this.elapsed = undefined;

   this.paused = false;
   this.startPause = 0;
   this.totalPausedTime = 0;
};
```

The stopwatch's methods reside in the Stopwatch object's prototype, listed in Example 8.8.

Example 8.8 Stopwatch methods

```
Stopwatch.prototype = {
   start: function () {
      var now = +new Date();

      this.startTime = now;
      this.running = true;
      this.totalPausedTime = 0;
      this.startPause = 0;
   },

   stop: function () {
      var now = +new Date();

      if (this.paused) {
         this.unpause();
      }

      this.elapsed = now - this.startTime - this.totalPausedTime;
      this.running = false;
   },

   pause: function () {
      var now = +new Date();

      this.startPause = now;
      this.paused = true;
   },
```

(Continues)

Example 8.8 *(Continued)*

```javascript
  unpause: function () {
    var now = +new Date();

    if (!this.paused) {
      return;
    }

    this.totalPausedTime += now - this.startPause;
    this.startPause = 0;
    this.paused = false;
  },

  getElapsedTime: function () {
    var now = +new Date();

    if (this.running) {
      return now - this.startTime - this.totalPausedTime;
    }
    else {
      return this.elapsed;
    }
  },

  isPaused: function() {
    return this.paused;
  },

  isRunning: function() {
    return this.running;
  },

  reset: function() {
    var now = +new Date();

    this.elapsed = 0;
    this.startTime = now;
    this.running = false;
    this.totalPausedTime = 0;
    this.startPause = 0;
  }
};
```

You can start, stop, pause, unpause, and reset stopwatches. You can also get their elapsed time, and you can determine whether they are running or paused.

In Section 4.5 on p. 107, you saw how to resume a paused game exactly where it left off by accounting for the amount of time the game was paused. Like the game itself, paused stopwatches must resume exactly where they leave off, so they also account for the amount of time they've been paused.

The stopwatch implementation, though simple, is important because it lets us implement behaviors that last for a finite amount of time.

NOTE: +new `Date()`. The current time according to stopwatches

`Stopwatch` methods access the current time with the construct +new `Date()`, which coerces a `Date` object into a number. The important thing, however, is not the construct, but the fact that—for the time being—the *concept of the current time is internal to stopwatches*. When we discuss time systems in Chapter 10, we modify the `Stopwatch` object so the current time is no longer defined inside `Stopwatch` methods, but is passed to those methods by the game itself.

NOTE: JavaScript timestamps

Most computer languages provide a convenient way to get a timestamp; for example, C++'s `time()` method. Typically, such timestamp methods return the number of seconds since the Epoch (00:00 at January 1, 1970). JavaScript, on the other hand, returns the number of milliseconds since the Epoch.

It's important to realize that a timestamp's actual value is irrelevant, as long as it represents the current time (however it's defined) and as long as the value consistently represents the same thing. Games are only interested in the flow of time, so elapsed times are important, not absolute time values.

8.5 Refine the Jump Behavior

Now that we have stopwatches, let's use them to time the jump behavior. First, we modify the `equipRunnerForJumping()` method from Example 8.4 on p. 211 as shown in Example 8.9.

Example 8.9 Revised equipRunnerForJumping() method

```
SnailBait.prototype = {
   ...

   equipRunnerForJumping: function () {
      var INITIAL_TRACK = 1;

      this.runner.JUMP_HEIGHT   = 120;  // pixels
      this.runner.JUMP_DURATION = 1000; // milliseconds

      this.runner.jumping = false;
      this.runner.track   = INITIAL_TRACK;

      this.runner.ascendTimer  = new Stopwatch();
      this.runner.descendTimer = new Stopwatch();

      this.runner.jump = function () {
         if (this.jumping) // 'this' is the runner
            return;

         this.jumping = true;

         this.runAnimationRate = 0; // Freeze the runner while jumping
         this.verticalLaunchPosition = this.top;
         this.ascendTimer.start();
      };

      this.runner.stopJumping = function () {
         this.jumping = false;
      };
   },
   ...
};
```

The revised implementation of equipRunnerForJumping() creates two stopwatches: runner.ascendTimer for the jump's ascent and runner.descendTimer for its descent.

When the jump begins, the jump() method starts the runner's ascend stopwatch; sets the runner's run animation rate to zero, to freeze her while she's in the air; and records the runner's vertical position, to return her to that position when the jump completes.

The runner properties set in Example 8.9 are summarized in Table 8.1.

Table 8.1 The runner's jump-related properties

Property	Description
JUMP_DURATION	A constant representing the jump's duration in milliseconds: 1000.
JUMP_HEIGHT	A constant representing the jump's height in pixels: 120. At the apex of her jump, the top of the runner's head is 20 pixels above the next track.
ascendTimer	A stopwatch that times the runner's ascent during a jump.
descendTimer	A stopwatch that times the runner's descent during a jump.
jumpApex	The highest point for the top of the runner's head during the runner's jump. During the runner's descent, the jump behavior uses the apex to determine how far to drop the runner for each animation frame.
jumping	A flag that's true while the runner is jumping. This is the trigger for the jump behavior.
verticalLaunchPosition	The top of the runner's head when a jump starts. The runner returns to that position at the end of a complete jump.

Next, in Example 8.10, we modify the jump behavior originally implemented in Example 8.6 on p. 213.

Example 8.10 The jump behavior, revisited

```
var SnailBait = function () {
   ...

   this.jumpBehavior = {
      ...

      execute: function(sprite, now, context,
                        fps, lastAnimationFrameTime) {
```

(Continues)

Example 8.10 *(Continued)*

```
        if ( ! sprite.jumping) {              // Not currently jumping
           return;                            // Nothing to do
        }

        if (this.isAscending(sprite)) {       // Ascending
           if ( ! this.isDoneAscending(sprite)) // Not done ascending
              this.ascend(sprite);            // Ascend
           else
              this.finishAscent(sprite);      // Finish ascending
        }
        else if (this.isDescending(sprite)) { // Descending
           if ( ! this.isDoneDescending(sprite))// Not done descending
              this.descend(sprite);           // Descend
           else
              this.finishDescent(sprite);     // Finish descending
        }
     }
  };
  ...
};
```

The jump behavior in Example 8.10 is the implementation of a high-level abstraction that leaves jumping details to other methods, such as ascend() and isDescending(). All that remains is to fill in those details by using the runner's ascend and descend stopwatches to implement the following eight methods:

- ascend()
- isAscending()
- isDoneAscending()
- finishAscent()
- descend()
- isDescending()
- isDoneDescending()
- finishDescent()

8.6 Implement Linear Motion

To begin, we implement jumping with linear motion, meaning the runner ascends and descends at a constant rate of speed, as depicted in Figure 8.3.

Figure 8.3 Linear jump sequence

Linear motion results in a jumping motion that's unnatural because gravity should constantly decelerate the runner when she's ascending and accelerate her as she descends. In Chapter 9, we modify time so the jump behavior results in nonlinear motion, as depicted in Figure 8.1 on p. 208, but for now we'll stick to the simpler case of linear motion.

8.6.1 Ascending

The jump behavior's methods dealing with ascending are shown in Example 8.11.

Example 8.11 Ascending

```
var SnailBait = function () {
   ...

   this.jumpBehavior = {
      isAscending: function (sprite) {
         return sprite.ascendTimer.isRunning();
      },

      ascend: function (sprite, now) {
         var elapsed = sprite.ascendTimer.getElapsedTime(now),
             deltaY  = elapsed / (sprite.JUMP_DURATION/2) *
                       sprite.JUMP_HEIGHT;

         sprite.top = sprite.verticalLaunchPosition - deltaY; // up
      },
```

(Continues)

Example 8.11   *(Continued)*

```
    isDoneAscending: function (sprite, now) {
        return sprite.ascendTimer.getElapsedTime(now) >
                sprite.JUMP_DURATION/2;
    },

    finishAscent: function (sprite, now) {
        sprite.jumpApex = sprite.top;
        sprite.ascendTimer.stop(now);
        sprite.descendTimer.start(now);
    },
    ...
};
    ...
};
```

The methods in Example 8.11 are summarized in Table 8.2.

Table 8.2 The jump behavior's ascend methods

Method	Description
isAscending()	Returns true if the runner's ascend stopwatch is running.
ascend()	Moves the runner up in accordance with the elapsed time of the last animation frame and the jump's duration and height.
isDoneAscending()	Returns true if the elapsed time on the runner's ascend stopwatch is greater than half the jump's duration.
finishAscent()	Finishes the ascent by stopping the runner's ascend stopwatch and starting its descend stopwatch. The jump behavior calls this method when the runner is at the highest point in the jump, so finishAscent() stores the runner's vertical position in the runner's jumpApex property. The descend() method uses that property to position the runner during her descent.

Recall that the runner's jump() method, listed in Example 8.9 on p. 218, starts the runner's ascend stopwatch. Subsequently, that running stopwatch causes the jump behavior's isAscending() method to temporarily return true. Also recall that until the runner is done ascending—meaning the jump is halfway over—the runner's jump behavior repeatedly calls the ascend() method, as you can see from Example 8.10.

The ascend() method calculates the number of pixels to move the runner vertically for each animation frame by dividing the stopwatch's elapsed time (milliseconds) by one-half of the jump's duration (milliseconds) and multiplying that value by the height of the jump (pixels). The milliseconds cancel out, yielding pixels as the unit of measure for the deltaY value.

When the runner finishes her ascent, the jump behavior's finishAscent() method records the sprite's position at the jump apex, stops the ascend stopwatch, and starts the descend stopwatch.

8.6.2 Descending

The jump behavior methods associated with descending are shown in Example 8.12.

Example 8.12 Descending

```
var SnailBait = function () {
   ...

   this.jumpBehavior = {
      ...

      isDescending: function (sprite) {
         return sprite.descendTimer.isRunning();
      },

      descend: function (sprite, now) {
         var elapsed = sprite.descendTimer.getElapsedTime(now),
             deltaY  = elapsed / (sprite.JUMP_DURATION/2) *
                       sprite.JUMP_HEIGHT;

         sprite.top = sprite.jumpApex + deltaY; // Moving down
      },

      isDoneDescending: function (sprite, now) {
         return sprite.descendTimer.getElapsedTime(now) >
               sprite.JUMP_DURATION/2;
      },

      finishDescent: function (sprite, now) {
         sprite.stopJumping();

         if (snailBait.platformUnderneath(sprite)) {
            sprite.top = sprite.verticalLaunchPosition;
         }
```

(Continues)

Example 8.12 *(Continued)*

```
        else {
            sprite.fall(snailBait.GRAVITY_FORCE *
                (sprite.descendTimer.getElapsedTime(now)/1000) *
                snailBait.PIXELS_PER_METER);
        }
    },
    ...
};
    ...
};
```

The methods in Example 8.12 are summarized in Table 8.3.

There's a lot of symmetry between the ascend methods in Table 8.2 and the descend methods in Table 8.3. Both ascend() and descend() calculate the number of pixels to move the runner in the vertical direction for the current frame in exactly the same manner. The descend() method, however, adds that value to the jump's apex, whereas ascend() subtracts it from the vertical launch position (recall that the Canvas Y axis increases from top to bottom).

When the jump's descent is finished, finishDescent() places the runner at the same vertical position at which she began the jump and restarts her run animation.

Table 8.3 The jump behavior's descend methods

Method	Description
isDescending()	Returns true if the runner's descend stopwatch is running.
descend()	Moves the runner down in accordance with the elapsed time of the last animation frame and the jump's duration and height.
isDoneDescending()	Returns true if the elapsed time on the runner's descend stopwatch is greater than half the jump's duration.
finishDescent()	Stops the descent, and the jump, by stopping the runner's descend stopwatch and setting the runner's jumping flag to false, respectively.
	After descending, the runner might not be at exactly the same height as she was when the jump began, so finishDescent() sets the runner's vertical position to what it was before the jump.
	Finally, finishDescent() sets the runner's animation rate to its normal value, causing the runner to start running.

8.7 Pause Behaviors

Behaviors that time their activities with stopwatches must pause and resume those stopwatches when the game in which they reside pauses and resumes; otherwise, behaviors can get out of sync with the rest of the game. For example, the preceding implementation of the jump behavior does not pause its stopwatches when Snail Bait pauses during a jump, causing jumps to move ahead in time while the game is paused. When the game resumes, therefore, the jump behavior jumps ahead in time.

To pause and resume sprite behaviors and therefore keep behaviors in sync with Snail Bait, we add a `togglePausedStateOfAllBehaviors()` method to Snail Bait. The game invokes that method from its `togglePaused()` method, as shown in Example 8.13.

Example 8.13 The `togglePaused()` method, revised

```
SnailBait.prototype = {
   ...

   togglePaused: function () {
      var now = +new Date();

      this.paused = !this.paused;

      this.togglePausedStateOfAllBehaviors();

      if (this.paused) {
         this.pauseStartTime = now;
      }
      else {
         this.lastAnimationFrameTime += (now - this.pauseStartTime);
      }
   },
   ...
};
```

The `togglePausedStateOfAllBehaviors()` method is listed in Example 8.14.

The `togglePausedStateOfAllBehaviors()` method iterates over all of Snail Bait's sprites and subsequently iterates over each sprite's behaviors, invoking each behavior's `pause()` or `unpause()` method. Those methods are optional; typically, if a behavior does not time its activities, it does not need to implement `pause()` or `unpause()`.

Example 8.14 Pausing and unpausing all of Snail Bait's sprite behaviors

```
SnailBait.prototype = {
   ...

   togglePausedStateOfAllBehaviors: function (now) {
      var behavior;

      for (var i=0; i < this.sprites.length; ++i) {
         sprite = this.sprites[i];

         for (var j=0; j < sprite.behaviors.length; ++j) {
            behavior = sprite.behaviors[j];

            if (this.paused) {
               if (behavior.pause) {
                  behavior.pause(sprite, now);
               }
            }
            else {
               if (behavior.unpause) {
                  behavior.unpause(sprite, now);
               }
            }
         }
      }
   },
   ...
};
```

Example 8.15 shows the implementations of pause() and unpause() for the jump behavior.

Example 8.15 Pausing the jump behavior

```
var SnailBait = function () {
   ...

   this.jumpBehavior = {
      ...

      pause: function (sprite) {
         if (sprite.ascendTimer.isRunning()) {
            sprite.ascendTimer.pause();
         }
         else if (sprite.descendTimer.isRunning()) {
            sprite.descendTimer.pause();
         }
      },
```

```
    unpause: function (sprite) {
        if (sprite.ascendTimer.isRunning()) {
            sprite.ascendTimer.unpause();
        }
        else if (sprite.descendTimer.isRunning()) {
            sprite.descendTimer.unpause();
        }
    },
    ...
};
    ...
};
```

The jump behavior's pause() and unpause() methods pause and unpause the behavior's timers if they are running.

8.8 Conclusion

Prior to this chapter we've dealt with time implicitly, mostly as a backdrop to animation; however, our need to time finite animations has led us to deal with time explicitly by implementing stopwatches and using them to time a jump's ascent and descent.

In this chapter, you saw how to use those stopwatches to implement a jump behavior with linear motion. As you also saw in this chapter, implementing linear motion is relatively straightforward; however, jumping with linear motion is unnatural, so the next thing to do is to make that linear motion nonlinear.

In the two chapters that follow, we delve more deeply into time as it pertains to video games. In the next chapter, we implement nonlinear motion for the runner's jump behavior by modifying the flow of time through that behavior, *without making any changes to the runner's jump behavior*. Then follows a chapter in which you will see how to implement a time system that lets you modify the flow of time throughout an entire game. That handy feature is the source of all kinds of interesting effects and features, such as slow-motion power-ups.

8.9 Exercises

1. Run Snail Bait and pause the game during a jump. When you resume the game, does the runner resume exactly where she left off? Comment out the pause() and unpause() methods in the jump behavior and try again. Does the runner still resume exactly where she left off?

2. There are other ways to get a timestamp in JavaScript. In the version of the game for this chapter, modify the Stopwatch object so that it uses another way besides +new Date() to get the current time and restart the game. Does the game work the same after the change? Explain.

3. Change the runner's JUMP_DURATION constant from 1000 ms to 2000 ms and restart the game. The runner should jump just as high, but the jump should take twice as long. Is that the case?

Time, Part II: Nonlinear Motion

Topics in This Chapter

From sprinting gazelles on the plains of Africa to someone reaching for a cup of coffee in a high-rise office building in Tokyo, natural motion is predominantly nonlinear, meaning it involves acceleration. In Snail Bait, the runner's jumping motion is nonlinear because gravity slows her down as she ascends and increases her speed as she descends.

In the previous chapter we implemented a jump behavior that resulted in linear motion, meaning the runner ascended and descended at a constant rate of speed. In this chapter, we turn that linear motion into nonlinear motion as depicted in Figure 9.1.

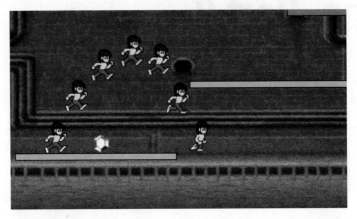

Figure 9.1 A natural jumping sequence

In this chapter, you will learn how to do the following:

- Use animation timers and easing functions to implement nonlinear jumping (Section 9.2 on p. 231)
- Implement animation timers—a stopwatch with an easing function (Section 9.3 on p. 233)
- Implement JavaScript functions, known as easing functions, that modify the flow of time (Section 9.4 on p. 235)
- Implement a realistic bouncing behavior (Section 9.6 on p. 241)
- Randomize behaviors (Section 9.7 on p. 245)
- Implement nonlinear color changes (Section 9.8 on p. 247)

9.1 Understand Time and Its Derivatives

To implement more realistic jumping than the linear motion we implemented in the last chapter, you might expect us to modify the runner's jump behavior, but we do not. *Instead of modifying the runner's jump behavior, we temporarily modify the underlying flow of time* as she jumps. *Because motion is derived from time, modifying time results in changes to motion.*

The reason we modify time to influence motion instead of modifying motion directly is that motion is not the only derivative of time. A pulsating platform, for example, involves nonlinear color change over time as an initial rapid pulse of color slowly fades, so the platform's color change is also a derivative of time.

If we directly implement derivatives of time—such as motion and color change—case by case, we end up implementing nonlinear behavior in multiple places. For example, we might implement nonlinear motion for jumping and later implement nonlinear color change for pulsating platforms. However, *if we instead modify the underlying flow of time, we automatically affect its derivatives* and we need modify time in only one place.

To manipulate the flow of time, we use animation timers and easing functions.

9.2 Use Animation Timers and Easing Functions to Implement Nonlinear Jumping

Recall the runner's jump behavior from the last chapter, when we used two stopwatches to time the runner's ascent and descent during a jump. Those stopwatches were created by Snail Bait's `equipRunnerForJumping()` method, as shown in Example 9.1.

Example 9.1 Jump stopwatches

```
SnailBait.prototype = {
   ...
   equipRunnerForJumping: function () {
      ...
      this.runner.ascendTimer  = new Stopwatch();
      this.runner.descendTimer = new Stopwatch();
      ...
   },
   ...
};
```

The runner's jump behavior uses those stopwatches to position the runner in the vertical direction when she's jumping. *To implement nonlinear motion for jumps, we simply swap stopwatches for animation timers with appropriate easing functions*, as shown in Example 9.2. By modifying the flow of time through the jump behavior, we don't have to modify the behavior's code at all.

Example 9.2 Using animation timers instead of stopwatches

```
SnailBait.prototype = {
    ...

    equipRunnerForJumping: function () {
        ...

        // On the ascent, the runner looses speed
        // due to gravity (ease out)

        this.runner.ascendTimer =
            new AnimationTimer(
                this.runner.JUMP_DURATION/2,
                AnimationTimer.makeEaseOutEasingFunction(1.0)
            );

        // On the descent, the runner gains speed
        // due to gravity (ease in)

        this.runner.descendTimer =
            new AnimationTimer(
                this.runner.JUMP_DURATION/2,
                AnimationTimer.makeEaseInEasingFunction(1.0)
            );
        ...
    },
    ...
};
```

The runner's ascend animation timer is created with an ease-out function, which means time flows quickly in the beginning and slows throughout the ascent. The ease-out function is created by another function—AnimationTimer. makeEaseOutEasingFunction()—which we illustrate in the next section.

The descend timer is created with an ease-in function. Time starts slowly and flows faster throughout the descent. Like the ease-out function, the ease-in function is created by an AnimationTimer method: AnimationTimer.makeEaseInEasing-Function().

You've seen how to use animation timers and easing functions to implement nonlinear motion during a jump. Realize that's all there is to implementing nonlinear jumping; the runner's jump behavior remains unchanged. Next, let's take a look at the implementation of those timers and easing functions.

NOTE: Cuckoo birds and animation timers

Cuckoos are one of several bird species known as brood parasites because they lay their eggs in another bird's nest, leaving the unsuspecting parent to raise the cuckoo's young. Cuckoos are masters at laying eggs that look almost like the adoptive parent's eggs.

The animation timer that we implemented in this chapter is like a cuckoo bird egg because we replaced stopwatches with animation timers, without any changes to the unsuspecting jump behavior, which uses those timers to time jumps. Just as the cuckoo's egg looks nearly identical to the adoptive parent's egg, our animation timer looks nearly identical to a stopwatch because it implements the same methods with identical signatures.

9.3 Implement Animation Timers

Animation timers are essentially stopwatches with two additional features:

- Animation timers run for a specific duration.
- You can attach an easing function to an animation timer to modify the flow of time through the timer.

Easing functions, which you create with `AnimationTimer` convenience methods such as `makeEaseInEasingFunction()` and `makeEaseOutEasingFunction()`, convert time from one value to another, as shown in Figure 9.2.

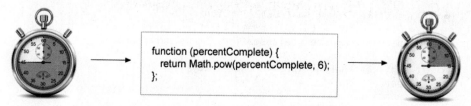

Figure 9.2 An easing function. Real time is on the left and the modified time is on the right.

Example 9.3 shows the implementation of the `AnimationTimer` constructor.

Example 9.3 Animation timer constructor

```
var AnimationTimer = function (duration, easingFunction) {
    this.easingFunction = easingFunction;
```

(Continues)

Example 9.3 *(Continued)*

```
    if (duration !== undefined) this.duration = duration;
    else                        this.duration = 1000;

    this.stopwatch = new Stopwatch();
};
```

The animation timer's duration and easing function are both optional; if you don't specify a duration it defaults to one second, and if you don't specify an easing function, it defaults to undefined. The most interesting part of the AnimationTimer constructor is the fact that it creates a stopwatch that it subsequently uses in its methods, which are listed in **Example 9.4**.

Example 9.4 Animation timer methods

```
AnimationTimer.prototype = {
       start: function () { this.stopwatch.start();             },
        stop: function () { this.stopwatch.stop();              },
       pause: function () { this.stopwatch.pause();             },
     unpause: function () { this.stopwatch.unpause();           },
    isPaused: function () { return this.stopwatch.isPaused();   },
   isRunning: function () { return this.stopwatch.running;      },
       reset: function () { this.stopwatch.reset();             },

    isExpired: function () {
       return this.stopwatch.getElapsedTime() > this.duration;
    },

    getElapsedTime: function (now) {
       var elapsedTime = this.stopwatch.getElapsedTime(now),
           percentComplete = elapsedTime / this.duration;

       if (this.easingFunction === undefined ||
           percentComplete === 0 ||
           percentComplete > 1) {
          return elapsedTime;
       }

       return elapsedTime *
              (this.easingFunction(percentComplete) / percentComplete);
    }
};
```

Nearly all AnimationTimer methods simply delegate to the animation timer's stopwatch. The signatures of those methods are identical to Stopwatch methods, so animation timers can masquerade as stopwatches, which is why we did not have to modify the jump behavior to turn linear motion into nonlinear.

Unlike stopwatches, animation timers have a duration. You can find out if a timer has expired, meaning it has run for its duration, with the `isExpired()` method. The most interesting difference between stopwatches and animation timers, however, is that you can attach an easing function to an animation timer.

The `AnimationTimer.getElapsedTime()` method gets the elapsed time from the timer's stopwatch and calculates the percent of the animation that has elapsed. If the animation timer has an easing function associated with it, `getElapsedTime()` passes the percent of the animation that has elapsed to the easing function, *which presumably returns a different percent, thereby modifying the flow of time.*

Subsequently, the `getElapsedTime()` method calculates and returns the elapsed time based on the modified percent returned from the easing function.

NOTE: The Decorator pattern

Animation timers are an example of the Decorator pattern, where one object masquerades as another (animation timers masquerade as stopwatches). The imposter (animation timer) delegates much of its functionality to an enclosed object (stopwatch) and selectively overrides functions, or, as in the case of animation timers, adds functionality to the enclosed object.

Decorators let you reuse code. Animation timers, for example, reuse the code in stopwatches. Another mechanism for code reuse is inheritance, a feature found in many object-oriented languages. JavaScript does not explicitly support inheritance.

9.4 Implement Easing Functions

Figure 9.3 illustrates two classic easing functions: ease-in and ease-out. To illustrate those effects, the application shown in Figure 9.3 draws a vertical timeline that represents real time.

Ease-in is illustrated by the screenshots in the left column in Figure 9.3 from top to bottom. Ease-in starts slowly, far behind the timeline, and gains speed at the end. Ease-out, illustrated in the right column, is the opposite effect, starting with a burst of speed and slowing at the end. In both cases, the runner is aligned with the timeline at the end of the animation. You can access the application shown in Figure 9.3 at corehtml5games.com/easing-functions.

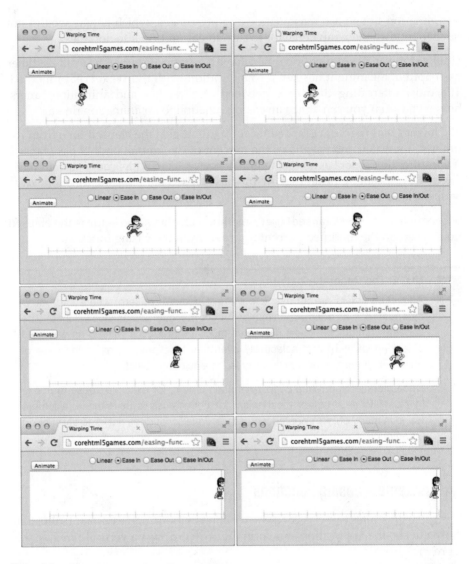

Figure 9.3 Ease-in (left) and ease-out (right)

The ease-in and ease-out effects, from a mathematical standpoint, are implemented by equations depicted by the graphs shown in Figures 9.4 and 9.5. In those graphs, the horizontal axis represents the actual percent of the animation that is complete and the vertical axis represents the percent returned from an appropriate easing function. The straight lines in the graphs represent real time, and the curves show how the easing functions warp time.

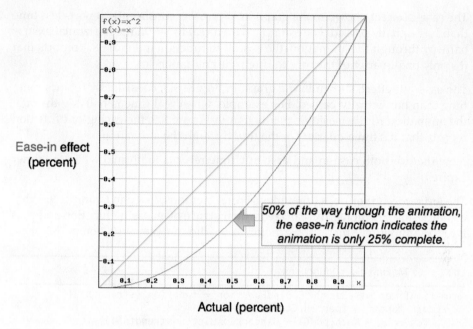

Ease-in **effect**
(percent)

Actual (percent)

Figure 9.4 A graph of the ease-in function

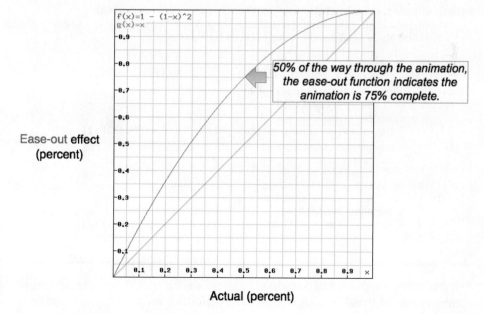

Ease-out **effect**
(percent)

Actual (percent)

Figure 9.5 A graph of the ease-out function

The ease-in effect, shown in the graph in Figure 9.4, consistently reports less time than has actually passed. For example, when real time (on the horizontal axis) is halfway through the animation, the easing-in function in Figure 9.4 reports that it's only one-quarter of the way through the animation.

The ease-out effect, shown in the graph in Figure 9.5, consistently reports more time than has actually passed. For example, when real time is halfway through the animation for the easing-out function in Figure 9.5, the easing-out function reports that it's three-quarters of the way through the animation.

Note that for both ease-in and ease-out, time returns to normal when the timer expires.

The `AnimationTimer` object provides several methods, listed in Example 9.5, that create easing functions. You can create an instance of an easing function and pass it to the animation timer's constructor, as we did in Example 9.2 on p. 232.

Example 9.5 Making easing functions

```
AnimationTimer.makeEaseOutEasingFunction = function (strength) {
    return function (percentComplete) {
        return 1 - Math.pow(1 - percentComplete, strength*2);
    };
};

AnimationTimer.makeEaseInEasingFunction = function (strength) {
    return function (percentComplete) {
        return Math.pow(percentComplete, strength*2);
    };
};

AnimationTimer.makeEaseOutInEasingFunction = function () {
    return function (percentComplete) {
        return percentComplete +
            Math.sin(percentComplete*2*Math.PI) / (2*Math.PI);
    };
};

AnimationTimer.makeEaseInOutEasingFunction = function () {
    return function (percentComplete) {
        return percentComplete -
            Math.sin(percentComplete*2*Math.PI) / (2*Math.PI);
    };
};
```

The preceding methods include algorithms for easing in and out, in addition to combinations of those two algorithms. In Section 9.6 on p. 241, you'll see how to use the easing function returned by `AnimationTimer.makeEaseOutInEasing-Function()` to implement a bouncing motion. In Section 9.8 on p. 247 you'll see how to use the function returned by `AnimationTimer.makeEaseInOutEasing-Function()` to implement pulsating platforms.

NOTE: Easing function equations on the Web

The equations used above for easing functions are well established and widely available; for example, see www.dzone.com/snippets/robert-penner-easing-equations for one online resource.

NOTE: Easing functions in UI toolkits

Many software developers are familiar with easing functions from user interface toolkits, such as jQuery, which provides a rich set of easing functions for animating user interface elements. See http://api.jqueryui.com/easings/ for more information.

9.5 Fine-tune Easing Functions

Because they use the power of a number to compute values, the curves shown in Figures 9.4 and 9.5 are known as power curves. Power curves are prevalent in many disciplines, from animation to economics. Figures 9.4 and 9.5 show curves for a power of 2; changing that number, as shown in Figure 9.6, results in different power curves.

Figure 9.6 shows three power curves for an ease-in effect. From left to right, they represent powers of 2, 3, and 4, respectively. Increasing the exponent exaggerates the ease-in effect.

The `AnimationTimer` methods that create the ease-in and ease-out functions in Example 9.5 take a `strength` argument representing one-half of the exponent for their power curves. The default `strength` value is 1, which results in a power of 2.

By modifying the `strength` value you pass to `AnimationTimer.makeEaseIn-EasingFunction()` and `AnimationTimer.makeEaseOutEasingFunction()`, you can control the effect's strength. For example, the modified version of `equipRunnerForJumping()`, listed in Example 9.6, increases the strength of the ease-in and ease-out effects during the runner's jump from `1.0` to `1.15`. That small change slightly exaggerates both effects, which makes the runner hang in the air a little longer at the apex of the jump.

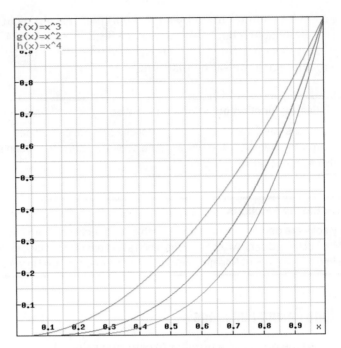

Figure 9.6 Power curves with varying exponents for an ease-in effect

---

Example 9.6 Increasing the easing effect

```
SnailBait.prototype = {
   ...

   equipRunnerForJumping: function () {
      ...

      this.runner.ascendTimer =
         new AnimationTimer(this.runner.JUMP_DURATION/2,
            AnimationTimer.makeEaseOutEasingFunction(1.15));

      this.runner.descendTimer =
         new AnimationTimer(this.runner.JUMP_DURATION/2,
            AnimationTimer.makeEaseInEasingFunction(1.15));
      ...
   },
   ...
};
```

9.6 Implement a Realistic Bounce Behavior

Animation timers encapsulate the ability to modify the flow of time for a given activity. To use them, as you saw in Section 9.2 on p. 231, you implement a behavior fitted with an animation timer with an appropriate easing function. That's how Snail Bait makes coins and jewels bounce on their platforms, as shown in Figure 9.7.

Figure 9.7 A bouncing coin

Besides a cycle behavior that makes coins appear to throb, coins have a bounce behavior, as shown in Example 9.7.

Example 9.7 Creating coins with bounce behaviors

```
SnailBait.prototype = {
   ...

   createCoinSprites: function () {
      var BLUE_THROB_DURATION = 100,  // milliseconds
          GOLD_THROB_DURATION = 500,  // milliseconds
          BOUNCE_DURATION = 800,      // milliseconds
          BOUNCE_HEIGHT = 50,         // pixels
          coin,
          i;

      for (i = 0; i < this.coinData.length; ++i) {
         if (i % 2 === 0) {
            coin = new Sprite('coin',
               new SpriteSheetArtist(this.spritesheet,
                                     this.goldCoinCells),
```

(Continues)

Example 9.7 *(Continued)*

```
                   [ new BounceBehavior(BOUNCE_DURATION, BOUNCE_HEIGHT),
                     new CycleBehavior(GOLD_THROB_DURATION)
                   ]
              );
         }
         else {
            coin = new Sprite('coin',
               new SpriteSheetArtist(this.spritesheet,
                                     this.blueCoinCells),

                  [ new BounceBehavior(BOUNCE_DURATION, BOUNCE_HEIGHT),
                    new CycleBehavior(BLUE_THROB_DURATION)
                  ]
               );
         }
         ...
      }
   },
   ...
};
```

The two arguments to the bounce behavior's constructor, which is listed in Example 9.8, represent the duration of an entire single bounce—both the ascent and descent—and the height of the bounce. Both values are optional, defaulting to 1000 milliseconds for the duration and 50 pixels for the height.

Example 9.8 Bounce behavior's constructor

```
var BounceBehavior = function (duration, height) {
   this.duration = duration || 1000;
   this.distance = height*2 || 100;
   this.bouncing = false;

   this.timer =
      new AnimationTimer(this.duration,
                         AnimationTimer.makeEaseOutInEasingFunction());

   this.paused = false;
};
```

The bounce behavior's constructor invokes AnimationTimer.makeEaseOutIn-EasingFunction() to create an easing function that mimics bouncing: easing out on the way up and easing in on the way down. The bounce behavior applies the easing function for the entire bounce, so it's more convenient for the behavior to deal with the entire distance of the bounce rather than the bounce's height; for that reason, the constructor calculates the distance by doubling the height.

The bounce behavior's `execute()` method is listed in Example 9.9.

Example 9.9 Bounce behavior's execute() method

```
BounceBehavior.prototype = {
   ...

   execute: function (sprite, now, fps, context,
                      lastAnimationFrameTime) {
      var elapsed,
          deltaY;

      if (!this.bouncing) {          // Not bouncing
         this.startBouncing(sprite); // Start bouncing
      }
      else {                         // Already bouncing
         elapsed = this.timer.getElapsedTime();

         if (this.timer.isExpired()) { // Bounce is complete
            this.resetTimer();         // Restart the bounce
            return;                    // Done
         }

         this.adjustVerticalPosition(sprite, elapsed);
      }
   }
};
```

If the sprite associated with the bounce behavior is not bouncing when Snail Bait invokes the behavior's `execute()` method, the behavior starts bouncing the sprite; otherwise, if the bounce has completed, the `execute()` method resets the timer and returns. Resetting the timer resets the timer's elapsed time to zero, and because the behavior's `bouncing` property is still `true`, the bouncing repeats endlessly.

If the sprite is already bouncing and the bounce is still in progress—which is the case nearly all of the time—the behavior gets the elapsed time from the its timer (fitted with the ease-in-out function) and uses that value to adjust the sprite's vertical position.

The bounce behavior's `execute()` method uses three helper methods:

- `startBouncing()`
- `resetTimer()`
- `adjustVerticalPosition()`

The implementation of the three methods is shown Example 9.10.

Example 9.10   Bounce behavior support methods

```javascript
BounceBehavior.prototype = {
   ...

   startBouncing: function (sprite) {
      this.baseline = sprite.top;
      this.bouncing = true;
      this.timer.start();
   },

   resetTimer: function () {
      this.timer.stop();
      this.timer.reset();
      this.timer.start();
   },

   adjustVerticalPosition: function (sprite, elapsed) {
      var rising = false,
         deltaY = this.timer.getElapsedTime() / this.duration *
                  this.distance;

      if (elapsed < this.duration/2)
         rising = true;

      if (rising) {
         // Move the sprite up
         sprite.top = this.baseline - deltaY;
      }
      else {
         // Move the sprite down
         sprite.top = this.baseline - this.distance + deltaY;
      }
   },
   ...
};
```

When the behavior's sprite starts bouncing, the behavior records the vertical position of the sprite, starts the timer, and sets a bouncing flag to true.

The most interesting method listed in Example 9.10 is adjustVerticalPosition(), which, as its name implies, adjusts the vertical position of the behavior's sprite. The distance to move the sprite in the vertical direction is easy to calculate. First, adjustVerticalPosition() divides the timer's elapsed time by the bounce's duration to calculate what percent of the bounce has elapsed, then the method multiplies that percent by the entire distance of the bounce.

Once the adjustVerticalPosition() method has calculated the delta to move the sprite in the vertical direction, it checks to see whether the sprite is currently rising or falling and adjusts the vertical position of the sprite accordingly.

Recall from Chapter 8 that behaviors with internal timers must implement pause() and unpause() methods so that the behaviors stay in sync with the game when players pause and unpause the game. The bounce behavior's pause() and unpause() methods are listed in Example 9.11.

Example 9.11 Pausing bounce behaviors

```
BounceBehavior.prototype = {
   ...

   pause: function(sprite) {
      if (!this.timer.isPaused()) {
         this.timer.pause();
      }
      this.paused = true;
   },

   unpause: function(sprite) {
      if (this.timer.isPaused()) {
         this.timer.unpause();
      }
      this.paused = false;
   },
   ...
};
```

 NOTE: Snail Bait has several bouncing sprites

Besides coins, Snail Bait's rubies and sapphires also bounce endlessly until the runner collides with them or they scroll out of view. Snail Bait adds bounce behaviors to its ruby and sapphire sprites similarly to how it adds bounce behaviors to coins. In the interest of brevity, that code is not listed in this book.

9.7 Randomize Behaviors

The implementation of Snail Bait's createCoinSprites() method in Example 9.7 on p. 241 created identical bounce behaviors for every coin. The game is more interesting, however, if coins bounce at different heights and rates of speed. Example 9.12 shows a revised listing of createCoinSprites() that creates behaviors with random bounce durations and heights.

Example 9.12 Creating coins with random bounce behaviors

```
SnailBait.prototype = {
   ...

   createCoinSprites: function () {
      var BLUE_THROB_DURATION  = 100,
          GOLD_THROB_DURATION  = 500,
          BOUNCE_DURATION_BASE = 800, // milliseconds
          BOUNCE_HEIGHT_BASE   = 50,  // pixels
          coin;

      for (var i = 0; i < this.coinData.length; ++i) {
         if (i % 2 === 0) {
            coin = new Sprite('coin',
               new SpriteSheetArtist(this.spritesheet,
                                     this.goldCoinCells),

               [ new BounceBehavior(BOUNCE_DURATION_BASE +
                           BOUNCE_DURATION_BASE * Math.random(),

                           BOUNCE_HEIGHT_BASE +
                           BOUNCE_HEIGHT_BASE * Math.random()),

                  new CycleBehavior(GOLD_THROB_DURATION)
               ]
            );
         }
         else {
            coin = new Sprite('coin',
               new SpriteSheetArtist(this.spritesheet,
                                     this.blueCoinCells),

               [ new BounceBehavior(BOUNCE_DURATION_BASE +
                           BOUNCE_DURATION_BASE * Math.random(),

                           BOUNCE_HEIGHT_BASE +
                           BOUNCE_HEIGHT_BASE * Math.random()),

                  new CycleBehavior(BLUE_THROB_DURATION)
               ]);
         }
         ...
      }
   },
   ...
};
```

The revised `createCoinSprites()` method creates random values by starting with a base—800 ms for the duration and 50 pixels for the height—and then adding a value between zero and the base. When JavaScript's `Math.random()`, which returns a number between `0.0` and `1.0`, returns zero, the value is equal to the base, and when `Math.random()` returns `1.0`, the value is equal to two times the base. As a result, durations lie somewhere between 800 and 1600 ms, and heights lie somewhere between 50 and 100 pixels.

Now that you've seen how to use animation timers and easing functions to implement nonlinear motion, let's use them to implement nonlinear effects for other derivatives of time.

9.8 Implement Nonlinear Color Changes with Animation Timers and Easing Functions

Up to now we've used animation timers and easing functions to modify time so we could influence motion. We can easily do the same to influence another derivative of time: color change.

Figure 9.8 shows a platform equipped with a pulse behavior. That behavior continuously modifies the opacity of the platform's colors to make it appear as though the platform is pulsating.

Figure 9.8 A pulsating platform

Example 9.13 shows how Snail Bait creates platforms, taking pulsating into account. Platforms don't do anything other than pulsate, and there's only one pulsating platform in the game, so Snail Bait's `createPlatformSprites()` method creates each platform sprite without any behaviors. Subsequently, if the platform's `pulsate` property is `true`, `createPlatformSprites()` adds a pulse behavior to the platform.

Example 9.13 Creating platforms with pulse behaviors

```
SnailBait.prototype = {
   ...

   createPlatformSprites: function () {
      var sprite, pd, // Sprite, Platform data
          PULSE_DURATION = 800,
          PULSE_OPACITY_THRESHOLD = 0.1;

      for (var i=0; i < this.platformData.length; ++i) {
         ...

         sprite = new Sprite('platform', this.platformArtist);
         ...

         if (sprite.pulsate) { // Add a behavior
            sprite.behaviors =
               [ new PulseBehavior(PULSE_DURATION,
                                   PULSE_OPACITY_THRESHOLD) ];
         }

         this.platforms.push(sprite);
      }
   },
   ...
};
```

When you create a pulse behavior, you can optionally specify the pulse duration in milliseconds and the opacity threshold for the pulse. That threshold represents the minimum opacity for a sprite during a pulse. The opacity threshold of 0.1 used by the preceding `createPlatformSprites()` method means that the platform will fade out until it's barely visible before fading back into view.

Pulse behaviors manipulate their sprite's opacity similar to the way bounce behaviors manipulate their sprite's position. Let's see how they do it.

9.8.1 The Pulse Behavior

The pulse behavior's constructor is listed in **Example 9.14**.

Example 9.14 The pulse behavior's constructor

```
var PulseBehavior = function (duration, opacityThreshold) {
   this.duration = duration || 1000;
   this.opacityThreshold = opacityThreshold || 0;

   this.timer =
      new AnimationTimer(this.duration,
                        AnimationTimer.makeEaseInOutEasingFunction());
   this.paused = false;
   this.pulsating = false;
};
```

The pulse behavior's duration represents the time it takes for an entire pulse to take place. A pulse is a flash of color that subsequently fades away. The opacity threshold is the minimum value for the behavior's associated sprite's opacity during the pulse. The defaults for those values are 1000 ms for the duration and zero for the opacity threshold.

The pulse behavior methods are listed in **Example 9.15**.

Example 9.15 The pulse behavior's methods

```
PulseBehavior.prototype = {
   pause: function(sprite, now) {
      if (!this.timer.isPaused()) {
         this.timer.pause(now);
      }
      this.paused = true;
   },

   unpause: function(sprite, now) {
      if (this.timer.isPaused()) {
         this.timer.unpause(now);
      }
      this.paused = false;
   },
```

(Continues)

Example 9.15 *(Continued)*

```javascript
   dim: function (sprite, elapsed) {
      sprite.opacity = 1 - ((1 - this.opacityThreshold) *
                            (parseFloat(elapsed) / this.duration));
   },

   brighten: function (sprite, elapsed) {
      sprite.opacity += (1 - this.opacityThreshold) *
                        parseFloat(elapsed) / this.duration;
   },

   startPulsing: function (sprite) {
      this.pulsating = true;
      this.timer.start();
   },

   resetTimer: function () {
      this.timer.stop();
      this.timer.reset();
      this.timer.start();
   },

   execute: function (sprite, now, fps, context,
                      lastAnimationFrameTime) {
      var elapsed;

      if (!this.pulsating) {                // Not pulsating
         this.startPulsing(sprite);         // Start pulsating
      }
      else {                                // Already pulsating
         elapsed = this.timer.getElapsedTime();

         if (this.timer.isExpired()) {      // Pulse is complete
            this.resetTimer();              // Restart pulsating
            return;                         // Done
         }

         if (elapsed < this.duration/2) {
            this.dim(sprite, elapsed);
         }
         else {
            this.brighten(sprite, elapsed);
         }
      }
   }
};
```

The pulse behavior methods are nearly identical to the bounce behavior discussed earlier in this chapter. Instead of adjusting a sprite's vertical position, as was the case for the bounce behavior, the pulse behavior dims and brightens the sprite by manipulating its opacity.

The pulse behavior's `dim()` and `brighten()` methods calculate the sprite's opacity based on what percent of the pulse is complete at the current time, similar to the way the bounce behavior calculated the delta in which to move its sprite in the vertical direction.

9.9 Conclusion

The most fundamental aspect of implementing a video game is how time flows through the game. Everything else in the game—the position of sprites, what they look like, and what they are doing—depends on the flow of time.

In this chapter you saw how to use animation timers and easing functions to temporarily modify the flow of time during sprite behaviors. By modifying the flow of time you automatically influence its derivatives such as motion and color change.

In the next chapter you will see how to modify the flow of time throughout an entire game; that capability is a powerful tool you can use for special effects and gameplay aspects.

9.10 Exercises

1. Comment out the assignment to `this.easingFunction` in the `AnimationTimer` constructor and restart the game. What happens when the runner jumps? Why?
2. Change the ease-out-in function used by the bounce behavior to an ease-in-out function by using `AnimationTimer.makeEaseInOut- EasingFunction()` instead of `AnimationTimer.makeEaseOutInFunction()`. Verify that changing the easing function makes it look like coins and jewels are bouncing upside down.
3. Modify the bounce behavior to use two timers—one for the bounce ascent and another for the descent—instead of one. Experiment with the strength parameters that you pass to `AnimationTimer.makeEaseInEasingFunction()` and `AnimationTimer.makeEaseOutEasingFunction()` to distort bouncing.

CHAPTER

10

Time, Part III: Time Systems

Topics in This Chapter

In the last chapter, we temporarily modified the flow of time for individual behaviors to influence time's derivatives—a powerful technique. In this chapter, we extend that technique to implement a time system that modifies the flow of time throughout an entire game.

Slowing or increasing the rate at which time flows through a game is useful for gameplay features and special effects. Snail Bait slows time during transitions between lives, for example, to emphasize that gameplay is suspended during the transition. Snail Bait's developer backdoor, discussed in Chapter 18 and shown in Figure 10.1, lets you modify the flow of time as the game proceeds, mostly so the developer can run the game in slow motion to make playtesting more productive.

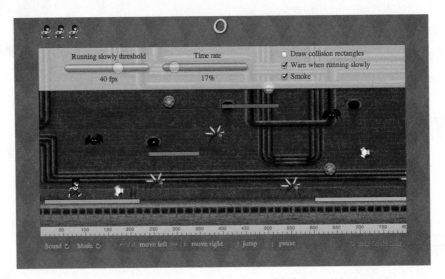

Figure 10.1 Snail Bait in slow motion

In this chapter, we explore the implementation and use of Snail Bait's simple but capable time system. That time system is less than 50 lines of JavaScript, so we won't need much time to discuss its implementation. Most of this chapter is concerned with how Snail Bait uses the time system and how the time system affects objects that already have their own notion of time, such as behaviors, animation timers, and stopwatches.

In this chapter, you will learn how to do the following.

- Create and start the time system (Section 10.2 on p. 257)
- Incorporate the time system into Snail Bait (Section 10.3 on p. 258)
- Implement a game method that slows time or speeds it up (Section 10.3.2 on p. 259)
- Redefine the current time for stopwatches and animation timers (Section 10.4 on p. 264)
- Implement the time system (Section 10.5 on p. 268)

 NOTE: Slow-motion power-ups

An interesting addition to Snail Bait would be a power-up that causes the game to run in slow motion, perhaps activated when the runner captures a particular coin or jewel. Playing the game in slow motion is significantly easier than playing at full speed, giving the player an advantage while the power-up is active.

BEST PRACTICE: Implement a time system early on

A time system is a fundamental aspect of any video game, so it's best to incorporate it into the game from the very start of the game's development.

10.1 Snail Bait's Time System

Snail Bait's time system has only three methods, listed in Table 10.1.

Table 10.1 Time system methods

Method	Description
`start()`	Starts the game timer. Snail Bait calls this method when the game starts.
`calculateGameTime()`	Returns a number representing the amount of time that has passed since the time system's `start()` method was called, accounting for any transducers that have been attached to the time system since it started.
`setTransducer(transducerFunction, duration)`	Sets a transducer function that modifies the flow of time through the game. The transducer stays in effect for the specified duration. The duration is optional; if you don't specify it, the time system uses the transducer until you replace it with another one.

You start the time system with its `start()` method and you access the current game time with `calculateGameTime()`. To modify the flow of time through the time system, you attach a *transducer* function to the time system with the `setTransducer()` method.

By default, the time system represents time as it really is; for example, `calculateGameTime()` returns 5000 milliseconds if you call it exactly 5 seconds after invoking the time system's `start()` method.

A time system isn't very interesting, however, if it's always truthful about how much time has elapsed since the game began. Things get interesting when the time system *purposely reports erroneous values to modify the flow of time*. In fact, that's exactly what we did in the last chapter with easing functions to control the flow of time through a behavior so we could indirectly affect a sprite's motion and color change over time.

The time system uses time transducer functions to affect the flow of time through an entire game. A transducer function is just like an easing function, except that easing functions modify the completion percentage of a finite behavior, whereas transducer functions modify a game's overall elapsed time. For example, Example 10.1 shows the implementation of a transducer function that, when passed to the setTransducer() method of Snail Bait's time system, makes the game run at half speed.

Example 10.1 A transducer that makes Snail Bait run at half speed

```
var halfSpeedTransducer = function (time) {
   return time / 2; // Half speed
};
```

Example 10.2 shows how to use the preceding transducer function to make Snail Bait run at half speed.

Example 10.2 Setting the half speed transducer function

```
snailBait.timeSystem.setTransducer(halfSpeedTransducer);
```

Snail Bait also provides a convenience method named setTimeRate() that lets you specify the rate at which time flows through the game, as you can see in Example 10.3.

Example 10.3 Using Snail Bait's setTimeRate() method

```
snailBait.setTimeRate(0.5); // Run at half speed
```

The value that you pass to setTimeRate() represents a percent of the normal rate at which time flows through the game. Passing a value of 2.0, for example, makes the game run at twice its normal rate.

The implementation of snailBait.setTimeRate() is discussed in Section 10.3.2 on p. 259.

In Section 10.5, "Implement the Time System," on p. 268, we look at the implementation of the methods in Table 10.1, but first let's see how Snail Bait creates and uses the time system.

NOTE: Transducers

Transducers in the physical world convert one form of energy into another. In the virtual world of games, our transducers convert time from one value to another.

Why `calculateGameTime()` instead of `getGameTime()`?

The names software developers assign to variables and methods are important because good names convey how code works. The time system implements a `calculateGameTime()` method because that method calculates game time by optionally modifying the current time through a transducer function instead of merely accessing it.

10.2 Create and Start the Time System

Snail Bait creates an instance of the time system in its constructor function, as you can see in Example 10.4, and sets a variable representing the current time rate to 1.0. That rate is intuitive: zero means time is standing still; 1.0 means time is flowing normally; 0.5 means time is flowing at half speed, and so forth.

Example 10.4 Creating the time system

```
var SnailBait = function () {
   ...

   this.timeSystem = new TimeSystem(); // See js/timeSystem.js
   this.timeRate = 1.0;
   ...
};
```

Snail Bait starts the time system in its `startGame()` method, as illustrated in Example 10.5.

Example 10.5 Starting the time system

```
SnailBait.prototype = {
   ...

   startGame: function () {
      ...
```

(Continues)

Example 10.5 *(Continued)*

```
        this.timeSystem.start(); // Start the time system
        ...
    },
    ...
};
```

Now that you've seen how Snail Bait creates and starts the time system, let's see how it subsequently uses the time system throughout the game.

10.3 Incorporate the Time System into Snail Bait

Fundamentally, using the time system is straightforward. Instead of getting the current time from the browser or a JavaScript expression such as +new Date(), we get it from the time system's calculateGameTime() method. Practically, however, we must do several things to ensure that the current time from the time system reverberates throughout the entire game:

- Use the time system to drive the game's animation
- Implement a game method that uses the time system to modify the flow of time
- Factor the rate at which time flows into the frame rate calculation
- Pause and resume the game by using the time system

Let's take a look at each of the preceding modifications to Snail Bait.

10.3.1 Use the Time System to Drive the Game's Animation

Recall that the browser passes the current time to Snail Bait's animate() method. Up to now, the animate() method used that time to calculate the frame rate and draw the next animation frame, as shown in **Example 10.6**.

Example 10.6 The original implementation of Snail Bait's animate() method

```
SnailBait.prototype = {
    ...

    animate: function (now) {
        // The browser passes the current
        // time in the now argument
        ...
```

```
        snailBait.fps = snailBait.calculateFps(now);
        snailBait.draw(now);
        ...
    },
    ...
};
```

From now on we overwrite the time the browser passes to the animate() *method with the time calculated by the game's time system,* as shown in Example 10.7.

Example 10.7 Snail Bait's animate() method, revised

```
SnailBait.prototype = {
    ...

    animate: function (now) {
        // Replace the time the browser passes into the method
        // with the time from Snail Bait's time system

        now = snailBait.timeSystem.calculateGameTime();
        ...

        snailBait.fps = snailBait.calculateFps(now);
        snailBait.draw(now);
        ...
    },
    ...
};
```

Instead of letting the browser dictate the current time to Snail Bait, we calculate it with the time system; in effect, we have hijacked time from the browser. Now that we have done so, it's time to tinker with time itself.

10.3.2 Implement a Game Method that Uses the Time System to Modify the Flow of Time

To affect the flow of time through the game, Snail Bait implements a setTimeRate() method, listed in Example 10.8. The lone argument to that method is a number that represents the rate at which time flows through the game.

The setTimeRate() method passes a function to the time system's setTransducer() method. That function returns the current time multiplied by Snail Bait's time rate. For example, if the actual elapsed time for the game is 10 seconds and the time rate is 0.5, the time returned by the transducer would be five seconds, making the game run at half speed. You can also specify values greater than 1.0 for Snail Bait's timeRate property. A value of 2.0, for example, makes the game run twice as fast as normal.

Example 10.8 Setting the time rate

```
SnailBait.prototype = {
   ...

   setTimeRate: function (rate) {
      this.timeRate = rate;

      this.timeSystem.setTransducer( function (now) {
         return now * snailBait.timeRate;
      });
   },
   ...
};
```

10.3.3 Factor the Time Rate into the Frame Rate Calculation

Up to now, Snail Bait calculated the game's frame rate as shown in Example 10.9.

Example 10.9 The original implementation of Snail Bait's calculateFps() method

---

```
SnailBait.prototype = {
   ...

   calculateFps: function (now) {
      var fps = 1 / (now - this.lastAnimationFrameTime) * 1000;
      ...

      return fps;
   },
   ...
};
```

Now, however, when Snail Bait sets a transducer function that modifies the current time, the value of the calculateFps() method's now parameter *does not reflect the actual elapsed time*, and therefore calculateFps() must account for the time rate so that the calculated frame rate is accurate, as shown in Example 10.10.

The revised version of Snail Bait's calculateFps() method simply multiplies the frame rate by the game's time rate to account for any transducers that are attached to the game's time system.

Example 10.10 Snail Bait's `calculateFps()` method, revised

```
SnailBait.prototype = {
   ...

   calculateFps: function (now) {
      var fps = 1 / (now - this.lastAnimationFrameTime) *
                1000 * this.timeRate;
      ...

      return fps;
   },
   ...
};
```

10.3.4 Pause and Resume the Game by Using the Time System

Recall that when Snail Bait resumes from a pause, it adjusts the time of the last animation frame to account for the pause, as you can see from the original implementation of the game's `togglePaused()` method, which is listed in Example 10.11.

Example 10.11 The original implementation of Snail Bait's `togglePaused()` method

```
SnailBait.prototype = {
   ...

   togglePaused: function () {
      var now = +new Date();

      this.paused = !this.paused;

      this.togglePausedStateOfAllBehaviors();

      if (this.paused) {
         this.pauseStartTime = now;
      }
      else {
         this.lastAnimationFrameTime += (now - this.pauseStartTime);
      }
   },
   ...
};
```

The `togglePaused()` method in the preceding listing calculates game time with the construct +new `Date()`, coercing a `Date` object into a number. The revised implementation of `togglePaused()` is shown in Example 10.12.

Example 10.12 Snail Bait's `togglePaused()` method, revised

```
SnailBait.prototype = {
   ...

   togglePaused: function () {
      var now = this.timeSystem.calculateGameTime();

      this.paused = !this.paused;

      this.togglePausedStateOfAllBehaviors(now);

      if (this.paused) {
         this.pauseStartTime = now;
      }
      else {
         this.lastAnimationFrameTime += (now - this.pauseStartTime);
      }
   },
   ...
};
```

The revised implementation of `togglePaused()` calculates game time with Snail Bait's time system. Besides using the time system to track the amount of time the game pauses, the revised implementation of `togglePaused()` passes the time calculated by the time system to `togglePausedStateOfAllBehaviors()`.

The revised implementation of Snail Bait's `togglePausedStateOfAllBehaviors()` method passes the current time to each behavior's `pause()` and `unpause()` methods, as you can see from Example 10.13.

Example 10.13 Snail Bait's `togglePausedStateOfAllBehaviors()` method, revised

```
SnailBait.prototype = {
   ...

   togglePausedStateOfAllBehaviors: function (now) {
      var behavior;

      for (var i=0; i < this.sprites.length; ++i) {
         sprite = this.sprites[i];

         for (var j=0; j < sprite.behaviors.length; ++j) {
            behavior = sprite.behaviors[j];

            if (this.paused) {
               if (behavior.pause) {
```

```
            behavior.pause(sprite, now);
         }
      }
      else {
         if (behavior.unpause) {
            behavior.unpause(sprite, now);
         }
      }
   }
},
...
};
```

Snail Bait passes the current time to the behavior's pause() and unpause() methods so that those methods can, in turn, forward the current time to any timers the behavior is using, as shown in **Example 10.14**, which lists the pulse behavior's pause() and unpause() methods.

Example 10.14 Pausing pulse behaviors, revised

```
PulseBehavior.prototype = {
   pause: function(sprite, now) {
      if (!this.timer.isPaused()) {
         this.timer.pause(now);
      }
      this.paused = true;
   },

   unpause: function(sprite, now) {
      if (this.timer.isPaused()) {
         this.timer.unpause(now);
      }

      this.paused = false;
   },
   ...
};
```

Up to now, the AnimationTimer.pause() and AnimationTimer.unpause() methods invoked in the preceding code calculated game time internally with the +new Date() JavaScript expression, so those methods did not take any arguments. Now, however, Snail Bait passes the current time that it obtains from its time system to those methods so that animation timers pause and unpause in concert with the game.

AnimationTimer.pause() and AnimationTimer.unpause() are not the only animation timer methods that use the current time. In fact, nearly all AnimationTimer methods use the current time, so we must revise `AnimationTimer` methods to take the current time as an argument instead of using +new `Date()`.

10.4 Redefine the Current Time for Stopwatches and Animation Timers

Snail Bait has several sprite behaviors that time their sprite's activities with animation timers. Those animation timers previously calculated game time internally with the +new `Date()` JavaScript expression; now, however, Snail Bait passes the game time to `AnimationTimer` methods, as illustrated in Example 10.15.

Example 10.15 Running the jump behavior on game time as opposed to system time

---

```
SnailBait.prototype = {
   ...

   equipRunnerForJumping: function () {
      this.runner.jump = function () {
         ...

         this.ascendAnimationTimer.start(
            snailBait.timeSystem.calculateGameTime());
         ...
      };
   },
   ...
};
```

As discussed in Chapter 8, the runner's `jump()` method starts the runner's ascend animation timer. With the time system installed, Snail Bait now passes the game time to the animation timer's `start()` method, whereas that `start()` method previously did not take any arguments.

To keep animation timers and stopwatches in sync with the game's time system, we must revise the implementations of those objects so that we can pass the current time to their methods. Example 10.16 shows the revised implementation of the `AnimationTimer`'s prototype object.

Example 10.16 Animation timers, revised

```
AnimationTimer.prototype = {
   start: function (now) {
      this.stopwatch.start(now);
   },
```

```
  stop: function (now) {
    this.stopwatch.stop(now);
  },

  pause: function (now) {
    this.stopwatch.pause(now);
  },

  unpause: function (now) {
    this.stopwatch.unpause(now);
  },

  isPaused: function () {
    return this.stopwatch.isPaused();
  },

  getElapsedTime: function (now) {
    var elapsedTime = this.stopwatch.getElapsedTime(now),
        percentComplete = elapsedTime / this.duration;

    if (this.easingFunction === undefined ||
        percentComplete === 0 ||
        percentComplete > 1) {
      return elapsedTime;
    }

    return elapsedTime *
          (this.easingFunction(percentComplete) / percentComplete);
  },

  isRunning: function() {
    return this.stopwatch.running;
  },

  isExpired: function (now) {
    return this.stopwatch.getElapsedTime(now) > this.duration;
  },

  reset: function(now) {
    this.stopwatch.reset(now);
  }
};
```

Animation timers just pass the current time through to their underlying stopwatch, as you can see from the preceding listing, so we must revise stopwatches in addition to animation timers. The revised implementation of the Stopwatch object's methods is shown in Example 10.17.

Example 10.17 Stopwatches, revised

```javascript
var Stopwatch = function () {
    this.startTime = 0;
    this.running = false;
    this.elapsed = undefined;

    this.paused = false;
    this.startPause = 0;
    this.totalPausedTime = 0;
};

Stopwatch.prototype = {
    start: function (now) {
        this.startTime = now ? now : +new Date();
        this.elapsedTime = undefined;
        this.running = true;
        this.totalPausedTime = 0;
        this.startPause = 0;
    },

    stop: function (now) {
        if (this.paused) {
            this.unpause();
        }

        this.elapsed = (now ? now : +new Date()) -
                       this.startTime -
                       this.totalPausedTime;
        this.running = false;
    },

    pause: function (now) {
        if (this.paused) {
            return;
        }

        this.startPause = now ? now : +new Date();
        this.paused = true;
    },

    unpause: function (now) {
        if (!this.paused) {
            return;
        }

        this.totalPausedTime += (now ? now : +new Date()) -
                                this.startPause;
        this.startPause = 0;
        this.paused = false;
    },
```

```
isPaused: function () {
  return this.paused;
},

getElapsedTime: function (now) {
  if (this.running) {
    return (now ? now : +new Date()) -
           this.startTime -
           this.totalPausedTime;
  }
  else {
    return this.elapsed;
  }
},

isRunning: function() {
  return this.running;
},

reset: function(now) {
  this.elapsed = 0;
  this.startTime = now ? now : +new Date();
  this.elapsedTime = undefined;
  this.running = false;
}
};
```

Initially, none of the Stopwatch or AnimationTimer methods took any arguments because they calculated the current game time internally with the +new Date() JavaScript expression. Now, nearly all the methods take a single argument representing the current game time, which comes from the time system. At this point, the time system has permeated throughout the entire game.

Now that you've seen how to incorporate the time system into Snail Bait, it's time to see how to implement the time system.

 NOTE: Passing the current time to stopwatch methods is optional

Stopwatch methods use the JavaScript expression now ? now : +new Date(). That expression evaluates to now when now is defined; otherwise, when now is undefined, the expression evaluates to the value of +new Date(). That lets you call stopwatch methods without passing the current time, and the time will default to +new Date(). The time system itself, which uses an animation timer, takes advantage of that fact.

10.5 Implement the Time System

Snail Bait's time system uses an animation timer that runs continuously to calculate game time. By default, that animation timer returns the actual elapsed time that the game has been running; however, by fitting the time system with a transducer function, you can modify the flow of time, as you've already seen in this chapter.

Example 10.18 shows the time system's constructor.

Example 10.18 The time system's constructor

```
var TimeSystem = function () {
   this.transducer = function (elapsedTime) { return elapsedTime; };
   this.timer = new AnimationTimer();
   this.lastTimeTransducerWasSet = 0;
   this.gameTime = 0;
}
```

The constructor assigns values to the time system's four properties, which are listed in Table 10.2.

Table 10.2 Time system properties

Property	Description
gameTime	The amount of time since the time system's start() method was invoked, accounting for any transducers that have been attached to the time system since it started. This is the value that calculateGameTime() updates and returns.
timer	An animation timer used by calculateGameTime() to calculate game time.
transducer	A function that takes the current time as a parameter and returns a (presumably different) value for the current time. Notice from Example 10.18 that the default transducer does not modify the flow of time.
lastTimeTransducerWasSet	The value of the gameTime property the last time a transducer was attached to the time system. The calculateGameTime() method uses that property to calculate game time.

The time system's methods are listed in Example 10.19.

Example 10.19 The time system's methods

```
TimeSystem.prototype = {
   start: function () {
      this.timer.start();
   },

   reset: function () {
      this.timer.stop();
      this.timer.reset();
      this.timer.start();
      this.lastTimeTransducerWasSet = this.gameTime;
   },

   setTransducer: function (fn, duration) {
      // Duration is optional. If you specify it, the transducer is
      // applied for the specified duration; after the duration ends,
      // the permanent transducer is restored. If you don't specify the
      // duration, the transducer permanently replaces the current
      // transducer.

      var lastTransducer = this.transducer,
          self = this;

      this.calculateGameTime();
      this.reset();
      this.transducer = fn;

      if (duration) {
         setTimeout( function (e) {
            self.setTransducer(lastTransducer);
         }, duration);
      }
   },

   calculateGameTime: function () {
      this.gameTime = this.lastTimeTransducerWasSet +
                    this.transducer(this.timer.getElapsedTime());
      this.reset();

      return this.gameTime;
   }
};
```

The time system invokes the methods of its animation timer with no arguments,
which means that the timer uses +new Date() to calculate the time.

By keeping track of the last time the game set a transducer function, the time system's `calculateGameTime()` method easily calculates game time by adding the elapsed time since the transducer was set—modified by the transducer function—to the last time the transducer was set.

By default, transducer functions stay in effect until the next time you set the transducer function. You can set the transducer function for a specific duration, however, by specifying the `duration` parameter for the time system's `setTransducer()` method.

10.6 Conclusion

Some video games are more sophisticated than others, but they all have a time system. Up to this chapter, our time system consisted of the browser, which passes the current time to our `animate()` method. In this chapter, we overwrote that value with time calculated from a time system that can modify the flow of time with transducer functions.

The ability to modify the flow of time through your game gives you more interesting options for user interface effects and gameplay mechanics. For example, at slower speeds most video games are easier to play, whereas they are more difficult at faster speeds, so if players can temporarily slow play during difficult areas of the game, they can progress more easily.

10.7 Exercises

1. Modify Snail Bait's `keydown` event handler to run the game in slow motion when the player presses the s key by invoking Snail Bait's `setTimeRate()` method. If the game is already running in slow motion when the player presses the s key, return the game to normal speed. The precise definition of slow motion is up to you.

2. After completing the first exercise, open Snail Bait's developer backdoor by typing CTRL-d and toggle the game between slow motion and regular speed as outlined in Exercise 1. As you toggle, watch the time slider in the developer backdoor. Does it respond when you press the s key? See Chapter 18 to see how Snail Bait keeps the time slider in sync with the game's time system.

3. Modify Snail Bait's `setTimeRate()` method to take a second argument: the duration, in milliseconds, that Snail Bait runs the game at the specified rate. If the rate is unspecified, set the time rate until it is reset. Recall that the time system's `setTransducer()` method already implements that functionality,

so you just need to pass the duration from Snail Bait's `setTimeRate()` to the time system's `setTransducer()` method.

4. Implement a slow-motion power-up that Snail Bait activates when the runner captures a coin. The power-up should cause the game to run at 20 percent of its normal rate for a duration of five seconds. After five seconds, de-activate the power-up and return the time rate to normal. Is that an effective power-up?

CHAPTER

Collision Detection

Topics in This Chapter

Nearly all computer games implement collision detection. Even games that are mostly static, such as puzzles, must detect collisions. Collision detection is a deep and varied topic, with entire books devoted to the subject. And the math required to implement certain types of collision detection can get pretty intense.

In spite of collision detection complexities, for many games it's relatively simple to implement. The level of difficulty depends to a great extent on how fast sprites move and how big they are; it's fairly easy to detect collisions between large and slow-moving sprites, but it's more challenging to detect collisions between small sprites moving at high speeds.

Besides detecting collisions, you must do something about them when they occur. Figure 11.1, for example, shows Snail Bait's runner exploding after colliding with a bee in the upper-left corner of the game.

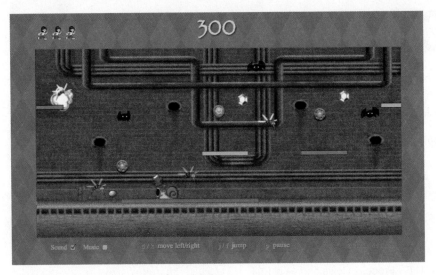

Figure 11.1 Detecting and reacting to collisions

In this chapter, you will learn how to do the following:

- Choose a particular type of collision detection for your game (Section 11.2 on p. 275)
- Implement collision detection as sprite behaviors (Section 11.3.2 on p. 279)
- Select sprites that are candidates for collision detection (Section 11.4 on p. 281)
- Use the HTML5 Canvas context for hit detection (Section 11.5 on p. 282)
- Process collisions (Section 11.6 on p. 284)
- Optimize collision detection (Section 11.7 on p. 286)
- Monitor collision detection performance (Section 11.8 on p. 289)
- Implement collision detection edge cases (Section 11.9 on p. 291)

11.1 The Collision Detection Process

Collision detection is a three-step process, one of which is the actual detection of collisions:

1. Disqualify sprites that are not candidates for collision detection.
2. Detect collisions between candidate sprites.
3. Process collisions.

Collision detection can be computationally expensive, so it's essential to avoid it for sprites that cannot possibly collide. For example, Snail Bait's runner runs through other sprites when they are exploding. Because it takes less time to check whether a sprite is exploding than it does to perform collision detection, Snail Bait excludes exploding sprites from collision detection.

Let's start with an overview of collision detection techniques.

11.2 Collision Detection Techniques

You can detect collisions between sprites in several ways. Three popular techniques, in order of increasing sophistication and complexity, are

- Bounding areas (bounding volumes for 3D games)
- Ray casting
- The Separating Axis Theorem

Collision detection with bounding areas detects intersections between circles or polygons. In the example in Figure 11.2, the smaller circle is the bounding area that represents the ball, and the larger circle is a bounding area representing the top of the bucket. When those two circular bounding areas intersect, the ball is in the bucket.

Detecting collisions between two circles is the simplest of all collision detection techniques: If the distance between the circles' centers is less than the circles' combined radii, the circles intersect and the associated sprites have collided.

Bounding area collision detection is simple, but it can fail when bounding areas are too small or are moving too fast. In either case, sprites can pass by each other in a single animation frame, thereby avoiding detection.

A more reliable technique for small, fast moving sprites is ray casting, illustrated in Figure 11.3. Ray casting detects the intersection of two sprites' velocity vectors. In each of the five frames in Figure 11.3, the ball's velocity vector is the diagonal line drawn in blue, and the velocity vector for the bucket is the red horizontal

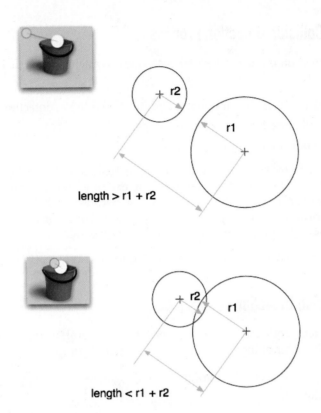

Figure 11.2 Bounding areas: Collisions between circles

Figure 11.3 Ray casting

line. The ball lands in the bucket when the intersection of those vectors lies within the opening at the top of the bucket and the ball is below the opening, as illustrated in the rightmost screenshot in Figure 11.3.

Ray casting works well for simple shapes under circumstances—such as the ball landing in the bucket in Figure 11.3—where it's easy to determine if two shapes have collided, given the intersection of their velocity vectors.

For more complicated scenarios, such as collisions between polygons of arbitrary size and shape, the Separating Axis Theorem is one of the most reliable—and most complicated—collision detection techniques. The Separating Axis Theorem is the mathematical equivalent of shining a light on two polygons from different angles, as shown in Figure 11.4. If the shadow on one of the walls behind the polygons reveals a gap, the polygons are not colliding.

separation between shadows

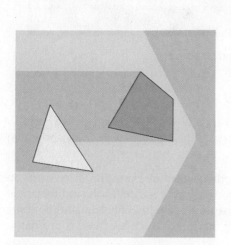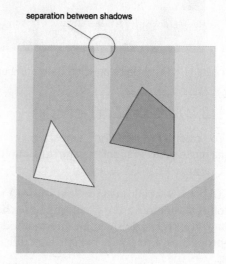

Figure 11.4 The Separating Axis Theorem

This book does not cover ray casting or the Separating Axis Theorem any further. You can read in-depth discussions of each approach in *Core HTML5 Canvas* (Prentice Hall, 2012).

11.3 Snail Bait's Collision Detection

Snail Bait's collision detection involves relatively large sprites moving at slow speeds, so the game detects collisions with bounding boxes. Those bounding boxes are shown in Figure 11.5.

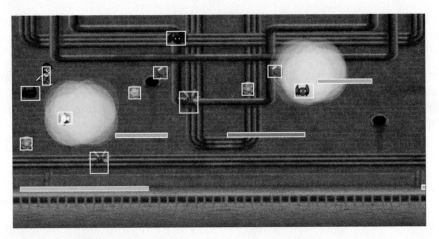

Figure 11.5 Snail Bait's collision detection bounding boxes

11.3.1 Sprite Collision Rectangles

To calculate collision detection bounding boxes for sprites, we add a `calculateCollisionRectangle()` method to the `Sprite` object, as shown in Example 11.1.

The `calculateCollisionRectangle()` method listed in Example 11.1 returns an object containing the positions of each corner of the sprite's collision rectangle and the rectangle's center. The method uses the sprite's `left`, `top`, and `hOffset` properties, along with the sprite's collision margin, to calculate those coordinates.

The `left` and `top` properties represent the coordinates of the upper-left corner of the sprite. The `hOffset` property represents the sprite's horizontal offset, which Snail Bait uses to scroll sprites horizontally (see Chapter 3 for more information about how Snail Bait scrolls sprites). A collision margin, discussed in Section 11.7, "Optimize Collision Detection," on p. 286, also factors into the sprite's collision rectangle calculation.

Example 11.1 Calculating sprite collision detection rectangles

---

```
Sprite.prototype = {
   ...

   calculateCollisionRectangle: function () {
      // Return an object with properties left,
      // right, top, bottom, centerX, and centerY
```

```
   return {
      left:     this.left   - this.hOffset + this.collisionMargin.left,

      right:    this.left   - this.hOffset +
                this.width  - this.collisionMargin.right,

      top:      this.top    + this.collisionMargin.top,

      bottom:   this.top    + this.collisionMargin.top +
                this.height - this.collisionMargin.bottom,

      centerX: this.left + this.width/2,

      centerY: this.top + this.height/2
   }
},
...
};
```

Initially, a sprite's collision margin has no effect on its collision rectangle because the margin's properties are all zero, as you can see in **Example 11.2**, which shows the initialization of collision margins in the `Sprite` constructor. Because those property values are all zero, they initially have no effect. In Section 11.7.1 on p. 286, we set collision margin properties to nonzero values when we refine Snail Bait's collision detection.

Example 11.2 Adding collision margins to sprites

```
var Sprite = function (type, artist, behaviors) {
   ...

   this.collisionMargin = {
      left:   0,
      right:  0,
      top:    0,
      bottom: 0
   };
   ...
};
```

Now that we've seen how sprites calculate their collision rectangles, let's see how Snail Bait implements a collide behavior for the runner.

11.3.2 The Runner's Collide Behavior

As you saw in previous chapters, Snail Bait implements sprite activities, such as running, jumping, and exploding, as sprite behaviors, and the same is true for collision detection. At this point in Snail Bait's development, the runner has three behaviors: she can run, jump, and collide with other sprites. Example 11.3 shows the instantiation of the runner sprite with those three behaviors.

Example 11.3 Adding the collide behavior to the runner's array of behaviors

```
var SnailBait = function () {
   ...

   this.runner = new Sprite('runner',          // type
                            this.runnerArtist,  // artist
                            [ this.runBehavior, // behaviors
                              this.jumpBehavior,
                              this.collideBehavior
                            ]);
   ...
};
```

Example 11.4 shows an excerpt from the runner's collide behavior.

Example 11.4 The runner's collide behavior (excerpt)

```
var SnailBait = function () {
   ...

   this.collideBehavior = {
      ...

      execute: function (sprite, time, fps, context,
                         lastAnimationFrameTime) {
         var otherSprite;

         for (var i=0; i < snailBait.sprites.length; ++i) {
            otherSprite = snailBait.sprites[i];

            // sprite is the runner

            if (this.isCandidateForCollision(sprite, otherSprite)) {
               if (this.didCollide(sprite, otherSprite, context)) {
                  this.processCollision(sprite, otherSprite);
               }
            }
         }
      },
      ...
   };
};
```

The collideBehavior object is a sprite behavior by virtue of its execute() method, meaning that Snail Bait invokes the behavior's execute() method for every animation frame. And because the collideBehavior object is associated with the runner, the sprite that Snail Bait passes to the execute() method is always the runner. See Chapter 7 for more information about sprite behaviors.

The collideBehavior object's execute() method encapsulates the three collision detection steps listed earlier with calls to the following methods:

- isCandidateForCollision(sprite, otherSprite)
- didCollide(sprite, otherSprite, context)
- processCollision(sprite, otherSprite)

The implementations of each of those methods are discussed in the following sections.

11.4 Select Candidates for Collision Detection

Sprites are eligible to collide with the runner when

- The sprite is not the runner
- Both the sprite and the runner are visible
- Neither the sprite nor the runner is exploding

The collideBehavior object's isCandidateForCollision() method, shown in Example 11.5, implements that logic.

Example 11.5 Selecting candidates for collision detection: isCandidateForCollision()

```
var SnailBait =  function () {
   ...

   this.collideBehavior = {
      ...

      isCandidateForCollision: function (sprite, otherSprite) {
         // sprite is the runner

         return sprite !== otherSprite &&
               sprite.visible && otherSprite.visible &&
               !sprite.exploding && !otherSprite.exploding;
      },
      ...
   };
```

(Continues)

Example 11.5 *(Continued)*

```
  ...
};
```

Next, let's see how to detect collisions between qualifying sprites.

11.5 Detect Collisions Between the Runner and Another Sprite

The collideBehavior object's didCollide() method, which determines whether the runner has collided with another sprite, is shown in Example 11.6.

Example 11.6 Check for collisions

```
var SnailBait = function () {
   ...

   this.collideBehavior = {
      ...

      didCollide: function (sprite, otherSprite, context) {
         var o = otherSprite.calculateCollisionRectangle(),
             r = sprite.calculateCollisionRectangle();

         // Determine if either of the runner's four corners or her
         // center lies within the other sprite's bounding box.

         context.beginPath();
         context.rect(o.left, o.top, o.right - o.left, o.bottom - o.top);

         return context.isPointInPath(r.left,    r.top)     ||
                context.isPointInPath(r.right,   r.top)     ||

                context.isPointInPath(r.centerX, r.centerY) ||

                context.isPointInPath(r.left,    r.bottom)  ||
                context.isPointInPath(r.right,   r.bottom);
      },
      ...
   };
   ...
};
```

Given the runner's collision rectangle, didCollide() checks to see whether one of the rectangle's corners or its center lies within the other sprite's bounding box, as illustrated in Figure 11.6.

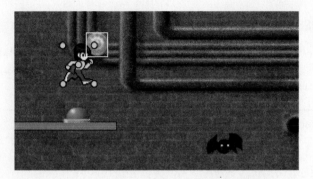

Figure 11.6 If one of the five points (yellow dots) lies within another sprite's collision rectangle (white rectangle), it's a collision.

Determining whether a point lies within a rectangle does not require a great deal of mathematical acuity. The HTML5 canvas element's 2D context makes it even easier with the isPointInPath() method, which returns true if a point lies within the canvas context's current path.

The didCollide() method creates a rectangular path representing the other sprite's bounding box with calls to beginPath() and rect(). The didCollide() method subsequently calls isPointInPath() to determine if any of the aforementioned five points within the runner lies within the other sprite's bounding box. The beginPath(), rect(), and isPointInPath() methods are all methods of the 2D context.

You've seen how to implement collision detection with bounding boxes, but the technique can be more accurate and perform better than we've done so far. In the sections that follow, you'll see how to refine Snail Bait's collision detection by modifying the runner's bounding box and partitioning the game's space.

Now that you've seen how to detect collisions, let's take a look at how to process them.

 NOTE: HTML5 Canvas 2D context hit detection

The canvas context's isPointInPath() method, which determines whether a point lies within an arbitrary path, is a useful method for game developers.

Snail Bait uses isPointInPath() to determine whether points lie within rectangles, which is easy to do on your own. However, determining whether a point lies within an irregularly shaped path is a more challenging task, and that makes isPointInPath() more valuable.

11.6 Process Collisions

Once you detect a collision, you must do something about it. The collide behavior's
processCollision() method processes collisions between the runner and other
sprites, as you can see from Example 11.7.

Example 11.7 Process collisions: processCollision()

```
var SnailBait = function () {
  ...

  this.collideBehavior = {
    ...

    processCollision: function (sprite, otherSprite) {
      if (sprite.jumping && 'platform' === otherSprite.type) {
        this.processPlatformCollisionDuringJump(sprite, otherSprite);
      }
      else if ('coin'     === otherSprite.type       ||
              'sapphire' === otherSprite.type       ||
              'ruby' === otherSprite.type       ||
              'snail' === otherSprite.type) {
        this.processAssetCollision(otherSprite);
      }

      if ('bat' === otherSprite.type       ||
          'bee' === otherSprite.type       ||
          'snail bomb' === otherSprite.type) {
        this.processBadGuyCollision(sprite);
      }
    },

    processBadGuyCollision: function (sprite) {
      snailBait.explode(sprite);   // sprite is the runner
      ...
    },

    processAssetCollision: function (sprite) {
      sprite.visible = false; // sprite is the asset
      ...
    },
    ...
  },
  ...
};
```

When the runner collides with assets—coins, sapphires, or rubies—the collide
behavior's processCollision() method invokes processAssetCollision(),

which makes the asset invisible by setting its visible attribute to false. In Chapter 17, we come back to processAssetCollision() to update the game's score when the runner captures an asset.

When the runner collides with bad guys—bats, bees, or the snail bomb—processBadGuyCollision() explodes the runner with Snail Bait's explode() method. That explode() method is discussed in Chapter 13.

Finally, the processPlatformCollisionDuringJump() method, shown in Example 11.8, processes platform collisions while the runner is jumping.

Example 11.8 processPlatformCollisionDuringJump()

```
var SnailBait = function () {
   ...

   this.collideBehavior = {
      ...

      processPlatformCollisionDuringJump: function (sprite, platform) {
         var isDescending = sprite.descendTimer.isRunning();

         sprite.stopJumping();

         if (isDescending) {
            snailBait.putSpriteOnTrack(sprite, platform.track);
         }
         else {
            sprite.fall();
         }
      },
      ...
   }
};

SnailBait.prototype = {
   ...

   putSpriteOnTrack: function(sprite, track) {
      var SPACE_BETWEEN_SPRITE_AND_TRACK = 2;

      sprite.track = track;
      sprite.top = this.calculatePlatformTop(sprite.track) -
                   sprite.height - SPACE_BETWEEN_SPRITE_AND_TRACK;
   },
   ...
};
```

When the runner collides with a platform while she's descending during a jump, she stops jumping and lands on the platform. If the runner was ascending, she collided with the platform from underneath it, so she falls. For now, the runner's `fall()` method is implemented as shown in Example 11.9.

Example 11.9 Stopgap method for falling

```
SnailBait.prototype = {
   ...

   // Snail Bait calls equipRunnerForFalling() at startup

   equipRunnerForFalling: function () {
      ...

      this.runner.fall = function () {
         snailBait.runner.track = 1;

         snailBait.runner.top =
            snailBait.calculatePlatformTop(snailBait.runner.track) -
                                    snailBait.runner.height;
      };
      ...
   },
   ...
};
```

The runner's `fall()` method immediately places the runner on the bottom track, meaning the top of the lowest platform. In Chapter 12, you'll see how to reimplement that method with realistic falling by incorporating gravity over time.

11.7 Optimize Collision Detection

There's always room for improvement when it comes to collision detection. Snail Bait employs two techniques to increase accuracy and performance: refine the size of sprite collision rectangles and use spatial partitioning.

11.7.1 Refine Bounding Boxes

As you can see from Figure 11.7, collision detection rectangles enclose the sprite they represent. The corners of those rectangles, however, are often transparent. That's the case for the runner, as Figure 11.7 illustrates. Those transparent corners can result in false collisions, that are especially noticeable when two transparent corners collide.

Figure 11.7 The runner's original bounding box

One way to eliminate false collisions resulting from transparent corner areas is to reduce the size of the sprite's collision rectangle, as shown in Figure 11.8.

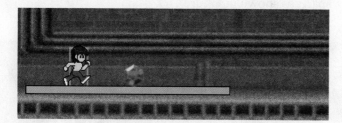

Figure 11.8 The runner's revised bounding box

Snail Bait reduces the size of the runner's collision rectangle by specifying a collision margin, shown in Example 11.10.

Example 11.10 Modifying the runner's collision rectangle

```
SnailBait.prototype = {
   ...

   createRunnerSprite: function () {
      ...

      this.runner.collisionMargin = { // All values represent pixels
         left:   20,
         top:    15,
         right:  15,
         bottom: 20
      };
      ...
   },
   ...
};
```

Sprites use their collision margins to shrink their collision rectangles, as discussed in Section 11.3.1, "Sprite Collision Rectangles," on p. 278.

Reducing the runner's bounding box makes Snail Bait's collision detection more accurate than previously described because it eliminates false collisions. Next, let's see how to make collision detection perform better.

11.7.2 Use Spatial Partitioning

Spatial partitioning involves partitioning a game's space into cells, so that only sprites in the same cell can possibly collide. By eliminating collision detection for sprites that reside in certain cells, spatial partitioning often results in substantial performance increases. Snail Bait gets just such a performance increase by partitioning space, as shown in Figure 11.9.

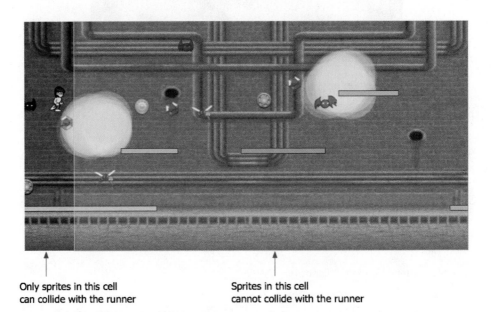

Only sprites in this cell   Sprites in this cell
can collide with the runner   cannot collide with the runner

Figure 11.9 Partitioning space into collision detection cells. In the screenshot, only three sprites are candidates for collision with the runner.

Example 11.11 shows a revised implementation of the collision behavior's isCandidateForCollision() method whereby Snail Bait excludes all sprites in the right-hand cell in Figure 11.9 from collision detection, thus greatly reducing the amount of collision detection the game performs.

Example 11.11 Refining the selection of sprites for collision detection

```
var SnailBait = function () {
    ...

    this.collideBehavior = {
        ...

        isCandidateForCollision: function (sprite, otherSprite) {
            var s, o;

            if (! sprite.calculateCollisionRectangle ||
                ! otherSprite.calculateCollisionRectangle) {
                return false;
            }

            s = sprite.calculateCollisionRectangle(),
            o = otherSprite.calculateCollisionRectangle();

            return o.left < s.right &&
                   sprite !== otherSprite &&
                   sprite.visible && otherSprite.visible &&
                   !sprite.exploding && !otherSprite.exploding;
        },
        ...
    };
    ...
};
```

NOTE: More on spatial partitioning

Snail Bait's spatial partitioning is as primitive as spatial partitioning gets. Other implementations of spatial partitioning such as octrees and binary space partitioning are appropriate for more complicated collision detection scenarios.

11.8 Monitor Collision Detection Performance

Collision detection can easily be a performance bottleneck, especially for more mathematically intense collision detection algorithms such as the Separating Axis Theorem. This chapter has illustrated simple techniques you can use to improve performance, such as refining bounding boxes and using spatial partitioning. But it's also a good idea to constantly monitor your game's performance so you can catch and fix performance problems soon after they appear.

All modern browsers come with sophisticated development environments; for example, Chrome, Safari, Firefox, Internet Explorer, and Opera all let you profile your code as it runs. Figure 11.10 shows Chrome's profiler, which depicts how much time, relative to the total, is spent in individual methods. See Chapter 2 for more about profilers and development tools in general.

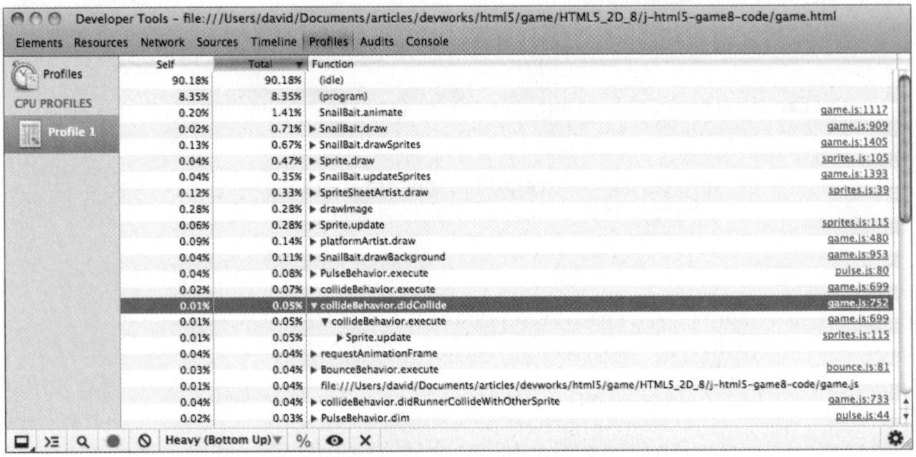

Figure 11.10 Collision detection performance

90% idle?

The top entry in the table displayed in Figure 11.10 means that when the profile was taken, Snail Bait was just waiting around for something to do 90 percent of the time. Snail Bait has such remarkable performance because the profile in Figure 11.10 was taken in the Chrome browser (version 26)—which, like all modern browsers—hardware accelerates the canvas element. Browser vendors typically implement hardware acceleration for the canvas element by translating calls to the Canvas API into WebGL, so you get the convenience of the Canvas API with the performance of WebGL.

NOTE: Snail Bait doesn't always idle 90% of the time

Remarkable performance from hardware acceleration for games that run in the ubiquitous browser can easily be degraded by other activities unrelated to the game; for example, if your system backup software runs while you are playing a game, the game's performance can degrade considerably.

HTML5 games, therefore, must be on constant lookout for unacceptably slow frame rates and should alert the player when the game runs too slowly. We discuss doing that in Chapter 17.

You can see in Figure 11.10 that Snail Bait's didCollide() method takes only 0.05 percent of the game's time. (The Self column, whose value for didCollide() is 0.01 percent, represents only the time spent directly in a method, not including time spent in methods that the method calls.)

11.9 Implement Collision Detection Edge Cases

Collision detection nearly always involves specific code for edge cases in addition to generalized code that accounts for collisions between arbitrary sprites. So far in this chapter, we discussed Snail Bait's generalized code for collision detection, and in this section, we discuss one of Snail Bait's collision detection edge cases.

Snail Bait has two edge cases that are not properly handled by its generalized collision detection code:

1. Collisions between the runner and the snail bomb
2. Collisions between the runner and platforms during a fall

In Chapter 12, we discuss the runner's falling and the consequent collisions between the runner and platforms. In this section we discuss collisions between the runner and the snail bomb, as illustrated in Figure 11.11, which shows the runner and the snail bomb shortly before they collide.

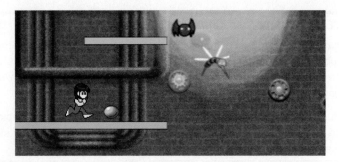

Figure 11.11 Detecting collisions between the runner and the snail bomb

Recall from Section 11.5, "Detect Collisions Between the Runner and Another Sprite," on p. 282 that the runner's collide behavior detects collisions between the runner and other sprites by testing to see if one of five points within the runner's collision rectangle lies within the collision rectangle of the other sprite. If so, a collision has occurred, as illustrated in Figure 11.6 on p. 283. That strategy, however, does not work when the other sprite is the snail bomb, as illustrated in Figure 11.12, which shows that the bomb can pass through the runner without any of the runner's five points intersecting the bomb's collision rectangle.

Figure 11.12 The snail bomb passes through the runner undetected

Because the generalized collision detection code in the runner's collide behavior does not always properly handle collisions between the runner and the snail bomb, we implement an edge case for that collision, as illustrated in Figure 11.13.

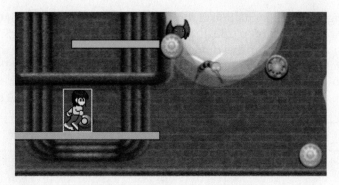

Figure 11.13 Invert collision detection for the snail bomb

We check for collisions between the runner and the snail bomb by effectively inverting the algorithm that we used to detect collisions between the runner and other types of sprites. Instead of checking to see whether points within the runner lie within the bomb's collision rectangle, we check to see if the center of the bomb lies within the runner's collision rectangle. We begin by modifying the runner's collide behavior, as shown in Example 11.12.

Example 11.12 Check for collisions, revised

```
var SnailBait = function () {
   ...

   this.collideBehavior = {
      ...

      didCollide: function (sprite, otherSprite, context) {
         var o = otherSprite.calculateCollisionRectangle(),
             r = sprite.calculateCollisionRectangle();

         if (otherSprite.type === 'snail bomb') {
            return this.didRunnerCollideWithSnailBomb(r, o, context);
         }
         else {
            return this.didRunnerCollideWithOtherSprite(r, o, context);
         }
      },
      ...
   };
   ...
};
```

Like the original implementation of the collide behavior's didCollide() method, listed in Example 11.6 on p. 282, the revised implementation obtains references to collision rectangles for the runner and the other sprite. Unlike the original implementation, however, the didCollide() method subsequently invokes one of two helper methods, depending on the type of the other sprite. The didRunnerCollideWithOtherSprite() method is listed in Example 11.13.

Example 11.13   Check for collision with sprites other than the snail bomb

```
var SnailBait = function () {
   ...

   this.collideBehavior = {
      ...

      didRunnerCollideWithOtherSprite: function (r, o, context) {
         // Determine if either of the runner's four corners or her
         // center lies within the other sprite's bounding box.

         context.beginPath();
         context.rect(o.left, o.top, o.right - o.left, o.bottom - o.top);

         return context.isPointInPath(r.left,   r.top)         ||
                context.isPointInPath(r.right,   r.top)         ||

                context.isPointInPath(r.centerX, r.centerY) ||

                context.isPointInPath(r.left,   r.bottom)      ||
                context.isPointInPath(r.right,   r.bottom);
      },
      ...
   };
   ...
};
```

The didRunnerCollideWithOtherSprite() method checks to see if any of the runner's five points lie within the collision rectangle of the other sprite, which is identical to the original implementation of didCollide(). The most interesting aspect of the revised didCollide() method is the didRunnerCollideWithSnailBomb() method, listed in Example 11.14.

The didRunnerCollideWithSnailBomb() method creates a rectangular path around the runner's collision rectangle. The method then checks to see whether the bomb's center lies inside that path; if so, the runner and the snail bomb have collided.

Example 11.14 Check for collision with the snail bomb

```javascript
var SnailBait = function () {
   ...

   this.collideBehavior = {
      ...

      didRunnerCollideWithSnailBomb: function (r, o, context) {
         // Determine if the center of the snail bomb lies
         // within the runner's bounding box.

         context.beginPath();
         context.rect(r.left + snailBait.spriteOffset,
                      r.top, r.right - r.left, r.bottom - r.top);

         return context.isPointInPath(o.centerX, o.centerY);
      },
      ...
   };
   ...
};
```

11.10 Conclusion

Collision detection can be one of the most challenging aspects of implementing video games.

In this chapter you saw an overview of collision detection techniques, followed by an examination of Snail Bait's bounding box collision detection. The collision detection that we implemented in this chapter has the curious distinction of not performing any math whatsoever other than addition and subtraction, which is rare among collision detection algorithms. The reason we were able to eschew mathematics of any complexity entirely in this chapter is because of the isPointInPath() method of the HTML5 canvas element's 2D graphics context. That method, which determines whether a point is in the current path, performs all the math that we needed in this chapter.

Optimizing collision detection is as important as implementing it in first place, so in this chapter we discussed two common techniques for making collision detection more accurate with better performance: refining bounding boxes and using spatial partition.

This chapter is the least of the collision detection arcana; indeed, entire books are available on the topic. When you implement collision detection for your own game, explore your options and select the simplest implementation that will suffice for your needs.

Finally, the collision detection that we implemented in this chapter cannot detect collisions between the runner and a platform when the runner falls from the topmost platform to the bottommost. In that case the runner is moving too fast and the platforms are too thin for the bounding box collision detection that we implemented in this chapter. At the end of Chapter 12 we will see how to implement collision detection for that edge case.

11.11 Exercises

1. Profile the final version of Snail Bait and note how much time Snail Bait is idle. Subsequently, remove spatial partitioning from Snail Bait's collision detection and run the profiler again. How does spatial partitioning affect performance?

2. In the version of the game for this chapter, implement a method that draws sprite collision rectangles as the game is in progress, as illustrated in Figure 11.5 on p. 278. Toggle the drawing of sprite collision rectangles with a hot key of your choice.

3. Experiment with bounding-box sizes by modifying the collision margins for different sprites.

4. In the `execute()` method of the runner's collide behavior, replace the call to `didRunnerCollideWithSnailBomb()` with `didRunnerCollideWithOther-Sprite()`. That causes Snail Bait to use its generalized collision detection for collisions between the runner and the snail bomb. Play the game and verify that the runner cannot be harmed by snail bombs unless she's jumping or falling. Explain why the runner is vulnerable while jumping or falling, but not when she's running on a platform.

5. Implement a power-up that's triggered when the runner captures an orange coin. Deactivate the power-up when the runner captures a blue coin. The power-up makes the runner invincible to snail bombs while she's running on platforms, but not while she's jumping or falling.

CHAPTER **12**

Gravity

Topics in This Chapter

In Chapter 9 you saw how to simulate gravity during a sprite's jumps and bounces by using easing functions that slow time on the sprite's ascent and accelerate it on the descent. That manipulation of time affects all time's derivatives, including motion, so sprites slow as they ascend and speed up as they descend, similar to how gravity acts on the objects the sprites represent.

Sometimes, however, an approximation of gravity is not enough; for example, an artillery game should be more precise about how gravity affects rounds as they fly through the air. In this short chapter, you will see how to directly affect a falling sprite's motion to simulate gravity. You will also see how to detect collisions between the runner and platforms when the runner is falling, a collision detection edge case that's not properly handled by the more general collision detection we implemented in Chapter 11.

12.1 Equip the Runner for Falling

Snail Bait's runner falls when she either runs off the edge of a platform or collides
with a platform from underneath it. Figure 12.1 shows the runner falling off the
edge of a platform.

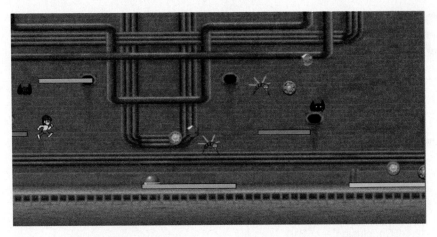

Figure 12.1 Falling off the edge of a platform

The runner also falls when she misses a platform at the end of a jump's descent,
as illustrated in Figure 12.2.

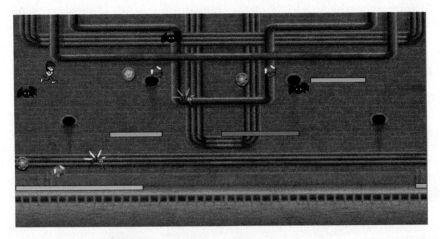

Figure 12.2 Falling at the end of a jump

The runner falls by virtue of her fall behavior. Example 12.1 shows the instantiation of the runner sprite, specifying her final array of behaviors.

Example 12.1 Creating the runner with a fall behavior

```
SnailBait.prototype = {
   ...

   createRunnerSprite: function () {
      ...

      this.runner = new Sprite(
                         'runner',

                         new SpriteSheetArtist(this.spritesheet,
                                               this.runnerCellsRight),

                         [
                             this.runBehavior,
                             this.jumpBehavior,
                             this.collideBehavior,
                             this.runnerExplodeBehavior,
                             this.fallBehavior
                         ]
                      );
      ...
   },
   ...
};
```

Recall that when the game starts, Snail Bait invokes the equipRunner() method, which equips the runner for both jumping and falling by invoking equipRunnerForJumping() and equipRunnerForFalling(). The latter method, listed in Example 12.2, contains the implementation of the runner's fall() and stopFalling() methods.

Example 12.2 The runner's fall() method

```
SnailBait.prototype = {
   ...

   equipRunner: function () {
      ...

      this.equipRunnerForJumping();
      this.equipRunnerForFalling();
   },
```

(Continues)

Example 12.2 *(Continued)*

```
equipRunnerForFalling: function () {
   this.runner.fallTimer = new AnimationTimer(); // this is snailBait
   this.runner.falling   = false;

   this.runner.fall = function (initialVelocity) {
      this.falling = true; // this is the runner

      this.velocityY       = initialVelocity || 0;
      this.initialVelocityY = initialVelocity || 0;

      this.fallTimer.start(snailBait.timeSystem.calculateGameTime());
   };

   this.runner.stopFalling = function () {
      this.falling  = false; // this is the runner
      this.velocityY = 0;

      this.fallTimer.stop(snailBait.timeSystem.calculateGameTime());
   };
},
...
};
```

The `fall()` method sets the runner's initial vertical velocity, sets her `falling` property to `true`, and starts an animation timer to track her fall's elapsed time.

The runner's fall behavior is triggered with the runner's `falling` property. The runner's `fall()` method sets that property to `true`, thereby triggering the fall behavior.

While the runner's `falling` property is `true`, the fall behavior takes action every animation frame. When the runner's `stopFalling()` method sets the property to `false`, the fall behavior is deactivated. The `stopFalling()` method also stops the animation timer and sets the runner's vertical velocity to zero.

We discuss the runner's fall behavior in Section 12.2.1, "The Runner's Fall Behavior," on p. 302, but first let's see how Snail Bait incorporates gravity in general.

12.2 Incorporate Gravity

Near the Earth's surface, falling objects accelerate quickly. Without allowing for wind resistance, a falling object's velocity increases by nearly 36 km/hr (or 21 miles/hr) every second. The consequence of gravity for game developers is that calculating a falling sprite's position means they must first calculate its constantly changing velocity.

Fortunately, calculating a falling object's velocity is straightforward. Multiply the force of gravity (9.81 m/s/s or 32 ft/s/s) by the sprite's elapsed fall time, and add that value to the sprite's initial vertical velocity when it began to fall. The equation is

$$v = v_i + G * t$$

v represents the sprite's vertical velocity, v_i is the initial vertical velocity, G is the force of gravity, and t is the elapsed time of the fall.

As is often the case for equations, the confusing part is not the math but the units, because the result of the preceding equation leaves you with meters (or feet) per second. To make that value more useful, Snail Bait converts it to pixels per second. First, the game calculates a pixels:meter ratio at the beginning of the game as follows.

1. In the game's HTML, define the width of the game in pixels. SnailBait's width is 800 pixels.
2. In the game's JavaScript, define the width of the game in meters. SnailBait's width is 13 meters.
3. Divide the width in pixels by the width in meters to get a ratio of pixels-to-meter.

With a pixel:meter ratio in hand, Snail Bait positions falling sprites as follows.

1. When the runner begins to fall, the runner's fall() method records her initial vertical velocity (see Example 12.2).
2. Subsequently, for every animation frame, Snail Bait uses the pixel:meter ratio to position the falling sprite.

   a) Use $v = v_i + G * t$ to calculate the sprite's velocity in meters/second.
   b) Convert the velocity to pixels/second by multiplying the velocity in meters/second by the pixel:meter ratio.
   c) Calculate the number of pixels to move the sprite in the vertical direction by multiplying the sprite's vertical velocity in pixels/second times the elapsed time of the preceding animation frame in seconds, which yields a value representing pixels. See Chapter 3 for more details on time-based motion.

Let's convert the preceding algorithm into code. The first step is to define the force of gravity and the game's pixel:meter ratio, as shown in Example 12.3.

Example 12.3 Constants pertaining to gravity and falling

```
var SnailBait = function () {
  ...

  this.GRAVITY_FORCE = 9.81; // meters/second/second
  this.CANVAS_WIDTH_IN_METERS = 13;  // Proportional to sprite sizes

  this.PIXELS_PER_METER = this.canvas.width /
                          this.CANVAS_WIDTH_IN_METERS;

  ...
};
```

The second step is to calculate the runner's vertical velocity—depending on her initial vertical velocity when the fall began and the amount of time she has been falling—and position her accordingly. That functionality is the responsibility of the runner's fall behavior, which we discuss next.

12.2.1 The Runner's Fall Behavior

The runner's fall behavior has four distinct responsibilities:

- Start falling when the runner is running without a platform underneath her
- Adjust the runner's vertical position as she falls
- When the runner falls on a platform, stop falling and place the runner's feet on the platform
- When the runner falls through the bottom of the game, invoke Snail Bait's loseLife() method

Like all behaviors, the runner's fall behavior has an execute() method, listed in Example 12.4, that Snail Bait invokes for every animation frame. Also, because the fall behavior is associated with the runner, the sprite that Snail Bait passes to the behavior's execute() method is always the runner. See Chapter 7 for more about sprite behaviors and how Snail Bait invokes them.

If the runner is falling and she's in play and not exploding, the fall behavior's execute() method adjusts her vertical position with the behavior's moveDown() method.

If the runner is exploding during a fall, she stops falling. If she's out of play, meaning she has fallen through the bottom of the canvas, she also stops falling and the player loses a life.

If the runner is neither falling nor jumping and does not have a platform underneath her, she starts falling.

Example 12.4 The fall behavior's execute() method

```
var SnailBait = function () {
    ...

    this.fallBehavior = {
        ...

        execute: function (sprite, now, fps, context,
                           lastAnimationFrameTime) {
            if (sprite.falling) {
                if (! this.isOutOfPlay(sprite) && !sprite.exploding) {
                    this.moveDown(sprite, now, lastAnimationFrameTime);
                }
                else { // Out of play or exploding
                    sprite.stopFalling();

                    if (this.isOutOfPlay(sprite)) {
                        snailBait.loseLife();
                        snailBait.runner.visible = false;
                        snailBait.playSound(snailBait.electricityFlowingSound);
                    }
                }
            }
            else { // Not falling
                if ( ! sprite.jumping &&
                     ! snailBait.platformUnderneath(sprite)) {
                    sprite.fall();
                }
            }
        },
        ...
    };
    ...
};
```

The fall behavior's moveDown() method is listed in Example 12.5.

The moveDown() method sets the runner's vertical velocity by invoking the behavior's setSpriteVelocity() method. The moveDown() method subsequently calculates the distance the runner will drop given the newly calculated velocity, the current time, and the time of the last animation frame, by invoking the behavior's calculateVerticalDrop() method.

If, given the drop distance, the runner will not fall below her current track (recall that platforms move on three horizontal tracks, as discussed in Chapter 3), moveDown() moves the runner down by that distance. And since the Y coordinates for the canvas coordinate system increase from top to bottom, moveDown() adds to the runner's Y coordinate to move her down, instead of subtracting, as you might think.

If the runner's feet will fall below her current track and a platform is underneath her, moveDown() puts the runner on the platform and stops her fall. If the runner will fall below her current track and no platform is underneath her, moveDown() decrements her track property and moves her down by the drop distance.

Example 12.5 The fall behavior's moveDown() method

```
var SnailBait = function () {
  ...

  this.fallBehavior = {
    ...

    moveDown: function (sprite, now, lastAnimationFrameTime) {
      var dropDistance;

      this.setSpriteVelocity(sprite, now);

      dropDistance = this.calculateVerticalDrop(
                        sprite, now, lastAnimationFrameTime);

      if ( ! this.willFallBelowCurrentTrack(sprite, dropDistance)) {
        sprite.top += dropDistance;
      }
      else { // Will fall below current track
        if (snailBait.platformUnderneath(sprite)) {
          this.fallOnPlatform(sprite);
          sprite.stopFalling();
        }
        else { // Below current track with no platform underneath
          sprite.track--;
          sprite.top += dropDistance;
        }
      }
    },
    ...
  };
  ...
};
```

The support methods invoked by the fall behavior's execute() and moveDown() methods are listed in Example 12.6.

Example 12.6 Fall behavior support methods

```
var SnailBait = function () {
    ...

    this.fallBehavior = {
        ...

        isOutOfPlay: function (sprite) {
            return sprite.top > snailBait.canvas.height;
        },

        setSpriteVelocity: function (sprite, now) {
            sprite.velocityY =
                sprite.initialVelocityY + snailBait.GRAVITY_FORCE *
                (sprite.fallTimer.getElapsedTime(now)/1000) *
                snailBait.PIXELS_PER_METER;
        },

        calculateVerticalDrop: function (sprite, now,
                                        lastAnimationFrameTime) {
            return sprite.velocityY * (now - lastAnimationFrameTime) / 1000;
        },

        willFallBelowCurrentTrack: function (sprite, dropDistance) {
            return sprite.top + sprite.height + dropDistance >
                snailBait.calculatePlatformTop(sprite.track);
        },

        fallOnPlatform: function (sprite) {
            sprite.stopFalling();
            snailBait.putSpriteOnTrack(sprite, sprite.track);
            snailBait.playSound(snailBait.thudSound);
        },
        ...
    };
    ...
};
```

The setSpriteVelocity() method calculates how much speed the runner has picked up since she started to fall by multiplying the force of gravity times the runner's elapsed fall time, yielding velocity in meters per second. The setSpriteVelocity() method subsequently multiplies that velocity by Snail Bait's pixels-to-meter ratio to turn the velocity's units into pixels per second. Finally, setSpriteVelocity() determines the runner's current velocity by adding the calculated velocity to the runner's initial velocity as she began to fall.

The calculateVerticalDrop() method uses the time-based motion discussed in Chapter 3 to calculate how far the runner should drop for the current animation frame: multiply the runner's velocity times the amount of time, in seconds, that has passed since the last animation frame.

The moveDown() method invokes Snail Bait's platformUnderneath() method, which is listed in Example 12.7. The platformUnderneath() method returns a reference to the platform underneath the runner if there is one, or undefined otherwise.

Example 12.7 Snail Bait's platformUnderneath() method

```
SnailBait.prototype = {
   ...

   platformUnderneath: function (sprite, track) {
      var platform,
          platformUnderneath,
          sr = sprite.calculateCollisionRectangle(), // Sprite rect
          pr; // Platform rectangle

      if (track === undefined) {
         track = sprite.track; // Look on sprite track only
      }

      for (var i=0; i < snailBait.platforms.length; ++i) {
         platform = snailBait.platforms[i];
         pr = platform.calculateCollisionRectangle();

         if (track === platform.track) {
            if (sr.right > pr.left  && sr.left < pr.right) {
               platformUnderneath = platform;
               break;
            }
         }
      }
      return platformUnderneath;
   },
   ...
};
```

Next let's see how to calculate the runner's initial velocity when she falls at the end of a jump.

12.2.2 Calculate Initial Falling Velocities

When the runner runs off the end of a platform or collides with one from underneath, she starts to fall with no vertical velocity. When she misses a platform at the end of a jump, however, she begins to fall with the vertical velocity she had at the end of the jump's descent. Example 12.8 shows how the runner's jump behavior uses the GRAVITY_FORCE and PIXELS_PER_METER constants that are defined in Example 12.3 on p. 302 to calculate that initial velocity.

Example 12.8 Falling at the end of a jump

```
var SnailBait = function () {
   ...

   this.jumpBehavior = {
      ...

      finishDescent: function (sprite, now) {
         sprite.stopJumping();

         if (snailBait.platformUnderneath(sprite)) {
            sprite.top = sprite.verticalLaunchPosition;
         }
         else {
            sprite.fall(snailBait.GRAVITY_FORCE *
               (sprite.descendTimer.getElapsedTime(now)/1000) *
               snailBait.PIXELS_PER_METER);
         }
      },
      ...
   };
   ...
};
```

The runner's vertical velocity as she's falling is the force of gravity times the elapsed descent time, times the game's pixel-to-meter ratio: (9.81 m/s/s) × (*elapsed descent time in seconds*) × (800 pixels / 13 m).

What about the runner's horizontal position?

The runner's fall behavior is only concerned with placing the runner vertically. The fall behavior doesn't need to modify the runner's horizontal position. Although it looks like the runner is moving horizontally, she never actually moves in the horizontal direction at all. Instead, the background moves beneath her to make it look as though she's moving horizontally. See Chapter 3 for more information on scrolling the game's background.

12.2.3 Pause When the Runner Is Falling

As we discussed in Chapter 8, behaviors that time their activities must implement
pause() and unpause() methods so that they can pause and resume in concert
with the game as a whole. The implementation of those methods for the runner's
fall behavior is shown in Example 12.9.

Example 12.9 Pausing and unpausing the fall behavior

```
var SnailBait = function () {
   ...

   this.fallBehavior = {
      pause: function (sprite, now) {
         sprite.fallTimer.pause(now);
      },

      unpause: function (sprite, now) {
         sprite.fallTimer.unpause(now);
      },
   }
   ...
}
```

The fall behavior tracks elapsed time during falls with the runner's fall timer.
Therefore, the behavior's pause() and unpause() methods simply pause and
unpause that timer.

 NOTE: Gravity is a special case

Gravity produces nonlinear motion. Previously, we implemented nonlinear
jumping by using easing functions that approximate gravity with ease-out and
ease-in functions. If you vary those functions, you can produce an infinite spec-
trum of nonlinear motion, meaning that gravity is a special case of nonlinear
motion in general.

12.3 Collision Detection, Redux

Recall that the fall behavior's moveDown() method listed in Example 12.5 on p. 304
detects when the runner collides with a platform while she's falling and places
her on that platform. In effect, the moveDown() method is dabbling in collision
detection, which may seem strange considering that we've already implemented
collision detection in the previous chapter. However, the collision detection we

implemented in the last chapter is insufficient to detect collisions between the falling runner and a platform underneath.

The collision detection we implemented in the last chapter checks to see if one of five points within the runner's collision rectangle lies within another sprite's collision rectangle; if so, the runner has collided with the other sprite, as shown in Figure 12.3.

Figure 12.3 The runner colliding with a coin (yellow dots represent points in the runner's collision rectangle)

Most of Snail Bait's sprites, such as bees, bats, and coins, are sufficiently wide and tall enough so that no matter how fast the runner is moving, the game reliably detects when one of the points within the runner's collision rectangle intersects another sprite's collision rectangle.

Platforms, however, are a different story because they are very thin, and *when the runner is moving fast enough, points in her collision rectangle can jump over a platform in a single animation frame.*

When the runner jumps and hits her head on a platform above her, as shown in Figure 12.4, *she is moving slowly enough* that the collision detection we implemented in the last chapter detects the collision.

However, when the runner is moving very fast, checking those five points for intersection with the platform's collision rectangle will not work; for example, Figure 12.5 shows the runner just as she starts to fall after a jump. When that screenshot was taken, the runner already had considerable vertical velocity from the descent of her jump, and by the time she reaches the bottommost platform, she will be moving at approximately 475 pixels per second. If the game is running at 60 frames per second, that means the runner is falling at 475 ÷ 60 = 8 pixels per frame. Because platforms are eight pixels high, the points in the runner's collision rectangle can—and regularly do—jump over a platform in a single animation frame, especially if the frame rate dips a little (for a frame rate of 30 frames per second, the runner falls at 16 pixels per frame). Because those collisions are not detected by the general collision detection we implemented in the last chapter, the runner's fall behavior implements that edge case.

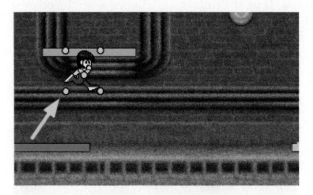

Figure 12.4 The runner collides with a platform from underneath.

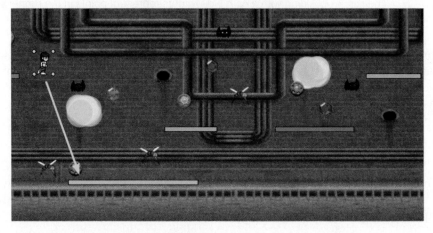

Figure 12.5 The runner falls after completing a jump.

12.4 Conclusion

In this chapter, you saw how to make sprites fall under the influence of gravity and how to detect collisions when one or more of the participants is very small or moving very fast. Both of those skills are essential for implementing just about any kind of video game, from pinball games to platformers.

Collision detection is one of the most difficult aspects of game development. Typically, game developers add refinements such as the spatial partitioning we discussed in the last chapter to proven collision detection techniques, for example, bounding boxes or ray casting, along with specialized code for edge cases. In this chapter you saw some specialized code in the fall behavior's moveDown() method to detect collisions between the runner and platforms when the runner is falling.

At this point we are nearly done with implementing gameplay. In the next chapter you will see how to implement sprite animations and add special effects to your games.

12.5 Exercises

1. Add a log statement to the end of the runner's fall() method that prints her initial vertical velocity, in pixels per second, after she starts to fall. You should see approximately 310 pixels per second. If the game is running at 60 frames per second, how many pixels per second is the runner falling for each animation frame?

2. Add a log statement to the beginning of the runner's stopFalling() method prints her vertical velocity, in pixels per second. How many pixels per second is she moving vertically at that time?

3. With the log statements from the preceding exercises intact, do something to slow Snail Bait enough so that you see the game's running slowly warning. Good ways to slow the game include running the browser's profiler during gameplay, running your system backup software, or opening an application that has semitransparent windows. When the game displays the running slowly warning, click the Do not show this warning again and play the game. Are the velocities in line with what you saw in Exercises 1 and 2? Why or why not?

4. With the log statements from the preceding exercises intact, modify Snail Bait so that it runs in slow motion (at 25% speed). See Section 10.3.2, "Implement a Game Method that Uses the Time System to Modify the Flow of Time," on p. 259 for details about how to do that with Snail Bait's setTimeRate() method. Subsequently, play the game, and check the log statements. Were the values roughly one-quarter of what they were before, or were they the same? Explain the numbers.

Sprite Animations and Special Effects

Sprites often animate through a temporary sequence of images; for example, Figure 13.1 shows, from top to bottom, the explosion animation that Snail Bait displays when the runner runs into a bee.

In addition to special effects, such as exploding bees, that affect one or more sprites at a time, games often implement special effects that affect the game as a whole. When the runner loses her life, for example, Snail Bait transitions to the next life by slowing time and fading the game's canvas almost entirely from view.

In this chapter you will learn how to do the following:

- Implement temporary sprite animations (Section 13.1 on p. 314)
- Create special effects for the game as a whole (Section 13.2 on p. 320)

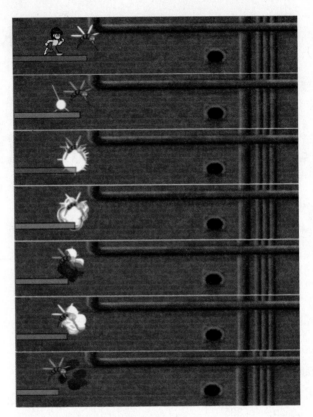

Figure 13.1 The runner exploding after a collision

- Transition between lives (Section 13.2.2 on p. 323)
- Choreograph effects between sprites by making bees explode when the runner lands on a button (Section 13.3 on p. 329)

13.1 Implement Sprite Animations

Snail Bait implements sprite animations, such as the one shown in Figure 13.1, with cell switch behaviors. A cell switch behavior, when triggered, temporarily changes the cells that a sprite's artist draws. For example, when the runner explodes, a cell switch behavior changes her animation cells to those shown in Figure 13.2 for 0.5 seconds.

Figure 13.2 The explosion images from Snail Bait's sprite sheet (shown with a gray background to make the white parts of the explosion visible)

The CellSwitchBehavior constructor is shown in Example 13.1.

Example 13.1 CellSwitchBehavior constructor

```
var CellSwitchBehavior = function (
        cells,       // An array of rectangles in the game's sprite sheet
        duration,    // The duration of the switch in milliseconds
        trigger,     // A function that triggers the behavior
        callback) {  // A function the behavior invokes after the animation

   this.cells    = cells;
   this.duration = duration || 1000;
   this.trigger  = trigger;
   this.callback = callback;
};
```

The CellSwitchBehavior constructor takes four arguments. The first is an array of bounding boxes in Snail Bait's sprite sheet. Those bounding boxes are the temporary animation cells, and the argument is mandatory. The remaining arguments are optional. The second argument is the duration of the cell switch in milliseconds. If you don't specify a duration, it defaults to one second.

The last two arguments are functions. The trigger function returns a Boolean value; when it returns a truthy value, the cell switch behavior takes action. If the trigger function returns a value that does not evaluate to true, then the cell switch behavior does nothing.

Cell switch behaviors invoke their callback function when the cell switch is complete, passing a reference to the associated sprite and the cell switch behavior itself.

If you don't specify a trigger function, the associated cell switch behavior never switches cells, and if you don't specify a callback function you won't receive any notification when the animation is complete.

Like all behaviors, cell switch behaviors implement an execute() method that Snail Bait invokes every animation frame. That method is shown in Example 13.2.

Example 13.2 The cell switch behavior's execute() method

```
CellSwitchBehavior.prototype = {
   ...

   execute: function(sprite, now, fps, context,
                      lastAnimationFrameTime) {
      if (this.trigger &&
          this.trigger(sprite, now, fps, lastAnimationFrameTime)) {

         if (sprite.artist.cells !== this.cells) {
            this.switchCells(sprite, now);
         }
         else if (now - sprite.switchStartTime > this.duration) {
            this.revert(sprite, now);
         }
      }
   }
};
```

The cell switch behavior takes action only when the behavior has a trigger function and that function returns true. In that case, if the switch hasn't taken place yet, the behavior switches the sprite's animation cells. If the switch has taken place and the elapsed time since the switch took place is greater than the animation's duration, then the cell switch behavior restores the cells to their original state.

The behavior's switchCells() and revert() methods are listed in Example 13.3.

Example 13.3 Switching and reverting animation cells

```
CellSwitchBehavior.prototype = {
   ...

   switchCells: function (sprite, now) {
      sprite.originalCells = sprite.artist.cells;
      sprite.originalIndex = sprite.artist.cellIndex;

      sprite.switchStartTime = now;

      sprite.artist.cells = this.cells;
      sprite.artist.cellIndex = 0;
   },

   revert: function (sprite, now) {
      sprite.artist.cells = sprite.originalCells;
      sprite.artist.cellIndex = sprite.originalIndex;
```

```
    if (this.callback) {
        this.callback(sprite, this);
    }
},
    ...
};
```

The cell switch behavior's `switchCells()` method switches cells by saving the original cells and the index pointing to the current cell, and replacing them with the temporary cells and zero, respectively. It also records the time of the switch.

Subsequently, after the switch's duration is over, the `revert()` method returns the sprite's cells and the index to what they were before the switch and invokes the cell switch behavior's callback function.

To animate through the cells that the sprite temporarily displays, the sprite must have some other behavior—such as the runner's run behavior discussed in Section 7.3 on p. 187 or cycle behaviors used by many of Snail Bait's other sprites—to cycle through those cells. For example, Example 13.4 shows the creation of the runner sprite with the runner's explode behavior.

Example 13.4 Creating the runner sprite, revised

```
SnailBait.prototype = {
    ...

    createRunnerSprite: function () {
        ...

        this.runner = new Sprite(
                        'runner',

                        new SpriteSheetArtist(this.spritesheet,
                                              this.runnerCellsRight),

                        [
                            this.runBehavior,
                            this.jumpBehavior,
                            this.collideBehavior,
                            this.runnerExplodeBehavior
                        ]
                    );
        ...
    },
    ...
};
```

Recall that the runner's run behavior continuously cycles through the runner's animation cells. The runner's explode behavior, listed in **Example 13.5**, temporarily changes those animation cells.

Example 13.5 Runner explode behavior

```
var SnailBait = function () {
   ...

   this.RUNNER_EXPLOSION_DURATION = 500; // milliseconds

   this.explosionCells = [
      {
         left: 3    top: 48,
         width: 50, height: this.EXPLOSION_CELLS_HEIGHT
      },

      {
         left: 63,  top: 48,
         width: 70, height: this.EXPLOSION_CELLS_HEIGHT
      },

      {
         left: 146, top: 48,
         width: 70, height: this.EXPLOSION_CELLS_HEIGHT
      },

      {
         left: 233, top: 48,
         width: 70, height: this.EXPLOSION_CELLS_HEIGHT
      },

      {
         left: 308, top: 48,
         width: 70, height: this.EXPLOSION_CELLS_HEIGHT
      },

      {
         left: 392, top: 48,
         width: 70, height: this.EXPLOSION_CELLS_HEIGHT
      },

      { left: 473, top: 48,
        width: 70, height: this.EXPLOSION_CELLS_HEIGHT
      }
   ];

   this.runnerExplodeBehavior = new CellSwitchBehavior(
      this.explosionCells,
      this.RUNNER_EXPLOSION_DURATION,
```

```
function (sprite, now, fps, lastAnimationFrameTime) { // Trigger
    return sprite.exploding;
},

function (sprite, animator) { // Callback
    sprite.exploding = false;
}
);
...
};
```

The runner's explode behavior is an instance of CellSwitchBehavior. The cells are the explosionCells, the duration of the switch is 500 ms, and the behavior's trigger is the runner's exploding property. The callback that the behavior invokes at the end of the animation sets the runner's exploding property to false, ensuring that the explosion does not repeat.

The trigger for the runner's explode behavior—meaning the exploding property of the runner—is set to true by Snail Bait's explode() method, listed in Example 13.6.

Example 13.6 Snail Bait's explode() method

```
SnailBait.prototype = {
    ...

    explode: function (sprite) {
        if ( ! sprite.exploding) {
            if (sprite.runAnimationRate === 0) {
                sprite.runAnimationRate = this.RUN_ANIMATION_RATE;
            }

            sprite.exploding = true;
            this.playSound(this.explosionSound);
        }
    },
    ...
};
```

Snail Bait explodes several types of sprites: the runner, bees, and bats. If the sprite is the runner and her run animation rate (stored in the runAnimationRate property) is zero, that means she is not cycling through her images because she's jumping. To ensure that the runner cycles through the explosion cells when she's exploding during a jump, the explode() method sets her animation rate to its normal value.

Subsequently, the `explode()` method sets the sprite's `exploding` property to `true`, which triggers its explode behavior. Snail Bait invokes its `explode()` method from several places. One of those places is the collide behavior, as shown in Example 13.7.

Example 13.7 Exploding the runner

```
var SnailBait = function () {
   ...

   this.collideBehavior = {
      ...

      processBadGuyCollision: function (sprite) {
         snailBait.explode(sprite);  // sprite is the runner
         ...
      },
      ...
   };
   ...
};
```

Cell switch behaviors let you implement many types of effects that are specific to one or more individual sprites. Games often have special effects that apply to the game as a whole, however, as we discuss next.

 NOTE: Although they maintain state, cell switch behaviors do not maintain state that directly affects their associated sprites. Instead, cell switch behaviors store sprite-specific state, such as the original cells and original index into those cells, in the sprites themselves. As a result, you can use cell switch behaviors as flyweights, as evidenced by the lone cell switch behavior that Snail Bait uses for all its bees. See Section 13.3.1 on p. 332 for more details.

13.2 Create Special Effects

Snail Bait has two special effects that apply to the entire game: shaking the game and transitioning between lives. When the runner collides with a bat, a bee, or the snail bomb, the runner explodes as you saw in the preceding section. When the explosion finishes, Snail Bait shakes the entire game back and forth before transitioning to either the next life or to the end game sequence.

In the previous section, you saw how cell switch behaviors neatly encapsulate the code to temporarily animate a sprite through a sequence of cells. To implement shaking the game and life transitions, we take a more ad hoc approach, using JavaScript's `setTimeout()` function for the relatively simple business of shaking the game and using CSS transitions for transitioning between lives.

13.2.1 Shake the Game

Snail Bait shakes the game with a `shake()` method. It invokes that method in the collide behavior's `processBadGuyCollision()` method, as shown in Example 13.8. See Chapter 11 for a discussion of the collide behavior.

Example 13.8 Shaking the game when colliding with bad guys

```
var SnailBait = function () {
   ...

   this.collideBehavior = {
      ...

      processBadGuyCollision: function (sprite) {
         snailBait.explode(sprite);  // sprite is the runner
         snailBait.shake();
         ...
      },
      ...
   };
};
```

The `processBadGuyCollision()` method explodes the runner and shakes the game.

Although they are not suitable for time-critical animations, as discussed in Chapter 3, the `setTimeout()` and `setInterval()` JavaScript functions are nonetheless useful for implementing special effects. When Snail Bait's runner explodes, for example, Snail Bait uses `setTimeout()` to shake the entire game back and forth with its `shake()` method, listed in Example 13.9.

Example 13.9 Shaking Snail Bait

```
SnailBait.prototype = {
   ...

   shake: function () {
      var SHAKE_INTERVAL = 80, // milliseconds
          v = snailBait.BACKGROUND_VELOCITY*1.5,
          originalVelocity = snailBait.bgVelocity;
```

(Continues)

Example 13.9 *(Continued)*

```
        this.bgVelocity = -v;

    setTimeout( function (e) {
     snailBait.bgVelocity = v;
     setTimeout( function (e) {
        snailBait.bgVelocity = -v;
        setTimeout( function (e) {
          snailBait.bgVelocity = v;
          setTimeout( function (e) {
            snailBait.bgVelocity = -v;
            setTimeout( function (e) {
              snailBait.bgVelocity = v;
              setTimeout( function (e) {
                snailBait.bgVelocity = -v;
                setTimeout( function (e) {
                  snailBait.bgVelocity = v;
                  setTimeout( function (e) {
                    snailBait.bgVelocity = -v;
                    setTimeout( function (e) {
                      snailBait.bgVelocity = v;
                      setTimeout( function (e) {
                        snailBait.bgVelocity = -v;
                        setTimeout( function (e) {
                          snailBait.bgVelocity = v;
                          setTimeout( function (e) {
                            snailBait.bgVelocity =
                              originalVelocity;
                          }, SHAKE_INTERVAL);
                        }, SHAKE_INTERVAL);
                      }, SHAKE_INTERVAL);
                    }, SHAKE_INTERVAL);
                  }, SHAKE_INTERVAL);
                }, SHAKE_INTERVAL);
              }, SHAKE_INTERVAL);
            }, SHAKE_INTERVAL);
          }, SHAKE_INTERVAL);
        }, SHAKE_INTERVAL);
      }, SHAKE_INTERVAL);
    }, SHAKE_INTERVAL);
  },
  ...
};
```

The shake() method shakes the game back and forth at a velocity equal to 1.5 times the game's normal background velocity. Every 80 milliseconds, Snail Bait reverses the sign of that velocity to move everything in the game in the opposite direction. When the shaking is finished, the `shake()` method restores the game's background velocity to what it was when the method was originally invoked.

Alternatively, you could implement the `shake()` method with a recursive function, as shown in Example 13.10.

Example 13.10 A recursive variant of the `shake()` method (functionality identical to Example 13.9)

```
SnailBait.prototype = {
   ...

   shake: function () {
      var NUM_SHAKES = 12,
          SHAKE_INTERVAL = 80, // milliseconds
          velocity = snailBait.BACKGROUND_VELOCITY*1.5,
          originalVelocity = snailBait.bgVelocity,
          i = 0;

      reverseDirection = function () {
         snailBait.bgVelocity = i % 2 ? velocity : -velocity;

         if (i < NUM_SHAKES) {
            setTimeout(reverseDirection, SHAKE_INTERVAL);
            ++i;
         }
         else {
            snailBait.bgVelocity = originalVelocity;
         }
      };

      reverseDirection();
   },
   ...
};
```

Now that you've seen how to shake the game, let's see how Snail Bait implements a more sophisticated special effect: transitioning between lives.

13.2.2 Transition Between Lives

After making the runner explode and subsequently shaking the game when the runner collides with a bat, a bee, or the snail bomb, Snail Bait transitions to the next life. That transition has three distinct phases:

1. The runner disappears, time slows to a crawl, and the game's canvas fades almost entirely from view.

2. At the moment the canvas stops fading out, Snail Bait resets the level, placing the background and all sprites except the runner at their original locations. The game makes the runner visible once again and leaves her at her usual horizontal position, but puts her on the third track with no platform directly underneath her.

3. When the runner appears, the canvas begins transitioning from barely visible to fully opaque, time returns to normal, and the runner falls, while running in place, from the third track to the platform on the first track. When she lands on the platform, the runner stops running in place.

Figure 13.3 shows the transition in the final phase after the runner has landed on the platform and the canvas is transitioning to fully opaque.

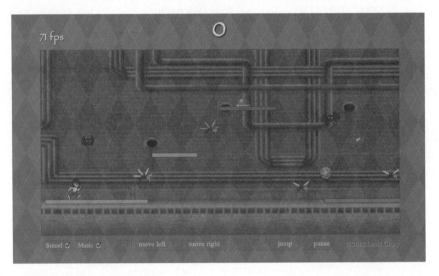

Figure 13.3 Transition between lives

The transition between lives starts in Snail Bait's loseLife() method, which the game invokes from the collide behavior's processBadGuyCollision() method, whose final implementation is shown in Example 13.11.

Example 13.11 Processing bad guy collisions (final implementation)

```
var SnailBait = function () {
    ...

    this.collideBehavior = {
        ...
```

```
    processBadGuyCollision: function (sprite) {
        snailBait.explode(sprite);  // sprite is the runner
        snailBait.shake();
        snailBait.loseLife();
    },
    ...
  };
  ...
};
```

The processBadGuyCollision() method explodes the sprite, shakes the game, and invokes Snail Bait's loseLife() method, listed in Example 13.12.

Example 13.12 Losing a life

```
var SnailBait = function () {
    ...

    this.RUNNER_EXPLOSION_DURATION = 500;
    ...
};

SnailBait.prototype = {
    ...

    loseLife: function () {
        var transitionDuration = 3000; // Same as canvas's transition time

        this.lives--;
        ...

        if (this.runner.exploding) {
            this.startLifeTransition(snailBait.RUNNER_EXPLOSION_DURATION);
            transitionDuration += snailBait.RUNNER_EXPLOSION_DURATION;
        }
        else {
            this.startLifeTransition();
        }
        ...

        setTimeout( function () { // After the canvas's transition
            snailBait.endLifeTransition();
        }, transitionDuration);
    },
    ...
};
```

The loseLife() method decrements the game's lives property and starts the life transition by invoking startLifeTransition(). The value that loseLife()

passes to startLifeTransition() when the runner is exploding represents a delay, in milliseconds, before startLifeTransition() actually starts the transition, so the transition does not start until the explosion is complete. If the runner is not exploding, meaning she fell through the bottom of the game, loseLife() starts the life transition immediately by invoking startLifeTransition() without passing a parameter.

Three seconds after the life transition begins, the loseLife() method ends the transition. That three second delay corresponds to the duration for the canvas's transition on its opacity property, as you can see in Example 13.13.

Example 13.13 The CSS transition for Snail Bait's canvas

```
#snailbait-game-canvas {
    ...

    -webkit-transition: opacity 3s;
    -moz-transition: opacity 3s;
    -o-transition: opacity 3s;
    transition: opacity 3s;
}
```

The startLifeTransition() method is listed in Example 13.14.

Example 13.14 Starting the life transition

```
SnaiBait.prototype = {
    ...

    startLifeTransition: function (delay) {
        var CANVAS_TRANSITION_OPACITY = 0.05,
            SLOW_MOTION_RATE = 0.1;

        if (delay === undefined) {
            delay = 0;
        }

        this.canvas.style.opacity = CANVAS_TRANSITION_OPACITY;
        this.playing = false;

        setTimeout( function () {
            snailBait.setTimeRate(SLOW_MOTION_RATE);
            snailBait.runner.visible = false;
        }, delay);
    },
    ...
};
```

The startLifeTransition() method starts the life transition by setting the opacity of the game's canvas to 0.05. The browser responds to that setting by smoothly animating the canvas from fully opaque to barely visible. The animation lasts three seconds.

The startLifeTransition() method also sets the game's playing property to false, which causes the game to disregard keyboard input until the playing property is subsequently reset to true, as you can see from Example 13.15.

Example 13.15 Disregarding keyboard input during transitions

```
window.addEventListener(
  'keydown',

  function (e) {
    var key = e.keyCode;

    if (! snailBait.playing || snailBait.runner.exploding) {
      return;
    }
    ...
  }
);
```

Using setTimeout(), the startLifeTransition() method in Example 13.14 waits for the specified delay—either 500 ms if the runner is exploding, or 0 ms if the runner has fallen through the bottom of the game—to make the runner disappear and slow the game's time rate to 1/10th of its normal rate.

Snail Bait ends life transitions, with the endLifeTransition() method listed in Example 13.16, three seconds after they begin, which coincides with the moment the game's canvas finishes fading out.

Example 13.16 Ending the life transition

```
SnaiBait.prototype = {
  ...

  endLifeTransition: function () {
    var TIME_RESET_DELAY = 1000,
        RUN_DELAY = 500;

    this.canvas.style.opacity = this.OPAQUE;

    if (this.lives === 0) this.gameOver();
    else                  this.restartLevel();
```

(Continues)

Example 13.16 *(Continued)*

```
      setTimeout( function () { // Reset the time
         snailBait.setTimeRate(1.0);

         setTimeout( function () { // Stop running
            snailBait.runner.runAnimationRate = 0;
         }, RUN_DELAY);
      }, TIME_RESET_DELAY);
   },
   ...
};
```

The endLifeTransition() method sets the opacity of the game's canvas to fully opaque and the browser responds by starting an animation from the current opacity of 0.05 to 1.0. That animation, as before, takes three seconds. The endLifeTransition() method subsequently invokes either gameOver() or restartLevel(), depending on the number of remaining lives.

Recall that startLifeTransition() slows Snail Bait's time rate to 1/10th of its normal rate at the beginning of the transition. The endLifeTransition() method waits one second, letting the runner effectively hang in the air running in place in slow motion, before setting the game's time rate back to normal. Subsequently, after 0.5 seconds, which is about how long it takes the runner to fall from the third track to the first, endLifeTransition() stops the runner's run animation by setting her runAnimationRate property to 0. Thus, the runner runs in place as she falls and stops running in place when she lands on the platform. The endLifeTransition() method also sets the game's playing property to true so that the game resumes handling keyboard input.

The restartLevel() method, listed in Example 13.17, restarts the level by resetting the game's offsets along with runner properties and making all sprites visible once again.

Example 13.17 Restarting the level

```
SnailBait.prototype = {
   ...

   restartLevel: function () {
      this.resetOffsets();
      this.resetRunner();
      this.makeAllSpritesVisible();

      this.playing = true;
   },
```

```
resetOffsets: function () {
    this.bgVelocity      = 0;
    this.backgroundOffset = 0;
    this.platformOffset  = 0;
    this.spriteOffset    = 0;
},

resetRunner: function () {
    this.runner.left     = snailBait.RUNNER_LEFT;
    this.runner.track    = 3;
    this.runner.hOffset  = 0;
    this.runner.visible  = true;
    this.runner.exploding = false;
    this.runner.jumping  = false;
    this.runner.falling  = false;
    this.runner.top      = this.calculatePlatformTop(3) -
                           this.runner.height;

    this.runner.artist.cells     = this.runnerCellsRight;
    this.runner.artist.cellIndex = 0;
},

makeAllSpritesVisible: function () {
    for (var i=0; i < this.sprites.length; ++i) {
        this.sprites[i].visible = true;
    }
},
    ...
};
```

When `restartLevel()` makes all sprites visible, the runner reappears. The last thing the runner did was explode, and as we discussed in Section 13.1 on p. 314, when the runner explodes, Snail Bait makes sure that her run animation rate is nonzero so that she cycles through her explosion animation cells. Therefore, when `restartLevel()` makes the runner visible again, she will be running in place.

Now that you've seen how to implement sprite animations and create special effects, let's see how to choreograph sprite behaviors to trigger sprite animations.

13.3 Choreograph Effects

A little more than halfway through the game's only level, the runner encounters two bees that block her path, as shown in Figure 13.4. It's possible for the runner to avoid the leftmost bee by running underneath it and jumping just before she falls off the platform; however, the space between the rightmost bee and the platform below it is too small for the runner to pass through.

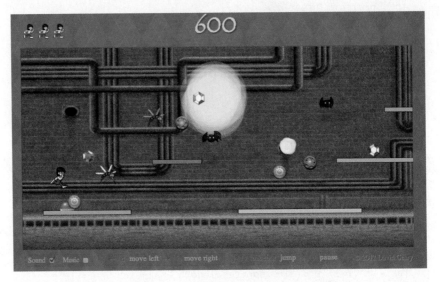

Figure 13.4 Detonating the blue button opens a pathway for the runner

To get past the bees shown in Figure 13.4, the runner must detonate the blue button by landing on it, as shown in Figure 13.4. That detonation triggers the sequence of events shown in Figure 13.5.

The top screenshot in Figure 13.5 shows the runner just before she lands on the blue button. In the screenshot below that, the runner has just landed on the button, causing the button to flatten and the leftmost bee to explode.

Shortly after the leftmost bee explodes, the rightmost bee also explodes, as shown in the third screenshot from the top in Figure 13.5.

The bottom screenshot in Figure 13.5 shows the runner passing by the exploding rightmost bee. When she lands on the platform, the runner must immediately jump over the bat in front of her, which never explodes.

That's how button detonation works, so let's see how it's implemented next.

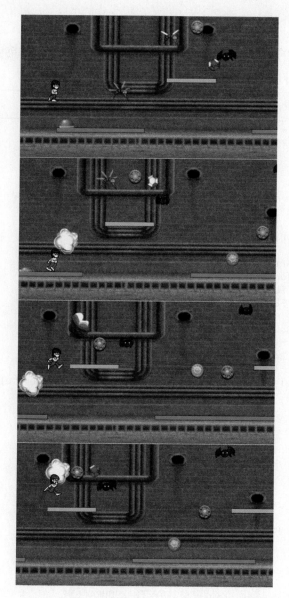

Figure 13.5 Landing on the blue button makes the bees explode (top to bottom).

13.3.1 Explode Bees

To make bees explode, we add a cell switch behavior to each bee, as shown in
Example 13.18.

Example 13.18 Making bees explode

```
var SnailBait = function () {
   this.BAD_GUYS_EXPLOSION_DURATION = 1500;
   ...
};

SnailBait.prototype = {
   ...

   createBeeSprites: function () {
      var bee,
          beeArtist,
          explodeBehavior,
          BEE_FLAP_DURATION = 100,
          BEE_FLAP_INTERVAL = 30;

      explodeBehavior = new CellSwitchBehavior(
         this.explosionCells,
         this.BAD_GUYS_EXPLOSION_DURATION,

         function (sprite, now, fps, lastAnimationFrameTime) { // Trigger
            return sprite.exploding;
         },

         function (sprite, animator) { // Callback
            sprite.exploding = false;
         }
      );

      for (var i = 0; i < this.beeData.length; ++i) {
         bee = new Sprite(
            'bee',

            new SpriteSheetArtist(this.spritesheet,
                                  this.beeCells),

            [ new CycleBehavior(BEE_FLAP_DURATION,
                                BEE_FLAP_INTERVAL),

              explodeBehavior // flyweight
            ]
         );

         bee.width = this.BEE_CELLS_WIDTH;
```

```
      bee.height = this.BEE_CELLS_HEIGHT;

      bee.collisionMargin = {
         left: 10, top: 10, right: 5, bottom: 10,
      };

      this.bees.push(bee);
   }
},
...
};
```

Cell switch behaviors for bees are nearly identical to the cell switch behavior for the runner listed in Example 13.5 on p. 318, except bees explode for a longer duration than the runner to give the runner a little extra time as she runs by an exploding bee before it reverts to being a bee.

Now that we have exploding bees, let's make them explode when the runner lands on the blue button.

13.3.2 Detonate Buttons

To detonate buttons when the runner lands on them, we modify the processCollision() method of the runner's collide behavior to process collisions between the runner and Snail Bait's buttons, as shown in Example 13.19.

Example 13.19 Tripping the detonate behavior's trigger

```
var SnailBait = function () {
   ...

   this.collideBehavior = {
      ...

      processCollision: function (sprite, otherSprite) {
         if (sprite.jumping && 'platform' === otherSprite.type) {
            ...
         }
         ...

         else if ('button' === otherSprite.type) {
            if (sprite.jumping && sprite.descendTimer.isRunning() ||
               sprite.falling) {
               otherSprite.detonating = true;
            }
         }
      },
```

(Continues)

Example 13.19 *(Continued)*

```
      ...
   };
      ...
};
```

When the runner collides with a button and she's either descending from a jump or falling, the revised processCollision() method sets the button's detonating property to true. That property is the trigger for the blue button's detonate behavior, listed in Example 13.20.

Example 13.20 Blue button detonate behavior

```
var SnailBait = function () {
   ...

   // Detonate buttons.................................................

   this.blueButtonDetonateBehavior = {
      execute: function(sprite, now, fps, lastAnimationFrameTime) {
         var BUTTON_REBOUND_DELAY = 1000,
             SECOND_BEE_EXPLOSION_DELAY = 400; // milliseconds

         // sprite is the blue button

         if ( ! sprite.detonating) { // trigger
            return;
         }

         sprite.artist.cellIndex = 1; // flatten the button

         snailBait.explode(snailBait.bees[5]);

         setTimeout( function () {
            snailBait.explode(snailBait.bees[6]);
         }, SECOND_BEE_EXPLOSION_DELAY);

         sprite.detonating = false; // reset trigger

         setTimeout( function () {
            sprite.artist.cellIndex = 0; // rebound
         }, BUTTON_REBOUND_DELAY);
      }
   };
   ...
};
```

The blue button's detonate behavior's execute() method, which is invoked by Snail Bait for every animation frame, takes action only when the detonating property of the sprite to which it is attached is true. If that's the case, the behavior flattens the button, makes the leftmost bee in Figure 13.4 on p. 330 explode, and sets the button's detonating property to false so that the behavior does not repeat.

Subsequently, after a 400 ms delay, the blue button detonate behavior's execute() method explodes the rightmost bee in Figure 13.4.

Finally, one second after the button detonates, the blue button detonate behavior makes the button pop back up by resetting the animation cell drawn by the button's artist.

Snail Bait creates the blue button's detonate behavior and attaches it to the blue button in the game's createButtonSprites() method, as shown in Example 13.21.

Example 13.21 Creating button sprites, revised

```
SnailBait.prototype = {
   ...

   createButtonSprites: function () {
      var button;

      for (var i = 0; i < this.buttonData.length; ++i) {
         if (i !== this.buttonData.length - 1) {
            button = new Sprite('button',
                     new SpriteSheetArtist(this.spritesheet,
                                             this.blueButtonCells),
                     [ this.paceBehavior,
                       this.blueButtonDetonateBehavior ]);
         }
         else {
            ...
         }
         ...
      }
   },
   ...
};
```

13.4 Conclusion

In this chapter you saw the implementation of a simple cell switch behavior that lets you temporarily animate sprites. You can use that behavior to make sprites do all sorts of things besides explode.

Although it's not reliable for time-critical animations, JavaScript's setTimeout() function is useful for special effects, as you saw in the final two-thirds of this chapter. You also saw how to implement special effects that apply to games as a whole, as opposed to sprite animations that involve only a single sprite.

In this chapter, you saw how to implement visual special effects. In the next chapter, we explore audio special effects by incorporating sound and music into Snail Bait.

13.5 Exercises

1. Experiment with the timing for life transitions by making them take a longer or shorter period of time. You will have to modify the game's CSS in addition to its JavaScript.

2. Instead of blowing up when she runs into a bat, turn the runner into a flapping bat for two seconds and continue play.

3. Instead of blowing up two bees in succession, blow up all bats and bees when the runner lands on the blue button.

CHAPTER **14**

Sound and Music

Topics in This Chapter

Music and sound effects set mood and heighten realism, and thus are essential elements for video games. In this chapter we discuss how to play music and multiple sound effects simultaneously, as illustrated in Figure 14.1, which shows Snail Bait just before the runner is about to collide with multiple sprites, resulting in multiple sound effects.

Games typically provide user interface controls to let players turn sound and music on and off. Additionally, games package their sound effects in a single audio file, known as an audio sprite sheet, to reduce startup time.

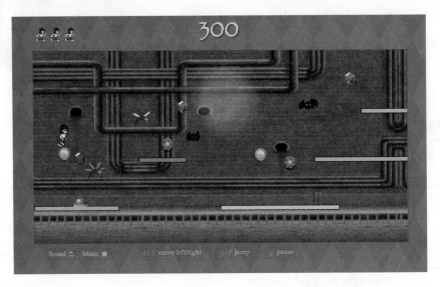

Figure 14.1 Playing multiple sounds at once

In this chapter you will learn how to do the following:

- Load audio files (Section 14.2 on p. 340)
- Implement controls that let players turn music and sound on and off (Section 14.3 on p. 342)
- Play music in a loop (Section 14.4 on p. 343)
- Pause music when the game pauses (Section 14.4 on p. 343)
- Create an audio sprite sheet (Section 14.6.1 on p. 350)
- Seek to locations in an audio sprite sheet (Section 14.6 on p. 347)
- Play sounds from an audio sprite sheet (Section 14.6 on p. 347)
- Implement multichannel sound (Section 14.6.3 on p. 353)

 NOTE: Audio has been notoriously difficult for browser vendors to implement

Audio has been one of the most difficult HTML5 APIs for browser vendors to implement reliably. An interesting case study in HTML5 audio is Microsoft's Cut the Rope HTML5 game. It uses HTML5 audio, but falls back to Flash audio for some browsers that don't properly implement audio. You can find Cut the Rope on the Web at www.cuttherope.ie.

NOTE: The Web Audio API

In this chapter, we use the rather simplistic HTML5 audio element for music and sound effects. Although it's limited in scope, the audio element is robust enough to play multiple sound effects simultaneously overlaid on a soundtrack on most platforms.

Some games, however, need more sophisticated audio support. HTML5's Web Audio API provides that support by letting you render audio by defining a graph of connected nodes.

At the time this book was written, the Web Audio API was not well supported among browsers, with only 57% support versus 83% for the audio element. See caniuse.com for more current figures.

NOTE: Audio on mobile devices

This chapter discusses how to implement Snail Bait's music and sound effects on the desktop. HTML5 audio on mobile devices has some peculiarities that are discussed in Chapter 15.

NOTE: Supported audio formats

See http://en.wikipedia.org/wiki/HTML5_Audio for a table of supported audio formats among browsers.

14.1 Create Sound and Music Files

Snail Bait uses two audio files, one for the game's music and another for its sound effects, as you can see in Figure 14.2. For each of those files, Snail Bait has an MP3 version and an Ogg version, which suffices for all modern browsers that support HTML5.

All Snail Bait's music and sound effects could reside in a single file, which would save an additional HTTP request at startup. As we discussed in Section 1.2.6, "Put All the Game's Images in a Single Sprite Sheet," on p. 15, it's important to keep HTTP requests at a minimum so that games load quickly.

In this case, however, placing everything in a single file puts the sound effects into a rather large file: 2.5MB for the MP3 version, instead of the much smaller 108KB file containing only audio sprites. As this book was being written, some browsers exhibited a considerable performance penalty when seeking for audio

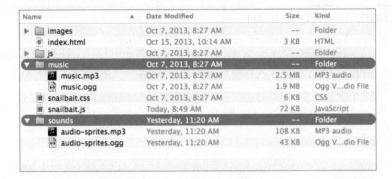

Name	▲	Date Modified	Size	Kind
▶ 📁 images		Oct 7, 2013, 8:27 AM	--	Folder
📄 index.html		Oct 15, 2013, 10:14 AM	3 KB	HTML
▶ 📁 js		Oct 7, 2013, 8:27 AM	--	Folder
▼ 📁 music		Oct 7, 2013, 8:27 AM	--	Folder
🎵 music.mp3		Oct 7, 2013, 8:27 AM	2.5 MB	MP3 audio
🎵 music.ogg		Oct 7, 2013, 8:27 AM	1.9 MB	Ogg V...dio File
📄 snailbait.css		Oct 7, 2013, 8:27 AM	6 KB	CSS
📄 snailbait.js		Today, 8:49 AM	72 KB	JavaScript
▼ 📁 sounds		Yesterday, 11:20 AM	--	Folder
🎵 audio-sprites.mp3		Yesterday, 11:20 AM	108 KB	MP3 audio
🎵 audio-sprites.ogg		Yesterday, 11:20 AM	43 KB	Ogg V...dio File

Figure 14.2 Sound and music directories

in a large file, so Snail Bait opts for separate files for sounds and music instead of one.

Now that you've seen Snail Bait's sound and music files, let's see how the game loads them.

 NOTE: Video formats

The HTML5 specification originally required the Ogg Theora format for video because it was freely available and open source and because the specification's authors believed it was better to specify a single format rather than many. Mozilla and Opera are big supporters of Ogg Theora.

Some companies, however, such as Apple and Nokia, were concerned about patent issues, and Apple didn't think it was a good idea to directly specify a video format in the specification. As a result, the specification was rewritten and the requirement for Ogg Theora was removed.

Subsequently, in 2010, Google acquired On2's VP8 format and released the software under an irrevocable free patent and BSD-like license. In January 2011, Google announced that it would end native support for MPEG-4 in Chrome.

14.2 Load Music and Sound Effects

Snail Bait loads audio files with the HTML shown in Example 14.1.

Like most games, Snail Bait prefers to load its audio when the game starts. Snail Bait signifies that preference with the preload attribute of the HTML5 audio tag, meaning the browser should load the files when the game's page loads, as you can see in Table 14.1.

Example 14.1 Loading Snail Bait's audio files

```html
<!DOCTYPE html>
<html>
   ...

   <body>
      <!-- The music soundtrack -->

      <audio id='snailbait-music' preload='auto'>
         <source src='music/music.ogg' type='audio/ogg'>
         <source src='music/music.mp3' type='audio/mp3'>
      </audio>

      <!-- Sound effects -->

      <audio id='snailbait-audio-sprites' preload='auto'>
         <source src='sound-effects/audio-sprites.ogg' type='audio/ogg'>
         <source src='sound-effects/audio-sprites.mp3' type='audio/mp3'>
      </audio>
      ...

   </body>
</html>
```

Table 14.1 The HTML5 `audio` tag's `preload` attribute values

Attribute	Description
auto	Load the entire audio file when the page loads.
metadata	Load only the metadata when the page loads.
none	Don't load the audio file when the page loads.

Unlike most HTML tag attributes, which are essentially directives, the audio tag's `preload` attribute is a mere suggestion for the browser. The browser can arbitrarily ignore the attribute.

 NOTE: iOS does not support the `preload` attribute

iOS ignores the `preload` attribute for the HTML5 `audio` tag because it only loads sounds as a result of direct user manipulation, such as clicking a button. See Chapter 15 for more details on the vagaries of sound on mobile devices.

14.3 Specify Sound and Music Controls

Snail Bait specifies the Sound and Music checkboxes shown in Figure 14.1 with the HTML listed in Example 14.2.

Example 14.2 Specifying Snail Bait's sound and music controls

```html
<!DOCTYPE html>
<html>
   ...

   <body>
      ...

      <!-- Sound and music.....................................-->

      <div id='snailbait-arena'>
         ...

         <div id='snailbait-sound-and-music'>
            <div id='snailbait-sound-checkbox-div'
                 class='snailbait-checkbox-div'>
               Sound <input id='snailbait-sound-checkbox'
                            type='checkbox' checked/>
            </div>

            <div class='snailbait-checkbox-div'>
               Music <input id='snailbait-music-checkbox'
                            type='checkbox' checked/>
            </div>
         </div>
         ...

      </div>
      ...

   </body>
</html>
```

In the sections that follow, we discuss how to access the Sound and Music checkboxes in JavaScript and attach event handlers to them. See Chapter 1 for a discussion of the CSS for the HTML shown in Example 14.2. Next, let's see how to play a game's soundtrack.

14.4 Play Music

To play the game's soundtrack, Snail Bait starts by accessing the soundtrack's HTML element in the game's constructor, as shown in Example 14.3. Snail Bait also obtains a reference to the Music checkbox.

Example 14.3 Accessing music elements in JavaScript

```
var SnailBait = function () {
   ...

   // Music.......................................................

   this.musicElement = document.getElementById('snailbait-music');

   this.musicCheckboxElement =
      document.getElementById('snailbait-music-checkbox');

   this.musicElement.volume = 0.1;
   this.musicOn = this.musicCheckboxElement.checked;
   ...
};
```

The preceding code sets the music element's volume to 0.1 (it's a loud soundtrack) and creates a Boolean variable named musicOn. That variable's initial value coincides with the Music checkbox element: If the Music checkbox is checked, music is on and the musicOn variable's value is true.

To keep the musicOn variable in sync with the checkbox, Snail Bait implements a change event handler, listed in Example 14.4. That event handler sets the musicOn variable and plays the soundtrack if the musicOn variable is true; otherwise, the event handler pauses the soundtrack.

Example 14.4 Music checkbox event handler

```
snailBait.musicCheckboxElement.addEventListener(
   'change',

   function (e) {
      snailBait.musicOn = snailBait.musicCheckboxElement.checked;

      if (snailBait.musicOn) {
         snailBait.musicElement.play();
      }
```

(Continues)

Example 14.4 *(Continued)*

```
      else {
         snailBait.musicElement.pause();
      }
   }
);
```

Snail Bait's `togglePaused()` method also pauses or plays the soundtrack according to what the value of the `musicOn` variable is and whether the game is paused, as you can see in **Example 14.5**.

Example 14.5 Pausing and resuming music

```
SnailBait.prototype = {
   ...

   togglePaused: function () {
      ...

      if (this.musicOn) {
         if (this.paused) {
            this.musicElement.pause();
         }
         else {
            this.musicElement.play();
         }
      }
   },
   ...
};
```

Now that you've seen how to access the soundtrack's HTML element and subsequently play and pause the element's associated audio, let's play music in a loop.

14.5 Play Music in a Loop

The HTML5 `audio` element has a `loop` attribute that causes the browser to endlessly loop through the element's audio, which is typically what you want for a game's soundtrack. Unfortunately, at the time this book was written, that attribute did not work in all browsers that supported HTML5, so Snail Bait implements looping by hand. Fortunately, looping in JavaScript is a relatively simple matter.

When the game begins, Snail Bait starts the game's music with the `startMusic()` method, listed in Example 14.6.

Example 14.6 Starting the music

```
SnailBait.prototype = {
   ...

   startMusic: function () {
      var MUSIC_DELAY = 1000;

      setTimeout( function () {
         if (snailBait.musicCheckboxElement.checked) {
            snailBait.musicElement.play();
         }

         snailBait.pollMusic(); // Restarts the soundtrack when it stops
                                // by invoking this method (startMusic())
      }, MUSIC_DELAY);
   },

   startGame: function () {
      ...

      this.startMusic();
      ...
   },
   ...
};
```

The `startMusic()` method waits one second and then, if the Music checkbox is checked, starts playing the music. The one-second delay serves two purposes. First, when Snail Bait calls `startMusic()` at the beginning of the game, the delay lets the game fade partially into view before the music starts. Second, when the soundtrack ends, Snail Bait calls `restartMusic()`, which is discussed below. That method restarts the music by once again calling `startMusic()`. In that case, the one second delay implemented by `startMusic()` provides a brief moment of silence before the soundtrack starts again.

To continuously loop over the game's soundtrack, Snail Bait's `startMusic()` method invokes a method named `pollMusic()`. That method uses the browser's built-in `setInterval()` method to poll the music element's `currentTime` property, as you can see in Example 14.7.

Example 14.7 Polling the soundtrack's `currentTime` property

```
SnailBait.prototype = {
   ...

   pollMusic: function () {
      var POLL_INTERVAL = 500,      // Poll every 1/2 second
          SOUNDTRACK_LENGTH = 132,  // seconds
          timerID;

      timerID = setInterval( function () {
         if (snailBait.musicElement.currentTime > SOUNDTRACK_LENGTH) {
            clearInterval(timerID);   // Stop polling
            snailBait.restartMusic(); // Restarts music and polling
         }
      }, POLL_INTERVAL);
   },
   ...
};
```

When the value of the soundtrack's `currentTime` property exceeds the length of the soundtrack, `pollMusic()` stops polling and invokes `restartMusic()`, which is listed in **Example 14.8**.

Example 14.8 Restarting music

```
SnailBait.prototype = {
   ...

   restartMusic: function () {
      snailBait.musicElement.pause();
      snailBait.musicElement.currentTime = 0;

      snailBait.startMusic();
   },
   ...
};
```

The `restartMusic()` method pauses the soundtrack and sets the music element's `currentTime` property to 0, which resets the soundtrack. Subsequently, `restartMusic()` invokes `startMusic()` to start playing the soundtrack once again.

To endlessly loop through its soundtrack, Snail Bait needs to know the length of the soundtrack. One way to ascertain the length of an audio file is to open it in Audacity and select the entire soundtrack, as shown in **Figure 14.3**.

As you can see from **Figure 14.3**, Snail Bait's soundtrack runs for 2 minutes and 12 seconds, which equates to the 132 seconds in **Example 14.7**.

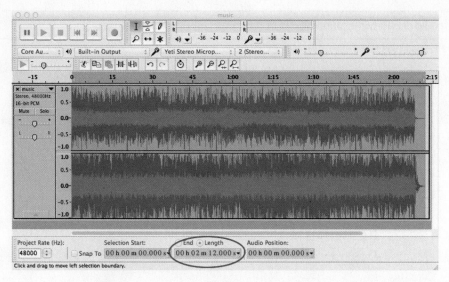

Figure 14.3 Audacity displays the length of Snail Bait's soundtrack.

Other than the minor nuisance of implementing looping by hand, starting, pausing, and playing music is straightforward. Playing sound effects, however, is a little more complicated, as you'll see in the next section.

14.6 Play Sound Effects

Snail Bait has six sound effects, listed in Table 14.2.

Table 14.2 Snail Bait's sounds

Sound	Snail Bait plays it when...
Cannon	The snail shoots a snail bomb
Coins	The runner captures a coin
Electricity flowing	The runner falls out of play
Explosion	A sprite explodes
Piano note	The runner captures a jewel
Thud	The runner falls on a platform

Snail Bait plays sounds with a playSound() method. Example 14.9 shows the various places in the game where Snail Bait plays sounds.

Example 14.9   Playing sound effects in Snail Bait

```
var SnailBait = function () {
   ...

   this.fallBehavior = {
      ...

      fallOnPlatform: function (sprite) {
         ...

         snailBait.playSound(snailBait.thudSound);
      },

      execute: function (sprite, now, fps, context,
                         lastAnimationFrameTime) {
         if (sprite.falling) {
            if (...) {
               ...
            }
            else { // Out of play or exploding
               ...

               if (this.isOutOfPlay(sprite)) {
                  ...

                  snailBait.playSound(
                     snailBait.electricityFlowingSound);
               }
            }
         }
         else { // Not falling
            ...
         }
      }
      ...
   };

   this.collideBehavior = {
      ...

      processPlatformCollisionDuringJump: function (sprite, platform) {
         var isDescending = sprite.descendTimer.isRunning();
         ...

         if (isDescending) {
            ...
         }
         else { // Collided with platform while ascending
            ...
```

```
            snailBait.playSound(snailBait.thudSound);
         }
      },

      processAssetCollision: function (sprite) {
         sprite.visible = false; // sprite is the asset

         if (sprite.type === 'coin')
            snailBait.playSound(snailBait.coinSound);
         else
            snailBait.playSound(snailBait.pianoSound);
      },
      ...
   };

   this.snailShootBehavior = { // sprite is the snail
      execute: function (sprite, now, fps, context,
                         lastAnimationFrameTime) {
         var bomb = sprite.bomb,
                 MOUTH_OPEN_CELL = 2;
         ...

         if ( ! bomb.visible &&
              sprite.artist.cellIndex === MOUTH_OPEN_CELL) {
            ...

            snailBait.playSound(snailBait.cannonSound);
         }
      }
   };
   ...
};

SnailBait.prototype = {
   ...

   explode: function (sprite) {
      if ( ! sprite.exploding) {
         ...

         this.playSound(this.explosionSound);
         ...
      }
   },
   ...
};
```

As the preceding code illustrates, to play sounds in Snail Bait you simply invoke the playSound() method, passing it an object representing a sound. The sections that follow show you how to implement the playSound() method and how to define sound objects. First, however, we need to discuss audio sprites.

14.6.1 Create Audio Sprites

Recall that Snail Bait puts all 63 of its images in a single sprite sheet. If each image resided in a separate file, the game would incur 62 more HTTP requests at startup, which would significantly degrade startup time. To draw individual images from the sprite sheet, Snail Bait uses simple objects to store the locations of each image in the sprite sheet. See Chapter 6 for more details.

Snail Bait does the same thing for sound effects by putting all the game's sounds in a single file and accessing them with objects containing the location and duration of each sound in the audio sprite sheet. Figure 14.4 shows Snail Bait's audio sprite sheet in Audacity.

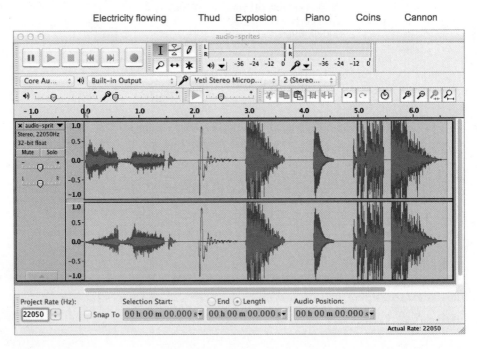

Figure 14.4 Snail Bait's audio sprite sheet. Individual sounds are identified at the top of the screenshot.

Creating audio sprite sheets is a simple matter. Next, let's define JavaScript objects that represent the individual sounds in an audio sprite sheet.

NOTE: Creating audio sprite sheets in Audacity

Audacity's File → Import → Audio… menu lets you import multiple files into one. You can export the resulting file to multiple formats with the File → Export… menu.

14.6.2 Define Sound Objects

Snail Bait's sound objects have three properties:

- `position`: Where the sound begins in the audio file (seconds)
- `duration`: How long the sound lasts (milliseconds)
- `volume`: A number from `0.0` (silent) to `1.0` (full volume)

You can determine the starting position and duration for a sound by selecting it in Audacity, as shown in Figure 14.5.

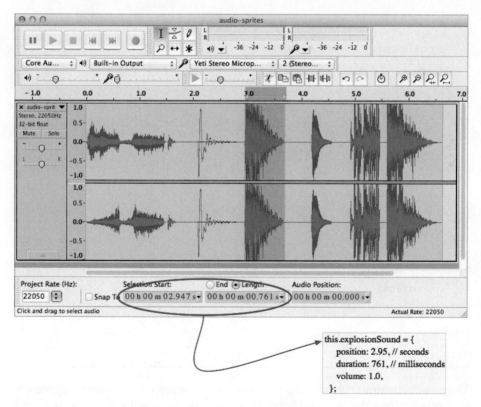

Figure 14.5 Determining the position and duration of a sound effect with Audacity

Example 14.10 shows the sound object definitions in Snail Bait's constructor.

Example 14.10 Creating sound objects

```
var SnailBait = function () {
   ...

   // Sounds.................................................................

   this.cannonSound = {
      position: 7.7,  // seconds
      duration: 1031, // milliseconds
      volume: 0.5
   };

   this.coinSound = {
      position: 7.1,  // seconds
      duration: 588,  // milliseconds
      volume: 0.5
   };

   this.electricityFlowingSound = {
      position: 1.03, // seconds
      duration: 1753, // milliseconds
      volume: 0.5
   };

   this.explosionSound = {
      position: 4.3,  // seconds
      duration: 760,  // milliseconds
      volume: 1.0
   };

   this.pianoSound = {
      position: 5.6,  // seconds
      duration: 395,  // milliseconds
      volume: 0.5
   };

   this.thudSound = {
      position: 3.1,  // seconds
      duration: 809,  // milliseconds
      volume: 1.0
   };
   ...
};
```

You can determine each sound's position and duration with a sound editor such as Audacity, but the volume level for each sound—a value between 0.0 and

1.0—is best determined empirically. Sounds are recorded at different volume levels, so volume settings can vary quite a bit.

You've seen how to create audio sprites and how to define JavaScript objects that represent the audio sprite's individual sounds, so the only remaining aspect of playing sound effects is implementing Snail Bait's playSound() method. That method plays sounds on multiple sound channels, as discussed in the next section.

14.6.3　Implement Multichannel Sound

Snail Bait frequently plays multiple sounds simultaneously, as illustrated in Figure 14.6.

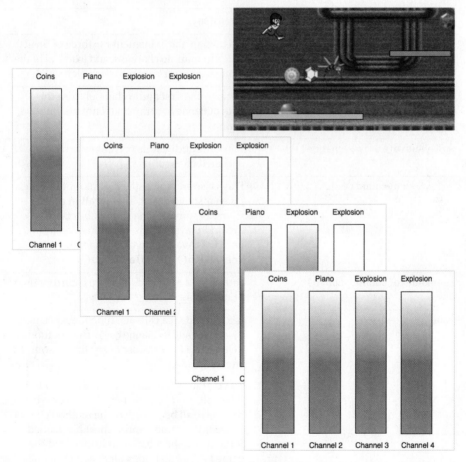

Figure 14.6　Snail Bait's four audio channels. Colored bars signify sound playing.

In the screenshot in Figure 14.6, the runner is about to land on the button, colliding with the coin and sapphire on her way down. From top to bottom, the illustrations in Figure 14.6 show the sequence of events as Snail Bait plays four sounds that overlap. First the runner collides with the coin and plays the coins sound. Subsequently she collides with the sapphire, playing the piano sound. Finally, the runner falls on the button, which explodes two of the game's bees in succession. With those final two explosions, all four of Snail Bait's audio channels are momentarily busy, as shown in the bottom illustration in Figure 14.6.

To play sound effects on multiple channels, Snail Bait implements the methods listed in Table 14.3.

Table 14.3 Snail Bait methods related to sound effects

Method	Description
createAudioChannels()	Creates an audio element for three of Snail Bait's four audio channels, and loads all of the game's audio sprites into each element.
getFirstAvailableAudioChannel()	Returns the first audio channel from the audioChannels array that's not playing a sound.
playAudio(audio, channel)	Plays the audio at its current time on the specified channel.
playSound(sound)	Plays a sound for a specific amount of time, given a sound object. The duration of the sound is stored in the sound object. This method plays sounds by calling getFirstAvailableAudioChannel(), seekAudio(), and playAudio().
seekAudio(sound, audio)	Pauses the sound and adjusts the current time of the audio.
soundLoaded()	Is a loadeddata callback function, specified by createAudioChannels(). This method is invoked by the browser every time a sound effect is loaded.
	The method maintains a countdown to track when all sound effects have been loaded; if they have all been loaded, the method checks to see if the game's sprite sheet has loaded. If the sprite sheet has been loaded and the game has not started, soundLoaded() calls Snail Bait's startGame().

Here's how Snail Bait uses the methods in Table 14.3:

- Initialization:

    1. Create audio elements (`createAudioChannels()`)
    2. Coordinate with sprite sheet loading to start the game (`soundLoaded()` callback)

- Play a sound:

    1. Get the first available audio channel (`getFirstAvailableAudioChannel()`)
    2. Seek to a sound's location in the audio sprite sheet (`seekAudio()`)
    3. Play the sound at the current location in the audio sprite sheet (`playSound()`)

In the sections that follow we look at each of the preceding methods in turn.

14.6.3.1 Create Audio Channels

Snail Bait's constructor accesses the `snailbait-audio-sprites` HTML element and declares an array of audio channels. Audio channels are JavaScript objects that keep track of an audio element and the status of that element: currently playing or not. Example 14.11 lists the channels.

Example 14.11 Snail Bait's audio channels

```
var SnailBait = function () {
   ...

   this.audioSprites =
       document.getElementById('snailbait-audio-sprites');

   this.audioChannels = [ // 4 channels
      { playing: false, audio: this.audioSprites, },
      { playing: false, audio: null, },
      { playing: false, audio: null, },
      { playing: false, audio: null  }
   ];
   ...
};
```

The HTML audio element for Snail Bait's first audio channel is the `snailbait-audio-sprites` element that Snail Bait declares in its HTML. The elements for the remaining channels are created programmatically by Snail Bait's `createAudioChannels()` method, which is listed in Example 14.12.

Example 14.12 Creating audio channels

```
SnailBait.prototype = {
  ...

  createAudioChannels: function () {
    var channel;

    for (var i=0; i < this.audioChannels.length; ++i) {
      channel = this.audioChannels[i];

      if (i !== 0) {
        channel.audio = document.createElement('audio');
        channel.audio.src = this.audioSprites.currentSrc;

        channel.audio.addEventListener(
          'loadeddata',     // event
          this.soundLoaded, // callback
          false             // use capture
        );
      }

      channel.audio.autobuffer = true;
    }
  },
  ...
};
```

The createAudioChannels() method uses the browser's built-in createElement() method to create three copies of the snailbait-audio-sprites element that Snail Bait declares in its HTML. For each of those copies and the snailbait-audio-sprites element itself, createAudioChannels() sets auto-buffering to true. The method also adds event handlers to the newly created audio elements. Those event handlers coordinate with sprite sheet loading to start the game.

 CAUTION: Downloads are initiated by the preceding code

The assignment to the src attribute of Snail Bait's audio elements in the preceding code listing causes the browser to download another copy of Snail Bait's sound effects.

14.6.3.2 Coordinate with Sprite Sheet Loading to Start the Game

Snail Bait doesn't start until all its graphics and sound effects are loaded. To monitor the loading of sound effects and graphics, Snail Bait maintains three variables, as shown in Example 14.13.

Example 14.13 Variables that coordinate loading graphics and sound effects

```
var SnailBait = function () {
    ...

    this.audioSpriteCountdown = this.audioChannels.length - 1;
    this.graphicsReady = false;
    this.gameStarted = false;
    ...
};
```

The audioSpriteCountdown variable represents the number of remaining audio files that Snail Bait must download. The game sets the graphicsReady variable to true after the browser loads the sprite sheet, and when the game starts, Snail Bait's startGame() method sets the gameStarted Boolean variable to true.

Recall that Snail Bait attached a listener to each audio element in Example 14.12. That listener is listed in Example 14.14.

Example 14.14 Sound loaded callback

```
SnailBait.prototype = {
    ...

    soundLoaded: function () {
        snailBait.audioSpriteCountdown--;

        if (snailBait.audioSpriteCountdown === 0) {
            if (!snailBait.gameStarted && snailBait.graphicsReady) {
                snailBait.startGame();
            }
        }
    },
    ...
};
```

The listener decrements Snail Bait's audioSpriteCountdown variable. If the variable's value is zero, and the game has not started and graphics are ready (meaning the sprite sheet has been loaded), then the event handler starts the game by invoking Snail Bait's `startGame()` method.

Example 14.15 lists the callback function that the browser invokes when it finishes loading Snail Bait's sprite sheet. That `spritesheetLoaded()` method starts the game if the game hasn't started and `audioSpriteCountdown` is zero. Whether it starts the game or not, `spritesheetLoaded()` sets the `graphicsReady` variable to `true`, signifying that the game's graphics have been loaded.

Example 14.15 Background loaded callback

```
SnailBait.prototype = {
   ...

   spritesheetLoaded: function () {
      var LOADING_SCREEN_TRANSITION_DURATION = 2000;

      this.graphicsReady = true;

      this.fadeOutElements(this.loadingElement,
         LOADING_SCREEN_TRANSITION_DURATION);

      setTimeout ( function () {
         if (! snailBait.gameStarted &&
             snailBait.audioSpriteCountdown === 0) {
            snailBait.startGame();
         }
      }, LOADING_SCREEN_TRANSITION_DURATION);
   },
   ...
};
```

We've taken care of initializing the sounds, so now let's play them.

14.6.3.3 Play Sounds

Example 14.16 shows the implementation of Snail Bait's `playSound()` method.

Example 14.16 Playing sounds

```
SnailBait.prototype = {
   ...

   playSound: function (sound) {
      var channel,
          audio;
```

```
    if (this.soundOn) {
        channel = this.getFirstAvailableAudioChannel();

        if (!channel) {
            if (console) {
                console.warn('All audio channels are busy. ' +
                             'Cannot play sound');
            }
        }
        else {
            audio = channel.audio;
            audio.volume = sound.volume;

            this.seekAudio(sound, audio);
            this.playAudio(audio, channel);

            setTimeout(function () {
                channel.playing = false;
                snailBait.seekAudio(sound, audio);
            }, sound.duration);
        }
    }
},
    ...
};
```

If the sound is on, playSound() invokes getFirstAvailableAudioChannel() to obtain a reference to the first audio channel in Snail Bait's audioChannels array that's not currently playing a sound. Snail Bait has four audio channels, all of which could be busy when Snail Bait invokes the playSound() method, so in that case, the playSound() method prints a warning to the console.

If an audio channel is available, playSound() invokes seekAudio(), which pauses the audio and seeks to the sound's position in the audio file. Subsequently, playSound() plays the sound with its playAudio() method. When the sound is done playing, playSound() seeks back to its starting position in the audio file in preparation for the next time the game plays the sound.

Snail Bait's getFirstAvailableAudioChannel() is listed in Example 14.17.

Example 14.17 Getting the first available audio channel

```
SnailBait.prototype = {
    ...

    getFirstAvailableAudioChannel: function () {
```

(Continues)

Example 14.17 *(Continued)*

```
        for (var i=0; i < this.audioChannels.length; ++i) {
            if (!this.audioChannels[i].playing) {
                return this.audioChannels[i];
            }
        }

        return null;
    },
    ...
};
```

Recall that audio channel objects have a `playing` property whose value is `true` when the channel's audio element is playing a sound. The `getFirst-AvailableAudioChannel()` method iterates over the audio channels and returns a reference to the first channel whose `playing` property's value is `false`. If all the channels are busy, `getFirstAvailableAudioChannel()` returns `null`.

Snail Bait's `seekAudio()` method is listed in Example 14.18.

Example 14.18 Seeking audio

```
SnailBait.prototype = {
    ...

    seekAudio: function (sound, audio) {
        try {
            audio.pause();
            audio.currentTime = sound.position;
        }
        catch (e) {
            if (console) {
                console.error('Cannot seek audio');
            }
        }
    },
    ...
};
```

The `seekAudio()` method pauses the audio element and sets its `currentTime` property to the sound's position in the audio file. If those actions cause an exception to be thrown—which can happen if, for example, the audio file failed to load—`seekAudio()` prints an error to the console.

Snail Bait's `playAudio()` method is listed in Example 14.19.

Example 14.19 Playing audio

```
SnailBait.prototype = {
   ...

   playAudio: function (audio, channel) {
      try {
         audio.play();
         channel.playing = true;
      }

      catch (e) {
         if (console) {
            console.error('Cannot play audio');
         }
      }
   },
   ...
};
```

The playAudio() method plays the audio element and sets the channel's playing property to true.

14.7 Turn Sound On and Off

Snail Bait lets players turn sound effects on and off with the Sound checkbox underneath the game. The game's JavaScript obtains a reference to that HTML element, as shown in Example 14.20.

Example 14.20 Accessing sound effect elements in JavaScript

```
var SnailBait = function () {
   ...

   this.soundCheckboxElement =
      document.getElementById('snailbait-sound-checkbox');

   this.soundOn = this.soundCheckboxElement.checked;
   ...
};
```

Snail Bait uses the event handler listed in Example 14.21 to keep the soundOn property in sync with the Sound checkbox.

Example 14.21 The Sound checkbox's event handler

```
snailBait.soundCheckboxElement.addEventListener(
   'change',

   function (e) {
      snailBait.soundOn = snailBait.soundCheckboxElement.checked;
   }
);
```

14.8 Conclusion

In this chapter, you saw how to implement multichannel sound to play multiple sounds simultaneously with a soundtrack running continuously in the background. We accomplished all that with HTML5's audio element, which is less capable but more widely supported than is the more sophisticated Web Audio API.

To reduce the number of HTTP requests your game incurs at startup, you should put all your sound effects in a single file, referred to as an audio sprite sheet because it resembles graphic sprite sheets that contain images.

The code that we discussed in this chapter pertains to Snail Bait running on the desktop; in the next chapter, we discuss how to deal with audio on mobile devices.

14.9 Exercises

1. Experiment with sound levels for Snail Bait's sound effects.
2. Add a sound to the game and play that sound when the runner jumps.
3. Open the browser's console and watch for output as you play Snail Bait. You should occasionally see warnings that Snail Bait could not play a sound. Add more channels to the audioChannels array until the warnings disappear.

Mobile Devices

Topics in This Chapter

As this book went to press in mid 2014, Gartner—a highly respected technology research and advisory company—predicted a staggering two billion mobile phones and tablets would be sold in that year alone. By comparison, Gartner expected that around 280,000 desktop-based PCs and notebooks would be sold. That's about 7,100 mobile devices for every PC and notebook, which is a compelling argument for making sure your game runs on mobile devices.

First, the good news. As of early 2014, lots of mobile devices can run HTML5 games such as Snail Bait at a rock-solid 60 frames per second. And players can add HTML5 applications to their home screens on iOS and Android, which means those applications open without browser chrome such as the address bar, making your games virtually indistinguishable from native games.

The bad news is that HTML5 games are not playable on less powerful devices, such as vintage 2010 iPods running iOS 4.X, or a first-generation Samsung Galaxy S3. And then there's HTML5 audio, which has been one of the biggest challenges for browser developers to implement reliably. It's not until recently, with the advent of iOS 6, that audio works reliably on iOS devices, but as you'll see in Section 15.7, "Work Around Sound Idiosyncrasies on Mobile Devices," on p. 400, both iOS 7 and Android 4.X sound support still require workarounds.

There is not a specific version of Snail Bait for mobile devices; instead, the game detects when it's running on a mobile device and configures itself appropriately. In this chapter we discuss how Snail Bait does that. Specifically, this chapter covers the following topics:

- Detect mobile devices (Section 15.2 on p. 368)
- Scale games to fit mobile device screens (Section 15.3 on p. 369)
- Change instructions when games run on mobile devices (Section 15.4 on p. 381)
- Implement alternative user interface controls (Section 15.5 on p. 383)
- Incorporate touch events (Section 15.6 on p. 396)
- Prevent zooming and inadvertent dragging during gameplay, but allow it otherwise (Section 15.6 on p. 396)
- Work around sound idiosyncrasies on mobile devices (Section 15.7 on p. 400)
- Run your game like a native app on iOS and Android (Section 15.8 on p. 402)

 NOTE: Gartner's predictions of PC and mobile device shipments for 2014

www.gartner.com/newsroom/id/2645115

TIP: Remote debugging iOS games from Mac OS X

You can remotely debug your game on Mac OS X . As shown in Figure 15.1, with your device connected via USB to your Mac, Safari adds your device to the Develop menu. After selecting the application to remotely debug, Safari opens a debugger window, as Figure 15.1 also illustrates. See http://bit.ly/1i954dV for explicit instructions on how to set up remote debugging on Safari.

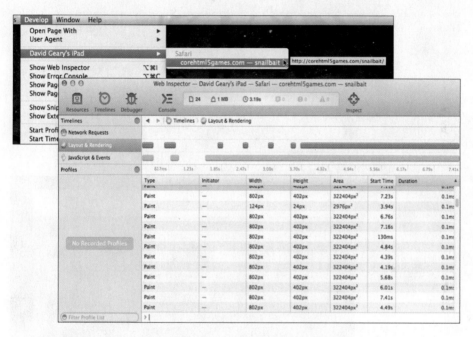

Figure 15.1 Remote debugging with Safari on Mac OS X

Note: To enable the Develop menu in Safari, go to the Advanced panel in Safari preferences and check the checkbox labeled Show Develop menu in menu bar.

 NOTE: Remote debugging for Android

You can also remotely debug Android applications. See https://developers. google.com/chrome-developer-tools/docs/remote-debugging?hl=de for more information.

15.1 Run Snail Bait on Mobile Devices

Snail Bait runs on mobile devices, as you can see in Figure 15.2, which shows Snail Bait running on an iPad and a Google Nexus 5.

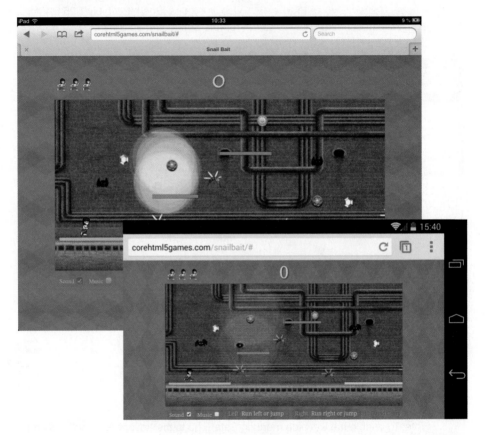

Figure 15.2 Snail Bait running in Safari on iOS (top) and Chrome on Android (bottom)

Table 15.1 shows the results of Snail Bait running on various mobile devices and operating systems.

As you would expect, the newer the mobile device and its operating system, the better Snail Bait performs.

Table 15.1 Snail Bait's mobile browser report card (grades are subjective)

Device	Grade	Pros	Cons
iPad 3 (iOS 6)	A+	Excellent performance and playability. The performance increase from the iPad 2 is significant, greatly increasing playability.	—
iPhone 5S (iOS 7.0.3)	A+	Excellent performance and playability.	—
Google Nexus 5 / 7 (Android 4.4 / Android 4.2.1)	A	Excellent performance and playability.	Sound takes a while to load initially.
iPhone 4S 16GB (iOS 7.0.3)	A	Excellent performance and playability.	Took over a minute to load the first time.
iPad 2 (iOS 6.1)	C	Good frame rate and great audio.	Display can be jittery at times, making it frustrating to play.
Samsung Galaxy Tab 2.0 (Android 4.1.1)	D	The game runs.	Too slow for enjoyable play.
Samsung Galaxy S3 (Android 4.1.2)	D	The game runs.	Too slow for enjoyable play. The game ran slowly on both Samsungs, despite running modern versions of Android.
iPod (iOS 4.2)	F	—	The game does not load.
Kindle original (Kindle browser)	F	The game loads and displays.	Required several refreshes to get the game to load. The Kindle does not respond to tapping, rendering the game unplayable.

Next, let's see how the game detects mobile devices.

15.2 Detect Mobile Devices

Because of alternative input controls and lack of a keyboard on most mobile devices, HTML5 games that run on both the desktop and mobile devices typically implement some code that runs on mobile devices only. For example, instead of controlling games with keyboards and mice, players on mobile devices use their fingers, which requires mobile-only code to detect and react to touch events.

The first order of business when tailoring your game to mobile devices is to determine whether the game is running on the desktop or on a mobile device. Example 15.1 shows the code that Snail Bait uses to make that determination.

Example 15.1 Detecting whether Snail Bait is running on a mobile device

```
SnailBait.prototype = {
   ...

   detectMobile: function () {
      snailBait.mobile = 'ontouchstart' in window;
   },
   ...
};
```

The preceding method sets a `snailBait.mobile` Boolean variable to `true` if the window object contains an `ontouchstart()` method; otherwise, `snailBait.mobile` is `false`. Snail Bait invokes the `detectMobile()` method when the game starts and subsequently uses the `snailBait.mobile` variable to implement mobile-specific code, as shown in Example 15.2.

Example 15.2 Using Snail Bait's mobile detection

```
snailBait = new SnailBait();
...

snailBait.detectMobile();

if (snailBait.mobile) {

   // Mobile-specific code goes here, such as touch
   // event handlers.

}
```

Now that you've seen how to detect features corresponding to mobile devices, let's see how to scale HTML5 games to snugly fit their display.

NOTE: Feature detection on mobile devices

You can read more about determining whether a JavaScript object has a particular property or method at www.nczonline.net/blog/2010/07/27/determining-if-an-object-property-exists.

NOTE: Feature detection vs. media queries

In simpler times, when mobile devices were still novelties, developers detected mobile devices with media queries to determine screen size. If a media query revealed that a game was running on a device with 320 x 480 pixels, for example, the device was an iPhone.

Today, there are many types of mobile devices; in fact, the line between computer and mobile device itself is significantly blurred. Feature detection, which probes APIs instead of hardware, is a better choice than media queries for detecting capabilities that browsers provide.

NOTE: Feature detection with Modernizr

Other than Node.js and socket.io, which Snail Bait uses to communicate between the client and server, the game eschews frameworks and libraries altogether, so you can learn how to develop your own HTML5 games entirely from scratch.

When you implement your own game, however, you should take full advantage of frameworks and libraries as you see fit. One useful library is Modernizr, which performs all sorts of feature detection in a manner similar to the feature detection discussed in this section.

15.3 Scale Games to Fit Mobile Devices

When Snail Bait runs on mobile devices, the browser scales the game so that it fits snugly, as shown in Figure 15.3, which shows the game running on Android in the Chrome browser.

Players can push the address bar up and out of the way to run full-screen, as shown in Figure 15.4. To start the game in full-screen mode, players can add Snail Bait to their home screen, as discussed in Section 15.8, "Add an Icon to the Home Screen and Run Without Browser Chrome," on p. 402.

As you can see from Figures 15.3 and 15.4, Snail Bait programmatically resizes the game when the amount of available screen real estate changes.

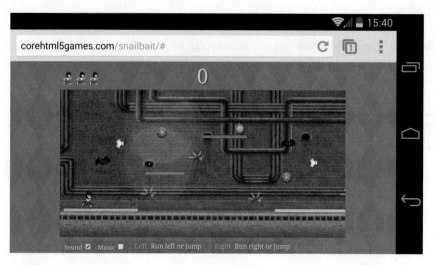

Figure 15.3 Android browser

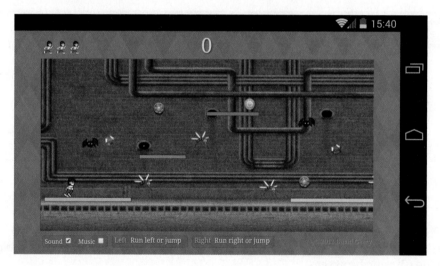

Figure 15.4 Android full-screen

Players can also pinch and zoom as they desire; for example, players can zoom in and concentrate entirely on the action if they wish, leaving the score and instructions behind as shown in Figure 15.5.

Once gameplay starts, Snail Bait prevents taps in the game's canvas from zooming the display. See Section 15.6, "Incorporate Touch Events," on p. 396 to see how Snail Bait disallows pinching and zooming.

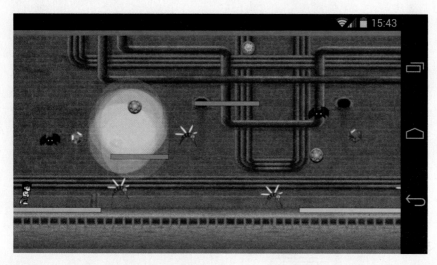

Figure 15.5 Zooming in on the game's canvas

Now that you've seen how Snail Bait scales to fit mobile device screens, let's see how it implements that functionality with the viewport meta tag and programmatic resizing.

15.3.1 The viewport Meta Tag

There's a lot more available screen real estate on desktops than on small mobile devices, as Figure 15.6 illustrates.

Because webpages meant for the desktop are too big for small mobile devices, mobile device browsers scale webpages to fit the screen, as shown in Figure 15.7.

When browsers display a webpage, they do not draw directly into the mobile device's screen, as you might expect. Instead, the browser draws into an off-screen viewport and subsequently copies the contents of the off-screen viewport to the screen. The off-screen viewport is known as the *layout viewport* because that's where the browser lays out the webpage, and the screen is known as the *visible viewport*. When the browser copies the contents of the layout viewport to the visible viewport, *it scales the contents of the layout viewport to fit the visible viewport*.

Layout viewports have different widths on different mobile operating systems, but for the most part they are close to the average width for a window on the desktop, meaning somewhere between 800 and 1,000 pixels. The layout viewport on iOS, for example, is 980 pixels wide, whereas it's 800 pixels on Android. That correlation to desktop window size means that on mobile devices, CSS

Figure 15.6 Most webpages don't fit on small screens.

Figure 15.7 Browsers scale webpages to fit small screens.

machinations result in websites that look proportionally similar to what you see on the desktop.

You can set the width of the layout viewport with the viewport meta tag, originally introduced by Apple. Figure 15.8 shows the effects of setting the width of Snail Bait's layout viewport to 800, 900, and 2,000 pixels, respectively, on an iPad.

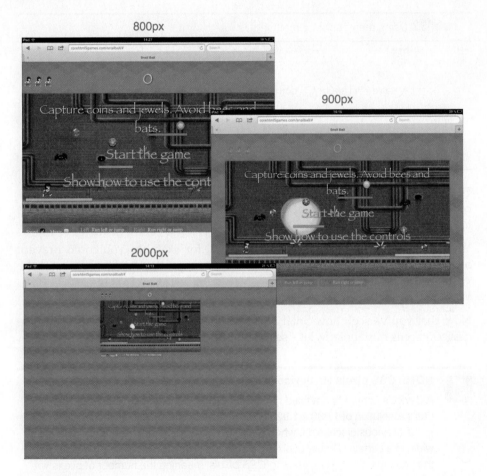

Figure 15.8 How the viewport meta tag's width directive affects scaling. Screenshots were taken on an iPad.

The width of Snail Bait's canvas is 800 pixels. When the layout viewport's width is also 800 pixels, the game fits snugly in the horizontal direction, as in the top screenshot in Figure 15.8.

When the layout viewport's width is 900 pixels, there are 50 pixels on either side of the canvas, as you can see in the middle screenshot in Figure 15.8. When the layout viewport's width is 2,000 pixels, there are 600 pixels on either side of the canvas, as you can see in the bottom screenshot in Figure 15.8.

Snail Bait chooses a layout viewport width of 900 pixels, as shown in Example 15.3.

Example 15.3 Using the `viewport` meta tag

```
<!DOCTYPE html>
<html>
   <head>
      <meta name="viewport" content="width=900"/>
      ...
   </head>
   ...

</html>
```

The `viewport` meta tag goes in the `head` section of your HTML page, as the preceding listing shows. Snail Bait uses only the `width` directive, but the `viewport` tag has several other directives, all of which are listed in Table 15.2.

You can combine the directives in Table 15.2; for example, you could prevent browsers from scaling when they copy the contents of the layout viewport to the visible viewport like this: `<meta name="viewport" width="initial-scale=1.0, minimum-scale=1.0, maximum-scale=1.0">`.

Now that you've seen how Snail Bait uses the `viewport` meta tag to fit mobile device screens horizontally, let's see how it fits the game vertically.

 NOTE: CSS pixels vs. device pixels

A device's screen has a fixed number of pixels. For example, Google's Nexus 5 has a resolution of 1,080 × 1,920 pixels. Those pixels are known as *device pixels*. In the previous discussion, when we talk about setting the `viewport` meta tag's width to a certain number of pixels, we're not talking about device pixels. Instead, the previous discussion refers to *CSS pixels*, meaning the number of pixels you specify in CSS for the sizes of HTML elements. High-resolution devices like the Nexus 5 use multiple device pixels to represent a single CSS pixel.

Table 15.2 `viewport` meta tag directives

Attribute	Description
`width`	A number specifying the layout viewport's width. On iOS, valid values are from 200 to 10,000, inclusive. A special value, `device-width`, sets the viewport's width to the width of the physical device.
`height`	The layout viewport's height. The browser sets the width. When this book went to press, no browsers implemented the `height` directive.
`initial-scale`	The initial scale at which the browser displays the webpage. iOS treats this directive differently than do other mobile browsers and it's nearly useless on Android. See the Caution below for more information.
`minimum-scale`	The minimum scale used by the browser when it scales a webpage to fit the display. On iOS, the valid range is from 0.01 to 10.0, and the default is 0.25. Android Webkit, when this book was published, did not implement this directive.
`maximum-scale`	The maximum scale used by the browser when it scales a webpage to fit the display. On iOS, the valid range is from 0.01 to 10.0, and the default is 0.25.
`user-scalable`	A Boolean value that controls whether the user can zoom the display. Valid values are yes and no. The default is yes.

NOTE: The browser infers `viewport` meta tag directives that you do not specify

Given the width you specify for the layout viewport with the `viewport` meta tag, the browser infers the layout viewport's height by maintaining the aspect ratio (width/height) of the webpage. The browser also infers the values of other directives you don't specify directly, so if you're not getting the results you expect, try specifying more directives directly.

NOTE: Other configurations for the viewport meta tag

You can find many recommendations on the Internet for the following use of the viewport tag: `<meta name="viewport" content="width=device-width, initial-scale=1, maximum-scale=1, user-scalable=0">`. That use of the tag sets the width of the layout viewport to the width of the physical device. In addition, the preceding use of the tag disallows scaling and zooming.

Snail Bait opts for a simpler use of the viewport meta tag because the game conditionally allows dragging and zooming and because it adds breathing room on either side of the game's canvas.

CAUTION: The viewport meta tag has many quirks

When this book went to press, browser implementations of the viewport meta tag were a mess, especially for Android WebKit. For example, even though you should be able to set the height of the viewport instead of the width, no browsers implement it correctly, even on iOS. Also, iOS pays attention to the initial-scale directive only when a page loads initially; as a result, if the user rotates the device from portrait to landscape mode, the page can puff up to 1.5 times its original size. Android WebKit pays attention to initial-scale only if the value is 1 and there is no width directive. And that's just the beginning of the problems with the viewport meta tag.

You can read more about the viewport meta tag at www.quirksmode.org/mobile/metaviewport and http://tech.bluesmoon.info/2011/01/device-width-and-how-not-to-hate-your.html.

NOTE: CSS Device Adaption

Instead of a meta tag, the W3C has specified a @viewport rule for CSS that provides functionality similar to the viewport meta tag; however, as this book went to press, the @viewport rule was not well supported among mobile browsers. You can read more about CSS Device Adaption at www.w3.org/TR/css-device-adapt.

15.3.2 Programmatically Resize Games to Fit Mobile Device Screens

Because aspect ratios differ among mobile device displays, it's not enough to merely use the viewport meta tag as discussed above to fit HTML5 games snugly in the horizontal direction. If the aspect ratio of a mobile device differs enough from your game's aspect ratio, the game will be cropped vertically, as illustrated in the top screenshot in **Figure 15.9**.

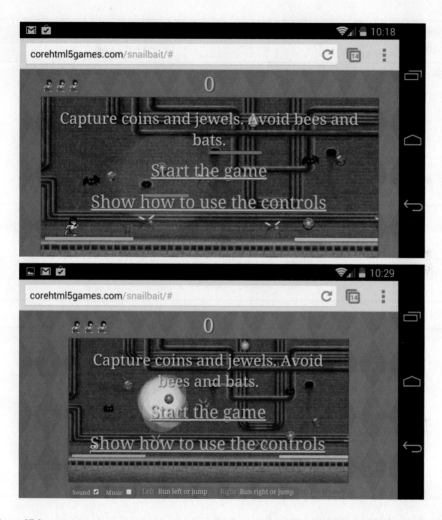

Figure 15.9 Aspect ratio cropping: Top screenshot is cropped; bottom screenshot accounts for aspect ratio.

To avoid aspect ratio cropping so the game is displayed as shown in the bottom screenshot in Figure 15.9, Snail Bait resizes the game to fit the screen at startup. Subsequently, Snail Bait also resizes the game whenever the window's size changes (such as when the player pushes the address bar out of the way) or when the player changes the device's orientation. Example 15.4 shows how Snail Bait does that.

Example 15.4 Resizing to fit the screen at startup and when window size or orientation change

```
snailBait.detectMobile();

if (snailBait.mobile) {
   ...

   snailBait.fitScreen();

   window.addEventListener("resize", snailBait.fitScreen);
   window.addEventListener("orientationchange", snailBait.fitScreen);
}
```

Snail Bait's fitScreen() method fits the game to mobile device screens when the game starts. Subsequently, Snail Bait specifies that method as a callback for the window's resize and orientationchange events. The fitScreen() method is listed in **Example 15.5**.

Example 15.5 Snail Bait's fitScreen() method

```
SnailBait.prototype = {
   ...

   fitScreen: function () {
      var arenaSize = snailBait.calculateArenaSize(
                        snailBait.getViewportSize());

      snailBait.resizeElementsToFitScreen(arenaSize.width,
                                          arenaSize.height);
   },
   ...
};
```

The fitScreen() method gets the size of the visible viewport, which it uses to calculate the size of the game's arena. Subsequently, fitScreen() resizes some of the game's HTML elements to fit the arena.

The getViewportSize() method is listed in **Example 15.6**.

Using document.documentElement is the preferred method of getting the width and height of the visible viewport (clientWidth and clientHeight), but if that's not available, getViewportSize() falls back to the inner width and height of the window.

Example 15.6 Snail Bait's `getViewportSize()` method

```
SnailBait.prototype = {
  ...

  getViewportSize: function () {
     return {
       width: Math.max(document.documentElement.clientWidth ||
                       window.innerWidth || 0),

       height: Math.max(document.documentElement.clientHeight ||
               window.innerHeight || 0)
     };
  },
  ...
};
```

The most interesting aspect of fitting Snail Bait to mobile device screens is the `calculateArenaSize()` method, listed in Example 15.7.

Example 15.7 Snail Bait's `calculateArenaSize()` method

```
SnailBait.prototype = {
  ...

  calculateArenaSize: function (viewportSize) {
     var DESKTOP_ARENA_WIDTH  = 800,   // Pixels
         DESKTOP_ARENA_HEIGHT = 520,   // Pixels
         arenaHeight,
         arenaWidth;

     arenaHeight = viewportSize.width *
                   (DESKTOP_ARENA_HEIGHT / DESKTOP_ARENA_WIDTH);

     if (arenaHeight < viewportSize.height) { // Height fits
        arenaWidth = viewportSize.width;      // Set width
     }
     else {                                   // Height doesn't fit
        arenaHeight = viewportSize.height;    // Set height
        arenaWidth  = arenaHeight *           // Calculate width
                   (DESKTOP_ARENA_WIDTH / DESKTOP_ARENA_HEIGHT);
     }

     if (arenaWidth > DESKTOP_ARENA_WIDTH) {  // Too wide
        arenaWidth = DESKTOP_ARENA_WIDTH;     // Limit width
     }
```

(Continues)

Example 15.7   *(Continued)*

```
    if (arenaHeight > DESKTOP_ARENA_HEIGHT) { // Too tall
        arenaHeight = DESKTOP_ARENA_HEIGHT;    // Limit height
    }

    return {
        width:  arenaWidth,
        height: arenaHeight
    };
  },
  ...
};
```

On the desktop, Snail Bait's arena, which contains all the game's HTML elements, is 800 pixels wide and 520 pixels high. The `calculateArenaSize()` method recalculates those values depending on the aspect ratio of the mobile device. The method returns an object with `width` and `height` properties that represent the width and height of the arena.

The `fitScreen()` method, listed in Example 15.5, passes the arena's width and height to `resizeElementsToFitScreen()`, which is listed in Example 15.8.

Example 15.8   Snail Bait's `resizeElementsToFitScreen()` method

```
SnailBait.prototype = {
  ...

  resizeElementsToFitScreen: function (arenaWidth, arenaHeight) {
    snailBait.resizeElement(
        document.getElementById('snailbait-arena'),
        arenaWidth,
        arenaHeight
    );

    snailBait.resizeElement(snailBait.mobileWelcomeToast,
                            arenaWidth, arenaHeight);

    snailBait.resizeElement(snailBait.mobileStartToast,
                            arenaWidth, arenaHeight);
  },
  ...
};
```

The `resizeElementsToFitScreen()` method resizes the arena, along with mobile toasts. Those toasts are discussed in Section 15.5, "Change the Welcome Screen," on p. 383.

Finally, `resizeElementsToFitScreen()` invokes Snail Bait's `resizeElement()` method, listed in Example 15.9.

Example 15.9 Snail Bait's `resizeElement()` method

```
SnailBait.prototype = {
   ...

   resizeElement: function (element, w, h) {
      element.style.width  = w + 'px';
      element.style.height = h + 'px';
   },
   ...
};
```

The `resizeElement()` method changes the `width` and `height` properties of an HTML element's `style` object. It's important to remember to add the *px* string to the values for width and height; without it, browsers ignore the value.

Now that you've seen how Snail Bait combines the `viewport` meta tag with resizing the game's arena in JavaScript, let's see how the game changes instructions when it runs on mobile devices.

 NOTE: Snail Bait uses the `viewport` meta tag and resizes the game

Snail Bait uses the `viewport` meta tag to fit the game initially in the horizontal direction. Subsequently, it resizes the game to fit the screen in both the vertical and horizontal directions.

15.4 Change Instructions Underneath the Game's Canvas

On the desktop, Snail Bait shows the instructions in the top screenshot in Figure 15.10. For mobile devices, Snail Bait changes those instructions to the ones shown in the bottom screenshot in Figure 15.10. Those instructions, unlike the instructions at the beginning of the game, are displayed all the time beneath the game's canvas.

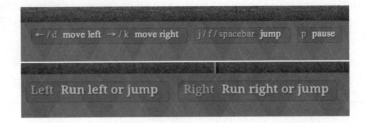

Figure 15.10 Snail Bait's instructions on desktop (top) and mobile (bottom)

The HTML for the mobile instructions is shown in Example 15.10.

Example 15.10 The HTML for the mobile instructions element

```
<div id='snailbait-mobile-instructions'>
   <div class='snailbait-keys'>
      Left
      <div class='snailbait-explanation'>Run left or jump</div>
   </div>

   <div class='snailbait-keys'>
      Right
      <div class='snailbait-explanation'>Run right or jump</div>
   </div>
</div>
```

At startup on mobile devices, Snail Bait sets its `instructionsElement` property to the HTML element listed above, as in Example 15.11. That assignment cancels a previous assignment of the `instructionsElement` to the desktop instructions.

Example 15.11 Swapping out the instructions element

```
if (snailBait.mobile) {

   // The following line of code overrides the instructionsElement

   snailBait.instructionsElement =
      document.getElementById('snailbait-mobile-instructions');

   ...
}
```

Now that you've seen how to change the instructions under the game, let's see how Snail Bait modifies the game's initial toasts for mobile devices.

15.5 Change the Welcome Screen

Implementing support for touch events is the most obvious aspect of implementing games for mobile devices. Often, that support results in different instructions for the game. In Section 15.6, "Incorporate Touch Events," on p. 396, we discuss the implementation of Snail Bait's support for touch events; in this section, we discuss the implementation of Snail Bait's instructions for mobile devices.

Recall from Chapter 1 that when Snail Bait runs on the desktop it initially displays a brief toast, as shown in Figure 15.11. The game's instructions showing which keys control the runner are always displayed beneath the game's canvas.

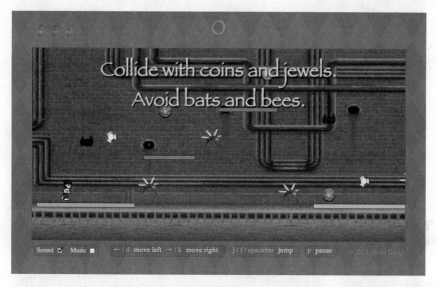

Figure 15.11 Snail Bait's initial toast on the desktop

When the game runs on a mobile device, Snail Bait modifies the game's initial toast as in the top screenshot in Figure 15.12. If the player taps on the Show how to use the controls link, Snail Bait displays a second toast, shown in the bottom screenshot in Figure 15.12, that describes the game's controls.

If players have played the game before, they probably don't want to see the instructions again, so the welcome toast gives the player the option to immediately start the game, as shown in the top screenshot in Figure 15.12.

Implementing the toasts shown in Figure 15.12 involves the following steps:

• Implement a welcome toast (shown in the top screenshot in Figure 15.12)

- Implement an instructions toast (shown in the bottom screenshot in Figure 15.12) with a Start link that starts the game

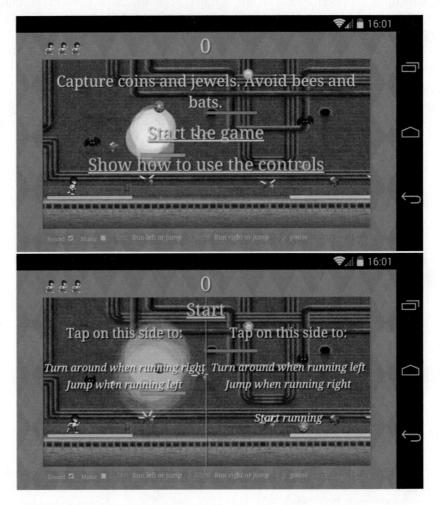

Figure 15.12 Snail Bait's initial toasts for mobile. Top: Welcome. Bottom: Instructions.

15.5.1 Implement the Welcome Toast

We implement the welcome toast shown in the top screenshot in Figure 15.12 with the following steps:

- Modify the game's start sequence

- Add HTML for the welcome toast
- Define CSS for the welcome toast
- Implement event handlers for the welcome toast's links

15.5.1.1 Modify the Game's Start Sequence

When Snail Bait runs on the desktop, the game's startGame() method starts the game's animation and displays the desktop welcome toast. We modify that method as shown in Example 15.12 to fade in the mobile welcome toast when the game is running on a mobile device.

Example 15.12 Snail Bait's startGame() method, revised

```
var SnailBait = function () {
   ...

   this.mobileWelcomeToast =
      document.getElementById('snailbait-mobile-welcome-toast'),
   ...
};

SnailBait.prototype = function () {
   ...

   startGame: function () {
      ...

      if (snailBait.mobile) {
         this.fadeInElements(snailBait.mobileWelcomeToast);
      }
      else {
         this.revealInitialToast();
         this.playing = true;
      }
      ...

      requestNextAnimationFrame(this.animate);
   },
   ...
};
```

Before it returns, the startGame() method invokes requestNextAnimationFrame(), the polyfill for requestAnimationFrame() discussed in Chapter 3, to kick off the game's animation. The screenshots in Figure 15.12 don't show the effect, but underneath the partially transparent toast a smoking hole smokes, and the coins and jewels sparkle and bob up and down.

15.5.1.2 Add HTML for the Mobile Welcome Toast

The mobile welcome toast is a DIV element whose identifier is snailbait-mobile-welcome-toast, as you can see from Example 15.13. That DIV contains the brief message and two links shown in the top screenshot in Figure 15.12.

Example 15.13 The HTML for the mobile welcome toast

```html
<!DOCTYPE html>
<html>
   ...

   <body>
      ...

      <!-- Arena....................................................-->

      <div id='arena'>
         ...

         <!-- mobile devices only -->

         <div id='snailbait-mobile-welcome-toast'
            class='snailbait-mobile-toast'>

            <div id='snailbait-welcome'>
               Capture coins and jewels. Avoid bees and bats.

               <div id='snailbait-welcome-instructions'>
                  <p><a href='#' class='snailbait-welcome-link'
                              id='snailbait-welcome-start-link'>
                     Start the game
                  </a>
                  </p>

                  <p><a href='#' class='snailbait-welcome-link'
                              id='snailbait-show-how-link'>
                     Show how to use the controls
                  </a>
                  </p>
               </div>
            </div>

         </div>
         ...
      </div>
      ...
   </body>
</html>
```

The preceding HTML is unremarkable, other than the `snailbait-mobile-welcome-toast` DIV's CSS class. Let's look at that CSS next.

15.5.1.3 Define CSS for the Mobile Toasts

Snail Bait has one other toast for mobile devices in addition to the welcome toast listed in Example 15.13. That other toast, which contains a lone Start link, is shown in the bottom screenshot in Figure 15.12. The welcome and start toasts have several CSS properties in common, so they reside in a CSS class, listed in Example 15.14.

Example 15.14 CSS for the mobile toasts

```
.snailbait-mobile-toast {
   position: absolute;
   border-radius: 10px;

   font: 30px fantasy;
   text-align: center;
   text-shadow: 1px 1px 1px rgb(0,0,0);

   color: yellow;

   -webkit-transition: opacity 1s;
   -moz-transition: opacity 1s;
   -o-transition: opacity 1s;
   transition: opacity 1s;

   display: none;
   z-index: 1;
   opacity: 0;
}
```

The preceding CSS exhibits the familiar pattern of HTML elements that Snail Bait fades in and out. The elements that have the `snailbait-mobile-toast` class are initially invisible and have a transition associated with their `opacity` property. See Chapter 5 for more information on how Snail Bait fades elements in and out.

Example 15.15 lists the CSS for the `snailbait-mobile-welcome-toast` element.

Example 15.15 CSS for the mobile welcome toast element

```
#snailbait-mobile-welcome-toast {
   width: 800px;
   height: 400px;
}
```

The preceding CSS sizes the snailbait-mobile-welcome-toast element to exactly fit the game's canvas. Next, we look at the event handlers for the links in the mobile welcome toast.

15.5.1.4 Implement Event Handlers for the Mobile Welcome Toast's Links

When the player taps the mobile welcome toast's Start the game link, the browser invokes the event handler listed in Example 15.16.

Example 15.16 The Start the game link's click event handler

```
var SnailBait = function () {
   ...

   this.welcomeStartLink =
      document.getElementById('snailbait-welcome-start-link');
   ...
};

snailBait.welcomeStartLink.addEventListener(
   'click',

   function (e) {
      var FADE_DURATION = 1000;

      snailBait.playSound(snailBait.coinSound);
      snailBait.fadeOutElements(snailBait.mobileWelcomeToast,
                                FADE_DURATION);
      snailBait.playing = true;
   }
);
```

The browser detects click events when players either click links with the mouse or tap them with a finger. The preceding click event handler plays a sound, fades out the initial start toast, and sets the game's playing property to true.

If the player taps the Show how to use the controls link, the browser invokes the event handler shown in Example 15.17.

Example 15.17 The Show how to use the controls link's `click` event handler

```
var SnailBait = function () {
    ...

    this.showHowLink =
        document.getElementById('snailbait-show-how-link');
    ...
};

snailBait.showHowLink.addEventListener(
    'click',

    function (e) {
        var FADE_DURATION = 1000;

        snailBait.fadeOutElements(snailBait.mobileWelcomeToast,
                                  FADE_DURATION);

        snailBait.drawMobileInstructions();
        snailBait.revealMobileStartToast();
        snailBait.mobileInstructionsVisible = true;
    }
);
```

The preceding event handler fades out the welcome toast and subsequently draws the mobile instructions and reveals the mobile Start toast. The event handler also sets a flag named `mobileInstructionsVisible` that Snail Bait uses to determine when to draw the game's mobile instructions.

15.5.2 Draw Mobile Instructions

Snail Bait draws instructions for mobile devices, shown in Figure 15.13, with a `drawMobileInstructions()` method. That method is listed in Example 15.18.

The `drawMobileInstructions()` method saves and restores the context for the game's canvas, so context settings made between those two calls are temporary. See Chapter 3 for more information about the context's `save()` and `restore()` methods.

Figure 15.13 Snail Bait's mobile instructions on Android

Example 15.18 Drawing mobile instructions

```
SnailBait.prototype = {
   ...

   drawMobileInstructions: function () {
      var TOP_LINE_OFFSET = 115,
          LINE_HEIGHT = 40;

      this.context.save();

      this.initializeContextForMobileInstructions();

      this.drawMobileDivider(cw, ch);

      this.drawMobileInstructionsLeft(this.canvas.width,
                                     this.canvas.height,
                                     TOP_LINE_OFFSET,
                                     LINE_HEIGHT);

      this.drawMobileInstructionsRight(this.canvas.width,
                                       this.canvas.height,
                                       TOP_LINE_OFFSET,
                                       LINE_HEIGHT);
      this.context.restore();
   },
   ...
};
```

The drawMobileInstructions() method initializes the context for the game's canvas with an initializeContextForMobileInstructions() method, which is listed in Example 15.19.

Example 15.19 Initializing the context for mobile instructions

```
SnailBait.prototype = {
   ...

   initializeContextForMobileInstructions: function () {
      this.context.textAlign = 'center';
      this.context.textBaseline = 'middle';

      this.context.font = '26px fantasy';

      this.context.shadowBlur = 2;
      this.context.shadowOffsetX = 2;
      this.context.shadowOffsetY = 2;
      this.context.shadowColor = 'rgb(0,0,0)';

      this.context.fillStyle = 'yellow';
      this.context.strokeStyle = 'yellow';
   },
   ...
};
```

As discussed in Chapter 3, the HTML5 canvas context has properties that control certain drawing aspects, such as where to place text and whether or not to add shadows to graphics and text.

The initializeContextForMobileInstructions() method listed above sets the context's textAlign and textBaseline properties so the context's fillText() method draws text centered horizontally. The initializeContextForMobile-Instructions() method also sets a fantasy font that's 26 pixels high and a black shadow for text and graphics. Finally, the method sets the context's fill and stroke styles to yellow.

After initializing context properties, Snail Bait draws the vertical divider in the center of the game's canvas with the drawMobileDivider() method, listed in Example 15.20.

Example 15.20 Drawing the divider

```
SnailBait.prototype = {
   ...
```

(Continues)

Example 15.20 *(Continued)*

```
drawMobileDivider: function (cw, ch) {
   this.context.beginPath();
   this.context.moveTo(cw/2, 0);
   this.context.lineTo(cw/2, ch);
   this.context.stroke();
},
...
};
```

Next, drawMobileInstructions() draws the instructions on the left side of the game's canvas with the drawMobileInstructionsLeft() method listed in Example 15.21.

Example 15.21 Drawing mobile instructions on the left

```
SnailBait.prototype = {
   ...

   drawMobileInstructionsLeft: function (cw, ch,
                                         topLineOffset,
                                         lineHeight) {
     this.context.font = '32px fantasy';

     this.context.fillText('Tap on this side to:',
                    cw/4, ch/2 - topLineOffset);

     this.context.fillStyle = 'white';
     this.context.font = 'italic 26px fantasy';

     this.context.fillText('Turn around when running right',
                    cw/4, ch/2 - topLineOffset + 2*lineHeight);

     this.context.fillText('Jump when running left',
                    cw/4, ch/2 - topLineOffset + 3*lineHeight);
   },
   ...
};
```

The preceding method primarily uses the context's fillText() method to draw text. The same is true for drawMobileInstructionsRight(), which draws the instructions on the right side of the canvas, listed in Example 15.22.

Example 15.22 Drawing mobile instructions on the right

```
SnailBait.prototype = {
   ...
```

```
drawMobileInstructionsRight: function (cw, ch,
                                  topLineOffset, lineHeight) {
   this.context.font = '32px fantasy';
   this.context.fillStyle = 'yellow';

   this.context.fillText('Tap on this side to:',
                  3*cw/4, ch/2 - topLineOffset);

   this.context.fillStyle = 'white';
   this.context.font = 'italic 26px fantasy';

   this.context.fillText('Turn around when running left',
                  3*cw/4, ch/2 - topLineOffset + 2*lineHeight);

   this.context.fillText('Jump when running right',
                  3*cw/4, ch/2 - topLineOffset + 3*lineHeight);

   this.context.fillText('Start running',
                  3*cw/4, ch/2 - topLineOffset + 5*lineHeight);
   },
   ...
};
```

As you saw in Example 15.17 on p. 389, Snail Bait invokes drawMobile-Instructions() when the player taps on the Show how to use the controls link in the mobile welcome screen. Snail Bait draws the mobile instructions directly into the game's canvas, which is the same canvas that Snail Bait redraws every animation frame. Because Snail Bait continuously redraws the game's canvas, it must do the same for the mobile instructions while they are visible. To do that, we modify the game's draw() method, as shown in Example 15.23.

Example 15.23 Drawing mobile instructions every animation frame

```
SnailBait.prototype = {
   ...

   draw: function (now) {
      ...

      if (this.mobileInstructionsVisible) {
         snailBait.drawMobileInstructions();
      }
   },
   ...
};
```

If the mobile instructions are visible, Snail Bait's draw() method draws them. Recall that the game sets the mobileInstructionsVisible flag when the player taps on the Show how to use the controls link, as shown in Example 15.17.

To start the game, players tap the Start button that the game displays, along with the mobile instructions. That Start button resides in a start toast, whose implementation we discuss next.

15.5.3 Implement the Mobile Start Toast

The HTML for the mobile start toast is shown in Example 15.24.

Example 15.24 The HTML for the mobile start toast

```html
<!DOCTYPE html>
<html>
   ...

   <body>
      ...

      <div id='snailbait-arena'>
         ...

         <!-- mobile devices only -->

         <div id='snailbait-mobile-start-toast'
              class='snailbait-mobile-toast'>
            <a href='#'
               class='snailbait-welcome-link'
               id='snailbait-mobile-start-link'>

               Start

            </a>
         </div>
         ...

      </div>
      ...
   </body>
</html>
```

The start toast contains only the Start link. The toast's CSS class is snailbait-mobile-toast, which is the class shared by the mobile welcome toast, as discussed in Section 15.5.1.3, "Define CSS for the Mobile Toasts," on p. 387.

The CSS for the start toast is listed in Example 15.25.

Example 15.25 The CSS for the start toast

```css
#snailbait-mobile-start-toast {
    width: 800px;
    height: 400px;
}
```

The start toast, like the mobile welcome toast, is the same size as the game's canvas.

Next, we implement the event handler for the mobile start toast's Start link.

15.5.3.1 Implement the Start Link's Event Handler

The event handler for the mobile start toast's Start link is shown in Example 15.26.

Example 15.26 The event handler for the Start link

```javascript
var SnailBait = function () {
    ...

    this.mobileStartToast =
        document.getElementById('snailbait-mobile-start-toast');
    ...
};
...

snailBait.mobileStartLink.addEventListener(
    'click',

    function (e) {
        var FADE_DURATION = 1000;

        snailBait.fadeOutElements(snailBait.mobileStartToast,
                            FADE_DURATION);

        snailBait.mobileInstructionsVisible = false;
        snailBait.playSound(snailBait.coinSound);
        snailBait.playing = true;
    }
);
```

The preceding event handler fades out the mobile start toast and sets the mobileInstructionsVisible property's value to false, which prevents the game's draw() method from drawing the instructions any further.

As was the case for the event handler for the Start the game link in the mobile welcome toast, the preceding event handler in Example 15.26 plays the coin sound when the player taps the Start link. Finally, the event handler sets Snail Bait's `playing` property to `true`, which activates the game's event handlers.

15.5.4 Reveal the Mobile Start Toast

Recall that the event handler for the Show how to use the controls link, listed in Example 15.17 on p. 389, invokes the `revealMobileStartToast()` method. That method is listed in Example 15.27.

Example 15.27 **Revealing the start toast**

```
SnailBait.prototype = {
   ...

   revealMobileStartToast: function () {
      snailBait.fadeInElements(snailBait.mobileStartToast);
      this.mobileInstructionsVisible = true;
   },
   ...
};
```

The `revealMobileStartToast()` method fades in the start toast containing the Start link and sets the `mobileInstructionsVisible` Boolean variable's value to `true`. The `revealMobileStartToast()` method is invoked by the Show how to use the controls link's event handler, which we discussed in Example 15.17.

You've seen how to modify Snail Bait's user interface for mobile devices, so now let's see how to incorporate touch events.

15.6 Incorporate Touch Events

When Snail Bait runs on mobile devices, it adds touch event handlers to the game, as you can see in Example 15.28.

Example 15.28 **Adding touch event handlers**

```
if (snailBait.mobile) {
   ...

   snailBait.addTouchEventHandlers();
   ...
}
```

Snail Bait's addTouchEventHandlers() method, listed in Example 15.29, adds two touch event handlers to the game, one for touchstart events and another for touchend events.

Example 15.29 Specifying mobile touch event handlers

```
SnailBait.prototype = {
   ...

   addTouchEventHandlers: function () {
      snailBait.canvas.addEventListener(
         'touchstart',
         snailBait.touchStart
      );

      snailBait.canvas.addEventListener(
         'touchend',
         snailBait.touchEnd
      );
   },
   ...
};
```

The touchstart event handler, which is listed in Example 15.30, is uneventful.

Example 15.30 The mobile touch start event handler

```
SnailBait.prototype = {
   ...

   touchStart: function (e) {
      if (snailBait.playing) {

         // Prevent players from inadvertently
         // dragging the game canvas

         e.preventDefault();
      }
   },
   ...
};
```

If gameplay is underway, the preceding event handler prevents the browser from reacting in its default manner for touch start events. In more practical terms, the call to preventDefault() prevents players from accidentally dragging the canvas.

The touchend event handler is listed in Example 15.31.

Example 15.31 The mobile touch end event handler

```
SnailBait.prototype = {
   ...

   touchEnd: function (e) {
      var x = e.changedTouches[0].pageX;

      if (snailBait.playing) {
         if (x < snailBait.canvas.width/2) {
            snailBait.processLeftTap();
         }
         else if (x > snailBait.canvas.width/2) {
            snailBait.processRightTap();
         }

         // Prevent players from double
         // tapping to zoom into the canvas

         e.preventDefault();
      }
   },
   ...
};
```

The touchend event handler calls either processLeftTap() or processRightTap(), depending on the location of the tap. The call to preventDefault() prevents players from zooming the display. The processRightTap() method is listed in Example 15.32.

Example 15.32 Processing taps on the right side of the screen

---

```
SnailBait.prototype = {
   ...

   processRightTap: function () {
      if (snailBait.runner.direction === snailBait.LEFT ||
          snailBait.bgVelocity === 0) {
         snailBait.turnRight();
      }
      else {
         snailBait.runner.jump();
      }
   },
   ...
};
```

The preceding event handler turns the runner to the right when she is moving left; otherwise, the event handler makes the runner jump. The processLeftTap() method is listed in Example 15.33.

Example 15.33 Processing taps on the left side of the screen

```
SnailBait.prototype = {
    ...

    processLeftTap: function () {
        if (snailBait.runner.direction === snailBait.RIGHT) {
            snailBait.turnLeft();
        }
        else {
            snailBait.runner.jump();
        }
    },
    ...
};
```

The processLeftTap() method is the mirror image of processRightTap(). The former turns the runner to the left when she is moving right; otherwise, the event handler makes the runner jump.

 NOTE: Touch event handlers lie dormant until gameplay starts

Both the touchstart and touchend event handlers only respond to events once gameplay is underway. That lets players pinch and zoom the display before starting to play.

 NOTE: Be careful of subtle distinctions between mouse and touch events

Mouse and touch events are similar, but not exactly the same. Not understanding the subtle distinctions between the two can be the source of bugs. You can read more about those subtleties at www.html5rocks.com/en/mobile/touchandmouse.

 NOTE: Preventing inadvertent dragging and zooming

Both the touch event handlers discussed in this section invoke the preventDefault() method on the event object the browser passes to those event handlers. For the touchStart() method, that call to preventDefault() prevents players from double-tapping to zoom in or out. The call to preventDefault() in the touchMove() method prevents players from inadvertently dragging the canvas.

NOTE: Preventing zooming and scrolling with `preventDefault()` also prevents other default actions

It's important to keep in mind that `preventDefault()` has side effects you may not anticipate. For example, if you prevent the default reaction for every mouse event, the browser will not allow the default behavior of setting focus in a text field.

15.7 Work Around Sound Idiosyncrasies on Mobile Devices

At the time this book was written, developers had to do the following two things, at a minimum, to get sound working reliably on mobile devices:

- Force the player to initiate a sound so that iOS will download sound files
- Adjust positions in the audio sprite sheet for Android

The HTML5 `audio` element on iOS downloads sound files only if a user activates a user interface control to make the first sound. From then on, the operating system will dutifully play sounds without user intervention.

That requirement on iOS is the reason the event handlers for the Start links discussed in this chapter played the coin sound; see Example 15.16 on p. 388 and Example 15.26 on p. 395. Without the player initiating the sound with a click, iOS will refuse to play any of Snail Bait's sounds at all.

For Snail Bait, iOS's refusal to download sounds without a user interaction causes a change to the game's startup code. Recall from Chapter 14 that the browser invokes Snail Bait's `spriteSheetLoaded()` method when Snail Bait's sprite sheet loads. That method starts the game only if all the game's sounds have been loaded. iOS, however, doesn't load the sounds until user clicks on one of the mobile Start buttons, so the game's `spriteSheetLoaded()` method must be revised as shown in Example 15.34.

Example 15.34 The `spriteSheetLoaded()` method (final implementation)

```
SnailBait.prototype = {
   ...

   spritesheetLoaded: function () {
      var LOADING_SCREEN_TRANSITION_DURATION = 2000;
```

```
    this.graphicsReady = true;

    this.fadeOutElements(this.loadingElement,
                    LOADING_SCREEN_TRANSITION_DURATION);

    setTimeout ( function () {
        if (! snailBait.gameStarted &&
            (snailBait.audioSpriteCountdown === 0 ||
            /(iPad|iPhone|iPod)/g.test(navigator.userAgent))) {
            snailBait.startGame();
        }
    }, LOADING_SCREEN_TRANSITION_DURATION);
},
    ...
};
```

On iOS, the revised implementation of `spriteSheetLoaded()` starts the game, regardless of whether the browser has loaded the game's sounds.

The second nuisance associated with getting sound to work reliably on mobile devices is Android's interpretation of where individual sounds lie in an audio sprite. Those sounds are offset anywhere from 0.2 seconds to 2.5 seconds. Because of those offsets, Snail Bait resets all the sound positions when the game runs on Android devices, as shown in Example 15.35. See Chapter 14 for more about how Snail Bait implements sound and music.

Example 15.35 Specifying different sound positions for Android

---

```
if (snailBait.mobile) {
    ...

    if (/android/i.test(navigator.userAgent)) {
        snailBait.cannonSound.position = 5.4;
        snailBait.coinSound.position = 4.8;
        snailBait.electricityFlowingSound.position = 0.3;
        snailBait.explosionSound.position = 2.8;
        snailBait.pianoSound.position = 3.5;
        snailBait.thudSound.position = 1.8;
    }
}
```

The preceding code uses a JavaScript regular expression to determine if the game is running on an Android device; if so, it adjusts the game's sound positions in the audio sprite sheet.

NOTE: JavaScript regular expressions

JavaScript regular expressions have many other uses besides detecting mobile devices. See www.w3schools.com/jsref/jsref_obj_regexp.asp for a reference to these handy objects.

15.8 Add an Icon to the Home Screen and Run Without Browser Chrome

Both iOS and Android make it easy for users to add an icon representing a website to the mobile device's home screen, as you can see from Figure 15.14, which shows a drop-down menu on Android.

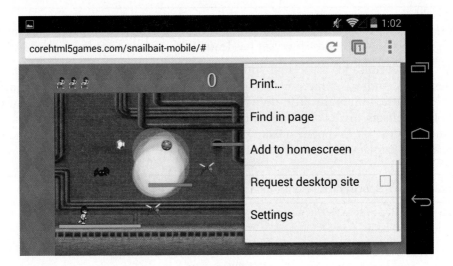

Figure 15.14 Add an icon to the Android home screen

When the player taps on the resulting icon, shown in the second row and third column of the left screenshot in Figure 15.15, the game begins without browser chrome, as you can see in the right screenshot in Figure 15.15.

NOTE: The full-screen API

As this book went to press, the W3C had released a working draft of a full-screen API, that lets your web application run full-screen without user intervention, but that functionality was not widely supported.

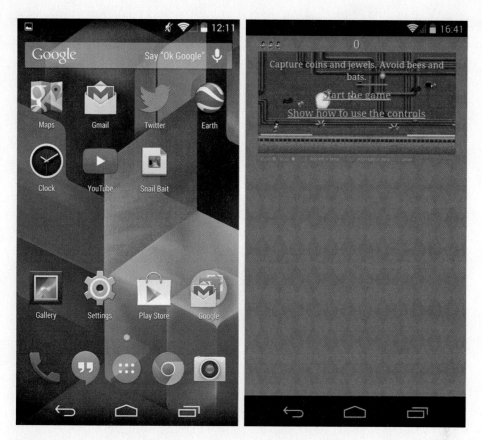

Figure 15.15 A Snail Bait icon on the Android home screen (left) and the ensuing game after a player taps the icon (right)

15.9 Conclusion

There are lots of mobile devices in the world, with more being sold all the time at a rate of two billion per year and climbing. And lots of those mobile device users play games on their devices.

In this chapter you saw how to customize Snail Bait so it runs on mobile devices. This chapter is far from a full-fledged exploration of implementing games for mobile devices; you will find entire books devoted to that topic. Instead, this chapter shows you how to get a nontrivial video game running on iOS and Android, pointing out some of the pitfalls of HTML5 mobile development in general.

In the next chapter you will see how to implement particle systems to represent real-world phenomena such as smoke and fire.

15.10 Exercises

1. Try Snail Bait on different mobile devices and see how the game performs.
2. Experiment with the `viewport` meta tag by setting different sizes for the width.
3. Set the `viewport` meta tag's width to `device-width` and restart the game on Android and iOS. Does the game initially scale the same on both operating systems?
4. Modify Snail Bait so that the resize event handler in this chapter also works on the desktop (in Example 15.4 on p. 378, move the calls to `addEventListener()` outside of the `if (snailBait.mobile)` block). Start the game on the desktop and resize the game's window so that the window is smaller than the game's canvas. Did the game resize as you resized the window?

Particle Systems

A smooth column of smoke rising from a cigarette quickly turns into turbulent, nondeterministic flow. You could easily represent the smooth column as a line, but nothing in Euclidean geometry is useful for modeling turbulent smoke. In fact, in the real world—as opposed to the virtual world of games—most physical phenomena exhibit chaotic behavior that can be challenging to represent graphically.

One way to represent chaotic physical systems, such as turbulent smoke or explosions, is to display a sequence of images; for example, Snail Bait implements explosions with a sequence of images. However, the sequence of images is always the same, making the next explosion look exactly like the last.

A more realistic way to represent chaotic physical systems is with particle systems.

A particle system is a collection of particles that together represent so-called fuzzy objects such as fire, water, or smoke. Fuzzy objects lack well-defined edges and, like most things in nature, do not conform to man-made geometric shapes such as rectangles, triangles, or circles.

In addition to particles, particle systems have *emitters* that create and emit particles. Once emitted, particles go through a well-defined life cycle as their attributes evolve over time. That evolution typically includes a random aspect to mimic the chaos that underlies even the simplest of natural systems. At the end of their life cycle, particles disappear.

In this chapter you will learn how to do the following:

- Use particle systems (Section 16.2 on p. 411)
- Implement particle systems (Section 16.3 on p. 414)
- Create a lifetime for particles that defines how they evolve (Section 16.3.3.4 on p. 432)
- Inject randomness into the creation of particles to emulate chaos in physical systems (Section 16.3.3.4 on p. 432)
- Pause and resume particle systems (Section 16.4 on p. 434)

 NOTE: Coining the term particle system

William T. Reeves coined the term particle system while working on the Genesis effect for the movie *Star Trek II: The Wrath of Khan.* You can see that effect at www.siggraph.org/education/materials/HyperGraph/animation/movies/genesisp.mpg.

16.1 Smoking Holes

In this chapter, we examine Snail Bait's smoking holes, shown in Figure 16.1, which are particle systems that contain fire particles and emit smoke bubbles. Over time, fire particles flicker and smoke bubbles dissipate.

Implementing particle systems may sound complicated, and some particle systems are indeed complicated; however, the hard part of implementing particle systems lies not so much in the programming, but in making particle systems look realistic. For example, Snail Bait's smoking holes first draw ten colored smoke bubbles—black, yellow, and orange—that dissipate more slowly than the ensuing ten grayscale bubbles that it draws on top of the colored bubbles. Those colored

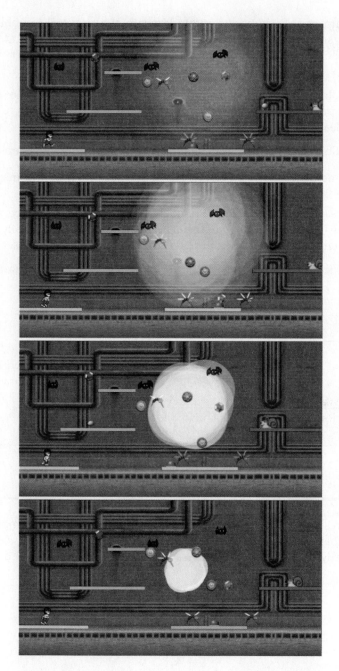

Figure 16.1 Smoke bubbles erupt from a smoking hole and dissipate (from bottom to top).

bubbles impart a fiery backdrop underneath the grayscale bubbles, which makes the smoke look more realistic. The colored bubbles expand slowly so that they don't overtake the grayscale bubbles, exposing the fiery backdrop illusion.

Drawing colored smoke bubbles underneath grayscale bubbles is not difficult to do from a programming standpoint, but it's not initially obvious. Coming up with the idea in the first place takes some experimentation.

Implementing particle systems in general involves the following steps:

1.   Implement an emitter that emits particles. The emitter may or may not have a graphical representation.

2.   Implement particles that continuously change their appearance depending on how long the particles have been in existence. Particles typically disappear at the end of their lifetime or are reset to their initial conditions.

Snail Bait's smoking holes consist of three objects, summarized in Table 16.1.

Table 16.1 Smoking hole objects

Object	Role	Description	Sprite?
Smoking hole	Emitter	Contains fire particles and emits smoke bubbles. Has no graphical representation.	No, but it implements `Sprite` methods so Snail Bait can treat it as a sprite.
Fire particles	Particle	Small circles filled with different shades of yellow.	Yes
Smoke bubbles	Particle	Filled circles that dissipate. Bubbles are either black, orange, yellow, or grayscale.	Yes

As you can see most clearly in the top screenshot in Figure 16.1, smoking holes look like holes in Snail Bait's background, but the game does not draw smoking holes directly. The holes in Snail Bait's background are part of the background itself.

Snail Bait creates smoking hole objects and adds them to its array of sprites, as depicted in Figure 16.2.

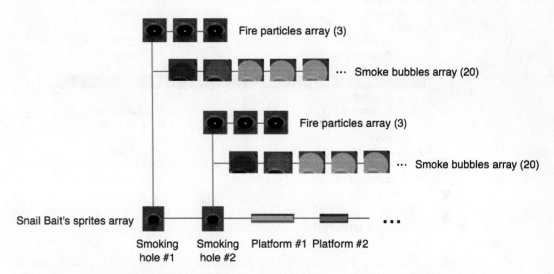

Figure 16.2 Smoking holes in Snail Bait's sprites array

Snail Bait's sprites array contains all the game's sprites, including two smoking hole objects at the beginning of the array. Although they reside in Snail Bait's sprites array, smoking holes are not actually sprites; instead, they are objects that contain sprites—fire particles and smoke bubbles—as you can see in Figure 16.2.

Smoking holes are not sprites because they don't draw anything directly; however, *because they contain sprites, it's most convenient if Snail Bait can treat smoking holes as if they are sprites instead of implementing special code to incorporate them into the game.* As a result, smoking holes disguise themselves as sprites by implementing the same methods as a sprite. The game, ignorant of the fact that smoking holes are not really sprites, treats them as though they are by updating and drawing all visible smoking holes every animation frame. The smoking holes, in turn, update and draw their fire particles and smoke bubbles, which are bona fide sprites.

The implementation of smoking holes resides in a JavaScript file of its own, so smoking holes can be used by games other than Snail Bait. That file is shown in Figure 16.3.

Figure 16.3 Snail Bait smoking hole JavaScript file

Snail Bait includes the smoking hole JavaScript file in its HTML, as shown in Example 16.1.

Example 16.1 Including smoking hole JavaScript

```
<!DOCTYPE html>
<html>
  ...

  <body>
    ...

    <!-- The final version of Snail Bait puts all the
         game's JavaScript into a single file. See
         Chapter 19 for more details about how
         Snail Bait is deployed. -->

    <script src='js/smokingHole.js'></script>
    ...

    <script src='snailbait.js'></script>
    ...
  </body>
</html>
```

Before we discuss the implementation of Snail Bait's smoking holes, let's look at how Snail Bait uses them.

NOTE: Sprite containers

Snail Bait's smoking holes are objects that contain sprites. Because they don't have a graphical representation, Snail Bait does not implement smoking holes themselves as sprites; however, Snail Bait treats them as sprites.

Smoking holes are a specialization of more general objects, which may or may not be sprites themselves, that contain other sprites.

16.2 Use Smoking Holes

Snail Bait incorporates smoking holes in four steps:

1. Define smoking hole data
2. Create smoking holes
3. Add smoking holes to Snail Bait's `sprites` array
4. Scroll smoking holes every animation frame

Let's look at each step.

16.2.1 Define Smoking Hole Data

As it does for its sprites, Snail Bait defines metadata for its smoking holes, as shown in Example 16.2. It also defines an array to store smoking hole objects.

Example 16.2 Smoking hole data

```
var SnailBait = function () {
   ...

   this.smokingHoleData = [
      { left: 250,  top: this.TRACK_2_BASELINE - 20 },
      { left: 850,  top: this.TRACK_2_BASELINE - 20 }
   ];

   this.smokingHoles = [];
   ...
};
```

Snail Bait defines the upper-left corner of each smoking hole. Those coordinates correspond to the locations of holes in the background.

That's all there is to defining smoking hole metadata. Next, let's see how Snail Bait creates smoking holes.

16.2.2 Create Smoking Holes

Snail Bait creates smoking holes with a `createSmokingHoles()` method, which it invokes from `createSprites()`, as shown in Example 16.3.

Example 16.3 Creating smoking holes

```
SnailBait.prototype = {
   ...

   createSmokingHoles: function () {
      var data,
          smokingHole,
          SMOKE_BUBBLE_COUNT  = 20,
          FIRE_PARTICLE_COUNT = 3,
          SMOKING_HOLE_WIDTH  = 10;

      for (var i=0; i < this.smokingHoleData.length; ++i) {
         data = this.smokingHoleData[i];

         smokingHole = new SmokingHole(SMOKE_BUBBLE_COUNT,
                                       FIRE_PARTICLE_COUNT,
                                       data.left, data.top,
                                       SMOKING_HOLE_WIDTH);

         this.smokingHoles.push(smokingHole);
      }
   },
   ...

   createSprites: function () {
      ...

      this.createSmokingHoles();
      ...
   },
   ...
};
```

The `createSmokingHoles()` method iterates over Snail Bait's smoking hole data, creating a `SmokingHole` object for each data instance and pushing that object onto the array declared in Example 16.2. Snail Bait's smoking holes have 3 fire particles and 20 smoke bubbles and are 10 pixels wide.

16.2.3 Add Smoking Holes to Snail Bait's `sprites` Array

Recall that even though smoking holes are not sprites, Snail Bait treats them as though they are sprites, which means it adds them to the game's `sprites` array, as shown in Example 16.4.

Example 16.4 `SnailBait.addSpritesToSpriteArray()`, revised

```
SnailBait.prototype = {
   ...

   addSpritesToSpriteArray: function () {
      // Smoking holes must be drawn first so that they
      // appear underneath all other sprites. Sprites
      // are drawn in the order of their appearance in the
      // sprites array.

      for (var i=0; i < this.smokingHoles.length; ++i) {
         this.sprites.push(this.smokingHoles[i]);
      }

      for (var i=0; i < this.platforms.length; ++i) {
         this.sprites.push(this.platforms[i]);
      }
      ...

      // Similar loops for adding other types of sprites
      // to the sprites array are omitted for brevity
   },
   ...
};
```

As you can see in Figure 16.1 on p. 407, a smoking hole's fire particles and smoke bubbles are drawn underneath the game's other sprites. Whatever you draw first appears underneath whatever you subsequently draw into an HTML5 canvas element, so Snail Bait adds smoking holes to the `sprites` array before adding the rest of the game's sprites. Because Snail Bait draws sprites in the order of their appearance in the `sprites` array, it draws smoking holes before it draws the other sprites.

16.2.4 Scroll Smoking Holes Every Animation Frame

As we discussed above, Snail Bait creates smoking holes and adds them to its array of sprites at startup. As the game is running, however, Snail Bait must

scroll smoking holes in concert with the background, so we revise the
setSpriteOffsets() method previously discussed in Chapter 3 as shown in
Example 16.5.

Example 16.5 Scrolling smoking holes in concert with the background

```
SnailBait.prototype = {
   ...

   setSpriteOffsets: function (now) {
      var sprite,
          i;

      for (i=0; i < this.sprites.length; ++i) {
         sprite = this.sprites[i];

         // Smoking holes scroll in concert with the background

         if ('smoking hole' === sprite.type) {
            sprite.hOffset = this.backgroundOffset;
         }
         ...
      }
   },
   ...
};
```

Recall that Snail Bait invokes setSpriteOffsets() every animation frame, so
each smoking hole's horizontal offset, represented by its hOffset property, stays
in sync with the background's offset. See Chapter 6 for more about sprites and
their hOffset property.

Now that you've seen how Snail Bait uses smoking holes, let's see how to
implement them.

16.3 Implement Smoking Holes

We implement smoking holes with the following steps:

• Disguise smoking holes as sprites
• Incorporate fire particles
• Incorporate smoke bubbles

16.3.1 Disguise Smoking Holes as Sprites

Smoking holes, like Snail Bait itself, are JavaScript objects, so they have a constructor function and a prototype. To disguise smoking holes as sprites, the SmokingHole constructor invokes the SmokingHole object's disguiseAsSprite() method, as shown in Example 16.6.

Example 16.6 Constructing smoking holes: Disguise as sprite

```
var SmokingHole = function (smokeBubbleCount, fireParticleCount,
                            left, top, width) {
   ...

   this.disguiseAsSprite(left, top, width);
   ...
};
```

Snail Bait disguises smoking holes as sprites by fitting them with properties, methods, and behaviors that correspond to the properties, methods, and behaviors in sprites, as you can see from Example 16.7.

Example 16.7 Disguising smoking holes as sprites

```
SmokingHole.prototype = {
   ...

   disguiseAsSprite: function (left, top, width) {
      this.addSpriteProperties(left, top, width);
      this.addSpriteMethods();
      this.addBehaviors();
   },
   ...
};
```

The SmokingHole object's disguiseAsSprite() method invokes methods that add sprite properties, methods, and behaviors to the SmokingHole object.

Recall that sprites have a type. A smoking hole's type is smoking hole. Sprites also keep track of their upper-left corner, how wide and tall they are, and whether or not they are visible. The SmokingHole object's addSpriteProperties() method adds those properties to smoking holes as shown in Example 16.8.

Example 16.8 Adding sprite properties to smoking holes

```
SmokingHole.prototype = {
   ...

   addSpriteProperties: function (left, top, width) {
      this.type   = 'smoking hole';
      this.top    = top;
      this.left   = left;
      this.width  = width;
      this.height = width; // Square
      this.visible = true;
   },
   ...
};
```

Sprites implement two mandatory methods: draw() and update(), so the SmokingHole object's addSpriteMethods() adds identical methods to the SmokingHole object's prototype, as shown in Example 16.9.

Example 16.9 Adding sprite methods to smoking holes

```
SmokingHole.prototype = {
   ...

   addSpriteMethods: function () {
      this.draw = function (context) {
         // TODO: Draw fire particles and smoke bubbles
      };

      this.update = function (now, fps,
                             context, lastAnimationFrameTime) {
         // TODO: 1. Update smoke bubbles
         //       2. Execute smoking hole behaviors
         //
         // It's not necessary to update fire particles because
         // they have no behaviors.
      };
   },
   ...
};
```

For now the SmokingHole object's draw() and update() methods are placeholders. In the sections that follow, we modify those methods to draw and update smoking holes. Besides updating smoke bubbles, the update() method executes smoking hole behaviors. Smoking holes have only one behavior that emits smoke bubbles. That smoking hole behavior is created in the SmokingHole object's addBehaviors() method, which is also initially a placeholder, as you can see in Example 16.10. Recall that the diguiseAsSprite() method invokes addBehaviors().

Example 16.10 Adding behaviors to smoking holes

```
SmokingHole.prototype = {
    ...

    addBehaviors: function () {
        // TODO: Add an array of behaviors to the smoking hole
    },
    ...
};
```

In Section 16.3.3.3, "Emit Smoke Bubbles," on p. 430 we modify the addBehaviors() method to add a smoking hole behavior that emits smoke bubbles.

 NOTE: A recap

So far we've created smoking holes, disguised them as sprites, and added them to the game. Because we added smoking holes to Snail Bait's array of sprites, Snail Bait invokes each visible smoking hole's update() and draw() methods every animation frame. For the remainder of this chapter, we flesh out the implementation of SmokingHole.draw() and SmokingHole.update() to draw and update fire particles and smoke bubbles. In addition, we implement two behaviors: one for smoking holes that emits smoke bubbles, and another for smoke bubbles that makes them dissipate.

16.3.2 Incorporate Fire Particles

Snail Bait's fire particles are small yellow circles that flicker, as shown in Figure 16.4.

Fire particles are simple, so we have only two things to do to incorporate them into Snail Bait:

- Create fire particles
- Draw and update fire particles every animation frame

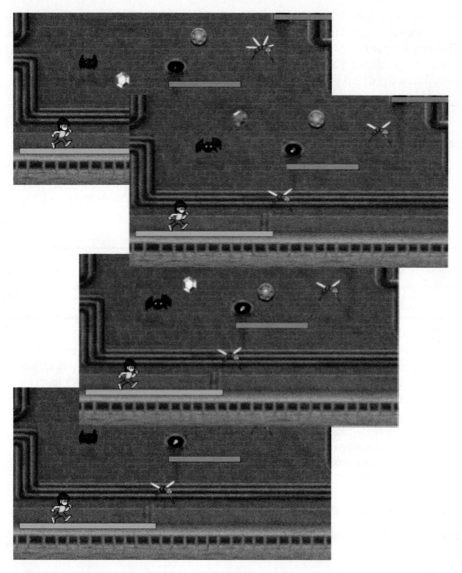

Figure 16.4 Fire particles flickering (in the smoking hole in the middle of the screenshots)

16.3.2.1 Create Fire Particles

Each smoking hole maintains an array of fire particles, which it creates with a createFireParticles() method, as shown in the revised SmokingHole constructor in Example 16.11.

Example 16.11 Constructing smoking holes: Incorporating fire particles

---

```
var SmokingHole = function (smokeBubbleCount, fireParticleCount,
                            left, top, width) {
    this.fireParticles = [];

    this.disguiseAsSprite   (left, top, width);
    this.createFireParticles(fireParticleCount, left, top);
    ...
};
```

The createFireParticles() method is listed in Example 16.12.

Example 16.12 Creating fire particles

```
SmokingHole.prototype = {
    ...

    createFireParticles: function (fireParticleCount, left, top) {
        var radius,
            offset;

        for (i = 0; i < fireParticleCount; ++i) {
            radius = Math.random() * 1.5;
            offset = Math.random() * (radius * 2);

            if (i % 2 === 0) {
                fireParticle = this.createFireParticle(left + offset,
                                                       top  - offset,
                                                       radius);
            }
            else {
                fireParticle = this.createFireParticle(left - offset,
                                                       top  + offset,
                                                       radius);
            }

            this.fireParticles.push(fireParticle);
        }
    },
    ...
};
```

---

createFireParticles() randomly varies both the size and position of the fire particles it creates. It then pushes each fire particle onto the smoking hole's array of fire particles. To create individual fire particles, createFireParticles() delegates to a createFireParticle() method, which is listed in Example 16.13.

Example 16.13   Creating individual fire particles

```
SmokingHole.prototype = {
   ...

   createFireParticle: function (left, top, radius) {
      var sprite = new Sprite(
               'fire particle',
               this.createFireParticleArtist(left, top, radius));

      sprite.left    = left;
      sprite.top     = top;
      sprite.radius  = radius;
      sprite.visible = true;

      return sprite;
   },
   ...
};
```

Recall that because they have no graphical representation, smoking holes are not sprites; however, fire particles and smoke bubbles do have graphical representations, so Snail Bait implements them as sprites.

Like all sprites, fire particles are drawn by an artist, which is created by the smoking hole's createFireParticleArtist() method. That method, which is listed in Example 16.14, is called from createFireParticle() in the previous listing.

Example 16.14   Creating fire particle artists

```
SmokingHole.prototype = {
   ...

   createFireParticleArtist: function (left, top, radius) {
      var YELLOW_PREAMBLE = 'rgba(255,255,0,';

      return { // Return a JavaScript object with a draw() method
         draw: function (sprite, context) {
            context.save();

            context.fillStyle = YELLOW_PREAMBLE +
                              Math.random().toFixed(2) + ');';

            context.beginPath();
            context.arc(sprite.left, sprite.top,
                     sprite.radius*1.5, 0, Math.PI*2, false);
```

```
        context.fill();

        context.restore();
      }
    };
  },
  ...
};
```

The createFireParticleArtist() method creates an object with a draw() method, as required by all sprite artists. That draw() method draws a yellow filled circle with a random opacity. It's that random opacity, which is different every time the draw() method draws the particle, that makes particles appear to flicker.

16.3.2.2 Draw and Update Fire Particles Every Animation Frame

Unlike its other sprites, Snail Bait does not draw or update fire particles or smoke bubbles directly. That's because fire particles and smoke bubbles reside in smoking holes, instead of in Snail Bait's sprites array; it's the smoking holes that Snail Bait updates and draws every animation frame. To draw fire particles, we modify the SmokingHole object's draw() method, as shown in Example 16.15.

Example 16.15 Adding sprite methods, revised for fire particles

---

```
SmokingHole.prototype = {
  ...

  addSpriteMethods: function () {
    this.draw = function (context) {
      // TODO: Draw smoke bubbles

      this.drawFireParticles(context);
      ...
    };
    ...
  },
  ...
};
```

The drawFireParticles() method is listed in Example 16.16.

Example 16.16 Drawing fire particles

```
SmokingHole.prototype = {
  ...
```

(Continues)

Example 16.16 *(Continued)*

```
drawFireParticles: function (context) {
    for (var i=0; i < this.fireParticles.length; ++i) {
        this.fireParticles[i].draw(context);
    }
},
...
};
```

`drawFireParticles()` iterates over the smoking hole's fire particles, drawing each one in turn. Recall that fire particles are sprites, so their `draw()` method delegates to the sprite's artist. For fire particles, that artist is the one listed in Example 16.14.

Now that you've seen how to incorporate fire particles into Snail Bait, let's see how to incorporate smoke bubbles.

 NOTE: Fire particles do not have behaviors

Fire particles are sprites, but they don't have any behaviors. A fire particle's apparent flickering is caused by its artist, which draws fire particles in yellow with a random alpha component. Smoke bubbles, on the other hand, which are considerably more complicated than fire particles, do have a behavior. That smoke bubble behavior makes the bubbles dissipate.

16.3.3 Incorporate Smoke Bubbles

As Figure 16.5 illustrates, smoke bubbles begin as small opaque circles that dissipate.

Smoke bubbles, which move, change size, and change opacity over time, are more complicated than fire particles which merely flicker. As a result of that added complexity, we break the task of incorporating smoke bubbles into four steps, as follows:

- Create smoke bubbles
- Draw and update smoke bubbles every animation frame
- Emit smoke bubbles from a smoking hole
- Dissipate smoke bubbles

Let's look at each step in turn.

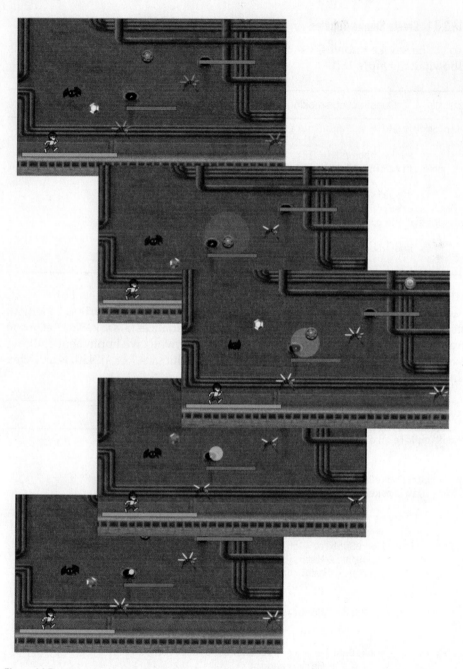

Figure 16.5 One smoke bubble dissipates (counterclockwise from bottom to top).

16.3.3.1 Create Smoke Bubbles

To create smoke bubbles, we once again revise the SmokingHole constructor as shown in **Example 16.17**.

Example 16.17 Constructing smoking holes: Incorporate smoke bubbles (final implementation)

```
var SmokingHole = function (smokeBubbleCount, fireParticleCount,
                           left, top, width) {
   this.smokeBubbles  = [];
   this.fireParticles = [];

   this.disguiseAsSprite    (left, top, width);
   this.createFireParticles(fireParticleCount, left, top);
   this.createSmokeBubbles (smokeBubbleCount, left, top);

   this.smokeBubbleCursor = 0;
};
```

The final version of the SmokingHole constructor declares a smokeBubbles array, which it fills with smoke bubble objects in the createSmokeBubbles() method, listed in **Example 16.18**. The constructor also initializes a smokeBubbleCursor variable to 0. That variable, which comes into play when we implement emitting smoke bubbles in Section 16.3.3.3, "Emit Smoke Bubbles," on p. 430, is an index into the smokeBubbles array.

Example 16.18 Creating smoke bubbles

```
SmokingHole.prototype = {
   ...

   createSmokeBubbles: function (smokeBubbleCount, left, top) {
      var smokeBubble; // smokeBubble is a sprite

      for (i = 0; i < smokeBubbleCount; ++i) {
         if (i % 2 === 0) { // i is an even number
            smokeBubble = this.createBubbleSprite(
               left + Math.random()*3,
               top - Math.random()*3,
               1,  // radius
               Math.random() * 8,  // velocityX
               Math.random() * 5); // velocityY
         }
         else {
            smokeBubble = this.createBubbleSprite(
               left + Math.random()*10,
```

```
        top + Math.random()*6,
        1,  // radius
        Math.random() * 8,  // velocityX
        Math.random() * 5); // velocityY
     }

     this.setInitialSmokeBubbleColor(smokeBubble, i);

     if (i < 10) {
        // Make sure colored smoke bubbles don't overtake
        // the grayscale bubbles on top.
        smokeBubble.dissipatesSlowly = true;
     }

     this.smokeBubbles.push(smokeBubble);
   }
  },
  ...
};
```

The createSmokeBubbles() method creates smoke bubbles with varying characteristics by invoking a helper method—createBubbleSprite()—that creates individual smoke bubbles. The createSmokeBubbles() method then sets the initial
colors for the smoke bubble with the setInitialSmokeBubbleColor() method
listed in Example 16.19 and sets the dissipatesSlowly flag for the first ten smoke
bubbles.

Example 16.19 Setting smoke bubble initial colors

```
SmokingHole.prototype = {
  ...

  setInitialSmokeBubbleColor: function (smokeBubble, i) {
     var ORANGE = 'rgba(255,104,31,0.3)',
         YELLOW = 'rgba(255,255,0,0.3)',
         BLACK  = 'rgba(0,0,0,0.5)';

     if (i <= 5)        smokeBubble.fillStyle = BLACK;
     else if (i <= 8)   smokeBubble.fillStyle = YELLOW;
     else if (i <= 10)  smokeBubble.fillStyle = ORANGE;
     else
        smokeBubble.fillStyle =
           'rgb(' + (220+Math.random()*35).toFixed(0) +
           ',' + (220+Math.random()*35).toFixed(0) +
           ',' + (220+Math.random()*35).toFixed(0) + ')';
  },
  ...
};
```

The first ten smoke bubbles are black-, yellow-, or orange-colored bubbles that the game draws underneath the grayscale bubbles, to make the smoke look more realistic by creating a fiery backdrop. Those first ten smoke bubbles also dissipate slowly so they don't expose the fiery backdrop illusion by overtaking the grayscale bubbles above them. The first ten smoke bubbles dissipate slowly because the SmokingHole constructor sets their dissipatesSlowly property to true.

As you saw in Example 16.18, individual smoke bubbles—which are sprites—are created by the SmokingHole.createBubbleSprite() method, listed in Example 16.20.

Example 16.20 Creating smoke bubble sprites

```
SmokingHole.prototype = {
   ...

   createBubbleSprite: function (left, top, radius,
                                 velocityX, velocityY) {
      var DEFAULT_BUBBLE_LIFETIME = 10000; // 10 seconds

      sprite = new Sprite('smoke bubble',
                          this.createBubbleArtist(),
                          [ this.createDissipateBubbleBehavior() ]);

      this.setBubbleSpriteProperties(sprite, left, top, radius,
                                     velocityX, velocityY);

      this.createBubbleSpriteTimer(sprite, DEFAULT_BUBBLE_LIFETIME);

      return sprite;
   },
   ...
};
```

The createBubbleSprite() method creates a new sprite whose type is smoke bubble, with a bubble artist and a behavior that dissipates the bubble. Subsequently, createBubbleSprite() sets initial values for the sprite's properties with setBubbleSpriteProperties(), listed in Example 16.21.

Example 16.21 Setting bubble sprite properties

```
SmokingHole.prototype = {
   ...

   setBubbleSpriteProperties: function (sprite, left, top, radius,
                                        velocityX, velocityY) {
```

```
    sprite.left   = left;
    sprite.top    = top;
    sprite.radius = radius;

    sprite.originalLeft   = left;
    sprite.originalTop    = top;
    sprite.originalRadius = radius;

    sprite.velocityX = velocityX;
    sprite.velocityY = velocityY;
  },
  ...
};
```

The createBubbleArtist() method, invoked from createBubbleSprite() in Example 16.20 and listed in Example 16.22, creates the smoke bubble's artist.

Example 16.22 Creating the bubble artist

```
SmokingHole.prototype = {
  ...

  createBubbleArtist: function () {
    return {
      draw: function (sprite, context) {
        var TWO_PI = Math.PI * 2;

        if (sprite.radius > 0) {
          context.save();
          context.beginPath();

          context.fillStyle = sprite.fillStyle;
          context.arc(sprite.left, sprite.top,
                      sprite.radius, 0, TWO_PI, false);

          context.fill();
          context.restore();
        }
      }
    };
  },
  ...
};
```

Smoke bubble artists simply draw a filled circle in the game's canvas. Recall that the circle's fill style was set by SmokingHole.setInitialSmokeBubbleColor(), listed in Example 16.19.

After setting the bubble sprite's properties, the `createBubbleSprite()` method listed in Example 16.20 creates a timer with the `createBubbleSpriteTimer()` method, listed in Example 16.23.

Example 16.23 Bubble sprite helper methods

```
SmokingHole.prototype = {
   ...

   createBubbleSpriteTimer: function (sprite, bubbleLifetime) {
      sprite.timer = new AnimationTimer(
         bubbleLifetime,
         AnimationTimer.makeEaseOutEasingFunction(1.5));
      ...
   },
   ...
};
```

The smoke bubble's timer is used by the smoke bubble's dissipate bubble behavior, discussed in Section 16.3.3.4, "Dissipate Smoke Bubbles," on p. 432.

The timer runs for ten seconds, during which it modifies the flow of time with an easing-out function. That easing-out function means that smoke bubbles expand more slowly as they become larger; see Chapter 9 for more information about easing functions.

Now that you've seen how Snail Bait creates smoke bubbles, let's see how the game draws and updates them.

16.3.3.2 Draw and Update Smoke Bubbles Every Animation Frame

Recall that Snail Bait treats smoking holes as sprites, even though they are not. That means Snail Bait invokes each visible smoking hole's `draw()` and `update()` methods every animation frame. In Example 16.24, we update those methods.

Example 16.24 `SmokingHole.addSpriteMethods()`, revised

```
SmokingHole.prototype = {
   ...

   addSpriteMethods: function () {
      this.draw = function (context) {
         this.drawFireParticles(context);
         this.drawSmokeBubbles(context);
      };
```

```
       this.update = function (now, fps,
                               context, lastAnimationFrameTime) {
          this.updateSmokeBubbles(now, fps, context,
                               lastAnimationFrameTime);
          ...
       };
    },
    ...
};
```

When Snail Bait draws smoking holes, smoking holes draw their fire particles and smoke bubbles. When Snail Bait updates smoking holes, smoking holes update their smoke bubbles (but don't update their fire particles because fire particles have no behaviors). The SmokingHole.drawSmokeBubbles() and SmokingHole.updateSmokeBubbles() methods are listed in Example 16.25.

Example 16.25 Drawing and updating smoke bubbles

```
SmokingHole.prototype = {
   ...

   drawSmokeBubbles: function (context) {
      for (var i=0; i < this.smokeBubbles.length; ++i) {
         this.smokeBubbles[i].draw(context);
      }
   },

   updateSmokeBubbles: function (now, fps, context,
                               lastAnimationFrameTime) {
      for (var i=0; i < this.smokeBubbles.length; ++i) {
         this.smokeBubbles[i].update(now, fps, context,
                               lastAnimationFrameTime);
      }
   },
   ...
};
```

The preceding methods are straightforward. Each iterates over the smoking hole's smokeBubbles array and either draws or updates individual smoke bubbles.

Now that you've seen how to create smoke bubbles and how Snail Bait draws and updates them, two things remain: emitting smoke bubbles from a smoking hole and subsequently dissipating the smoke bubble. First, let's look at emitting smoke bubbles.

16.3.3.3 Emit Smoke Bubbles

Smoking holes emit smoke bubbles with a behavior, and because smoking holes are not really sprites, we must manually execute their behaviors. We do that in `SmokingHole.update()`, as shown in Example 16.26.

Example 16.26 `SmokingHole.update()`'s final implementation

```
SmokingHole.prototype = {
   ...

   addSpriteMethods: function () {
      this.draw = function (context) {
         this.drawFireParticles(context);
         this.drawSmokeBubbles(context);
      };

      this.update = function (now, fps,
                             context, lastAnimationFrameTime) {

         this.updateSmokeBubbles(now, fps, context,
                             lastAnimationFrameTime);

         for (var i=0; i < this.behaviors.length; ++i) {
            this.behaviors[i].execute(this, now, fps,
                                   context, lastAnimationFrameTime);
         }
      };
   },
   ...
};
```

Next, we create the smoking hole's behavior with the `SmokingHole.`
`addBehaviors()` method that we introduced in Section 16.3.1, "Disguise Smoking Holes as Sprites," on p. 415. That method, as you can see in Example 16.27, creates an array with a single behavior.

Example 16.27 Emitting smoke bubbles

```
SmokingHole.prototype = {
   ...

   addBehaviors: function () {
      this.behaviors = [
         {
            ...
            execute: function (sprite, now, fps,
                             context, lastAnimationFrameTime) {
```

```
        // Reveal a smoke bubble every animation frame
        // until all the smoking hole's smoke bubbles have
        // been revealed.

        if (sprite.hasMoreSmokeBubbles()) {
            sprite.emitSmokeBubble();
            sprite.advanceCursor();
        }
      }
    }
  ];
  },
  ...
};
```

Snail Bait invokes the preceding behavior's execute() method for every animation frame in which the smoking hole is visible, passing to the execute() method the smoking hole to which the behavior is attached. The execute() method checks to see if the smoking hole has more smoke bubbles to emit; if so, it emits the next smoke bubble and advances the cursor into the smoking hole's array of smoke bubbles. The helper methods invoked in Example 16.27 are listed in Example 16.28.

Example 16.28 Smoking hole behavior support methods

```
SmokingHole.prototype = {
  ...

  hasMoreSmokeBubbles: function () {
    return this.smokeBubbleCursor !== this.smokeBubbles.length-1;
  },

  emitSmokeBubble: function () {
    this.smokeBubbles[this.smokeBubbleCursor].visible = true;
  },

  advanceCursor: function () {
    if (this.smokeBubbleCursor <= this.smokeBubbles.length - 1) {
      ++this.smokeBubbleCursor;
    }
    else {
      this.smokeBubbleCursor = 0;
    }
  },
  ...
};
```

That's all there is to emitting smoke bubbles. Next, let's see how they dissipate.

16.3.3.4 Dissipate Smoke Bubbles

As you saw in the preceding section, smoking holes emit smoke bubbles with a behavior. Likewise, a smoke bubble behavior dissipates the bubble. That behavior's execute() method is listed in Example 16.29.

Example 16.29 Create the dissipate bubble behavior

```
SmokingHole.prototype = {
   ...

   createDissipateBubbleBehavior: function () {
      return {
         FULLY_OPAQUE: 1.0,
         BUBBLE_EXPANSION_RATE: 15,
         BUBBLE_SLOW_EXPANSION_RATE: 10,
         BUBBLE_X_SPEED_FACTOR: 8,
         BUBBLE_Y_SPEED_FACTOR: 16,

         execute: function (sprite, now, fps, context,
                            lastAnimationFrameTime) {
            if ( ! sprite.timer.isRunning()) {
               sprite.timer.start(now);
            }
            else if ( ! sprite.timer.isExpired(now)) {
               this.dissipateBubble(sprite, now,
                                 fps, lastAnimationFrameTime);
            }
            else { // timer is expired
               sprite.timer.reset();
               this.resetBubble(sprite, now); // resets the timer
            }
         },
         ...
      };
   },
   ...
};
```

The preceding behavior's execute() method dissipates bubbles when the bubble's timer is running and has not expired. If the timer is not running, the execute() method starts it, and if the timer has expired, the execute() method resets the timer and the bubble.

The dissipateBubble() and resetBubble() helper methods used in Example 16.29 are listed in Example 16.30.

Example 16.30 The dissipate bubble behavior's helper methods

```javascript
SmokingHole.prototype = {
   ...

   createDissipateBubbleBehavior: function () {
      return {
         ...

         dissipateBubble: function (sprite, now, fps,
                                    lastAnimationFrameTime) {
            var elapsedTime = sprite.timer.getElapsedTime(now),
                velocityFactor = (now - lastAnimationFrameTime) / 1000;

            sprite.left += sprite.velocityX * velocityFactor;
            sprite.top  -= sprite.velocityY * velocityFactor;

            sprite.opacity = this.FULLY_OPAQUE - elapsedTime /
                             sprite.timer.duration;

            if (sprite.dissipatesSlowly) {
               sprite.radius +=
                  this.BUBBLE_SLOW_EXPANSION_RATE * velocityFactor;
            }
            else {
               sprite.radius += this.BUBBLE_EXPANSION_RATE *
                                velocityFactor;
            }
         },

         resetBubble: function (sprite, now) {
            sprite.opacity = this.FULLY_OPAQUE;
            sprite.left    = sprite.originalLeft;
            sprite.top     = sprite.originalTop;
            sprite.radius  = sprite.originalRadius;

            sprite.velocityX = Math.random() *
                               this.BUBBLE_X_SPEED_FACTOR;

            sprite.velocityY = Math.random() *
                               this.BUBBLE_Y_SPEED_FACTOR;

            sprite.opacity = 0;
         }
      };
   },
   ...
};
```

The dissipateBubble() method dissipates bubbles by adjusting their location, size, and opacity to make bubbles grow larger and less opaque. Recall from Example 16.20 on p. 426 that the smoke bubble's timer runs for ten seconds and uses an easing-out function, which causes a smoke bubble's expansion to slow as it grows.

The resetBubble() method resets smoke bubbles to their initial configurations, with a random component mixed in for their velocity.

At this point, smoking holes are spewing smoke according to plan; however, if you pause the game and resume it, the smoking holes will not resume exactly where they left off. We take care of that last implementation detail in the next section.

16.4 Pause Smoking Holes

Recall that behaviors that time their activities should implement pause() and unpause() methods to stay in sync with the game. As you can see from Example 16.31, smoking hole behaviors implement pause() and unpause() methods, which iterate over the smoking hole's smoke bubbles, pausing or unpausing each one.

Example 16.31 Adding pause() and unpause() methods to smoke bubbles

```
SmokingHole.prototype = {
   ...
   addBehaviors: function () {
      this.behaviors = [
         {
            pause: function (sprite, now) {
               for (i=0; i < sprite.smokeBubbles.length; ++i) {
                  sprite.smokeBubbles[i].pause(now);
               }
            },

            unpause: function (sprite, now) {
               for (i=0; i < sprite.smokeBubbles.length; ++i) {
                  sprite.smokeBubbles[i].unpause(now);
               }
            },
            ...
         }
      ];
   },
   ...
};
```

The smoke bubble pause() and unpause() methods pause and unpause the smoke bubble's timer. The createBubbleSpriteTimer() method creates the timer and implements the methods, as shown in Example 16.32.

Example 16.32 Adding pause() and unpause() methods to smoke bubble behaviors

```
SmokingHole.prototype = {
    ...

    createBubbleSpriteTimer: function (sprite, bubbleLifetime) {
        sprite.timer = new AnimationTimer(
            bubbleLifetime,
            AnimationTimer.makeEaseOutEasingFunction(1.5));

        sprite.pause = function (now) {
            this.timer.pause(now);
        };

        sprite.unpause = function (now) {
            this.timer.unpause(now);
        };
    },
    ...
};
```

16.5 Conclusion

This chapter is ostensibly about particle systems. In this case the particle system is a smoking hole that displays fire particles and emits smoke bubbles, but the concepts easily translate to other types of particle systems that emit other kinds of particles.

An underlying theme in this chapter is the implementation of sprites that contain other sprites. In our case, smoking holes, which strictly speaking are not sprites but behave like them, contain fire particles and smoke bubbles, which are sprites.

Another underlying theme in this chapter is the use of *duck typing*. Because smoking holes themselves do not have a graphical representation, we did not implement them as sprites; however, it was convenient for the game to treat them as though they were sprites, and to do that we used duck typing.

Some programming languages force objects to conform to specific interfaces; for example, if you want to treat something as a sprite, it must actually be a sprite. Duck typing, on the other hand, does not force objects to conform to interfaces; for example, if you want to treat something as a sprite, it doesn't actually have to be a sprite, it just needs to act like one. If something looks like a duck and acts like a duck, duck typing treats it like a duck without requiring duck credentials.

Duck typing let us disguise smoking holes as sprites by merely adding methods and properties that look identical to sprite methods and properties. Perhaps most importantly, we did not have to modify a class hierarchy to get Snail Bait to accept smoking holes as sprites. Although they have benefits, maintaining class hierarchies can become cumbersome.

16.6 Exercises

1. Change the number of smoke bubbles to 10 and run the game. What happened to the smoke? Why?

2. For the version of the game corresponding to this chapter, increment the number of smoke bubbles by 5, run the game, and watch the fps meter in the upper-left corner. Did it change considerably after you added 5 smoke bubbles? If not, add 5 more and keep adding 5 at a time until you see an impact on performance.

3. As implemented in this chapter, smoking holes immediately start smoking after they are created. Modify the SmokingHole constructor in the final version of Snail Bait to introduce a delay by setting the smoking hole's visibility to false, and then, after a time-out lasting for a specific number of seconds, reset the smoking hole's visibility to true.

CHAPTER 17

User Interface

Topics in This Chapter

Great games are not merely games, they are experiences. All aspects of a game, including sound, music, user interface, and gameplay, combine to create that experience, so it's important to apply as much polish as you can to each aspect to create the best experience.

In this chapter we explore the implementation of Snail Bait's user interface, starting with the simple task of tracking and displaying the game's score and ending with something a little more complicated: displaying a winning animation when the player wins the game. In between, we discuss how to let players tweet their score, how to warn players when the game runs slowly, and how to show credits at the end of the game.

In this chapter you will learn how to do the following:

- Keep score (Section 17.1)
- Add a lives indicator to the game (Section 17.2 on p. 442)
- Display credits (Section 17.3 on p. 448)
- Tweet player scores (Section 17.4 on p. 455)
- Warn players when the game runs slowly (Section 17.5 on p. 458)
- Implement a winning animation (Section 17.6 on p. 467)

17.1 Keep Score

When the runner collides with an asset, meaning a coin, ruby, or sapphire, Snail Bait increases the game's score, which it displays above the game's canvas, as shown in Figure 17.1.

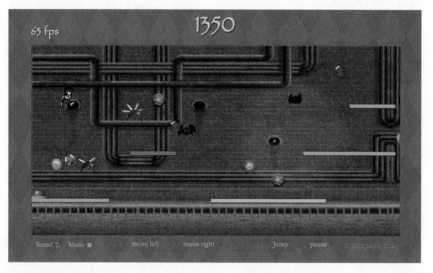

Figure 17.1 The snailbait-score element

Snail Bait keeps track of the score as follows:

- Adds a snailbait-score HTML element
- Specifies CSS for the snailbait-score element
- Accesses the snailbait-score element in JavaScript
- Creates a score variable and initializes it to zero

- Assigns values to sprites that are assets
- Updates the `score` variable and `snailbait-score` element when the runner collides with an asset

First, we add a `DIV` HTML element to Snail Bait's HTML and initialize its value to zero, as shown in Example 17.1.

Example 17.1 Add a `snailbait-score` HTML element

```html
<!DOCTYPE html>
<html>
   ...

   <body>
      ...

      <div id='snailbait-arena'>
         ...

         <div id='snailbait-score'>
            0
         </div>
         ...

      </div>
   </body>
</html>
```

The CSS for the `snailbait-score` element is listed in Example 17.2.

Example 17.2 Specify CSS for the `snailbait-score` element

```css
#snailbait-score {
   font: 46px fantasy;
   text-align: center;
   color: yellow;
   text-shadow: 2px 2px 4px navy;

   -webkit-transition: opacity 5s;
   -moz-transition: opacity 5s;
   -o-transition: opacity 5s;
   transition: opacity 5s;

   opacity: 0;
   display: none;
}
```

The preceding CSS configures the snailbait-score element's font, specifies a CSS transition, and makes the element initially invisible. That transition takes effect when Snail Bait sets the snailbait-score element's opacity property to 1.0 after gameplay begins, as discussed in Section 5.5 on p. 140.

With the HTML and CSS in place for the snailbait-score element, Snail Bait accesses the element in the game's constructor, as shown in Example 17.3. The constructor declares the score variable and initializes it to zero.

Example 17.3 Declare the score variable and access the snailbait-score HTML element

```
var SnailBait = function () {
   ...

   this.scoreElement = document.getElementById('snailbait-score');
   this.score = 0;
   ...
};
```

Snail Bait assigns values to assets in its setSpriteValues() method. The game invokes that method from initializeSprites(), as you can see from Example 17.4.

Example 17.4 Assign values to coins, rubies, and sapphires

```
SnailBait.prototype = {
   ...

   setSpriteValues: function() {
      var sprite,
          COIN_VALUE      = 100,
          SAPPHIRE_VALUE = 500,
          RUBY_VALUE      = 1000;

      for (var i = 0; i < this.sprites.length; ++i) {
         sprite = this.sprites[i];

         if (sprite.type === 'coin') {
            sprite.value = COIN_VALUE;
         }
         else if (sprite.type === 'ruby') {
            sprite.value = RUBY_VALUE;
         }
         else if (sprite.type === 'sapphire') {
            sprite.value = SAPPHIRE_VALUE;
         }
      }
   },
```

```
   initializeSprites: function() {
      ...

      this.setSpriteValues();
      ...
   },
   ...
};
```

When the runner collides with an asset, the runner's collide behavior increments the game's score and updates the snailbait-score element, as shown in Example 17.5.

Example 17.5 Adjust the score

```
var SnailBait = function () {
   ...

   this.collideBehavior = {
      adjustScore: function (sprite) {
         if (sprite.value) {
            snailBait.score += sprite.value;
            snailBait.updateScoreElement();
         }
      },

      processAssetCollision: function (sprite) {
         sprite.visible = false; // sprite is the asset

         if (sprite.type === 'coin')
            snailBait.playSound(snailBait.coinSound);
         else
            snailBait.playSound(snailBait.chimesSound);

         this.adjustScore(sprite);
      },
      ...
   };
   ...
};

SnailBait.prototype = {
   ...

   updateScoreElement: function () {
      this.scoreElement.innerHTML = this.score;
   },
   ...
};
```

When the runner collides with an asset, the collide behavior's `processAssetCollision()` method plays a sound and adjusts the game's score.

Now that you've seen how to keep score, let's see how to add a lives indicator.

17.2 Add a Lives Indicator

When Snail Bait begins, players have three lives. When the runner collides with a bat or a bee or falls through the bottom of the game, the player loses a life. Snail Bait displays the number of remaining lives above and to the left of the game's canvas, as shown in Figure 17.2.

Figure 17.2 The lives indicator

Adding the lives indicator involves the following steps:

- Add HTML elements for each life indicator and their containing DIV
- Specify CSS for the elements
- Access the elements in JavaScript
- Reveal the elements when the game starts
- Update the elements when the player loses a life

As you can see from Example 17.6, each life indicator is an image. The images, three in all, reside in a DIV with the identifier `snailbait-lives`.

Example 17.6 Add HTML elements for life indicators

```html
<!DOCTYPE html>
<html>
   ...

   <body>
      ...

      <div id='snailbait-arena'>
         ...

         <div id='snailbait-lives'>
            <img id='snailbait-life-icon-left'
               src='images/runner-small.png'/>

            <img id='snailbait-life-icon-middle'
               src='images/runner-small.png'/>

            <img id='snailbait-life-icon-right'
               src='images/runner-small.png'/>
         </div>
         ...
      </div>
      ...
   </body>
</html>
```

The three images and the DIV are shown in Figure 17.3 with white borders around each element.

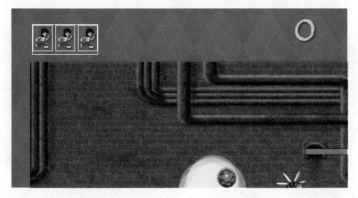

Figure 17.3 Life indicator HTML elements

The CSS for those elements (without the white borders) is shown in Example 17.7.

Example 17.7 Specify CSS for the elements

```css
#snailbait-lives {
    position: absolute;
    margin-top: 20px;
    margin-left: 5px;

    -webkit-transition: opacity 5s;
    -moz-transition: opacity 5s;
    -o-transition: opacity 5s;
    transition: opacity 5s;

    display: none;
    opacity: 0;
}

#snailbait-life-icon-left {
    -webkit-transition: opacity 5s;
    -moz-transition: opacity 5s;
    -o-transition: opacity 5s;
    transition: opacity 5s;
}

#snailbait-life-icon-middle {
    -webkit-transition: opacity 5s;
    -moz-transition: opacity 5s;
    -o-transition: opacity 5s;
    transition: opacity 5s;
}

#snailbait-life-icon-right {
    -webkit-transition: opacity 5s;
    -moz-transition: opacity 5s;
    -o-transition: opacity 5s;
    transition: opacity 5s;
}
```

All four elements have a CSS transition on the `opacity` property. When Snail Bait changes that property's value, the browser smoothly animates the associated element from the current opacity to the new opacity. Snail Bait sets the opacity for the `snailbait-lives` element when the game starts, fading it in, and fades it out temporarily when a player loses a life.

Snail Bait's constructor function obtains references to the four elements as shown in Example 17.8.

Example 17.8 Access the elements in Snail Bait's constructor

```
var SnailBait = function () {
   ...

   this.livesElement =
      document.getElementById('snailbait-lives');

   this.lifeIconLeft =
      document.getElementById('snailbait-life-icon-left');

   this.lifeIconMiddle =
      document.getElementById('snailbait-life-icon-middle');

   this.lifeIconRight =
      document.getElementById('snailbait-life-icon-right');
   ...
};
```

As Snail Bait loads resources, the score element and the lives indicator elements—collectively referred to as the game's top chrome—fade in, but only to 0.25 opacity to focus the player's attention on the game's bottom chrome, which contains the game's instructions. A short time later, the game fades the top chrome to 1.0 opacity.

Example 17.9 shows the revised listings of Snail Bait's `revealTopChrome()` and `revealTopChromeDimmed()` methods, originally discussed in Chapter 5, which now manipulate the `snailbait-lives` element instead of the defunct frames/second indicator that has occupied the upper-left corner of the game until now.

Example 17.9 Snail Bait's `revealTopChrome()` and `revealTopChromeDimmed()`, final version

```
SnailBait.prototype = {
   ...

   revealTopChrome: function () {
      this.fadeInElements(this.livesElement,
                          this.scoreElement);
   },

   revealTopChromeDimmed: function () {
      var DIM = 0.25;

      this.scoreElement.style.display = 'block';
```

(Continues)

Example 17.9   *(Continued)*

```
    this.livesElement.style.display = 'block';

    setTimeout( function () {
        snailBait.scoreElement.style.opacity = DIM;
        snailBait.livesElement.style.opacity = DIM;
    }, this.SHORT_DELAY); // 50 ms
  },
  ...
};
```

The revealTopChrome() method invokes Snail Bait's fadeInElements() method, which takes a variable-length list of elements. The fadeInElements() method fades elements in by setting their opacity to 1.0; for the fade-in animation, the method relies on CSS transitions attached to the elements.

The revealTopChromeDimmed() method sets the opacity for the snailbait-score and snailbait-lives elements to 0.25 instead of 1.0, so instead of invoking fadeInElements(), which makes elements fully opaque, revealTopChromeDimmed() fades elements in by hand. Like revealTopChrome(), revealTopChromeDimmed() relies on CSS transitions attached to the elements it manipulates.

When the player loses a life, Snail Bait's loseLife() method decrements the lives property and updates the snailbait-lives element, as shown in Example 17.10.

Example 17.10   Update the lives variable and the snailbait-lives element when the player loses a life

---

```
SnailBait.prototype = {
    ...

    loseLife: function () {
        ...

        this.lives--;
        this.updateLivesElement();
        ...
    }
    ...
};
```

The updateLivesElement() method is listed in Example 17.11.

Example 17.11 Update the snailbait-lives element

```
SnailBait.prototype = {
   ...

   updateLivesElement: function () {
      if (this.lives === 3) {
         this.lifeIconLeft.style.opacity   = snailBait.OPAQUE;
         this.lifeIconMiddle.style.opacity = snailBait.OPAQUE;
         this.lifeIconRight.style.opacity  = snailBait.OPAQUE;
      }
      else if (this.lives === 2) {
         this.lifeIconLeft.style.opacity   = snailBait.OPAQUE;
         this.lifeIconMiddle.style.opacity = snailBait.OPAQUE;
         this.lifeIconRight.style.opacity  = snailBait.TRANSPARENT;
      }
      else if (this.lives === 1) {
         this.lifeIconLeft.style.opacity   = snailBait.OPAQUE;
         this.lifeIconMiddle.style.opacity = snailBait.TRANSPARENT;
         this.lifeIconRight.style.opacity  = snailBait.TRANSPARENT;
      }
      else if (this.lives === 0) {
         this.lifeIconLeft.style.opacity   = snailBait.TRANSPARENT;
         this.lifeIconMiddle.style.opacity = snailBait.TRANSPARENT;
         this.lifeIconRight.style.opacity  = snailBait.TRANSPARENT;
      }
   },
   ...
};
```

The updateLivesElement() method sets the opacity for each life indicator according to the number of lives remaining, which triggers a smooth animation from the previous opacity by virtue of the elements' CSS transition. Snail Bait's OPAQUE and TRANSPARENT constants are 1.0 and 0, respectively.

Now that you've seen how Snail Bait implements the lives indicator, let's see how it displays credits.

 NOTE: Fading elements in and out

The user interface effects in this chapter use Snail Bait's fadeInElements() and fadeOutElements() methods. Those methods, which in turn rely on CSS transitions attached to the elements they manipulate, are discussed in Chapter 5.

17.3 Display Credits

Snail Bait displays credits at the end of the game, as shown in Figure 17.4.

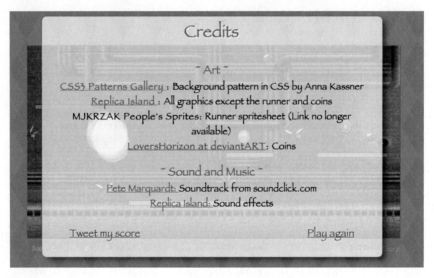

Figure 17.4 Credits

The game implements credits with the following steps:

- Add HTML elements for the credits
- Specify CSS for the credits HTML elements
- Access credits HTML elements in JavaScript
- Implement hideCredits() and revealCredits() methods
- Modify gameOver() to reveal credits
- Modify restartGame() to hide credits
- Add a click event handler for the Play again link that calls restartGame()

As it does for keeping score and displaying life indicators, Snail Bait implements credits by specifying HTML elements and their corresponding CSS and subsequently accessing those elements in the game's constructor. The HTML for the credits is listed in Example 17.12.

Example 17.12	Add HTML elements for the credits

```html
<!DOCTYPE html>
<html>
   ...

   <body>
      ...

      <div id='snailbait-arena'>
         <!-- Credits...............................................-->

         <div id='snailbait-credits' class='snailbait-credits'>
            <div class='snailbait-heading'>Credits</div>

            <hr></hr>

            <div class='snailbait-credit'>
               <div id='snailbait-art-title'
                  class='snailbait-title'>

                  ~ Art ~

               </div>

               <div class='snailbait-attribution'><b>
                  <a href='http://lea.verou.me/css3patterns'>
                     CSS3 Patterns Gallery
                  </a>:

                  </b> Background pattern in CSS by Anna Kassner
               </div>

               <div class='snailbait-attribution'><b>
                  <a href='http://bit.ly/kNzDVc'>
                     Replica Island
                  </a>:

                  </b> All graphics except the runner and coins
               </div>

               <div class='snailbait-attribution'>
                  <b>MJKRZAK People's Sprites:</b>
                  Runner spritesheet (Link no longer available)
               </div>

               <div class='snailbait-attribution'><b>
```

(Continues)

Example 17.12 *(Continued)*

```
                <a href='http://bit.ly/QvGRVR'>
                LoversHorizon at deviantART
                </a>:

                </b> Coins
            </div>
        </div>

        <div class='snailbait-credit'>
            <div id='snailbait-sound-and-music-title'
                class='snailbait-title'>

                ~ Sound and Music ~

            </div>

            <div class='snailbait-attribution'>
                <a href='http://bit.ly/LFtwr8'>
                Pete Marquardt:
                </a>

                Soundtrack from soundclick.com
            </div>

            <div class='snailbait-attribution'>
                <a href='http://bit.ly/kNzDVc'>
                Replica Island:
                </a>

                Sound effects
            </div>
        </div>

        <p>
            <!-- Tweet my score link omitted -->

            <a id='snailbait-play-again-link'
                href='#'>Play again</a>
        </p>

    </div> <!-- end of credits -->
    ...
    </div> <!-- end of arena -->
  </body>
</html>
```

The preceding HTML creates a hierarchy of DIVs where an enclosing snailbait-credits DIV contains snailbait-credit DIVs. The snailbait-credit

DIVs in turn contain snailbait-attribution DIVs. At the end of the snailbait-credits DIV, a paragraph element contains the Tweet my score and Play again links. The HTML for the Tweet my score link is omitted from Example 17.12; instead, it is discussed in Section 17.4 on p. 455.

The CSS for the credits elements is listed in Example 17.13.

Example 17.13 Specify CSS for the credits HTML elements

```css
.snailbait-credits {
   position: absolute;
   margin-left: 50px;
   margin-top: 10px;
   padding-bottom: 30px;
   font: 20px fantasy;
   text-align: center;
   width: 650px;
   height: 23em;
   background: rgba(255,255,230,0.75);
   border: thin solid blue;
   padding-top: 10px;
   padding-left: 40px;
   padding-right: 40px;

   -webkit-transition: opacity 2s;
   -moz-transition: opacity 2s;
   -o-transition: opacity 2s;
   transition: opacity 2s;

   -webkit-box-shadow: rgba(0,0,0,0.5) 8px 8px 16px;
   -moz-box-shadow: rgba(0,0,0,0.5) 8px 8px 16px;
   -o-box-shadow: rgba(0,0,0,0.5) 8px 8px 16px;
   box-shadow: rgba(0,0,0,0.5) 8px 8px 16px;

   border-radius: 10px;

   opacity: 0;
   display: none;
   z-index: 1;
}

#snailbait-credits a:hover {
   color: blue;
   text-shadow: 1px 1px 1px rgba(0,0,200,0.5);
}

#snailbait-credits p {
   margin-top: 20px;
```

(Continues)

Example 17.13 *(Continued)*

```
   margin-bottom: 10px;
   font: 24px fantasy;
   text-shadow: 1px 1px 1px rgba(0,0,0,0.8);
   color: blue;
   text-shadow: 1px 1px 1px rgba(255,255,255,0.6);
}

#snailbait-credits .attribution {
   font: 18px fantasy;
   color: blue;
   text-shadow: 1px 1px 1px rgba(255,255,255,0.6);
}

#snailbait-credits .title {
   margin-bottom: 10px;
   font-size: 22px;
   color: blue;
   text-shadow: 1px 1px 1px rgba(255,255,255,0.6);
}

#snailbait-new-game-link {
  margin-top: 10px;
  float: right;
  margin-right: 20px;
  font-size: 0.9em;
}

#snailbait-art-title {
   margin-top: 20px;
}

#snailbait-sound-and-music-title {
   margin-top: 20px;
}

#snailbait-credits .snailbait-heading {
   margin-bottom: 10px;
   font-size: 35px;
   font-family: fantasy;
   color: blue;
   text-shadow: 2px 2px 2px rgba(255,255,255,0.8);
}

.snailbait-tweet-link {
  margin-top: 10px;
  margin-left: 20px;
  float: left;
  font-size: 0.9em;
}
```

```
#snailbait-play-again-link {
  margin-top: 10px;
  float: right;
  margin-right: 20px;
  font-size: 0.9em;
}
```

As we've done previously with other DIVs that the game fades in and out, the snailbait-credits DIV is initially invisible. A CSS transition smoothly animates the DIV's opacity when the game sets that property. Additionally, the border-radius and box-shadow properties give the snailbait-credits element rounded corners and a drop shadow.

Besides the two links, Snail Bait does not manipulate any of the elements inside the snailbait-credits element because those elements merely display static information. In its constructor function, Snail Bait obtains references to the snailbait-credits element and the Play again link, as shown in Example 17.14.

Example 17.14 Snail Bait's constructor accesses credits HTML elements

---

```
var SnailBait = function () {
   ...

   // Credits......................................................

   this.creditsElement =
      document.getElementById('snailbait-credits');

   this.playAgainLink =
      document.getElementById('snailbait-play-again-link');
   ...
};
```

Snail Bait's revealCredits() and hideCredits() methods, listed in Example 17.15, use the game's fadeInElements() and fadeOutElements() methods, respectively.

Example 17.15 Implement revealCredits() and hideCredits() methods

---

```
SnailBait.prototype = {
   ...

   revealCredits: function () {
      this.fadeInElements(this.creditsElement);
      ...
   },
```

(Continues)

Example 17.15 *(Continued)*

```
  hideCredits: function () {
    var FADE_DURATION = 1000;

    this.fadeOutElements(this.creditsElement, FADE_DURATION);
  },
  ...
};
```

The gameOver() method, listed in Example 17.16, reveals the game's credits, drastically slows the rate at which the background scrolls, and sets the game's playing property to false, which causes the game to disregard player input.

Example 17.16 Modify gameOver() to reveal credits

```
SnailBait.prototype = {
  ...

  gameOver: function () {
    this.revealCredits();
    this.bgVelocity = this.BACKGROUND_VELOCITY / 20;
    this.playing = false;
    ...
  },
  ...
};
```

When the game restarts, it hides credits, as shown in Example 17.17. The restartGame() method also restarts the level, returning the game's background velocity and input handling to normal.

Example 17.17 Modify restartGame() to hide credits

```
SnailBait.prototype = {
  ...

  restartGame: function () {
    this.hideCredits();
    ...

    this.restartLevel();
  },
  ...
};
```

The game restarts when the player clicks the Play again link, as shown in Example 17.18.

Example 17.18 Add a click event handler for the Play again link that calls `restartGame()`

```
snailBait.playAgainLink.AddEventListener(
    'click',

    function (e) {
        snailBait.restartGame();
    }
);
```

Next, let's see how to implement the functionality behind the Tweet my score link.

> **NOTE: The z-index property for UI elements**
>
> The credits and running slowly warning both have a `z-index` of one. That places those elements above the game's canvas, which, by default, has a `z-index` of zero.

17.4 Tweet Player Scores

Twitter's Web Intents are the simplest way to let players tweet about your game. Snail Bait lets players tweet their scores by clicking the Tweet my score link in the game's credits, as shown in Section 17.3, "Display Credits," on p. 448.

Figure 17.5 shows Twitter's documentation for Web Intents.

Using Web Intents is simple. Create a link that points to the Web Intents URL, with parameters for things such as the tweet's text. As you can see from Figure 17.6, when players click the link, the Twitter intent opens a webpage that makes it easy for them to sign into their Twitter account and tweet (the sign in is not necessary if the player is already logged into Twitter).

Snail Bait implements the Tweet my score link with the following steps:

- Add a link to the game's HTML
- Access the link in JavaScript
- Set the link's `href` property to a twitter intent URL

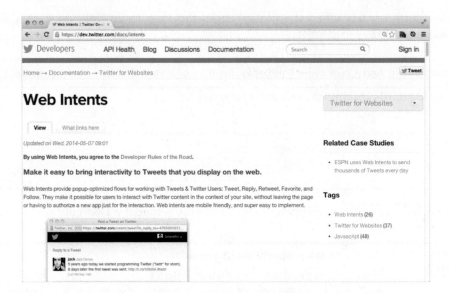

Figure 17.5   Twitter Web Intents (see https://dev.twitter.com/docs/intents)

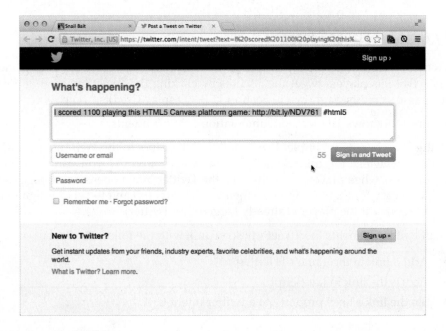

Figure 17.6   Tweeting scores

Example 17.19 shows the Tweet my score link in the game's HTML. The link's target property is _blank, so the browser opens the linked page in a new window or tab, as you can see in Figure 17.6.

Example 17.19 The Tweet my score link

```
<!DOCTYPE html>
<html>
   ...

   <body>
      ...

      <div id='snailbait-arena'>
         ...

         <div id='snailbait-credits'>
            ...

            <p>
               <a id='snailbait-tweet'
                  hashtags='#html5' target='_blank'
                  class='snailbait-tweet-link'>
                  Tweet my score</a>
               ...
            </p>

         </div> <!-- end of credits -->
      </div>
      ...
   </body>
</html>
```

Snail Bait's constructor accesses the link and declares two string constants, as shown in Example 17.20.

Example 17.20 Access the tweet link in JavaScript

```
var SnailBait = function () {
   ...

   this.tweetElement = document.getElementById('snailbait-tweet');

   this.TWEET_PREAMBLE = 'https://twitter.com/intent/tweet?text=' +
                         'I scored ';
```

(Continues)

Example 17.20   *(Continued)*

```
this.TWEET_EPILOGUE = ' playing this HTML5 Canvas platform game: ' +
                       'http://bit.ly/NDV761 &amp;hashtags=html5';
   ...
};
```

Example 17.21 lists the final version of the revealCredits() method that constructs the link's hypertext reference, which Snail Bait accesses with the href property.

Example 17.21   Set the tweet link's hypertext reference

```
SnailBait.prototype = {
   ...

   revealCredits: function () {
      this.fadeInElements(this.creditsElement);
      this.tweetElement.href = this.TWEET_PREAMBLE + this.score +
                               this.TWEET_EPILOGUE;
   },
   ...
};
```

From Snail Bait's perspective, that's all the code that's necessary to let players tweet their scores. Snail Bait's end of the bargain is merely to provide a properly configured link that points to the Twitter intent. The intent takes care of the rest.

 NOTE: The power of Web Intents

Web applications are typically implemented as a collection of services, ranging from simple services such as saving a document to more sophisticated services such as tweeting a game's score. Web Intents let web applications hand off services to third parties to implement the intent.

In this section Snail Bait handed off the service of tweeting the game's score to a Twitter web intent, which is orders of magnitude easier than implementing the same functionality on your own.

17.5 Warn Players When the Game Runs Slowly

HTML5 game developers are fortunate because their games run on virtually any computer platform with a browser, including, with a little extra work, mobile devices. HTML5 game developers are unfortunate, however, because their games, which run in an unpredictable environment, can easily be brought to their knees by all sorts of other applications, from backup software running in the background to YouTube videos running in another window.

No matter how fast your HTML5 game runs, there will be times when a player's computer won't be able to give your game the time it needs and the game will run too slowly to be playable. When that happens, you must warn the user that the game is running too slowly. Figure 17.7 shows Snail Bait's running slowly warning.

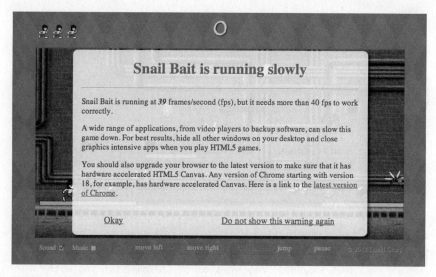

Figure 17.7 The running slowly warning

Snail Bait's running slowly warning includes the game's current frame rate (which the game constantly updates while the running slowly warning is displayed) and an option to dismiss the warning for good. The warning also explains why HTML5 games sometimes run slowly and what the user can do about it.

Snail Bait implements the running slowly warning with the following steps:

- Add HTML elements for the running slowly warning
- Specify CSS for the running slowly warning elements
- Access the HTML elements in JavaScript
- Implement a `revealRunningSlowlyWarning()` method

Example 17.22 shows the HTML for Snail Bait's running slowly warning.

Example 17.22 Add HTML elements for the running slowly warning

```html
<!DOCTYPE html>
<html>
   ...

   <body>
      ...

      <div id='snailbait-arena'>
         ...

         <div id='snailbait-running-slowly'>

            <h1>Snail Bait is running slowly</h1>

            <hr>

            <p id='snailbait-slowly-warning'></p>

            <p>
               A wide range of applications, from video players to
               backup software, can slow this game down. For best
               results, hide all other windows on your desktop and
               close graphics-intensive apps when you play HTML5 games.
            </p>

            <p>
               You should also upgrade your browser to the latest
               version to make sure that it has hardware-accelerated
               HTML5 Canvas. Any version of Chrome starting with
               version 18, for example, has hardware-accelerated
               Canvas. Here is a link to the
               <a href='http://www.google.com/chrome/'>
                  latest version of Chrome
               </a>.
            </p>

            <a id='snailbait-slowly-okay' href='#'>
               Okay
            </a>

            <a  id='snailbait-slowly-dont-show' href='#'>
               Do not show this warning again
            </a>
         </div> <!-- End of running-slowly -->
         ...
      </div> <!-- End of snailbait-arena -->
```

```
    ...
  </body>
</html>
```

The interesting part of the preceding HTML is the empty paragraph element near the top of the listing with the identifier `snailbait-slowly-warning`. Snail Bait fills in the contents of that paragraph element on the fly because the warning contains the game's current frame rate.

The CSS for the running slowly warning is listed in Example 17.23.

Example 17.23 Specify CSS for the running slowly warning elements

```css
#snailbait-running-slowly {
    position: absolute;
    margin-left: 82px;
    margin-top: 75px;
    width: 600px;
    background: rgba(255,255,255,0.85);
    padding: 0px 20px 20px 20px;
    color: navy;
    text-shadow: 1px 1px 1px rgba(255,255,255,0.5);

    -webkit-transition: opacity 1s;
    -moz-transition: opacity 1s;
    -o-transition: opacity 1s;
    transition: opacity 1s;

    border-radius: 10px 10px 10px;

    -webkit-box-shadow: rgba(0,0,0,0.5) 4px 4px 8px;
    -moz-box-shadow: rgba(0,0,0,0.5) 4px 4px 8px;
    -o-box-shadow: rgba(0,0,0,0.5) 4px 4px 8px;
    box-shadow: rgba(0,0,0,0.5) 4px 4px 8px;

    opacity: 0;
    display: none;

    z-index: 1;
}

#snailbait-running-slowly h1 {
    padding-top: 0;
    text-align: center;
    color: rgb(50,50,250);
}
```

(Continues)

Example 17.23   *(Continued)*

```
#snailbait-running-slowly p {
   color: navy;
   font-size: 1.05em;
}

#snailbait-slowly-okay {
   margin-top: 20px;
   float: left;
   margin-left: 50px;
   font-size: 1.2em;
}

#snailbait-slowly-okay:hover {
   color: blue;
}

#snailbait-slowly-dont-show {
   margin-top: 20px;
   float: right;
   margin-right: 50px;
   font-size: 1.2em;
}

#snailbait-slowly-dont-show:hover {
   color: blue;
}
```

Once again, we combine initial invisibility with CSS transitions to fade the running slowly warning in and out as needed by modifying its opacity with Snail Bait's `fadeInElements()` and `fadeOutElements()`. Example 17.24 shows how Snail Bait's constructor accesses the running slowly warning HTML elements.

Example 17.24   Access HTML elements in JavaScript

```
var SnailBait = function () {
   ...

   // Running slowly warning.........................................

   this.runningSlowlyElement =
      document.getElementById('snailbait-running-slowly');

   this.slowlyOkayElement =
      document.getElementById('snailbait-slowly-okay');
```

```
this.slowlyDontShowElement =
   document.getElementById('snailbait-slowly-dont-show');

this.slowlyWarningElement =
   document.getElementById('snailbait-slowly-warning');

this.lastSlowWarningTime = 0;
this.showSlowWarning = false;

this.runningSlowlyThreshold = this.DEFAULT_RUNNING_SLOWLY_THRESHOLD;
   ...
};
```

Snail Bait obtains references to some of the elements in the running slowly warning and creates three variables: showSlowWarning, runningSlowlyThreshold, and lastSlowWarningTime. Snail Bait uses showSlowWarning to control whether the game shows the running slowly warning, and the runningSlowlyThreshold defines the slowest acceptable frame rate. Snail Bait uses lastSlowWarningTime to determine when to next check the game's frame rate.

Snail Bait's revealRunningSlowlyWarning() method is listed in Example 17.25.

Example 17.25 Implement a revealRunningSlowlyWarning() method

```
SnailBait.prototype = {
   ...

   revealRunningSlowlyWarning: function (now, averageSpeed) {
      this.slowlyWarningElement.innerHTML =
         "Snail Bait is running at <i><b>"    +
         averageSpeed.toFixed(0) + "</i></b>"              +
         " frames/second (fps), but it needs more than " +
         this.runningSlowlyThreshold                       +
         " fps to work correctly."

      this.fadeInElements(this.runningSlowlyElement);
      this.lastSlowWarningTime = now;
   },
   ...
};
```

The revealRunningSlowlyWarning() method constructs the variable part of the warning with the game's current frame rate and fades in the running slowly element. The method also updates the lastSlowWarningTime, which records the last time the warning was revealed.

17.5.1 Monitor Frame Rate

When the average frame rate drops below the game's running slowly threshold—represented by the runningSlowlyThreshold variable declared in Example 17.26— Snail Bait invokes the revealRunningSlowlyWarning() method discussed above. Snail Bait's constructor declares an array of ten speed samples and an index into that array.

Example 17.26 Constants and variables for monitoring frame rate

```
var SnailBait = function () {
    ...

    // Running slowly warning.........................................

    this.FPS_SLOW_CHECK_INTERVAL = 2000; // Check every 2 seconds

    this.DEFAULT_RUNNING_SLOWLY_THRESHOLD = 40;   // fps
    this.MAX_RUNNING_SLOWLY_THRESHOLD     = 60;   // fps
    this.RUNNING_SLOWLY_FADE_DURATION     = 2000; // seconds

    this.speedSamples = [60,60,60,60,60,60,60,60,60,60];
    this.speedSamplesIndex = 0;

    this.NUM_SPEED_SAMPLES = this.speedSamples.length;

    this.runningSlowlyThreshold = this.DEFAULT_RUNNING_SLOWLY_THRESHOLD;
    ...
};
```

To monitor frame rate, we revise Snail Bait's animate() method as shown in Example 17.27.

Example 17.27 Revise Snail Bait's animate() method to check frame rate

```
SnailBait.prototype = {
    ...

    animate: function (now) {
        // Replace the time passed to this method by the browser
        // with the time from Snail Bait's time system

        now = snailBait.timeSystem.calculateGameTime();
        ...

        if (snailBait.paused) {
            ...
        }
```

```
    else { // not paused
        snailBait.fps = snailBait.calculateFps(now);

        if (snailBait.windowHasFocus  &&
            snailBait.playing         &&
            snailBait.showSlowWarning &&
            now - snailBait.lastSlowWarningTime >
            snailBait.FPS_SLOW_CHECK_INTERVAL) {

            snailBait.checkFps(now);
        }
        ...
    }
},
...
};
```

Snail Bait's `animate()` method checks the frame rate when play is underway and two seconds have elapsed since the last check. It checks the frame rate with the `checkFps()` method, listed in Example 17.28.

Example 17.28 Monitoring Snail Bait's frame rate

```
SnailBait.prototype = {
   ...

   checkFps: function (now) {
      var averageSpeed;

      this.updateSpeedSamples(snailBait.fps);

      averageSpeed = this.calculateAverageSpeed();

      if (averageSpeed < this.runningSlowlyThreshold) {
         this.revealRunningSlowlyWarning(now, averageSpeed);
      }
   },
   ...
};
```

The `checkFps()` method updates the game's speed samples and subsequently calculates an average speed from those samples. If the average speed is less than the running slowly threshold, `checkFps()` reveals the running slowly warning.

The helper methods used by `checkFps()` are listed in Example 17.29.

Example 17.29 Frame rate checking helper methods

```
SnailBait.prototype = {
   ...

   calculateAverageSpeed: function () {
      var i,
          total = 0;

      for (i=0; i < this.NUM_SPEED_SAMPLES; i++) {
         total += this.speedSamples[i];
      }

      return total/this.NUM_SPEED_SAMPLES;
   },

   updateSpeedSamples: function (fps) {
      this.speedSamples[this.speedSamplesIndex] = fps;
      this.advanceSpeedSamplesIndex();
   },

   advanceSpeedSamplesIndex: function () {
      if (this.speedSamplesIndex !== this.NUM_SPEED_SAMPLES-1) {
         this.speedSamplesIndex++;
      }
      else {
         this.speedSamplesIndex = 0;
      }
   },
   ...
};
```

17.5.2 Implement the Running Slowly Warning Event Handlers

When a player clicks the Do not show this warning again button, the browser invokes the element's click event handler, which is listed in Example 17.30.

Example 17.30 The Do not show this warning again button's event handler

---

```
snailBait.slowlyDontShowElement.addEventListener(
   'click',

   function (e) {
      snailBait.fadeOutElements(snailBait.runningSlowlyElement,
                                snailBait.RUNNING_SLOWLY_FADE_DURATION);
```

```
        snailBait.showSlowWarning = false;
        ...
    }
);
```

The preceding event handler fades the running slowly warning from view for a duration of two seconds. It then sets the showSlowWarning variable to false so that Snail Bait no longer monitors frame rate.

The click event handler for the running slowly warning's Okay button is listed in Example 17.31.

Example 17.31 The Okay button's event handler

```
SnailBait.prototype {
    ...

    resetSpeedSamples: function () {
        snailBait.speedSamples = [60,60,60,60,60,60,60,60,60,60];
    },
    ...
};

snailBait.slowlyOkayElement.addEventListener(
    'click',

    function (e) {
        snailBait.fadeOutElements(snailBait.runningSlowlyElement,
                            snailBait.RUNNING_SLOWLY_FADE_DURATION);
        snailBait.resetSpeedSamples();
    }
);
```

The Okay button's event handler fades out the running slowly warning and resets the game's speed samples array, discarding the frame rates the game recorded before the warning was revealed.

17.6 Implement a Winning Animation

If a player lands on the gold button at the end of the game, as shown in Figure 17.8, Snail Bait displays the winning animation shown in Figure 17.9.

The winning animation fades the game's canvas, replaces the score with *Winner!*, and shows the animated GIF the game displays when it loads. The game's

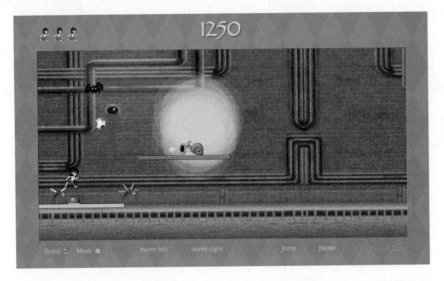

Figure 17.8   Falling on the gold button

Figure 17.9   Winning animation

revealWinningAnimation() method reveals the animation. That method is invoked by a behavior attached to the gold button.

Snail Bait implements the winning animation with the following steps:

- Implement a behavior for the gold button that invokes revealWinning-Animation()
- Detonate the button in the runner's fall behavior when the runner falls on the button
- Implement a revealWinningAnimation() method that fades in the winning animation; after displaying the animation for five seconds, end the game

Snail Bait has two buttons. The first is blue and the second is gold, as you can see from Example 17.32.

Example 17.32 Creating buttons, revised

```
SnailBait.prototype = {
   ...

   createButtonSprites: function () {
      var button;

      for (var i = 0; i < this.buttonData.length; ++i) {
         if (i !== this.buttonData.length - 1) {
            button = new Sprite('button',
                     new SpriteSheetArtist(this.spritesheet,
                                           this.blueButtonCells),
                     [ this.paceBehavior,
                       this.blueButtonDetonateBehavior ]);
         }
         else {
            button = new Sprite('button',
                     new SpriteSheetArtist(this.spritesheet,
                                           this.goldButtonCells),
                     [ this.paceBehavior,
                       this.goldButtonDetonateBehavior ]);
         }
         ...
      }
   },
   ...
};
```

Both buttons pace back and forth on their platforms. Recall from Chapter 13 that the blue button's detonate behavior blows up two bees to clear a path for the runner. The gold button's detonate behavior reveals the winning animation.

As required by all behaviors, the gold button's detonate behavior implements an execute() method, as you can see in Example 17.33. Snail Bait invokes that execute() method for every animation frame in which the gold button is visible.

Example 17.33　The gold button's detonate behavior

```
var SnailBait = function () {
   ...

   this.goldButtonDetonateBehavior = {
      execute: function(sprite, now, fps,
                        lastAnimationFrameTime) {
         var BUTTON_REBOUND_DELAY = 1000;

         if ( ! sprite.detonating) { // trigger
            return;
         }

         sprite.artist.cellIndex = 1; // flatten the button

         snailBait.revealWinningAnimation();
         sprite.detonating = false;

         setTimeout( function () {
            sprite.artist.cellIndex = 0; // rebound
         }, BUTTON_REBOUND_DELAY);
      }
   };
   ...
};
```

The execute() method first checks to see if the sprite—which is always the gold button because the behavior is attached to it—is detonating; if not, there's nothing to do and the method returns. If the button is detonating, the execute() method reveals the winning animation and resets the button's detonating property to false. Like the blue button, Snail Bait flattens the gold button when the runner lands on it and restores the button to normal after a one-second delay.

The gold button's detonating property, which is the trigger for the gold button's detonate behavior, is false until the runner lands on the gold button. In that case, the runner's fall behavior sets the detonating property to true, as you can see in Example 17.34.

Example 17.34　Detonate the gold button

```
SnailBait.prototype = {
   ...

   this.fallBehavior = {
      ...
```

```
    processCollision: function (sprite, otherSprite) {
        if (sprite.jumping && 'platform' === otherSprite.type) {
            this.processPlatformCollisionDuringJump(sprite, otherSprite);
        }
        else if ('button' === otherSprite.type) {
            if (sprite.jumping && sprite.descendTimer.isRunning() ||
                sprite.falling) {
                otherSprite.detonating = true;
            }
        }
    },
    ...
};
```

When the runner's fall behavior sets the gold button's detonating property to true, the gold button's detonate behavior invokes Snail Bait's revealWinningAnimation() method, as you saw in Example 17.33. That method is listed in Example 17.35.

Example 17.35 Reveal the winning animation

```
SnailBait.prototype = {
    ...

    revealWinningAnimation: function () {
        var WINNING_ANIMATION_FADE_TIME = 5000,
            SEMI_TRANSPARENT = 0.25;

        this.bgVelocity = 0;
        this.playing = false;
        this.loadingTitleElement.style.display = 'none';

        this.fadeInElements(this.runnerAnimatedGIFElement,
                            this.loadingElement);

        this.scoreElement.innerHTML = 'Winner!';
        this.canvas.style.opacity = SEMI_TRANSPARENT;

        setTimeout( function () {
            snailBait.runnerAnimatedGIFElement.style.display = 'none';
            snailBait.fadeInElements(snailBait.canvas);
            snailBait.gameOver();
        }, WINNING_ANIMATION_FADE_TIME);
    },
    ...
};
```

The revealWinningAnimation() method fades in the loading screen elements, without the Loading... text that the game displays when it loads resources. As the animated GIF fades in, the canvas fades out to an opacity of 0.25. After five seconds, revealWinningAnimation() hides the animated GIF, fades the canvas in to fully opaque, and ends the game. At that point, Snail Bait either shows the credits toast or, as you'll see in Chapter 19, displays high scores stored on the server.

17.7 Conclusion

In this chapter you saw how to implement most of Snail Bait's user interface. Not all game programming involves programming gameplay, and as a result, game developers spend a significant amount of time implementing features that don't affect gameplay.

At this point we've implemented all Snail Bait's gameplay and most of its user interface. The remaining chapters show you how to implement a developer backdoor, how to store high scores and in-game metrics on the server, and how to deploy your games.

17.8 Exercises

1. When a player captures an asset, change the color of the game's snailbait-score element to red. Subsequently, after a delay of 200 ms, restore the element's color to yellow, making the score flash. Experiment with the duration of the color change to fine-tune the effect.

2. In this chapter we replaced the frame rate (fps) indicator with the lives indicator. Restore the fps indicator to the final version of Snail Bait, this time placing it on the right side of the game instead of the left. Leave the lives indicator intact. Update the fps indicator in Snail Bait's calculateFps() and fade the fps indicator in with the rest of the game's top chrome, meaning you'll need to modify both revealTopChrome() and revealTopChrome-Dimmed().

3. If the frame rate dips below 40 frames/second, display the fps indicator's value in red; otherwise, display it in yellow. Do something to slow the game so you see the red indicator and running slowly warning simultaneously. Compare the frame rate shown in the warning to the frame rate shown by the fps indicator. Are they the same? Why or why not?

4. After performing Exercises 2 and 3, change the fps indicator so that it shows the game's average frame rate instead of the current frame rate calculated by `calculateFps()`. Again, do something to make the running slowly warning appear, and watch the frame rate in the warning versus the rate in the fps indicator.

Developer Backdoor

Topics in This Chapter

Game development is easier if you grant yourself special powers that are unavailable to other players. Those special powers make playtesting more efficient and can reveal insights into your game. For example, Figure 18.1 shows Snail Bait drawing collision rectangles and running in slow motion. Additionally, the developer has zoomed in on the action by using the browser's hot key for zooming.

Turning on collision rectangles and running the game in slow-motion makes it easier to implement collision detection. With the game running at full speed without collision rectangles, it's difficult to see exactly how collision detection takes place.

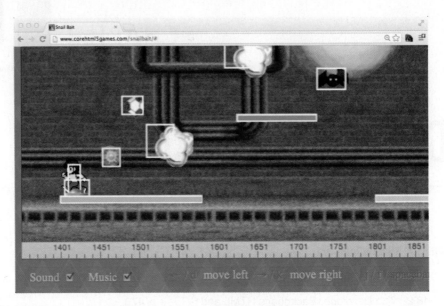

Figure 18.1 Turning on collision rectangles and zooming in

Snail Bait lets you turn on collision rectangles and run the game in slow-motion with a developer backdoor that you activate by pressing CTRL-d when the game is running. The backdoor's features make it easier to playtest, and therefore to implement, the game. In this chapter, we explore the implementation of Snail Bait's developer backdoor. More specifically, you will learn how to do the following:

- Reveal and hide a developer backdoor with a hot key (Section 18.3 on p. 481)
- Keep backdoor elements in sync with the game (Section 18.4 on p. 483)
- Draw collision detection bounding boxes (Section 18.5.1 on p. 487)
- Playtest slow frame rates and tempos faster than the default (Section 18.6.4 on p. 498)
- Calibrate the running slowly threshold (Section 18.6.4 on p. 498)
- Run the game in slow motion (Section 18.6.5 on p. 498)
- Move directly to a location in a level (Section 18.7 on p. 502)
- Drag the game's canvas (Section 18.7.5 on p. 507)

We start with an overview of Snail Bait's developer backdoor before discussing its implementation.

NOTE: A backdoor is a good breeding ground for game features

Besides making it easier to implement games, developer backdoors can also be a source of inspiration for new game features. For example, running the game in slow motion could be the impetus for a power-up that temporarily runs the game in slow motion, making it easier for players to navigate the level.

NOTE: Backdoors vs. Easter eggs

Snail Bait's developer backdoor has a lot in common with Easter eggs, which reveal hidden features for players instead of the developer. Some Easter eggs are rewards for some achievement, and others just offer random fun.

18.1 Snail Bait's Developer Backdoor

Snail Bait's developer backdoor is shown in Figure 18.2.

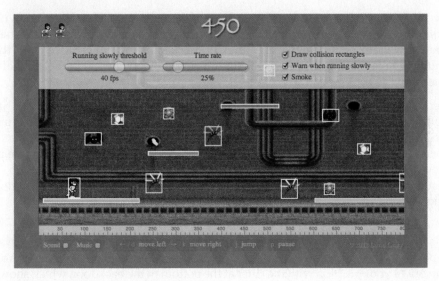

Figure 18.2 The developer backdoor

The screenshot in Figure 18.2 shows Snail Bait with visible collision rectangles, running at 1/4 speed.

Besides the controls at the top of the game, the developer backdoor also displays a ruler at the bottom of the game's canvas. That ruler, which the developer backdoor constantly updates, shows the horizontal offset in pixels from the beginning of the level.

The developer backdoor does not interfere in any way with gameplay, and its background is semitransparent so you can see the action underneath as you play the game.

The developer backdoor lets you do the following:

- Change Snail Bait's running slowly threshold from the default of 40 frames per second (fps)
- Turn off the running slowly warning entirely
- Change the rate at which time flows through the game
- Draw collision rectangles
- Toggle smoke visibility
- Drag the game's canvas horizontally

Recall from Chapter 11 that Snail Bait implements collision detection with bounding boxes. The developer backdoor makes those rectangles visible when the Draw collision rectangles checkbox is checked. And if the smoke from the smoking holes obscures your view, you can get rid of it by deselecting the Smoke checkbox.

Perhaps the most important feature of Snail Bait's developer backdoor is its ability to modify the rate at which time flows through the game. That feature makes it possible to run the game in slow motion, which in turn makes it easier to see exactly how events unfold during the game. Besides running the game in slow motion, the developer backdoor also lets you run the game up to twice as fast as normal, which is useful for calibrating the rate at which the game's action takes place.

One thing you can't see in Figure 18.2 is the developer's ability to drag the game's canvas horizontally when the developer backdoor is visible. Dragging the canvas repositions the runner, so you can go directly to specific sections of the level. You can orient your position with the ruler at the bottom of the backdoor, which shows how many pixels the game has scrolled horizontally. The game constantly updates those values when the backdoor is visible.

Now that we've seen the developer backdoor's features, let's see how to implement them.

BEST PRACTICE: Cut development time with a developer backdoor

For most nontrivial games, a developer backdoor should cut your development time by making it easier to implement error-prone or mathematically intensive code, such as collision detection.

CAUTION: Keep the cost/benefit ratio in mind

Developer backdoors are useful tools that can be fun and rewarding to implement, but they are not free. Implementing a developer backdoor can take a considerable amount of work, so you want to ensure that the backdoor adds substantially more value than the amount of work you put into it.

18.2 The Developer Backdoor's HTML and CSS

We start with a nascent developer backdoor that's devoid of features, as shown in Figure 18.3.

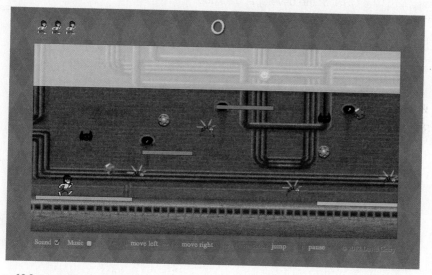

Figure 18.3 Revealing the developer backdoor

Inside the game's arena (a DIV that contains everything in the game) we add a DIV whose identifier is `snailbait-developer-backdoor`, as shown in Example 18.1. To begin, that element is empty.

Example 18.1 The HTML for the developer backdoor

```html
<!DOCTYPE html>
<html>
    ...

   <body>
      ...

      <div id='snailbait-arena'>
         <div id='snailbait-developer-backdoor'>
            ...
         </div>
         ...
      </div>
   </body>
</html>
```

The CSS for the snailbait-developer-backdoor element is shown in Example 18.2.

Example 18.2 The CSS for the developer backdoor

```css
#snailbait-developer-backdoor {
    color: navy;
    position: absolute;
    margin: 0 auto;
    margin-top: 72px;
    margin-left: 1px;
    width: 800px;
    height: 90px;
    border: thin solid brickred;
    background: rgba(255, 255, 200, 0.7);

    -webkit-transition: opacity 1s;
    -moz-transition: opacity 1s;
    -o-transition: opacity 1s;
    transition: opacity 1s;

    display: none;
    opacity: 0;
    z-index: 1;
}
```

The preceding CSS sizes and positions the developer backdoor, in addition to specifying an opacity transition and making the element initially invisible. The developer backdoor, when visible, is partially transparent. That transparency is a result of the element's background property; the alpha component of the background color is set to 0.7, as you can see in Example 18.2.

Snail Bait accesses the `snailbait-developer-backdoor` element as shown in Example 18.3.

Example 18.3 Accessing the backdoor element

```
var SnailBait = function () {
   ...

   this.developerBackdoorElement =
      document.getElementById('snailbait-developer-backdoor');

   this.developerBackdoorVisible = false;
   ...
};
```

Besides accessing the `snailbait-developer-backdoor` element, Snail Bait's constructor also declares a variable named `developerBackdoorVisible` whose value corresponds to the backdoor's visibility.

Now that we've seen the HTML element for the developer backdoor and how Snail Bait accesses that element in JavaScript, let's see how the game reveals and hides the backdoor.

 NOTE: Snail Bait's developer backdoor is a heads-up display

By providing a see-through background, Snail Bait's developer backdoor lets the developer play the game with the backdoor visible. That's what's known as a heads-up display (HUD). In Chapter 19, we implement another HUD with an entirely transparent background for displaying high scores.

18.3 Reveal and Hide the Developer Backdoor

With a reference to the developer backdoor in hand, Snail Bait implements a `revealDeveloperBackdoor()` method, listed in Example 18.4.

The `revealDeveloperBackdoor()` method uses Snail Bait's `fadeInElements()` method, which we discussed in Chapter 5, to fade the `snailbait-developer-backdoor` element into view. Recall that `fadeInElements()` relies on the elements it manipulates having a CSS transition on their `opacity` property. Without the CSS transition on the `snailbait-developer-backdoor` element, the element would not fade into view. The `revealDeveloperBackdoor()` method also sets the game's `developerBackdoorVisible` property to `true` and sets the cursor for the game's canvas to the `move` cursor.

Example 18.4 Revealing the developer backdoor

```
SnailBait.prototype = {
   ...

   revealDeveloperBackdoor: function () {
      this.fadeInElements(this.developerBackdoorElement,
                          this.rulerCanvas);

      ...

      this.canvas.style.cursor = 'move';
      this.developerBackdoorVisible = true;
   },
   ...
};
```

Hiding the developer backdoor is the inverse of revealing it, as you can see in Example 18.5.

Example 18.5 Hiding the developer backdoor

```
SnailBait.prototype = {
   ...

   hideDeveloperBackdoor: function () {
      var DEVELOPER_BACKDOOR_FADE_DURATION = 1000;

      this.fadeOutElements(this.developerBackdoorElement,
                           this.rulerCanvas,
                           DEVELOPER_BACKDOOR_FADE_DURATION);

      this.canvas.style.cursor = this.initialCursor;
      this.developerBackdoorVisible = false;
   },
   ...
};
```

Snail Bait's hideDeveloperBackdoor() method invokes the game's fadeOutElements() method, sets the developerBackdoorVisible property to false, and restores the cursor for the game's canvas. See Section 18.7.5, "Drag the Canvas," on p. 507 for more about the developer backdoor's cursor.

Snail Bait invokes the revealDeveloperBackdoor() and hideDeveloperBackdoor() methods from its keydown event handler, which is partially listed in Example 18.6.

Example 18.6 Activating the developer backdoor by pressing CTRL-d

---

```
window.addEventListener(
  'keydown',

  function (e) {
    var key = e.keyCode;
    ...

    if (key === 68 && e.ctrlKey) { // CTRL-d
      if ( ! snailBait.developerBackdoorVisible) {
        snailBait.revealDeveloperBackdoor();
      }
      else {
        snailBait.hideDeveloperBackdoor();
      }
      return;
    }
    ...
  }
);
```

When a player presses CTRL-d, Snail Bait reveals the developer backdoor if it's not visible. If the developer backdoor was visible when the player pressed CTRL-d, the game makes it invisible.

18.4 Update the Developer Backdoor's Elements

At this point, the developer backdoor doesn't have any elements, but by the end of this chapter, it will have sliders, checkboxes, and readouts, as you saw in Figure 18.2 on p. 477.

To update those elements when Snail Bait reveals the developer backdoor, the game calls three methods—updateDeveloperBackdoorSliders(), update-DeveloperBackdoorCheckboxes(), and updateDeveloperBackdoorReadouts()—in the revised revealDeveloperBackdoor() method listed in Example 18.7.

As we implement the backdoor's features throughout the rest of this chapter, we fill in the implementation of those three methods to keep the developer backdoor's elements in sync with the game when the backdoor is revealed.

Example 18.7 Revealing the developer backdoor, revised

```
SnailBait.prototype = {
   ...

   updateDeveloperBackdoorSliders: function () {
      // TODO
   },

   updateDeveloperBackdoorCheckboxes: function () {
      // TODO
   },

   updateDeveloperBackdoorReadouts: function () {
      // TODO
   },

   revealDeveloperBackdoor: function () {
      this.fadeInElements(this.developerBackdoorElement,
                          this.rulerCanvas);

      this.updateDeveloperBackdoorSliders();
      this.updateDeveloperBackdoorCheckboxes();
      this.updateDeveloperBackdoorReadouts();

      this.canvas.style.cursor = 'move';
      this.developerBackdoorVisible = true;
   },
   ...
};
```

At this point we have an empty backdoor with a semitransparent background that we can reveal and hide by pressing CTRL-d. Next, let's add some features.

18.5 Implement the Developer Backdoor's Checkboxes

Figure 18.4 shows the developer backdoor with checkboxes.

The developer backdoor's checkboxes let the developer do the following:

- Turn collision rectangles on and off
- Enable or disable the game's running slowly warning
- Show or hide smoking holes

The HTML for the backdoor's checkboxes is listed in Example 18.8.

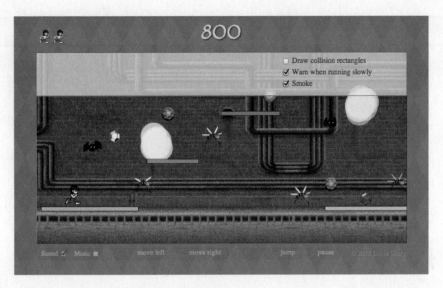

Figure 18.4 The developer backdoor's checkboxes

Example 18.8 The HTML for the developer backdoor's checkboxes

```
<!DOCTYPE html>
<html>
   ...

   <body>
      ...

      <div id='snailbait-arena'>
         ...

         <div id='snailbait-developer-backdoor'>
            ...

            <div class='snailbait-group'
                  id='snailbait-collision-rectangles'>
               <input type='checkbox'
                     id='snailbait-collision-rectangles-checkbox'/>
               Draw collision rectangles
            </div>

            <div class='snailbait-group'
                  id='snailbait-detect-running-slowly'>
```

(Continues)

Example 18.8 *(Continued)*

```
                 <input type='checkbox'
                     id='snailbait-detect-running-slowly-checkbox'
                     checked/>
                 Warn when running slowly
             </div>

             <div class='snailbait-group'
                     id='snailbait-smoking-holes'>
                 <input type='checkbox'
                     id='snailbait-smoking-holes-checkbox'
                     checked/>
                 Smoke
             </div>
         </div>
         ...
     </div>
   </body>
</html>
```

The preceding HTML has three DIVs, each of which contains a checkbox. The CSS for those elements is listed in Example 18.9.

Example 18.9 The CSS for the developer backdoor's checkboxes

```
.snailbait-group {
    position: absolute;
    text-align: center;
}

#snailbait-collision-rectangles {
    margin-left: 540px;
    margin-top: 0.5em;
    text-shadow: 1px 1px 1px rgba(255,255,255,0.5);
}

#snailbait-detect-running-slowly {
    margin-left: 540px;
    margin-top:  2.0em;
    text-shadow: 1px 1px 1px rgba(255,255,255,0.5);
}

#snailbait-smoking-holes {
    margin-left: 540px;
    margin-top: 3.5em;
    text-shadow: 1px 1px 1px rgba(255,255,255,0.5);
}
```

The CSS class for the DIVs that contain checkboxes is snailbait-group. The browser positions groups absolutely and center aligns their contents. The preceding CSS also specifies a white shadow for the checkboxes's text to make it appear as though the navy blue text has been pressed into the backdoor's yellow background.

Now that we've created the checkboxes and added them to the developer backdoor, let's implement their functionality.

18.5.1 Show and Hide Collision Rectangles

When you're debugging collision detection with bounding boxes, it's helpful if you can see collision rectangles for all the game's sprites, as shown in Figure 18.2 on p. 477. As it currently stands, a sprite's calculateCollisionRectangle() method returns a JavaScript object representing the sprite's collision rectangle as discussed in Section 11.3.1, "Sprite Collision Rectangles," on p. 278, but sprites cannot draw the rectangle. We give sprites that ability with a Sprite.drawCollisionRectangle() method, listed in Example 18.10.

Example 18.10 Drawing collision rectangles

```
Sprite.prototype = {
    ...

    drawCollisionRectangle: function (context) {
        var COLLISION_RECTANGLE_COLOR = 'white',
            COLLISION_RECTANGLE_LINE_WIDTH = 2.0,
            r = this.calculateCollisionRectangle();

        context.save();

        context.beginPath();

        context.strokeStyle = COLLISION_RECTANGLE_COLOR;
        context.lineWidth    = COLLISION_RECTANGLE_LINE_WIDTH;

        context.strokeRect(r.left + this.hOffset, r.top,
                           r.right - r.left, r.bottom - r.top);

        context.restore(); // resets strokeStyle and lineWidth
    },
    ...
};
```

The drawCollisionRectangle() method draws a white, two-pixel-wide rectangle representing the sprite's collision rectangle.

Sprites draw their collision rectangles only some of the time, so we add a showCollisionRectangle Boolean property to sprites that controls whether they draw the rectangle or not. That property is initially false, as shown in Example 18.11.

Example 18.11 Sprites keep track of whether they draw their collision rectangle.

```
var Sprite = function () {
   ...

   this.showCollisionRectangle = false;
   ...
};
```

Finally we revise Sprite.draw() to draw the collision rectangle if the sprite's showCollisionRectangle property is true, as listed in Example 18.12.

Example 18.12 Sprite.draw(), revised to draw collision rectangles

---

```
Sprite.prototype = {
   ...

   draw: function (context) {
      context.save();

      context.globalAlpha = this.opacity;

      if (this.visible && this.artist) {
         this.artist.draw(this, context);
      }

      if (this.showCollisionRectangle) {
         this.drawCollisionRectangle(context);
      }

      context.restore();
   },
   ...
};
```

As a result of the preceding additions to sprites, we can now draw a sprite's collision rectangle simply by setting its showCollisionRectangle property to true; subsequently, the sprite will draw its collision rectangle in subsequent animation frames until the property is reset to false.

To toggle the visibility of sprite collision rectangles when the developer clicks the Draw collision rectangles checkbox, Snail Bait first obtains a reference to the Draw collision rectangles checkbox as shown in Example 18.13.

Example 18.13 Accessing the collision rectangles checkbox element

```
var SnailBait = function () {
  ...

  this.collisionRectanglesCheckboxElement =
     document.getElementById(
        'snailbait-collision-rectangles-checkbox');
  ...
};
```

Snail Bait adds a change event handler to the checkbox, as you can see in Example 18.14.

Example 18.14 Handling change events for the collision rectangles checkbox

```
snailBait.collisionRectanglesCheckboxElement.addEventListener(
   'change',

   function (e) {
      var show = snailBait.collisionRectanglesCheckboxElement.checked;

      for (var i=0; i < snailBait.sprites.length; ++i) {
         snailBait.sprites[i].showCollisionRectangle = show;
      }
   }
);
```

When the developer clicks the Draw collision rectangles checkbox, the preceding event handler iterates over Snail Bait's sprites, synchronizing each one's showCollisionRectangle property with the checkbox.

18.5.2 Enable and Disable the Running Slowly Warning

Recall that Snail Bait shows a warning, whose implementation we discussed in Chapter 17, when the game runs slowly. By default, Snail Bait defines *slowly* as "less than 40 frames per second." The developer backdoor lets you modify that threshold or turn off the warning entirely, which lets you playtest slow frame rates without interruption and calibrate the running slowly threshold.

To get rid of the running slowly warning, Snail Bait first obtains a reference to the Warn when running slowly checkbox, as shown in Example 18.15.

Example 18.15 Accessing the running slowly checkbox element

```
var SnailBait = function () {
   ...

   this.detectRunningSlowlyCheckboxElement =
      document.getElementById(
         'snailbait-detect-running-slowly-checkbox');
   ...
};
```

When you click the checkbox, the event handler listed in **Example 18.16** kicks in.

Example 18.16 Handling change events for the running slowly checkbox

---

```
snailBait.detectRunningSlowlyCheckboxElement.addEventListener(
   'change',

   function (e) {
      snailBait.showSlowWarning =
         snailBait.detectRunningSlowlyCheckboxElement.checked;
   }
);
```

The preceding event handler keeps Snail Bait's showSlowWarning property in sync with the Warn when running slowly checkbox. That property is the Boolean variable discussed in Chapter 17 that controls whether the game displays the running slowly warning.

18.5.3 Show and Hide Smoking Holes

The developer backdoor lets the developer hide smoking holes. Snail Bait's constructor obtains a reference to the Smoke checkbox, as shown in **Example 18.17**.

Example 18.17 Accessing the smoking holes element

```
var SnailBait = function () {
   ...

   this.smokingHolesCheckboxElement =
      document.getElementById('snailbait-smoking-holes-checkbox');
   ...
};
```

Snail Bait adds a change event handler to the Smoke checkbox. That event handler is listed in Example 18.18.

Example 18.18 Handling change events for the smoking holes checkbox

```
snailBait.smokingHolesCheckboxElement.addEventListener(
  'change',

  function (e) {
    snailBait.showSmokingHoles =
      snailBait.smokingHolesCheckboxElement.checked;
  }
);
```

The preceding event handler keeps Snail Bait's showSmokingHoles property—which determines whether Snail Bait draws smoking holes—in sync with the Smoke checkbox.

18.5.4 Update Backdoor Checkboxes

To synchronize the backdoor's sliders with the game when Snail Bait reveals the backdoor, Snail Bait updates two of its checkboxes with the updateDeveloperBackdoorCheckboxes() method, which is invoked by revealDeveloperBackdoor(). The updateDeveloperBackdoorCheckboxes() method is listed in Example 18.19.

Example 18.19 Updating the developer backdoor checkboxes

```
SnailBait.prototype = {
  ...

  updateDeveloperBackdoorCheckboxes: function () {
    this.detectRunningSlowlyCheckboxElement.checked =
      this.showSlowWarning;

    this.smokingHolesCheckboxElement.checked =
      this.showSmokingHoles;
  },
  ...
};
```

The preceding method ensures that the Warn when running slowly and Smoke checkboxes represent the current state of the game when Snail Bait reveals the developer backdoor. Snail Bait doesn't keep track of whether sprites draw their collision rectangles, so the game does not update the Draw collision rectangle's checkbox when Snail Bait reveals the developer backdoor.

18.6 Incorporate the Developer Backdoor Sliders

Snail Bait uses custom sliders for setting the running slowly threshold and the game's time rate. The developer can change a slider's value by dragging the slider's knob or clicking in its rail, as shown in Figure 18.5.

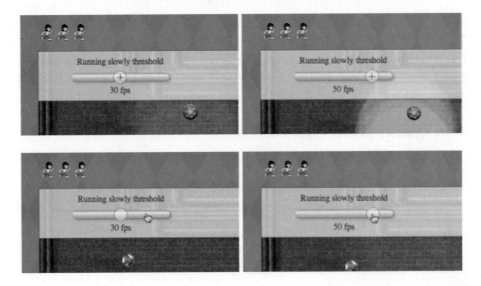

Figure 18.5 Manipulating the slider knob by dragging (top) and clicking (bottom)

The implementation of the backdoor's sliders is far afield from game development and so is not discussed in this book. See *Core HTML5 Canvas* (Prentice Hall, 2012) to learn how sliders are implemented with the canvas element.

In this section, we focus on how Snail Bait uses sliders in the developer backdoor. First, we add the code for the slider implementation, which resides in a file of its own, to Snail Bait's js (JavaScript) directory, as you can see from Figure 18.6.

Sliders are simple to use. As you can see from Table 18.1, which lists the slider methods that Snail Bait uses, you can draw and erase sliders, add change listeners to them, and append them to HTML elements.

Sliders do not keep track of a value; instead, they have a knobPercent property that represents the percentage of the slider's maximum value. The knobPercent is a number from 0.0 to 1.0. To calculate a slider's value, multiply the knobPercent by the slider's maximum value; for example, the Running slowly threshold slider's maximum value is 60 (fps), so when the knob is positioned in the middle of the slider, the slider's knobPercent is 0.5, so you would calculate the value as 30.

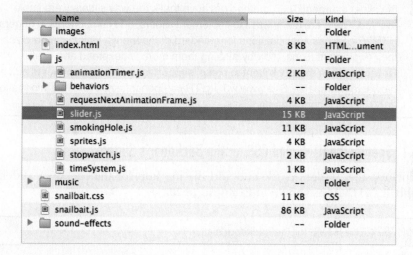

Name	Size	Kind
▶ 📁 images	--	Folder
📄 index.html	8 KB	HTML...ument
▼ 📁 js	--	Folder
📄 animationTimer.js	2 KB	JavaScript
▶ 📁 behaviors	--	Folder
📄 requestNextAnimationFrame.js	4 KB	JavaScript
📄 slider.js	15 KB	JavaScript
📄 smokingHole.js	11 KB	JavaScript
📄 sprites.js	4 KB	JavaScript
📄 stopwatch.js	2 KB	JavaScript
📄 timeSystem.js	1 KB	JavaScript
▶ 📁 music	--	Folder
📄 snailbait.css	11 KB	CSS
📄 snailbait.js	86 KB	JavaScript
▶ 📁 sound-effects	--	Folder

Figure 18.6 The sliders.js file

Table 18.1 Slider methods

Method	Description
appendTo(elementId)	Appends the slider to a DOM element and resizes the slider to fit snugly in the element.
draw(percent)	Draws the slider with the specified knob percent.
erase()	Erases the slider.
addChangeListener(callbackFunction)	Adds a change listener to the slider.

To incorporate sliders into Snail Bait's backdoor, we do the following:

- Specify the HTML and CSS for the backdoor's sliders
- Access slider readouts in Snail Bait's JavaScript
- Create and initialize the backdoor's sliders
- Wire the running slowly slider to the game

- Wire the time rate slider to the game
- Wire the game to the time rate slider

 NOTE: Snail Bait creates sliders and appends them to HTML elements with the slider's appendTo() method because that's the way sliders were implemented. There are many ways to implement sliders, and components in general. HTML5 now has specifications for standard components, which standardizes their implementations, thereby making them more widespread and useful. However, when this book went to press, support for HTML5 components among browsers was sparse. See www.w3.org/TR/components-intro for more information about HTML5 components.

18.6.1 Specify the HTML and CSS for the Backdoor's Sliders

We include the slider.js file and add the markup for the backdoor sliders to Snail Bait's HTML, as shown in Example 18.20.

Example 18.20 The HTML for the backdoor's sliders

```html
<!DOCTYPE html>
<html>
    ...

    <body>
        ...

        <div id='snailbait-arena'>
            ...

            <div id='developer-backdoor'>
                ...

                <div class='snailbait-group'
                      id='snailbait-running-slowly-threshold'>
                    <span class='snailbait-prompt'
                          id='snailbait-running-slowly-prompt'>
                      Running slowly threshold
                    </span>

                    <div id='snailbait-running-slowly-slider'></div>

                    <span class='snailbait-readout'
                          id='snailbait-running-slowly-readout'>
                            40
                    </span> fps
                </div>
```

```
            <div class='snailbait-group'
                  id='snailbait-time-rate'>
              <span class='snailbait-prompt'
                    id='snailbait-time-rate-prompt'>
                Time rate</span>

              <div id='snailbait-time-rate-slider'></div>

              <span class='snailbait-readout'
                    id='snailbait-time-rate-readout'>100</span>%
            </div>
            ...
          </div>
          ...
        </div>
        ...

        <script src='js/slider.js'></script>
        ...
      </body>
    </html>
```

Each slider resides in a DIV whose class is snailbait-group. As discussed in Section 18.5 on p. 484, groups are absolutely positioned and their elements are center aligned. Each DIV contains a title above the slider, an empty DIV into which Snail Bait inserts a slider, and the slider's readout.

The preceding HTML uses four DIVs and four span elements. The CSS for the DIVs is listed in Example 18.21 (there is no CSS for the span elements).

Example 18.21 The CSS for the backdoor's sliders

```css
#snailbait-running-slowly-threshold {
   margin-left: 30px;
   margin-top: 10px;
   width: 250px;
   height: 50px;
}

#snailbait-running-slowly-slider {
   margin-left: 20px;
   width: 200px;
   height: 30px;
}
```

(Continues)

Example 18.21 *(Continued)*

```css
#snailbait-time-rate {
    margin-left: 245px;
    margin-top: 10px;
    width: 250px;
    height: 50px;
}

#snailbait-time-rate-slider {
    margin-left: 20px;
    width: 200px;
    height: 30px;
}
```

Now that you've seen the HTML and CSS for the developer backdoor's sliders, let's see how Snail Bait accesses those elements and uses them in the game's JavaScript.

18.6.2 Access Slider Readouts in Snail Bait's JavaScript

Snail Bait manipulates the sliders and their readouts, so the game's JavaScript is concerned with the following elements:

- `snailbait-running-slowly-readout`
- `snailbait-time-rate-readout`
- `snailbait-running-slowly-slider`
- `snailbait-time-rate-slider`

The game accesses the readout elements as shown in Example 18.22.

Example 18.22 Accessing the slider readout elements

```javascript
var SnailBait = function () {
    ...

    this.runningSlowlyReadoutElement =
        document.getElementById('snailbait-running-slowly-readout');

    this.timeRateReadoutElement =
        document.getElementById('snailbait-time-rate-readout');
    ...
};
```

Snail Bait does not directly access the HTML elements containing the sliders (the `running-slowly-slider` and `time-rate-slider` DIVs); instead, it merely references their identifiers, as you'll see in the next section.

18.6.3 Create and Initialize the Backdoor's Sliders

Sliders are implemented as JavaScript objects, so you create them with the new operator, as shown in Example 18.23.

Example 18.23 Creating the backdoor sliders

```
var SnailBait = function () {
  ...

  this.runningSlowlySlider =
    new COREHTML5.Slider('blue',        // stroke style
                         'royalblue'); // fill style
  this.timeRateSlider =
    new COREHTML5.Slider('brickred',    // stroke style
                         'red');        // fill style
  ...
};
```

Snail Bait's constructor creates two instances of COREHTML5.Slider, and subsequently the initializeDeveloperBackdoorSliders() method appends them to their appropriate HTML elements, as shown in Example 18.24.

Example 18.24 Initializing the backdoor's sliders

```
var SnailBait = function () {

  ...

  this.developerBackdoorSlidersInitialized = false;
  ...
};

SnailBait.prototype = {
  ...

  initializeDeveloperBackdoorSliders: function () {
    this.timeRateSlider.appendTo(
      'snailbait-time-rate-slider'
    );
```

(Continues)

Example 18.24 *(Continued)*

```
        this.runningSlowlySlider.appendTo(
          'snailbait-running-slowly-slider'
        );

        this.developerBackdoorSlidersInitialized = true;
    },
    ...
};
```

Given the identifier of an HTML element, a slider's appendTo() method obtains a reference to the associated element, appends the slider to that element, and resizes the slider to fit snugly within its element.

Snail Bait appends each slider to its appropriate HTML element only once, so the game uses a Boolean variable to keep track of whether it has initialized the sliders. How Snail Bait invokes the initializeDeveloperBackdoorSliders() method is discussed in Section 18.6.7 on p. 500.

18.6.4 Wire the Running Slowly Slider to the Game

Snail Bait adds a change listener to the running slowly slider that sets the game's running slowly threshold to the slider's current value and updates the running slowly readout element, as shown in Example 18.25.

Example 18.25 The running slowly slider's change listener

```
snailBait.runningSlowlySlider.addChangeListener(function (e) {
    var threshold =
        (snailBait.runningSlowlySlider.knobPercent *
            snailBait.MAX_RUNNING_SLOWLY_THRESHOLD).toFixed(0);

    snailBait.runningSlowlyThreshold = threshold;
    snailBait.runningSlowlyReadoutElement.innerHTML = threshold;
});
```

18.6.5 Wire the Time Rate Slider to the Game

Snail Bait also implements a change listener that synchronizes the game's time rate with the position of the slider's knob (represented by the slider's knobPercent property), as shown in Example 18.26. The change listener also updates the backdoor's time rate readout.

Example 18.26 The time rate slider's change listener

```
snailBait.timeRateSlider.addChangeListener(function (e) {
   // Enforce a minimum value

   if (snailBait.timeRateSlider.knobPercent < 0.01) {
      snailBait.timeRateSlider.knobPercent = 0.01;
   }

   // Set time rate

   snailBait.setTimeRate(snailBait.timeRateSlider.knobPercent *
                         (snailBait.MAX_TIME_RATE));

   // Update the time rate readout

   snailBait.timeRateReadoutElement.innerHTML =
      (snailBait.timeRate * 100).toFixed(0);
});
```

18.6.6 Wire the Game to the Time Rate Slider

Snail Bait's running slowly threshold is a fixed commodity. Once the developer sets its value by manipulating the running slowly slider in the developer backdoor, the value does not change until the developer manipulates the slider again.

That's not the case for the game's time rate, however. For example, recall that Snail Bait slows time to ten percent of its normal speed during transitions between lives. To make the developer-backdoor's time rate slider reflect any changes to the game's time rate, we modify Snail Bait's setTimeRate() method, as shown in Example 18.27.

Example 18.27 Synchronizing the time rate

```
SnailBait.prototype = {
   ...

   setTimeRate: function (rate) {
      this.timeRate = rate;

      this.timeRateReadoutElement.innerHTML =
         (this.timeRate * 100).toFixed(0);

      this.timeRateSlider.knobPercent =
         this.timeRate / this.MAX_TIME_RATE;
```

(Continues)

Example 18.27 *(Continued)*

```
        if (this.developerBackdoorVisible) {
            this.timeRateSlider.erase();
            this.timeRateSlider.draw(this.timeRate /
                                        this.MAX_TIME_RATE);
        }

        this.timeSystem.setTransducer( function (percent) {
            return percent * snailBait.timeRate;
        });
    },
    ...
};
```

The revised implementation of the setTimeRate() method updates both the time rate slider's knob position and the text displayed by the associated readout element.

Because sliders are not sprites, Snail Bait does not automatically draw them every animation frame. So if the backdoor is visible, setTimeRate() manually erases and redraws the time rate slider with the new value. The setTimeRate() method also sets the transducer function for the game's time system. See Chapter 10 for more information on Snail Bait's time system.

 CAUTION: By keeping the time rate slider in sync with the game's time rate— which is a somewhat frivolous feature—we are close to violating the Caution on p. 479. Snail Bait implements that feature solely for it's instructional value.

18.6.7 Update Sliders Before Revealing the Backdoor

To synchronize the backdoor's sliders with the game when Snail Bait reveals the backdoor, the revealDeveloperBackdoor() method discussed in Section 18.4 on p. 483 invokes the game's updateDeveloperBackdoorSliders() method, listed in Example 18.28.

Example 18.28 Update the backdoor sliders just before revealing the backdoor

```
SnailBait.prototype = {
    ...

    updateDeveloperBackdoorSliders: function () {
```

```
    if ( ! this.developerBackdoorSlidersInitialized) {
      this.initializeDeveloperBackdoorSliders();
    }

    this.updateRunningSlowlySlider();
    this.updateTimeRateSlider();
  },
  ...
};
```

Besides updating the backdoor's two sliders with the `updateRunningSlowly-`
`Slider()` and `updateTimeRateSlider()` methods listed in Example 18.29, the
preceding method initializes the sliders if they haven't been initialized.

Example 18.29 Initializing the running slowly slider

```
SnailBait.prototype = {
   ...

   updateRunningSlowlySlider: function () {
      this.runningSlowlySlider.knobPercent =
         this.runningSlowlyThreshold /
         this.MAX_RUNNING_SLOWLY_THRESHOLD;

      this.runningSlowlySlider.erase();
      this.runningSlowlySlider.draw(this.runningSlowlyThreshold /
                                    this.MAX_RUNNING_SLOWLY_THRESHOLD);
   },

   updateTimeRateSlider: function () {
      this.timeRateSlider.knobPercent =
         this.timeRate * this.MAX_TIME_RATE;

      this.timeRateSlider.erase();
      this.timeRateSlider.draw(this.timeRate / this.MAX_TIME_RATE);
   },
   ...
};
```

The two preceding methods update their respective sliders by setting the slider's
knobPercent property and subsequently erasing and redrawing the slider.

At this point we've discussed the implementation of the controls at the top of the
developer backdoor. We close out this chapter by discussing the implementation
of the ruler at the bottom of the backdoor and the associated dragging of the
game's canvas.

18.7 Implement the Backdoor's Ruler

When playtesting near the middle or end of a level, it's tedious to play through preceding sections to get to your section of interest. Playtesting is more efficient if you can move directly to any location in a level.

Recall that Snail Bait scrolls the background by continuously translating the canvas context and redrawing the background in the horizontal location. The background's location is fixed, but the coordinate system of the canvas context moves horizontally, so it appears as though the background is scrolling. See Chapter 3 for more details on how Snail Bait scrolls the background.

As the game runs, Snail Bait keeps track of the horizontal offset by which it scrolls the background. Initially, that offset is zero, represented by the game's STARTING_BACKGROUND_OFFSET constant. If you change that constant and restart Snail Bait, the game will start at the offset you specify. To start the game at a specific location, set STARTING_BACKGROUND_OFFSET to the preferred offset and restart the game.

The ruler at the bottom of Snail Bait's developer backdoor, illustrated in Figure 18.7, shows the horizontal offset from the start of the game. While the developer backdoor is visible, Snail Bait continuously updates the values displayed by the ruler.

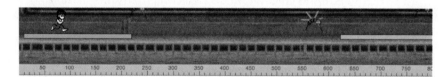

Figure 18.7 The ruler

Creating the ruler and incorporating it into the game requires the following four steps:

- Create and access the ruler canvas
- Fade the ruler
- Draw the ruler
- Update the ruler

Let's look at each in turn.

18.7.1 Create and Access the Ruler Canvas

The ruler is implemented with a canvas element, as shown in Example 18.30.

Example 18.30 Adding the ruler canvas

```html
<!DOCTYPE html>
<html>
   <body>
      ...

      <div id='snailbait-arena'>

         ...

         <div id='snailbait-developer-backdoor'>
            ...

            <canvas id='snailbait-ruler-canvas'
                    width='800' height='20'>
               Your browser does not support HTML5 Canvas.
            </canvas>
         </div>
         ...
      </div>
   </body>
</html>
```

The backdoor's ruler is 800 pixels wide, which is the same width as the game's canvas. The ruler's height, however, is only 20 pixels high. Snail Bait accesses the ruler's canvas and context in the game's constructor, as shown in Example 18.31.

Example 18.31 Accessing the ruler canvas and its context

```javascript
var SnailBait = function () {
   ...

   this.rulerCanvas = document.getElementById('snailbait-ruler-canvas');
   this.rulerContext = this.rulerCanvas.getContext('2d');
   ...
};
```

The CSS for the ruler is shown in Example 18.32.

Example 18.32 The ruler's CSS

```css
#snailbait-ruler-canvas {
   position: absolute;
   margin-top: -22px;
   border-top: thin solid rgba(255,255,0,0.5);
   border: thin solid rgba(0,0,255,0.5);
   background: rgba(255, 255, 200, 0.7);

   -webkit-transition: opacity 1s;
   -moz-transition: opacity 1s;
   -o-transition: opacity 1s;
   transition: opacity 1s;

   opacity: 0;
   display: none;
   z-index: 1;
}
```

18.7.2 Fade the Ruler

The ruler's CSS in Example 18.32 exhibits the familiar pattern of initial invisibility with an opacity transition. Snail Bait's `revealDeveloperBackdoor()` and `hideDeveloperBackdoor()` methods take advantage of that pattern by invoking the game's `fadeInElements()` and `fadeOutElements()` methods, as in Example 18.33.

Example 18.33 Fading the ruler in and out

```javascript
SnailBait.prototype = {
   ...

   revealDeveloperBackdoor: function () {
      this.fadeInElements(this.developerBackdoorElement,
                          this.rulerCanvas);
      ...
   },

   hideDeveloperBackdoor: function () {
      var DEVELOPER_BACKDOOR_FADE_DURATION = 1000;
      ...

      this.fadeOutElements(this.developerBackdoorElement,
                           this.rulerCanvas,
                           DEVELOPER_BACKDOOR_FADE_DURATION);
   },
```

```
      ...
};
```

Recall from Chapter 5 that Snail Bait's `fadeInElements()` and `fadeOutElements()` methods take a variable-length argument list, meaning they can simultaneously fade multiple elements in or out. To fade the ruler in concert with the backdoor's controls, we pass a reference to the ruler's canvas to the `fadeInElements()` and `fadeOutElements()` methods.

We specified the ruler canvas in Snail Bait's HTML, accessed the canvas and its context in Snail Bait's constructor function, and made the canvas fade in and out in concert with the backdoor's controls. Next we draw the ruler's contents.

18.7.3 Draw the Ruler

Snail Bait draws the backdoor's ruler with the `drawRuler()` method listed in Example 18.34.

Example 18.34 Drawing the ruler

```
SnailBait.prototype = {
   ...

   drawRuler: function () {
      var majorTickSpacing = 50,
          minorTickSpacing = 10,
          TICK_LINE_WIDTH = 0.5,
          TICK_FILL_STYLE = 'blue',
          i;

      this.rulerContext.lineWidth = TICK_LINE_WIDTH;
      this.rulerContext.fillStyle = TICK_FILL_STYLE;

      for (i=0; i < this.BACKGROUND_WIDTH; i += minorTickSpacing) {
         if (i === 0) {
            continue;
         }

         if (i % majorTickSpacing === 0) {
            this.drawRulerMajorTick(i);
         }
         else {
            this.drawRulerMinorTick(i);
         }
      }
   },
   ...
};
```

The `drawRuler()` method draws major and minor tick marks with the `drawRulerMajorTick()` and `drawRulerMinorTick()` methods, which are listed in **Example 18.35**.

Example 18.35 Drawing the ruler tick marks

```
SnailBait.prototype = {
   ...

   drawRulerMajorTick: function (i) {
      var MAJOR_TICK_BOTTOM = this.rulerCanvas.height,
          MAJOR_TICK_TOP = this.rulerCanvas.height/2 + 2,
          text = (this.spriteOffset + i).toFixed(0);

      this.rulerContext.beginPath();
      this.rulerContext.moveTo(i + 0.5, MAJOR_TICK_TOP);
      this.rulerContext.lineTo(i + 0.5, MAJOR_TICK_BOTTOM);

      this.rulerContext.stroke();
      this.rulerContext.fillText(text, i-10, 10);
   },

   drawRulerMinorTick: function (i) {
      var MINOR_TICK_BOTTOM = this.rulerCanvas.height,
          MINOR_TICK_TOP = 3*this.rulerCanvas.height/4;

      this.rulerContext.beginPath();
      this.rulerContext.moveTo(i + 0.5, MINOR_TICK_TOP);
      this.rulerContext.lineTo(i + 0.5, MINOR_TICK_BOTTOM);
      this.rulerContext.stroke();
   },
   ...
};
```

The preceding methods use the `moveTo()` and `lineTo()` methods of the ruler's canvas context to create a linear path, and the `stroke()` method to draw each line. The `drawRulerMajorTick()` method draws the text associated with the tick with the canvas context's `fillText()` method. See Chapter 3 for more information on drawing with the HTML5 canvas element.

Example 18.36 shows the `eraseRuler()` method, which clears the ruler canvas.

Example 18.36 Erasing the ruler

```
SnailBait.prototype = {
   ...
```

```
eraseRuler: function () {
   this.rulerContext.clearRect(0, 0, this.rulerCanvas.width,
                                     this.rulerCanvas.height);
   },
   ...
};
```

18.7.4 Update the Ruler

As the developer plays the game with the developer backdoor visible, Snail Bait continuously updates the backdoor's ruler with a simple addition to the game's draw() method, as shown in Example 18.37.

Example 18.37 Snail Bait's draw() method, revised

```
SnailBait.prototype = {
   ...

   draw: function (now) {
      ...

      if (this.developerBackdoorVisible) {
         this.eraseRuler();
         this.drawRuler();
      }
   },
   ...
};
```

Every time Snail Bait calls its draw() method—meaning for every animation frame—it checks to see if the developer backdoor is visible; if so, it redraws the ruler.

Now that you've seen how Snail Bait implements the backdoor's ruler, let's look at the backdoor's final feature: dragging the game canvas.

18.7.5 Drag the Canvas

The developer backdoor's ruler lets the developer restart Snail Bait at an exact location in the game's only level by setting the background offset to a nonzero initial value, as discussed at the start of Section 18.7 on p. 502. The developer can discover the offset from the backdoor's ruler. It's more efficient, however, to simply drag the game's canvas to a new location, as shown in Figure 18.8.

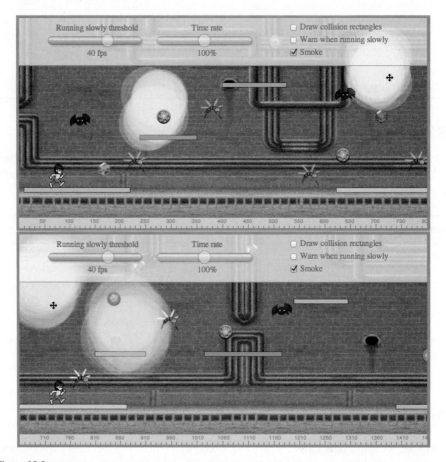

Figure 18.8 Dragging the game canvas from right to left (note the move cursor just below the backdoor)

To signify that the developer can drag the game's canvas horizontally when the developer backdoor is visible, Snail Bait changes the cursor for the game's canvas to a move cursor, as you can see in the upper right of the top screenshot and the upper left in the bottom screenshot in Figure 18.8.

Snail Bait's constructor records the original cursor for the game's canvas as shown in Example 18.38.

When Snail Bait reveals the developer backdoor, it sets the cursor to the move cursor. When it hides the backdoor, it restores the cursor to the original cursor recorded by the game's constructor, as shown in Example 18.39.

Example 18.38 Recording the game's original cursor

```
var SnailBait = function () {
   ...

   this.initialCursor = this.canvas.style.cursor;
   ...
};
```

Example 18.39 Changing the game's cursor when the developer backdoor is visible

```
SnailBait.prototype = {
   ...

   revealDeveloperBackdoor: function () {
      ...

      this.canvas.style.cursor = 'move';
   },

   hideDeveloperBackdoor: function () {
      ...

      this.canvas.style.cursor = this.initialCursor;
   },
   ...
};
```

Snail Bait implements mouse event handlers to let the developer drag the game's canvas when the backdoor is visible, as shown in Example 18.40.

Example 18.40 Snail Bait's mouse event handlers

```
snailBait.canvas.addEventListener(
   'mousedown',

   function (e) {
      if (snailBait.developerBackdoorVisible) {
         snailBait.startDraggingGameCanvas(e);
      }
   }
);

snailBait.canvas.addEventListener(
   'mousemove',
```

(Continues)

Example 18.40 *(Continued)*

```
    function (e) {
        if (snailBait.developerBackdoorVisible && snailBait.dragging) {
            snailBait.dragGameCanvas(e);
        }
    }
);

window.addEventListener(
    'mouseup',

    function (e) {
        if (snailBait.developerBackdoorVisible) {
            snailBait.stopDraggingGameCanvas();
        }
    }
);
```

Notice the mouse down and mouse move event handlers are attached to the game's canvas, whereas the mouse up event handler is attached to the game's window. If the developer inadvertently drags the mouse outside the canvas and then releases the mouse, attaching the mouse up event handler to the window ensures that we capture that mouse up event.

When the backdoor is visible, the preceding mouse down event handler starts dragging the game's canvas by invoking Snail Bait's startDraggingGameCanvas() method, which is listed in **Example 18.41**.

Example 18.41 Start dragging the game canvas

```
SnailBait.prototype = {
    ...

    startDraggingGameCanvas: function (e) {
        this.mousedown = { x: e.clientX, y: e.clientY };
        this.dragging = true;
        this.runner.visible = false;

        this.backgroundOffsetWhenDraggingStarted =
            this.backgroundOffset;

        this.spriteOffsetWhenDraggingStarted =
            this.spriteOffset;

        e.preventDefault();
    },
```

```
    . . .
};
```

The single argument to startDraggingGameCanvas() is the event object the browser passes to Snail Bait's mouse down event handler. That event object contains the location of the mouse down event in its clientX and clientY properties. The startDraggingGameCanvas() method records that location in a mousedown object.

The game is live as the developer drags the game's canvas, so to keep the runner from colliding with other sprites during the drag, the startDraggingGameCanvas() method makes the runner disappear by setting her visibility to false. The method also sets a dragging Boolean variable to true, and records the game's offsets for the sprites and the background.

Before the startDraggingGameCanvas() method returns, it invokes the event object's preventDefault() method. As its name implies, the preventDefault() method prevents the browser from reacting to the event as it normally would by default. Without the call to preventDefault(), the browser selects elements as the developer drags the mouse over them, as you can see in Figure 18.9.

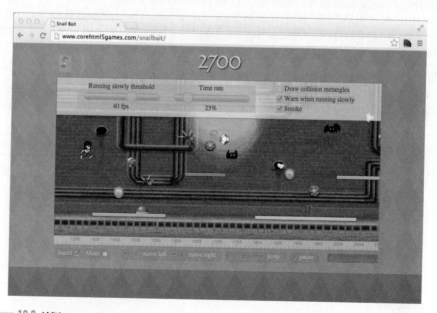

.Figure 18.9 Without calling preventDefault(): Accidentally selecting elements when dragging the game's canvas is an unwanted effect.

Snail Bait's mouse move event handler invokes the game's dragGameCanvas() method when the backdoor is visible and dragging is underway. The dragGameCanvas() method is listed in Example 18.42.

Example 18.42 Dragging the game canvas

```
SnailBait.prototype = {
   ...

   dragGameCanvas: function (e) {
      var deltaX = e.clientX - this.mousedown.x;

      this.backgroundOffset =
         this.backgroundOffsetWhenDraggingStarted - deltaX;

      this.spriteOffset =
         this.spriteOffsetWhenDraggingStarted - deltaX;
   },
   ...
};
```

The dragGameCanvas() method calculates how far the mouse has moved horizontally since the developer began dragging the canvas. The method then subtracts the delta from the start-of-dragging values of the game's background and sprite offsets, respectively, to set their new values.

When the developer releases the mouse after dragging the canvas, the window object's mouse up event handler invokes the game's stopDraggingGameCanvas(), which is listed in Example 18.43.

Example 18.43 Stop dragging the game canvas

```
SnailBait.prototype = {
   ...

   stopDraggingGameCanvas: function () {
      this.dragging = false;
      this.runner.visible = true;
   },
   ...
};
```

Snail Bait's `stopDraggingGameCanvas()` method turns dragging off by resetting the `dragging` flag to `false` and makes the runner visible once again.

18.8 Conclusion

A backdoor with the right features can significantly reduce the time it takes to implement your game. On the other hand, it can take a significant amount of time to implement a backdoor in the first place, so you must be cognizant of the cost-to-benefit ratio of implementing your backdoor.

With the exception of obscuring smoking holes, the features implemented by Snail Bait's developer backdoor—modifying the flow of time, changing the running slowly threshold, and drawing collision rectangles—are useful for facilitating the development of most games. It should be straightforward to implement a custom developer backdoor based on the code discussed in this chapter.

18.9 Exercises

1. Play the game with the developer backdoor visible. Watch the time rate slider when you lose a life. Recall that the slider responds to time rate changes.

2. Remove the call to `e.preventDefault()` from `startDraggingGameCanvas()`, restart the game, and see if you can re-create the effect shown in Figure 18.9. Then restore the line of code and try again.

3. Reveal the developer backdoor by pressing CTRL-d and drag the canvas to reposition the runner on the platform with the gold button. Now you can win the game with (relative) ease by jumping straight up and down to stomp on the gold button. Remember that you can slow time to help you avoid snail bombs while jumping. Also, notice that it's a bit tricky to reposition the runner because she must reappear at a safe location. Would you implement repositioning the runner differently? Keep in mind that time spent implementing the backdoor is time spent not implementing the game.

4. Snail Bait's `draw()` method first erases, then draws, the ruler when the developer backdoor is visible. Comment out the line of code that erases the ruler, restart the game, and activate the backdoor. What does the ruler look like? Why?

5. With the developer backdoor visible, change the time rate to more than 100% to determine the fastest you can comfortably play the game. If you can play

at 200%, modify the game's code so that you can adjust the rate higher than 200%. What happens to the time rate after you lose a life?

6. Change the game's MAX_TIME_RATE constant so that the developer backdoor's time rate slider lets you adjust the time up to five times the default time rate. Start the game and verify that the default position for the time rate slider's thumb has changed. See how far you can progress in the game when the time rate is 500%.

CHAPTER 19

On the Server: In-game Metrics, High Scores, and Deployment

Topics in This Chapter

The most important aspect of any game is how much fun it is to play. One way to make your game more fun is to adjust gameplay based on in-game metrics. For example, if you see that very few players advance past a particular point, you can make it easier to get past that point.

Many games send in-game metrics to a server as players play the game, especially during beta-testing. Games have other reasons to transfer data to a server; for example, most games store high scores on a server.

Sending data to a server as a game progresses seems like a difficult thing to do, in addition to also being a drag on performance. Fortunately, for HTML5 game developers, neither is true. Two popular JavaScript frameworks, whose popularity stems from their ease of use, make it easy to transfer data between clients and a server with virtually no impact on performance.

In this chapter, we use Node.js and socket.io to communicate between clients and the server to store high scores, depicted in Figure 19.1, and in-game metrics, on a server. You will also see how to deploy your game to a server.

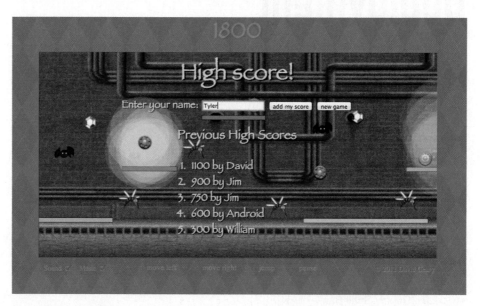

Figure 19.1 High scores

In this chapter you will learn how to do the following:

- Import socket.io JavaScript on the client (Section 19.2 on p. 518)
- Implement a simple server with Node.js (Section 19.3 on p. 520)
- Create a socket on the server (Section 19.4 on p. 520)
- Connect to the server when the game starts (Section 19.6 on p. 522)
- Send in-game metrics to the server as the game runs (Section 19.7 on p. 523)
- Store and retrieve high scores from the server (Section 19.8 on p. 526)
- Minify and obfuscate your game's JavaScript (Section 19.9 on p. 540)
- Use gzip compression to reduce the size of your text-based resources (Section 19.9 on p. 540)
- Deploy to a server (Section 19.10 on p. 542)

19.1 Node.js and socket.io

Most web applications, games included, implement code on the server. For web applications implemented in client-side JavaScript, it's most convenient if they can implement server-side code in the same language. Node.js is a platform built on Chrome's JavaScript runtime that runs JavaScript on the server.

Besides running JavaScript on the server, Node.js has a vibrant ecosystem of modules, which are pluggable pieces of functionality that you can use with Node.js; for example, the Passport module provides a simple way to add authentication to web applications.

Snail Bait uses several modules, most notably a module named socket.io that lets you communicate with the greatest of ease between your clients—where players play your game—and your server. The websites for Node.js and socket.io are shown in Figure 19.2.

NOTE: Installing Node.js and socket.io

Node.js is easy to install. Click the Install button on the Node.js website (shown in Figure 19.2) to download a package you can install. You can also download the code for Node.js and build it yourself, if you prefer. See http://bit.ly/1ah2ArA for instructions on the latter. Once you have Node.js installed, you can use its package manager to install socket.io, like this: npm install socket.io.

Figure 19.2   Node.js and socket.io

NOTE: Other Node.js modules used by Snail Bait

Besides socket.io, Snail Bait uses the http, io (input/output), fs (file system), and validator Node.js modules.

19.2 Include socket.io JavaScript in Snail Bait

Here's how Snail Bait implements high scores and in-game metrics:

- On the server, a Node.js application uses the socket.io module to send and retrieve high scores and in-game metrics to and from clients. The application stores those values in files on the server.

- On the client, Snail Bait also uses socket.io to send and retrieve high scores and in-game metrics to and from the server. That code is part of the game itself, implemented with `SnailBait` properties and methods, just like the rest of the game.

Snail Bait not only uses JavaScript on both the client and server, it also uses the same socket.io module to transfer data, which makes writing code on the server similar to writing code on the client. Additionally, it's a simple matter to transfer data via sockets using socket.io, making it even easier to accomplish the seemingly formidable task of communicating between a player's computer and the game's server.

There's one catch, however. Snail Bait uses socket.io on the client and therefore needs to include socket.io JavaScript into the game. As it turns out, the task of including socket.io JavaScript on the client is simple but not well documented. The trick is to include a `script` element in your game's HTML file before you include the game's main JavaScript file, as shown in Example 19.1.

Example 19.1 *Client:* Including socket.io JavaScript

```html
<!DOCTYPE html>

<html>
    ...

    <body>
        ...

        <script
            src='http://corehtml5canvas.com:98/socket.io/socket.io.js'>
        </script>

        <script src='snailbait.js'></script>
        ...
    </body>
</html>
```

The `src` attribute of the `script` element points to the game's host (http://corehtml5canvas.com) and port (98). *The socket.io/socket.io.js at the end of the src attribute causes the server to automatically send the socket.io JavaScript to the client.*

Once we have the socket.io JavaScript on the client, and Node.js and socket.io installed on the server, we're ready to write some code. Here's what we're going to do:

- Create a simple server with Node.js
- Create a socket on the server
- Start the server
- Create a socket on the client
- Connect the socket on the client to the socket on the server
- Send data between the client and server to implement in-game metrics and high scores

19.3 Create a Simple Server

Creating a server and subsequently listening to a port is about as easy as it gets. Use Node.js's http module, as shown in Example 19.2.

Example 19.2 *Server:* A simple server running on port 98

```
var http = require('http'),
    server = http.createServer();

server.listen(98);
```

 NOTE: Requiring modules with `require()`

If you require a module in Node.js, you simply invoke the `require()` method, as shown in Example 19.2. That method returns an object whose methods represent the functionality provided by the module; for example, creating servers with the `createServer()` method is part of the functionality provided by the http module. See http://nodejs.org/api/http.html#http_http for more information about Node.js's http module.

19.4 Create a Socket on the Server

Now that we have a server, let's create a socket as shown in Example 19.3.

Example 19.3 *Server:* Creating a socket with socket.io

```
var io = require('socket.io'),
    socket = io.listen(server);
```

Once again we require a Node.js module; this time, it's socket.io. That module has a listen() method that opens a socket on the specified server.

Sockets are communication endpoints, so we need another one on the client. We will see how to create that socket in the next section, but first we need to start the server.

NOTE: CommonJS, require, and nodejs modules

Modules and the require() method are defined by CommonJS, which is a JavaScript ecosystem for web servers that's implemented by Node.js. You can also use CommonJS for command line applications or apps that run in a browser. See http://wiki.commonjs.org/wiki/CommonJS for more about CommonJS.

NOTE: Debugging on the server

You can debug your server-side Node.js code in Chrome's debugger just like you can for your client-side code with Node Inspector. See http://bit.ly/1ah6bWr for more information.

19.5 Start the Server

Once we've implemented the preceding code to create the server and socket, we must run the code on the server. Example 19.4 shows how to run the code with Node.js, assuming the code resides in a file named game-server.js.

Example 19.4 *Server:* Running the server code

```
> node game-server.js
```

Some operating systems, such as UNIX and its variants, kill your processes when you log off. For those operating systems, you can use the nohup command (short for no hangup), as shown in Example 19.5, so that your Node.js application continues to run when you log off.

Example 19.5 *Server:* Using UNIX's nohup to prevent hangups

```
> nohup node game-server.js
```

Now that we've started the server, let's go to the client and connect back to the server.

19.6 Create a Socket on the Client and Connect to the Server

Snail Bait connects to the server in the game's constructor function, as shown in Example 19.6.

Example 19.6 *Client:* Opening a socket and connecting to the server

---

```
var SnailBait = function () {
    ...

    this.serverAvailable = true;

    try {
        this.socket =
            new io.connect('http://corehtml5canvas.com:98');
    }
    catch(err) {
        this.serverAvailable = false;
    }
    ...
};
```

Recall we have a socket on the server that listens to port 98. The preceding code connects to that port and gives us a socket on the client. Snail Bait keeps track of whether it successfully connected to the server with a serverAvailable property. If the connection fails, Snail Bait sets that property to false; otherwise, it's true.

At this point, we have the server running with connected sockets on both the server and client. With those preliminaries out of the way, it's time to implement in-game metrics and high scores by sending data between those sockets.

 CAUTION: The port numbers must match on the server and client.

Where did the `io` object come from on the client?

At first glance it may appear as though the `io` JavaScript object in Example 19.6 is the same as the object with the same name in Example 19.3, but that's not the case because the code in Example 19.6 runs on the client, whereas the code in Example 19.3 runs on the server.

In fact, Snail Bait never explicitly declares the `io` object on the client. That object, whose properties are shown in Figure 19.3, is created by the socket.io code that Snail Bait downloads from the server, as discussed in Section 19.2, "Include socket.io JavaScript in Snail Bait," on p. 518.

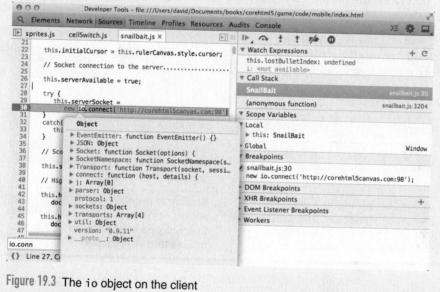

Figure 19.3 The `io` object on the client

19.7 Record In-game Metrics

A great way to gain insights into making your games more fun to play is to analyze in-game metrics. For example, every time a player loses a life, Snail Bait sends the location at which the runner lost her life to the server. That simple metric is useful for calibrating the level of difficulty at certain points in the game.

Snail Bait maintains a file named lives-lost.txt, partially listed in Example 19.7, that contains (X,Y) locations where players lost their lives.

Example 19.7 The lives-lost.txt file

```
(1703, 160)(284, 169)(59, 153)(271, 111)(685, 258)(1975, 169)...
```

When the player loses a life:

1. Snail Bait **emits** a *life lost* message to the server, passing the location where the runner lost her life.

2. **On** receiving the *life lost* message, the server appends the location where the player lost a life to the end of lives-lost.txt.

The sockets that we previously created on the client and server have an `emit()` method for emitting messages, and an `on()` method for receiving messages. Those methods are summarized in Table 19.1.

Table 19.1 Socket methods used by Snail Bait

Method	Description
`socket.emit(String messageId, Object data)`	Emits a message to the socket's endpoint. Messages consist of an identifier (`String`) and data (`Object`).
`socket.on(String messageId, function processData())`	Receives a message sent with `socket.emit()`. Socket.io passes the data that you pass to `socket.emit()` to the `processData()` function.

On the client, Snail Bait uses the socket's `emit()` method to emit a life lost message to the server. The data for that message is an object with `left` and `top` properties that represent the location at which the runner lost her life, as you can see in Example 19.8.

Example 19.8 *Client:* Emit the life lost message

```
SnailBait.prototype = function () {
   ...

   loseLife: function () {
      ...

      if (this.serverAvailable) {
         this.socket.emit(
```

```
            'life lost',

            {
                left: this.spriteOffset + this.runner.left,
                top:  this.runner.top
            }
        );
    }
    ...
},
...
};
```

Subsequently on the server, Snail Bait processes the life lost message as shown in Example 19.9.

Example 19.9 *Server:* Handle the life lost message

```
var fs = require('fs'); // require file system module

socket.on('connection', function (client) {
    ...

    client.on(
        'life lost',

        function (data) {
            fs.appendFile(
                'lives-lost.txt',

                '(' + data.left.toFixed(0) + ', ' +
                data.top.toFixed(0)  + ')',

                function (err) {
                    if (err) throw err;
                }
            );
        }
    );
    ...
});
```

When the client connects to the server, socket.io invokes the function Snail Bait passes to socket.on() in the preceding listing. That function implements handlers with calls to client.on() that receive messages from client sockets.

In the preceding code, on a life lost message from the client (thus client.on('life lost', ...)), the associated function appends data to a file. That data comes from the JavaScript object Snail Bait passed to `socket.emit()` in Example 19.8. The preceding code uses the `fs` module, which lets you do file-system-related things, so Snail Bait requires that module and calls its `appendFile()` method, passing the filename and the string to append to the file.

With the server running and connected sockets on the client and server, all that's required to implement in-game metrics is the code listed in Example 19.8 on the client and the code in Example 19.9 on the server. You can easily send other in-game metrics—for example, the amount of time it takes players to complete a level—by emitting another message on the client with the appropriate data and adding code on the server to receive the message.

Sending in-game metrics from the client to the server and subsequently processing them on the server is straightforward, as you've seen in this section. In the next section we look at a more complicated scenario that involves several round trips to the server to implement high scores.

19.8 Manage High Scores

At the end of the game, Snail Bait emits a message to the server. On receiving that message, the server returns the last high score. If the player's score exceeds the last high score, Snail Bait emits another message to the server requesting the top five high scores, and the server obliges. With the top five high scores in hand, Snail Bait displays the heads-up display (HUD) shown in Figure 19.4.

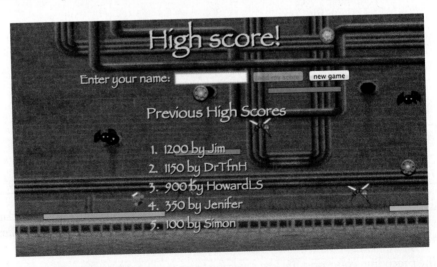

Figure 19.4 High scores display

At this point the player has a choice: add his or her name to the list of high scores or decline to do so and start a new game. Notice that the button to add the player's score to the list of high scores is initially disabled to prevent someone from entering a blank name. Once the player types a character in the text field, Snail Bait enables the add my score button.

When the player activates the add my score button from the high scores display, Snail Bait emits a message to the server, passing the new high score and the player's name. On receiving that message, the server adds the high score to the file containing the game's high scores.

In this section we discuss the implementation of Snail Bait's high scores, starting with the HTML and CSS for the high scores HUD display.

19.8.1 The High Scores User Interface

The HTML for Snail Bait's high scores is shown in Example 19.10.

Example 19.10 The HTML for the high scores HUD display

```html
<!DOCTYPE html>
<html>
   ...

   <body>
      ...

      <!-- Arena.............................................-->

      <div id='snailbait-arena'>

         <!-- High scores.............................................-->

         <div id='snailbait-high-score-toast'>
            <p class='snailbait-title'>High score!</p>

         Enter your name:

         <input id='snailbait-high-score-name'
                class='snailbait-textfield'>

         <input id='snailbait-high-score-add-score'
                type='button' value='add my score' disabled='true'>

         <input id='snailbait-high-score-new-game'
                type='button' value='new game'>
```

(Continues)

Example 19.10   *(Continued)*

```
            <p id='snailbait-previous-high-scores-title'>
                Previous High Scores
            </p>

            <div id='snailbait-previous-high-scores'>
                <ol id='snailbait-high-score-list'></ol>
            </div>
        </div>
        ...
    </div>
    </body>
</html>
```

The preceding HTML is uneventful. The most interesting aspect of that HTML is the ordered list of high scores at the end of the listing, which is initially empty. That list is filled in by the game's JavaScript.

The CSS for the game's high scores is shown in Example 19.11.

Example 19.11 The CSS for the high score HUD display

```
#snailbait-high-score-toast {
    position: absolute;
    padding: 5px;
    margin-left: 135px;
    margin-top: 32px;
    color: yellow;
    font: 20px fantasy;
    text-shadow: 1px 1px 1px black;
    text-align: center;
    width: 520px;
    height: 390px;
    z-index: 1;

    opacity: 0;
    display: none;

    -webkit-transition: opacity 1s;
    -moz-transition: opacity 1s;
    -o-transition: opacity 1s;
    transition: opacity 1s;
}

#snailbait-high-score-toast .snailbait-title {
```

```
    font-size: 45px;
    text-shadow: 2px 2px 2px black;
    margin-bottom: 10px;
}

#snailbait-previous-high-scores-title {
    font-size: 25px;
}

#snailbait-previous-high-scores {
    text-align: left;
    margin: 0 auto;
    padding-left: 130px;
}
```

Most of the attributes in the preceding CSS are involved in the mundane business of positioning elements and specifying how they look. The most interesting aspect of the preceding CSS is the by now familiar footprint of elements that fade in and out: the opacity transition and corresponding initial invisibility for the high scores. We will see how to fade in the high scores in Section 19.8.2, "Retrieve High Scores from the Server," on p. 530.

Example 19.12 shows how Snail Bait accesses the high score elements in its JavaScript.

Example 19.12 Accessing the high scores HTML elements in JavaScript

```
var SnailBait = function () {
    ...

    // High scores.......................................................

    this.highScoreElement =
        document.getElementById('snailbait-high-score-toast');

    this.highScoreListElement =
        document.getElementById('snailbait-high-score-list');

    this.highScoreNameElement =
        document.getElementById('snailbait-high-score-name');

    this.highScoreNewGameElement =
        document.getElementById('snailbait-high-score-new-game');

    this.highScoreAddScoreElement =
        document.getElementById('snailbait-high-score-add-score');
```

(Continues)

Example 19.12 *(Continued)*

```
    this.highScoreNamePending = false;
    ...
};
```

The game also declares a highScoreNamePending variable, discussed in the next section. Now that you've seen the HTML and CSS for the game's high scores display, let's look behind the scenes of the action.

19.8.2 Retrieve High Scores from the Server

Snail Bait stores high scores as comma-separated values (CSVs) in a file on the server, as shown in Example 19.13.

Example 19.13 The high-scores.txt file

```
Jim,1200,DrTfnH,1150,HowardLS,900,Jenifer,350,Simon,100
...
```

When the game is over, the client checks the current high score as follows:

1. The client emits a get high score message to the server.
2. On receiving the get high score message, the server emits a high score message containing the current high score to the client.
3. On receiving the high score message, the client checks to see if the player exceeded the current high score; if so, the client emits a get high scores message to retrieve the top-five high scores.
4. On receiving the get high scores message, the server reads the high scores file and emits a high scores message containing a list of the current high scores to the client.
5. The client updates the heads-up display with the high scores from the server.

Let's see what the preceding steps look like in code. First, Example 19.14 shows how the gameOver() method emits a get high score message to the server, using the socket that Snail Bait created previously on the client.

Example 19.14 *Client:* Emit a get high score message to the server

---

```
SnailBait.prototype = {
    ...

    checkHighScores: function () {
```

```
        this.socket.emit('get high score');
    },

    gameOver: function () {
        ...

        if (this.serverAvailable) {
            this.checkHighScores();
        }
        else {
            this.revealCredits();
        }
    },
    ...
};
```

The server handles the get high score message with the file system module's
readFile() method, as shown in **Example 19.15**. That method takes the name of
the file, the file's encoding, and a function that receives the file's data.

Example 19.15 *Server:* Emit the high score to the client

```
socket.on('connection', function (client) {
    ...

    client.on(
        'get high score',

        function (data) {
            var highScoreEntries = [];

            fs.readFile(
                'high-scores.txt',       // Filename

                'utf-8',                 // Encoding

                function (err, data) { // Handler
                    if (err) throw err;/

                    highScoreEntries = data.splitCSV();

                    client.emit('high score',
                                { score: highScoreEntries[1] });
                }
            );
        }
    );
    ...
});
```

The function that receives the data from the high scores file splits that data into an array with the string's splitCSV() method listed in **Example 19.16**. The function in the preceding listing then emits a high score message whose data object contains a lone score property. That property's value is the current high score—highScoreEntries[0] refers to the name of the person with the high score, whereas highScoreEntries[1] refers to that person's score.

Example 19.16 *Server:* Adding a splitCSV() method to all strings that turns a list of CSVs into an array

```
String.prototype.splitCSV = function() {
    // Add a splitCSV() function to strings

    var regex = /(\s*'[^']+'|\s*[^,]+)(?=,|$)/g;
    return this.match(regex);
};
```

On the client, Snail Bait handles the high score message from the server as shown in **Example 19.17**.

Example 19.17 *Client:* Emit a get high scores message to the server

```
snailBait.socket.on(
    'high score',

    function (data) {
        // data is the current high score

        if (snailBait.score > data.score) {
            snailBait.socket.emit('get high scores');
            snailBait.highScoreNamePending = true;
        }
        else {
            snailBait.revealCredits();
            ...
        }
    }
);
```

Recall from **Example 19.15** that when the server emits the high score to the client, it sends a data object with a lone score property whose value represents the last high score. The preceding code checks to see if the current player's score exceeds that high score; if so, Snail Bait requests all high scores by emitting a get high scores message back to the server. The preceding code also sets the value of the game's highScoreNamePending property to true. We discuss that property in Section 19.8.4, "Monitor Name Input," on p. 534.

Example 19.18 shows how the server handles the get high scores message.

Example 19.18 *Server:* Emit high scores to the client

```
socket.on('connection', function (client) {
   ...

   client.on(
      'get high scores',

      function (data) {
         fs.readFile(
            'high-scores.txt',       // Filename

            'utf-8',                  // Encoding

            function (err, data) {  // Handler
               if (err) {
                  throw err;
               }

               client.emit('high scores', { scores: data.splitCSV() });
            }
         );
      }
   );
});
```

The preceding code reads the high scores file and emits a high scores message back to the client. The data object for that message contains an array of names and high scores. Now let's see how Snail Bait displays those high scores on the client.

19.8.3 Display High Scores on the Client

Example 19.19 shows how Snail Bait handles the high scores message from the server.

Example 19.19 *Client:* Create HTML for the high score list

```
snailBait.socket.on(
    'high scores',

    function (data) {
        snailBait.highScoreListElement.innerHTML = "";

        for(var i=0; i < data.scores.length; i += 2) {
            snailBait.highScoreListElement.innerHTML +=
                "<li>" + data.scores[i+1] + " by " +
                data.scores[i] + "</li>";
        }

        snailBait.revealHighScores();
    }
);
```

When it receives a list of high scores from the server, Snail Bait adds list elements to the high scores HTML element and subsequently reveals the high scores, as you can see from the preceding code. Example 19.20 shows the implementation of the game's revealHighScores() method.

Example 19.20 *Client:* Reveal high scores

```
SnailBait.prototype = {
    ...

    revealHighScores: function () {
        this.highScoreNameElement.value = '';
        this.fadeInElements(snailBait.highScoreElement);
        this.highScoreNameElement.focus();
    },
    ...
};
```

The revealHighScores() method clears the name text field, fades in the high score element, and gives the name text field focus.

19.8.4 Monitor Name Input

At this point, if the player has exceeded the previous high score, Snail Bait has displayed the list of high scores, placed the cursor in the name text field, and disabled the add my score button, as shown in the top screenshot in Figure 19.5.

When the player types the first character of their name, Snail Bait enables the add my score button, as you can see from the bottom screenshot in Figure 19.5.

Figure 19.5 The name input field

Initially, the add my score button is disabled by default. When the player subsequently types a name's first character, the snailbait-high-score-name element's keypress event handler enables the button by setting its disabled property to false, as shown in Example 19.21.

Example 19.21 The name element's keypress event handler

```
snailBait.highScoreNameElement.addEventListener(
   'keypress',

   function () {
      if (snailBait.highScoreNamePending) {
         snailBait.highScoreAddScoreElement.disabled = false;
         snailBait.highScoreNamePending = false;
      }
   }
);
```

The preceding event handler does something only if the highScoreNamePending property is true. When that's the case, the event handler immediately resets the property to false so that the event handler's code executes only for the first character in the player's name.

Any time a web application receives input from its users, the application must validate that input. Let's see how to do that next.

19.8.5 Validate and Set the High Score on the Server

Recall the *player entered a name, which means we must validate that input to prevent breaches of security* such as cross-site scripting (XSS) or SQL injection. It's also easy to intercept HTTP requests and change values sent from the client on their way to the server, so Snail Bait also validates the score in addition to the player's name.

To do that validation, Snail Bait uses the validator module for Node.js. The validator, as you can see from Example 19.22, is simple to install with Node.js's package manager, known as npm.

Example 19.22 Installing Node.js's validator module

```
> npm install validator
npm http GET https://registry.npmjs.org/validator
npm http 200 https://registry.npmjs.org/validator
npm http GET https://registry.npmjs.org/validator/-/validator-3.1.0.tgz
npm http 200 https://registry.npmjs.org/validator/-/validator-3.1.0.tgz
validator@3.1.0 node_modules/validator
```

When the player activates the add my score button to send a name and score to the server:

1. The client emits a set high score message to the server, passing the new high score and the player's name.
2. On receiving the set high score message, the server validates the player's name to make sure it contains only alphanumeric characters. It also validates the score to make sure it contains only numeric characters.
3. Subsequently, if the name and score are valid, the server adds the high score to the file containing high scores and emits a high score set message to the client.

The add my score button's click event handler, which emits the set high score message to the server, is listed in Example 19.23.

Example 19.23 *Client:* Emit the set high score message to the server

---

```
snailBait.highScoreAddScoreElement.addEventListener(
   'click',

   function () {
      snailBait.highScoreAddScoreElement.disabled = true;

      snailBait.socket.emit(
         'set high score',
```

```
        {
            name: snailBait.highScoreNameElement.value,
            score: snailBait.score
        }
    );
  }
);
```

The data object emitted to the server by the event handler contains the player's name and score.

The server validates the player's name and score; if they pass inspection, the server stores the name and score in the game's high scores file, as shown in Example 19.24.

Example 19.24 *Server:* Setting the high score

```
var validator = require('validator');

socket.on('connection', function (client) {
   ...

   client.on('set high score', function (data) {
      var MAX_EXISTING_ENTRIES = 4,
          highScoreEntries = [],
          numExistingEntries,
          newEntries = data.name + ',' + data.score;

      if (validator.isAlphanumeric(data.name) &&
          validator.isNumeric(data.score)) {

         fs.readFile(
            'high-scores.txt',

            'utf-8',

            function (err, data) {
               if (err)
                  throw err;

            highScoreEntries = data.splitCSV();

            numExistingEntries = highScoreEntries.length / 2;

            if (numExistingEntries > MAX_EXISTING_ENTRIES) {
               numExistingEntries = MAX_EXISTING_ENTRIES;
            }
```

(Continues)

Example 19.24 *(Continued)*

```
            for(var i=0; i < numExistingEntries*2; i+=2) {
               newEntries += ',' + highScoreEntries[i] + ',' +
                                    highScoreEntries[i+1];
            }

            fs.writeFile('high-scores.txt',

                     newEntries,

                     function (err) {
                        if (err)
                           throw(err);
                     }
                  );

         client.emit('high score set',
                     { score: data.score });
      });
   }
});
...
});
```

After validating the name and score, the preceding code reads data from the high scores file. It subsequently creates a new array of high score entries containing the new high score and writes them back out to the same file. Finally, the code emits a high score set message back to the client.

19.8.6 Redisplay High Scores

On receiving the high score set message from the server, the client emits a get high scores message back to the server, causing the client, as before, to redisplay the high scores.

Example 19.25 *Client:* Redisplaying high scores

```
snailBait.socket.on(
   'high score set',

   function (data) {
      snailBait.socket.emit('get high scores'); // redisplay scores
   }
);
```

NOTE: Snail Bait could redisplay high scores without going back to the server

In the interests of simplicity, Snail Bait makes another round trip to the server to redisplay high scores even though that redisplay could be handled entirely on the client. In this case, Snail Bait opts for simplicity over performance because even though it's crucial to keep HTTP requests to a minimum when games load, once games are running, asynchronous calls to the server are inexpensive.

19.8.7 Start a New Game

When the player activates the new game button, the browser invokes the button's click event handler, listed in **Example 19.26**.

Example 19.26 *Client:* The new game button's click event handler

```
snailBait.highScoreNewGameElement.addEventListener(
   'click',

   function () {
      snailBait.highScoreAddScoreElement.disabled = true;
      snailBait.hideHighScores();
      snailBait.restartGame();
   }
);
```

The click event handler for the new game button disables the add my score button, hides the high scores, and restarts the game. The hideHighScores() method, listed in **Example 19.27**, uses Snail Bait's fadeOutElements() method to fade out the high scores.

Example 19.27 *Client:* Hiding high scores

```
SnailBait.prototype = {
   ...

   hideHighScores: function () {
      var HIGH_SCORE_TRANSITION_DURATION = 1000;

      snailBait.fadeOutElements(snailBait.highScoreElement,
                                HIGH_SCORE_TRANSITION_DURATION);
   },
   ...
};
```

Now that you've seen how to store in-game metrics and high scores on a game's server with Node.js and socket.io, let's turn our attention to the final topic in this chapter: deploying Snail Bait.

19.9 Deploy Snail Bait

To keep your game's loading time to a minimum, make as few HTTP requests and download as few bytes as possible. We've already addressed minimizing HTTP requests throughout this book. To keep your files as small as possible, you should minify your text resources and use gzip to further compress your files.

A good resource for minifying your text files is the YUI Compressor, shown in Figure 19.6.

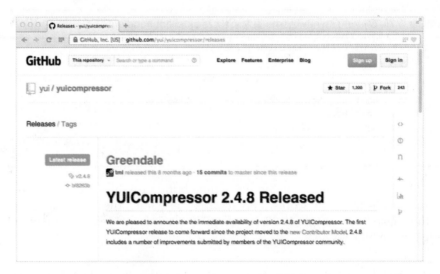

Figure 19.6 The YUI Compressor

The YUI Compressor, which is implemented and maintained by Yahoo!, lets you minify and obfuscate your code. It's a Java application, so you must have Java (version 1.4 or greater) installed on your computer. You run the application as shown in Example 19.28.

Example 19.28 The compress.sh script

```bash
#!/bin/bash

for f in `find . -name "*.css"`
   do
      echo 'Minifying and obfuscating ' $f
      java -jar ~/Utilities/yuicompressor-2.4.7.jar $1 $f >> all.css
   done

for f in `find . -name "*.js"`
   do
      echo 'Minifying and obfuscating ' $f
      java -jar ~/Utilities/yuicompressor-2.4.7.jar $1 $f >> all.js
   done
```

The preceding listing shows a UNIX script that iterates over Snail Bait's JavaScript and CSS files, minifying and obfuscating each in turn with the YUI Compressor, redirecting the JavaScript output to the end of a file named all.js and the CSS output to the end of all.css. Those are the files that the final version of Snail Bait includes, as you can see from Example 19.29, instead of the snailbait.css file and the myriad JavaScript files that the game previously included individually.

Example 19.29 Snail Bait's revised HTML file

```html
<!DOCTYPE html>
<html>
   ...

   <head>
      <title>Snail Bait</title>
      <link rel='stylesheet' href='all.css'/>
      ...
   </head>

   <body>
      ...

      <script src='all.js'></script>
   </body>
</html>
```

Snail Bait has a simple deploy script, shown in Example 19.30, that removes the previous all.js and all.css files and runs the preceding script to re-create them.

Example 19.30 The `deploy.sh` script

```bash
#!/bin/bash

rm all.js
rm all.css

echo 'Minifying and obfuscating...'
echo

compress.sh
```

That's all there is to minifying your text-based resources and obfuscating your JavaScript.

NOTE: Implementing scripts on operating systems other than UNIX

The shell script discussed in this section is a UNIX script. You can easily write equivalent scripts for other operating systems, such as Windows. You can also use many UNIX commands in general on Windows with MKS. See www.mkssoftware.com for details.

NOTE: The problems with obfuscation

Obfuscation seems like a pretty good idea. You make your JavaScript code more difficult to decipher and you reduce the size of your JavaScript files. However, obfuscation has two serious drawbacks. First, obfuscating your code can introduce bugs into your code. Second, the most determined hackers—which are the only ones you really need to worry about—can figure out what your code is doing anyway.

19.10 Upload Files to a Server

With minified and obfuscated text-based resources, we're ready to upload Snail Bait's files to the server. Example 19.31 shows the files and directories stored on the server.

Example 19.31 Snail Bait files on the server

```
> ls -al

total 116
-rw-r--r-- 1 root root  9274 Jan 12 19:17 all.css
-rw-r--r-- 1 root root 77385 Jan 12 19:17 all.js
-rw-r--r-- 1 root root  1150 Jan 12 19:17 favicon.ico
drwxr-xr-x 2 root root  4096 Jan 12 19:18 images
-rw-r--r-- 1 root root 10265 Jan 12 19:17 index.html
drwxr-xr-x 2 root root  4096 Jan 12 19:17 sounds

./images:
total 1272
-rw-r--r-- 1 root root    4297 Jan 12 19:23 runner-small.png
-rw-r--r-- 1 root root    7990 Jan 12 19:17 snail.gif
-rw-r--r-- 1 root root 1286324 Jan 12 19:17 spritesheet.png

./sounds:
total 4680
-rw-r--r-- 1 root root  314716 Jan 12 19:17 audio-sprites.mp3
-rw-r--r-- 1 root root  114140 Jan 12 19:17 audio-sprites.ogg
-rw-r--r-- 1 root root 2463196 Jan 12 19:17 music.mp3
-rw-r--r-- 1 root root 1876471 Jan 12 19:17 music.ogg
```

 NOTE: Using gzip

As a final step to reduce the size of your files, you should take advantage of gzip compression. To do so, simply configure your server to gzip your files on the fly and deliver them to clients—you don't even need to zip the files yourself. Zipping on the fly may sound slow, but it's blazingly fast on the server.

19.11 Conclusion

In this chapter you saw how to communicate between clients and your game's server with Node.js and socket.io, to implement in-game metrics and high scores. Additionally, we discussed how to deploy your game to a server.

In the next chapter, which is the last chapter in the book, we take a step back and apply what we've learned previously in the book to implement another video game.

19.12 Exercises

1. Modify Snail Bait's in-game metrics to include the game's elapsed time when the player lost a life, in addition to the location.

2. Add another metric to Snail Bait's in-game metrics that tracks the percent of assets that the runner captured. For example, if the runner ran past ten assets (coins, rubies, or sapphires) and collected seven of the assets, the metric would be 0.7.

3. Once every 0.5 seconds, send the game's current frame rate to the server. On the server, append the frame rate to a file named frame-rates.txt.

4. Play the game and achieve the high score. Enter a name with nonalpha-numeric characters and click the add my score button. What happens when you click the add my score button? Can you re-enter your name?

CHAPTER **20**

Epilogue: Bodega's Revenge

Topics in This Chapter

This book devotes entire chapters to implementing various aspects of 2D games such as graphics and animation, sprites and sprite behaviors, and collision detection, by examining the implementation of a nontrivial HTML5 video game.

This chapter provides a more holistic perspective by showing you how to combine those aspects of 2D game development to implement a simpler video game, shown in Figure 20.1.

Figure 20.1 Bodega's Revenge

In Bodega's Revenge, the player shoots advancing birds with a turret gun. Players rotate the turret by sliding their fingers up and down on mobile devices. On the desktop, players use either the left and right arrow keys or the *d* and *k* keys to rotate the turret. The player shoots bullets from the turret by pressing the spacebar on the desktop or tapping the screen on mobile devices.

When the turret fires a bullet, the circular part of the turret darkens and fire erupts from the end of the turret, as shown in Figure 20.1. When a bullet collides with a bird, the bird explodes and the bullet disappears.

The player starts the game with 20 bullets. When a bullet goes out of view, the game immediately reloads it in the turret and if the player holds down the spacebar on the desktop, the turret shoots bullets in rapid succession as shown in Figure 20.1.

Birds fly from right to left a little faster than the background scrolls, creating a mild parallax effect (see Chapter 3 for more about parallax). When a bird flies behind the turret and off the left edge of the game's canvas, the player loses a bullet. Above the canvas, the game displays the number of bullets that remain. The game ends when the turret runs out of bullets.

In this chapter we implement Bodega's Revenge with the following steps:

- Design the user interface (Section 20.1 on p. 547)

- Create the sprite sheet (Section 20.2 on p. 551)
- Instantiate the game (Section 20.3 on p. 552)
- Implement sprites (Section 20.4 on p. 553)
- Implement sprite behaviors (Section 20.5 on p. 563)
- Draw the bullet canvas (Section 20.6 on p. 580)
- Implement touch-based controls for mobile devices (Section 20.7 on p. 582)

Let's begin our discussion of Bodega's Revenge by looking at its user interface.

NOTE: Starting a game of your own

Bodega's Revenge was implemented from a stripped-down version of Snail Bait, without sprites and many of Snail Bait's extraneous features such as smoking holes. You can download that stripped-down version of Snail Bait, which you can use as the basis for your own game, at corehtml5games.com/snailbait-stripped-down.

NOTE: The rest of this book is a prerequisite for this chapter

This chapter focuses on implementing the gameplay of Bodega's Revenge and spends no time discussing the fundamentals of the game's underlying infrastructure such as implementing sprites and sprite behaviors in general. Discussions about implementing 2D game fundamentals take place elsewhere in this book and are not repeated in this chapter.

NOTE: Play Bodega's Revenge

You can play Bodega's Revenge online at www.corehtml5games.com/bodegas-revenge.

20.1 Design the User Interface

Bodega's Revenge uses CSS to draw the carbon fiber background for the game's webpage, as shown in Figure 20.2. The CSS for that background comes from the CSS3 Patterns Gallery, discussed in Chapter 2.

The game's favicon, shown in Figure 20.3, was generated at genfavicon.com.

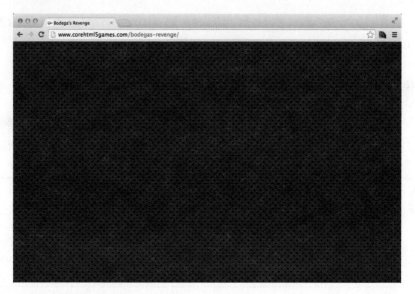

Figure 20.2 Bodega's CSS background

Figure 20.3 Bodega's favicon

As Bodega's Revenge loads resources, it displays the loading screen shown in Figure 20.4, which is an animated GIF of the firing turret. That animated GIF was created at picasion.com.

The game's start screen, shown in Figure 20.5, fades in after the game loads. When the player clicks the Start button, the game begins.

Figure 20.6 shows the running slowly warning for Bodega's Revenge. When the game's average frame rate drops below 40 frames per second, the game displays the warning.

Figure 20.4 Bodega's loading screen

Figure 20.5 Bodega's start screen

Figure 20.6 Bodega's running slowly warning

When the game completes, Bodega's Revenge displays the credits screen shown in Figure 20.7.

Figure 20.7 Bodega's credits

The implementation details of the game's loading and start screens, running slowly warning, and credits are discussed elsewhere in this book. The differences between those screens in Snail Bait versus Bodega's Revenge are entirely cosmetic, relegating them to HTML and CSS that is not discussed in this chapter.

20.2 Create the Sprite Sheet

The sprite sheet for Bodega's Revenge is shown in Figure 20.8.

Figure 20.8 Bodega's sprite sheet

As is the case for Snail Bait, the graphics for Bodega's Revenge comes from Replica Island. The sprite sheet for Bodega's Revenge was created by dragging individual images from Replica Island into a diagramming tool (Omni Graffle for the Mac) and then exporting the project as a PNG file.

 NOTE: Transparent backgrounds for sprite sheets

When you export a sprite sheet from a diagramming tool or drawing software, it's important to specify a transparent background; otherwise, you end up with sprites embedded in blocks of the default background color, usually white. In Figure 20.8, the sprite sheet's transparent background is gray so that you can see the white part of the explosion and the fire at the end of the turret.

20.3 Instantiate the Game

Bodega's Revenge is a JavaScript object with a constructor function and prototype, as shown in **Example 20.1**.

Example 20.1 Creating the game object

```
var BodegasRevenge = function () { // constructor
   this.CLOCKWISE = 0;
   this.COUNTER_CLOCKWISE = 1;
   ...

   this.canvas  = document.getElementById('game-canvas');
   this.context = this.canvas.getContext('2d');
   ...
};

BodegasRevenge.prototype = { // methods
   createSprites: function () {
      ...
   },
   ...
};
```

The game creates an instance of `BodegasRevenge` with the JavaScript new operator, as shown in **Example 20.2**.

Example 20.2 Instantiating the game

```
var game = new BodegasRevenge();
```

With user interface preliminaries out of the way and a game object in hand, let's see how to implement Bodega's Revenge, starting with the implementation of its sprites.

 NOTE: From here on out, it's all sprites and behaviors

Using the techniques discussed in this book, implementing gameplay consists almost entirely of implementing sprites and their behaviors. The rest of this chapter concentrates on the implementation of the sprites of Bodega's Revenge.

20.4 Implement Sprites

Bodega's Revenge has three types of sprites: a turret, bullets, and birds. Those sprites are created by the game's createSprites() method, listed in Example 20.3.

```
BodegasRevenge.prototype = {
   ...

   createSprites: function () {
      this.createTurret();
      this.createBullets();
      this.createBirds();
   },
   ...
};
```

We discuss the three methods that createSprites() invokes in the sections that follow.

20.4.1 The Turret

The turret rotates around the center of the circular part of the turret and shoots bullets. The game creates the turret with the createTurret() method, listed in Example 20.4.

```
var BodegasRevenge = function () {
   ...

   this.turretData = { left: 50, top: 180 };

   this.TURRET_WIDTH   = 68;
   this.TURRET_HEIGHT = 40;

   this.TURRET_CENTER_X = 20;
   this.TURRET_CENTER_Y = 20;

   this.TURRET_CYCLE_DURATION = 10;
   ...
};
```

(Continues)

Example 20.4 *(Continued)*

```
BodegasRevenge.prototype = {
    ...

    createTurret: function () {
        this.turret = new Sprite('turret',              // type
                        this.createTurretArtist(),  // artist
                        [                            // behaviors
                           this.createTurretRotateBehavior(),
                           this.createTurretBarrelFireBehavior(),
                           this.createTurretShootBehavior(),
                           new CycleBehavior(this.TURRET_CYCLE_DURATION)
                        ]
                    );

        this.turret.left   = this.turretData.left;
        this.turret.top    = this.turretData.top;
        this.turret.width  = this.TURRET_WIDTH;
        this.turret.height = this.TURRET_HEIGHT;
        this.turret.radius = this.TURRET_WIDTH - this.TURRET_CENTER_X;
    },
    ...
};
```

The createTurret() method creates the turret sprite with its artist and array of behaviors and sets the sprite's properties. The artist is discussed in the next section and the turret's behaviors are discussed in Section 20.5.1, "Turret Behaviors," on p. 564.

20.4.1.1 Create the Turret Sprite's Artist

The createTurretArtist() method, which creates the turret's artist, is listed in Example 20.5.

Example 20.5 Creating the turret sprite's artist

```
var BodegasRevenge = function () {
    ...

    this.turretRotation = 0;

    this.turretCell = [
        {left: 12,  top: 120, width: 68, height: 40}
    ];
};
```

```
BodegasRevenge.prototype = {
   ...

   createTurretArtist: function () {
      var turretArtist = new SpriteSheetArtist(this.spritesheet,
                                               this.turretCell);

      // Override the turret artist's draw() method to rotate the turret
      // before drawing it

      turretArtist.draw = function (sprite, context) {
         context.translate(sprite.left + game.TURRET_CENTER_X,
                           sprite.top  + game.TURRET_CENTER_Y);

         context.rotate(game.turretRotation);

         context.drawImage(this.spritesheet, // image
                           this.cells[this.cellIndex].left, // source x
                           this.cells[this.cellIndex].top,  // source y
                           game.TURRET_WIDTH,       // source width
                           game.TURRET_HEIGHT,      // source height
                           -game.TURRET_CENTER_X, // destination x
                           -game.TURRET_CENTER_Y, // destination y
                           game.TURRET_WIDTH,       // destination width
                           game.TURRET_HEIGHT);     // destination height
      };

      return turretArtist;
   },
   ...
};
```

The turret's artist is a sprite sheet artist. Recall from Chapter 7 that sprite sheet artists draw their sprites by copying a rectangular region from a sprite sheet into the game's canvas.

20.4.1.2 Draw the Turret

Because the turret can rotate, drawing the turret is not as simple as merely copying a rectangular region from the game's sprite sheet; instead, the turret artist's draw() method, listed in Example 20.5, translates the coordinate system of the game's canvas to the center of rotation and subsequently rotates it through the game's turret rotation angle, depicted in Figure 20.9, before copying the rectangle from the sprite sheet. See Chapter 3 for more about translating and rotating the canvas context.

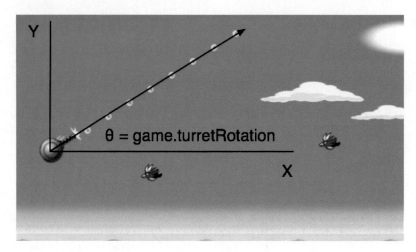

Figure 20.9 Tracking the turret's rotation

The turret rotation angle, stored in the game's turretRotation property, is set by the turret's behaviors, which we discuss in Section 20.5.1, "Turret Behaviors," on p. 564.

NOTE: Apparent horizontal motion vs. apparent rotation

Recall that Snail Bait's apparent horizontal motion is the result of translating the coordinate system of the game's canvas. In a similar fashion, Bodega's Revenge makes it appear as though the game's turret is rotating by translating and rotating the coordinate system of the game's canvas. The turret is the only thing that rotates because the Sprite.draw() method, which invokes the turret artist's draw() method, saves the canvas context before calling the artist's draw() method, and restores it afterward. See Chapter 3 for more about saving and restoring canvas contexts.

20.4.2 Bullets

Bodega's Revenge creates bullet sprites with its createBullets() method, listed in Example 20.6.

Example 20.6 Creating bullet sprites

```javascript
var BodegasRevenge = function () {
    ...

    this.NUM_BULLETS      = 20;

    this.BULLET_WIDTH     = 11;
    this.BULLET_HEIGHT    = 11;

    this.BULLET_CELL_LEFT = 18;
    this.BULLET_CELL_TOP  = 4;

    this.bulletCell = {
        left:   this.BULLET_CELL_LEFT,
        top:    this.BULLET_CELL_TOP,
        width:  this.BULLET_WIDTH,
        height: this.BULLET_HEIGHT
    };
    ...
};

BodegasRevenge.prototype = {
    ...

    createBullet: function (artist, moveBehavior) {
        bullet = new Sprite('bullet',
                            artist,
                            [ moveBehavior ]);

        bullet.width   = this.BULLET_WIDTH;
        bullet.height  = this.BULLET_HEIGHT;
        bullet.visible = false;

        return bullet;
    },

    createBullets: function () {
        var artist = this.createBulletArtist(this.bulletCell,
                                             this.BULLET_WIDTH,
                                             this.BULLET_HEIGHT),

            moveBehavior = this.createBulletMoveBehavior(),
            bullet,
            i;

        this.bullets = [];
```

(Continues)

Example 20.6 *(Continued)*

```
        for (i=0; i < this.NUM_BULLETS; ++i) {
            this.bullets[i] = this.createBullet(artist, moveBehavior);
        }

        this.lostBulletIndex = this.bullets.length;
    },
    ...
};
```

The preceding `createBullets()` method creates the game's bullets, all of which are drawn by a single bullet artist. Bullets have a single behavior—also shared by all bullets—that moves them along their initial trajectory when they left the turret.

Bodega's Revenge uses the `lostBulletIndex` property to track which bullets have been lost as a result of birds flying behind the turret and off the left edge of the canvas. We discuss the `lostBulletIndex` property in Section 20.5.3.1, "The Bird Move Behavior," on p. 575.

The bullet artist is created by the `createBulletArtist()` method, listed in Example 20.7.

Example 20.7 Creating the bullet artist

```
BodegasRevenge.prototype = {
    ...

    createBulletArtist: function (bulletCell) {
        return {
            draw: function (sprite, context) {
                context.translate(game.turret.left + game.TURRET_CENTER_X,
                                  game.turret.top  + game.TURRET_CENTER_Y);

                context.rotate(sprite.trajectory);

                context.drawImage(game.spritesheet,
                    bulletCell.left, bulletCell.top,        // sourcex, sourcey
                    sprite.width, sprite.height,            // sourcew, sourceh
                    sprite.distanceAlongTrajectory, 0,      // destx, desty
                    sprite.width, sprite.height);           // destw, desth
            }
        };
    },
    ...
};
```

Bullets maintain two interesting properties that their artist uses to draw them: trajectory and distanceAlongTrajectory, as illustrated in Figure 20.10.

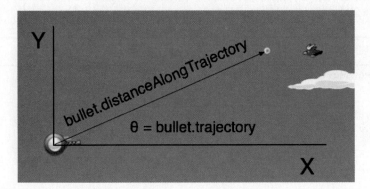

Figure 20.10 A bullet's trajectory and distance

The bullet's trajectory property represents the game's turret rotation at the time the turret fired the bullet. The distanceAlongTrajectory property represents how far the bullet has moved along the trajectory.

To draw a bullet, the bullet artist translates the coordinate system of the game's canvas to the center of the circular part of the turret and rotates the coordinate system through the bullet's trajectory. That translation and subsequent rotation let the bullet artist use the bullet's distanceAlongTrajectory property as the X coordinate in the call to the canvas context's drawImage() method.

NOTE: Flyweights

The bullet artist and its lone behavior are both flyweights, meaning one object that can be used by many other objects simultaneously. The use of flyweights reduces memory consumption, sometimes drastically. See Chapter 7 for more about flyweights and how to implement them.

NOTE: Temporary translations and rotations

The HTML5 canvas context's translate() and rotate() methods translate and rotate the canvas's coordinate system thus affecting graphics operations such as drawing images with drawImage(). The underlying sprite implementation saves the graphics context before drawing sprites and restores it afterwards, so calls such as translate() and rotate() are temporary instead of permanent. See Chapter 3 for more information about saving and restoring the graphics context.

20.4.3 Birds

The createBirds() method, which creates the game's birds, is listed in Example 20.8.

Example 20.8 Creating birds

```javascript
var BodegasRevenge = function () {
    ...

    this.BIRD_WIDTH  = 40;
    this.BIRD_HEIGHT = 40;

    this.BIRD_CYCLE_RATE_BASE = 500;
    this.BIRD_CYCLE_RATE_MAX_ADDITION = 500;

    this.EXPLOSION_CYCLE_DURATION = 50;

    this.birdCells = [
        {
            left:   9,
            top:    20,
            width:  this.BIRD_WIDTH,
            height: this.BIRD_HEIGHT
        },

        {
            left:   49,
            top:    30,
            width:  this.BIRD_WIDTH,
            height: this.BIRD_HEIGHT
        },

        {
            left:   89,
            top:    15,
            width:  this.BIRD_WIDTH,
            height: this.BIRD_HEIGHT
        }
    ];
    ...
};

BodegasRevenge.prototype = {
    ...
```

```
createBird: function () {
    var cycleRate = (game.BIRD_CYCLE_RATE_BASE +
                     game.BIRD_CYCLE_RATE_MAX_ADDITION *
                     Math.random()).toFixed(0),

        bird = new Sprite('bird',
                          new SpriteSheetArtist(game.spritesheet,
                                                game.birdCells),
                          [
                              this.createExplosionBehavior(),
                              this.createBirdMoveBehavior(),
                              this.createBirdCollideBehavior(),
                              new CycleBehavior(cycleRate)
                          ]);
    return bird;
},

createBirds: function () {
    var i;

    this.birds = [];

    for (i=0; i < this.NUM_BIRDS; ++i) {
        this.birds[i] = this.createBird();
        this.initializeBirdProperties(this.birds[i]);
    }
},
...
};
```

Birds fly, collide with bullets, and explode, so they have three behaviors that implement that functionality. Additionally, birds have a cycle behavior, discussed in Chapter 7, that continuously cycles birds through their animation cells to make it appear as though the birds are flapping their wings and bobbing up and down as they fly.

To make it appear as though the birds flap their wings at different rates of speed, Bodega's Revenge uses a technique, discussed in Section 9.7, "Randomize Behaviors," on p. 245, that adds a random amount to a fixed base to randomly vary the rate at which birds cycle through their animation cells and, as a result, flap their wings.

Bodega's Revenge uses the same technique to randomly vary each bird's position and velocity, as you can see in Example 20.9, which lists the game's initializeBirdProperties() method.

Example 20.9 Initializing bird properties

```
var BodegasRevenge = function () {
   ...

   this.BIRD_LEFT_BASE         = 800;
   this.BIRD_LEFT_MAX_ADDITION = 800;

   this.BIRD_TOP_BASE          = 35;
   this.BIRD_TOP_MAX_ADDITION = 330;

   this.BIRD_VELOCITY_BASE          = 50;
   this.BIRD_VELOCITY_MAX_ADDITION = 50;

   this.BIRD_VALUE = 50;
   ...
};

BodegasRevenge.prototype = {
   ...

   initializeBirdProperties: function (bird) {
      bird.width   = this.BIRD_WIDTH;
      bird.height  = this.BIRD_HEIGHT;
      bird.visible = true;

      bird.left = this.BIRD_LEFT_BASE +
                  this.BIRD_LEFT_MAX_ADDITION * Math.random();

      bird.top  = this.BIRD_TOP_BASE  +
                  this.BIRD_TOP_MAX_ADDITION  * Math.random();

      bird.velocity = this.BIRD_VELOCITY_BASE +
                      this.BIRD_VELOCITY_MAX_ADDITION * Math.random();

      bird.value = this.BIRD_VALUE;

      bird.flying = false;
      bird.exploding = false;
   },
   ...
};
```

Up to this point, you've seen how Bodega's Revenge creates and draws its sprites. Now lets see how the game implements sprite behaviors.

20.5 Implement Sprite Behaviors

Sprites have a sprite artist. The artist draws the sprite with a draw() method. Every animation frame, the game iterates over its sprites and, for every visible sprite, invokes the sprite artist's draw() method.

Sprites also have an array of behaviors. Behaviors manipulate the sprite with an execute() method. Every animation frame, the game invokes the execute() method of each behavior for every visible sprite.

Most sprite behaviors do nothing until they are tripped by a trigger. Triggers are conditions that cause behaviors to take action. They are typically Boolean variables attached to sprites; for example, the turret's shoot behavior shoots bullets only when the turret's shooting property is true. The game temporarily sets that property to true when the player presses the spacebar to shoot a bullet.

Because behavior-based games encapsulate actions associated with sprites, much of a game's gameplay is implemented in sprite behavior objects. See Chapter 7 for a more in-depth discussion of sprite behaviors.

Bodega's Revenge has a total of eight behaviors:

- Turret

  - Rotate
  - Barrel fire
  - Shoot
  - Cycle

- Bullets

  - Move

- Birds

  - Move
  - Collide
  - Explode

The rest of this chapter discusses the implementation of the preceding behaviors.

20.5.1 Turret Behaviors

Turret behaviors are summarized in Table 20.1.

Table 20.1 Turret behaviors

Behavior	Description	Trigger
Rotate	Rotates the turret clockwise or counterclockwise.	The `rotating` property of the turret sprite, which the game sets to `true` when the player presses the left or right arrow keys (or alternatively, d or k). The game resets the turret's `rotating` property to `false` when the player releases the key.
Barrel fire	Animates through a sequence of animation cells to make it look as though fire shoots out of the barrel when the turret shoots bullets.	The `shooting` property of the turret sprite, which the game sets to `true` when the player presses the spacebar (or is holding it down). The barrel fire behavior sets the turret's `shooting` property to `false` when its animation is finished.
Shoot	Makes the first available bullet visible, plays the turret firing sound, and records the current time as the last time the turret fired a shot.	The turret's `shooting` property must be `true` and enough time must have passed since the last time the turret fired a shot.
Cycle	Cycles through the turret's animation cells. This is a general behavior, as discussed in Chapter 7. It is not turret specific.	No trigger: this behavior is always executing.

Let's look at the implementation of each behavior.

20.5.1.1 The Turret's Rotate Behavior

The game attaches a `keydown` event handler to the `window` object. That event handler sets the turret's `rotating` and `direction` properties, as shown in Example 20.10. A corresponding `keyup` event handler sets the `rotating` property back to `false`.

Example 20.10 Tripping the rotate behavior

```
window.addEventListener(
    'keydown',

    function (e) {
        ...

        if (key === 68 || key === 37) { // 'd' or left arrow
            game.turret.rotating  = true;
            game.turret.direction = game.CLOCKWISE;
        }
        else if (key === 75 || key === 39) { // 'k' or right arrow
            game.turret.rotating  = true;
            game.turret.direction = game.COUNTER_CLOCKWISE;
        }
        ...
    }
);

window.addEventListener(
    'keyup',

    function (e) {
        game.turret.rotating = false;
    }
);
```

The turret's rotate behavior takes action depending on the values of the turret's rotating and direction properties, as shown in Example 20.11.

Example 20.11 Creating the turret rotate behavior

```
BodegasRevenge.prototype = {
    ...

    createTurretRotateBehavior: function () {
        return {
            execute: function (sprite, now, fps, context,
                               lastAnimationFrameTime) {
                var ROTATE_INCREMENT = Math.PI/100;

                if (sprite.rotating) {
                    if (sprite.direction === game.CLOCKWISE) {
                        game.turretRotation -= ROTATE_INCREMENT;
                    }
```

(Continues)

Example 20.11 *(Continued)*

```
            else if (sprite.direction === game.COUNTER_CLOCKWISE) {
                game.turretRotation += ROTATE_INCREMENT;
            }
        }
    };
},
...
};
```

Recall from Section 20.4.1.1, "Create the Turret Sprite's Artist," on p. 554 that the turret's artist rotates the coordinate system for the game's canvas through the game.turretRotation angle. When the turret's rotating property is true, the rotate behavior increments or decrements that angle depending on the value of the turret's direction property.

20.5.1.2 The Turret's Barrel Fire Behavior

When the turret shoots bullets, its barrel fire behavior darkens the center of the turret and shoots fire from the tip of the turret's barrel, as shown in Figure 20.11.

Figure 20.11 The turret's barrel fire

The game's sprite sheet contains the five images of the turret shown in Figure 20.12. When the turret is not firing bullets, the game displays the image on the far left in Figure 20.12. When it fires a bullet, the turret's barrel fire behavior displays the remaining four images in succession from left to right.

Figure 20.12 Turret cells

Both the barrel fire behavior and the turret's shoot behavior, which we discuss in the next section, are triggered by the game's shooting property. When the player presses the spacebar, the window object's keydown event handler sets the property's value to true, as you can see in Example 20.12.

Example 20.12 Tripping the shoot and barrel fire behaviors

```
window.addEventListener(
    'keydown',

    function (e) {
        var key = e.keyCode;
        ...

        else if (key === 32) {  // spacebar
            game.turret.shooting = true;
        }
        ...

    }
);
```

The barrel fire behavior is created by the game's createTurretBarrelFire-Behavior() method, listed in Example 20.13.

Example 20.13 Creating the turret barrel fire behavior

```
var BodegasRevenge = function () {
    ...

    this.turretFiringCells = [
        {left: 91,  top: 120, width: 68, height: 40},
        {left: 170, top: 121, width: 68, height: 40},
        {left: 250, top: 122, width: 68, height: 40},
        {left: 329, top: 123, width: 68, height: 40}
    ];

    this.TURRET_CYCLE_DURATION  = 10; // Cycle every 10 ms
```

(Continues)

Example 20.13 *(Continued)*

```
    this.TURRET_FIRING_DURATION = this.TURRET_CYCLE_DURATION *
                                  this.turretFiringCells.length;
    ...
};

BodegasRevenge.prototype = {
    ...

    createTurretBarrelFireBehavior: function () {
        return new CellSwitchBehavior(
            game.turretFiringCells,         // Temporary animation cells
            game.TURRET_FIRING_DURATION,  // Duration in ms

            function (sprite, now, fps, lastAnimationFrameTime) { // Trigger
                return sprite.shooting;
            },

            function (sprite) { // Callback
                sprite.shooting = false;
            }
        );
    },
    ...
};
```

The barrel fire behavior is an instance of CellSwitchBehavior, which temporarily switches the cells that a sprite's artist uses to draw the sprite. Cell switch behaviors have a trigger function. If that function returns true, the cell switch behavior takes action, either setting the animation cells for the associated sprite's artist or cycling through those cells. When a cell switch behavior is done cycling through the temporary animation cells, it restores the original cells and invokes its callback function. Cell switch behaviors are discussed in more detail in Chapter 13.

NOTE: The turret's cycle behavior

The turret has a cycle behavior that continuously cycles through the turret's animation cells. Initially, however, as you can see from Example 20.5 on p. 554, the turret has only one animation cell, so the cycle behavior has no noticeable effect. The cycle behavior does have an effect, however, when the turret's barrel fire behavior switches the turret's animation cells to the four cells shown on the right in Figure 20.12. Without the cycle behavior, the barrel fire behavior would still switch the turret's animation cells, but it would not cycle through those cells and therefore would show only the second cell from the left in Figure 20.12.

20.5.1.3 The Turret's Shoot Behavior

The turret's shoot behavior, listed in Example 20.14, shoots bullets by obtaining a reference to the first available bullet, making it visible, and placing it at the tip of the turret's barrel.

As long as the turret's shooting property is true, the shoot behavior, which the game invokes every animation frame, shoots bullets, provided that enough time has elapsed since the behavior fired the last bullet. That pause between shots, which is 1.5 times longer than it takes for the turret to fire, puts a space between bullets when the player holds down the spacebar and shoots bullets in rapid succession.

Example 20.14 Creating the turret shoot behavior

```
var BodegasRevenge = function () {
   ...

   this.TURRET_SHOT_INTERVAL = this.TURRET_FIRING_DURATION * 1.5;
   ...
};

BodegasRevenge.prototype = {
   ...

   createTurretShootBehavior: function () {
      return {
         lastTimeShotFired: 0,
         ...

         execute: function (sprite, now, fps, context,
                            lastAnimationFrameTime) {
            var elapsed = now - this.lastTimeShotFired;

            if(sprite.shooting && elapsed > game.TURRET_SHOT_INTERVAL) {
               bullet = this.getBullet();

               if (bullet) {
                  bullet.visible = true;
                  bullet.trajectory = game.turretRotation;
                  bullet.distanceAlongTrajectory = game.turret.radius;

                  this.lastTimeShotFired = now;
```

(Continues)

Example 20.14 *(Continued)*

```
                    game.playSound(game.turretFiringSound);
                }
            }
        }
    };
  },
  ...
};
```

The turret's shoot behavior obtains a reference to the first available bullet with the getBullet() method, listed in Example 20.15.

Example 20.15 Getting the first available bullet

```
BodegasRevenge.prototype = {
    ...

    createTurretShootBehavior: function () {
        return {
            ...

            getBullet: function () {
                var bullet,
                    i;

                for (i=0; i < game.lostBulletIndex; ++i) {
                    bullet = game.bullets[i];

                    if (!bullet.visible) {
                        return bullet;
                    }
                }
                return null;
            }
        };
    },
    ...
};
```

The getBullet() method iterates over the game's bullets array up to the lostBulletIndex and returns the first invisible bullet. If the lostBulletIndex is zero or all available bullets are visible, the getBullet() method returns null and the turret fires a blank. We discuss the lostBulletIndex property in Section 20.5.3.1, "The Bird Move Behavior," on p. 575.

NOTE: Incorporate sounds into the game

Bodega's Revenge plays a sound when the turret fires a bullet and another sound when a bird explodes. Like the game's graphics, those sounds come from Replica Island.

20.5.2 Bullet Behaviors

Bullets have only one behavior. That behavior, which moves bullets along their trajectory, is created by the createBulletMoveBehavior() method, listed in Example 20.16.

Example 20.16 Creating the bullet move behavior

```
BodegasRevenge.prototype = {
    ...

    createBulletMoveBehavior: function () {
        return {
            ...

            execute: function (sprite, now, fps, context,
                               lastAnimationFrameTime) {
                var BULLET_VELOCITY = 450, // pixels/second
                    location;

                sprite.distanceAlongTrajectory +=
                    BULLET_VELOCITY * (now - lastAnimationFrameTime) / 1000;

                location = this.getBulletLocation(sprite);

                if (this.isBulletOutOfPlay(location)) {
                    sprite.visible = false;
                }
                else {
                    sprite.left = location.left;
                    sprite.top  = location.top;
                }
            }
        };
    },
    ...
};
```

When bullets are visible, the bullet's move behavior moves them along their trajectory at a constant rate of 450 pixels/second regardless of the frame rate of the game's underlying animation. The behavior decouples the bullet's speed from the animation's frame rate with time-based motion—discussed in Chapter 3—to calculate how far to move the bullet along its trajectory. The behavior moves the bullet to that location when the bullet is in play or makes it invisible when it goes out of play. Making the bullet invisible makes it immediately available for firing.

The bullet's move behavior invokes two helper methods—getBulletLocation() and isBulletOutOfPlay(); the former is listed in Example 20.17.

Example 20.17 Getting a bullet's location

```
BodegasRevenge.prototype = {
    ...

    createBulletMoveBehavior: function () {
        return {
            ...

            getBulletLocation: function (bullet) {
                return game.polarToCartesian(
                    game.turret.left + game.TURRET_CENTER_X,  // x
                    game.turret.top  + game.TURRET_CENTER_Y,  // y
                    bullet.distanceAlongTrajectory,           // radius
                    bullet.trajectory);                       // angle
            },
            ...
        };
    },
    ...
};
```

Recall from Figure 20.10 on p. 559 that bullets store their position as the angle of their trajectory and the distance along that trajectory from the center of the turret. Mathematically speaking, that angle and trajectory, which are depicted in Figure 20.13 as θ and r, respectively, are known as polar coordinates.

Because the rest of the game, along with the HTML5 canvas context, deals strictly in Cartesian coordinates, we convert the polar coordinates stored in each bullet to Cartesian coordinates with the more general polarToCartesian() method, listed in Example 20.18.

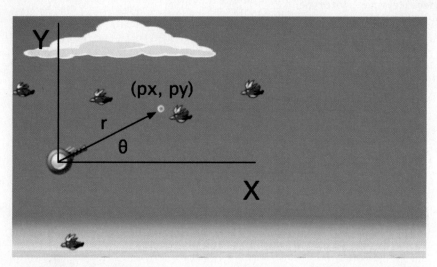

Figure 20.13 Polar coordinates

Example 20.18 Converting polar coordinates

```
BodegasRevenge.prototype = {
    ...

    polarToCartesian: function (px, py, r, angle) {
        var x = px + r * Math.cos(angle),
            y = py + r * Math.sin(angle);

        return { left: x, top: y };
    },
    ...
};
```

The polarToCartesian() method implements the math for converting polar coordinates to Cartesian coordinates. Given the location of a bullet in Cartesian coordinates, it's a simple matter to determine if a bullet is out of play, as shown in Example 20.19.

Example 20.19 Determining if a bullet is out of play

```
BodegasRevenge.prototype = {
    ...

    createBirdMoveBehavior: function () {
        return {
            execute: function (sprite, now, fps, context,
                                 lastAnimationFrameTime) {
                if (!sprite.exploding) {
                    sprite.left -= sprite.velocity *
                                 (now - lastAnimationFrameTime) / 1000;

                    if (sprite.left + sprite.width < 0) {
                        sprite.left = game.canvas.width - sprite.width;
                        game.loseOneBullet();
                    }
                }
            }
        }
    },
    ...
};
```

Now that you've seen how bullets behave, let's turn our attention to the birds of Bodega's Revenge.

20.5.3 Bird Behaviors

Birds have four behaviors, listed in Table 20.2.

Table 20.2 Bird behaviors

Behavior	Description
Move	Moves birds horizontally from right to left. When a bird goes off the left edge of the canvas, the behavior invokes the game's loseOneBullet() method.
Collide	When a bullet collides with a bird, explodes the bird, makes the bullet invisible, and increments the game's score.
Explode	Changes the bird's animation cells to a series of cells that look like an explosion.
Cycle	Cycles through the bird's animation cells to make it appear as though the bird is flapping its wings or exploding.

With the exception of the cycle behavior, whose implementation is discussed in Section 7.5.1, "The Cycle Behavior," on p. 193, let's look at the implementations of each of the preceding behaviors.

20.5.3.1 The Bird Move Behavior

Like bullets, birds have a move behavior. That behavior, which moves birds from right to left horizontally, is listed in **Example 20.20.**

Example 20.20 Creating the bird move behavior

```javascript
BodegasRevenge.prototype = {
   ...

   createBirdMoveBehavior: function () {
      return {
         execute: function (sprite, now, fps, context,
                            lastAnimationFrameTime) {
            if (!sprite.exploding) {
               sprite.left -= sprite.velocity / fps;

               if (sprite.left + sprite.width < 0) {
                  sprite.left = game.canvas.width - sprite.width;
                  game.loseOneBullet();
               }
            }
         }
      }
   },
   ...
};
```

The bird move behavior, like the bullet move behavior, moves birds by using time-based motion to ensure that birds move at a constant rate of speed regardless of the frame rate of the game's underlying animation.

The `loseOneBullet()` method, which the move behavior calls when the bird moves off the left edge of the canvas, is listed in **Example 20.21.**

Example 20.21 Losing a bullet

```javascript
BodegasRevenge.prototype = {
   ...

   loseOneBullet: function () {
```

(Continues)

Example 20.21 *(Continued)*

```
      if (this.lostBulletIndex === 0) {
         this.gameOver();
      }
      else {
         this.lostBulletIndex--;
      }
      ...
   },
   ...
};
```

Players lose a bullet—meaning the bullet is no longer in play—when a bird flies behind the turret and off the left edge of the canvas. The game keeps track of lost bullets with the lostBulletIndex property, as depicted in Figure 20.14.

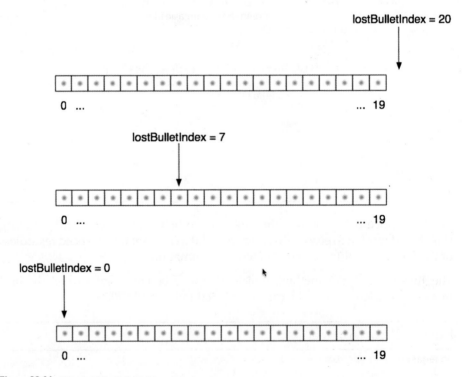

Figure 20.14 The lost bullet index

The `lostBulletIndex` is originally 20, which places it beyond the end of the bullets array, as shown in the top picture in Figure 20.14. That value for `lostBulletIndex` means all bullets are initially in play.

Every time a bird flies behind the turret and off the left edge of the game's canvas, the `loseOneBullet()` method decrements the `lostBulletIndex` property. The middle illustration in Figure 20.14 shows the `lostBulletIndex` after the player has lost 12 bullets. The game ends when, as shown in the bottom illustration in Figure 20.14, the `lostBulletIndex` is zero.

The value of the `lostBulletIndex` influences the game because methods such as `getBullet()`, listed in Example 20.15 on p. 570, and the bird's collide behavior, discussed in the next section, iterate over the game's `bullets` array like this: `for (i=0; i < game.lostBulletIndex; ++i) { ... }`; instead of iterating over the entire `bullets` array.

20.5.3.2 The Bird Collide Behavior

The bird collide behavior, listed in Example 20.22, iterates over the game's bullets (up to the `lostBulletIndex` as discussed in the previous section), checking for collisions between the bullets and the bird under consideration.

Example 20.22 Creating the bird collide behavior

```
var BodegasRevenge = function () {
   ...

   this.BIRD_EXPLOSION_TOP_DELTA  = 20;
   this.BIRD_EXPLOSION_LEFT_DELTA = 20;
   ...
};

BodegasRevenge.prototype = {
   ...

   createBirdCollideBehavior: function () {
      return {
         ...

         execute: function (sprite, now, fps, context,
                            lastAnimationFrameTime) {
            var bullet,
                i;

            for (i=0; i < game.lostBulletIndex; ++i) {
               bullet = game.bullets[i];
```

(Continues)

Example 20.22 *(Continued)*

```
                    if (bullet.visible && !sprite.exploding) {
                        if (this.isBulletInsideBird(context,
                                                    bullet,
                                                    sprite)) {
                            sprite.left -= game.BIRD_EXPLOSION_LEFT_DELTA;
                            sprite.top  -= game.BIRD_EXPLOSION_TOP_DELTA;

                            game.explode(sprite);

                            bullet.visible = false;

                            game.score += sprite.value;
                            game.updateScoreElement();

                            break;
                        }
                    }
                }
            }
        };
    },
    ...
};
```

A collision between bullet and bird takes place when the bullet is visible, the bird is not exploding, and the bullet is inside the bird. In that case, the bird collide behavior adjusts the bird's position to account for the size difference between bird animation cells and explosion animation cells (without adjusting the bird's positions, explosions appear below and to the right of the bird that's exploding).

After adjusting the bird's position, the bird collide behavior explodes the bird, makes the bullet invisible, and updates the game's score.

The isBulletInsideBird() method, listed in **Example 20.23**, determines whether a bullet lies within a bird by using the HTML5 canvas context's isPointInPath() method, which we discussed in Chapter 11.

Example 20.23 Hit detection with the HTML5 canvas context

```
BodegasRevenge.prototype = {
    ...

    createBirdCollideBehavior: function () {
        return {
            ...
```

```
    isBulletInsideBird: function (context, bullet, bird) {
        context.beginPath();

        context.rect(bird.left,  bird.top,
                    bird.width, bird.height);

        return context.isPointInPath(bullet.left + bullet.width/2,
                                    bullet.top + bullet.height/2);
    },
    ...
  };
 },
 ...
};
```

20.5.3.3 The Bird Explosion Behavior

Birds explode with an explosion behavior, listed in **Example 20.24**. That behavior is an instance of `CellSwitchBehavior`, which temporarily changes the bird's animation cells to the game's explosion cells for the specified duration. The behavior takes action when the bird's `exploding` property is `true`; when the bird is finished exploding, the behavior invokes its callback, which initializes the bird's properties to their initial state.

Example 20.24 Creating the explosion behavior

```
BodegasRevenge.prototype = {
  ...

  createExplosionBehavior: function () {
    return new CellSwitchBehavior(
        game.explosionCells,
        game.EXPLOSION_DURATION,

        function (sprite, now, fps,
                  lastAnimationFrameTime) { // trigger
          return sprite.exploding;
        },

        function (sprite) { // callback
          game.initializeBirdProperties(sprite);
        }
    );
  },
  ...
};
```

20.6 Draw the Bullet Canvas

Bodega's Revenge displays the number of remaining bullets above the game's canvas, as shown in Figure 20.15, by drawing bullets. In this section we take a look at the implementation of that bullet canvas.

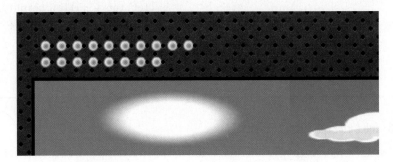

Figure 20.15 The bullet canvas

The bullet canvas is an HTML5 canvas element, declared in the game's HTML file, as shown in Example 20.25.

Example 20.25 The bullet canvas element

```
<canvas id='bullet-canvas' width='450' height='30'>
   Your browser does not support HTML5 Canvas.
</canvas>
```

Bodega's Revenge redraws the bullet canvas every time the player loses a bullet, as you can see in Example 20.26, which shows the final listing of the game's loseOneBullet() method.

Example 20.26 Losing a bullet, revised

```
BodegasRevenge.prototype = {
   ...

   loseOneBullet: function () {
      if (this.lostBulletIndex === 0) {
         this.gameOver();
      }
      else {
         this.lostBulletIndex--;
      }
```

```
        this.eraseBulletCanvas();
        this.drawBulletCanvas();
    },
    ...
};
```

The eraseBulletCanvas() method is listed in Example 20.27.

Example 20.27 Erasing the bullet canvas

```
BodegasRevenge.prototype = {
    ...

    eraseBulletCanvas: function () {
        this.bulletContext.clearRect(
            0,0,
            this.bulletCanvas.width,
            this.bulletCanvas.height);
    },
    ...
};
```

The eraseBulletCanvas() method erases the canvas by invoking the canvas context's clearRect() method to clear the entire canvas.

The drawBulletCanvas() method is listed in Example 20.28.

Example 20.28 Drawing the bullet canvas

```
BodegasRevenge.prototype = {
    ...

    drawBulletCanvas: function () {
        var context = this.bulletContext,
            firstBullet = game.bullets[0],
            TOP_EDGE = 0,
            LEFT_EDGE = 6,
            HORIZONTAL_SPACING = 16,
            VERTICAL_SPACING = 16,
            row = 0,
            col = 0,
            i;

        for (i=0; i < game.lostBulletIndex; ++i) {
            context.drawImage(game.spritesheet,
                game.bulletCell.left,           // sourcex
                game.bulletCell.top,            // sourcey
```

(Continues)

Example 20.28   *(Continued)*

```
                  firstBullet.width, firstBullet.height, // sourcew, sourceh
                  LEFT_EDGE + HORIZONTAL_SPACING*col,    // destx
                  TOP_EDGE  + VERTICAL_SPACING*row,      // desty
                  firstBullet.width, firstBullet.height);// destw, desth

        if (i === game.bullets.length / 2 - 1) { // middle
            col = 0;
            row++;
        }
        else {
            col++;
        }
    }
  },
  ...
};
```

The `drawBulletCanvas()` method iterates over the game's bullets up to the
`lostBulletIndex`, and draws each bullet in the canvas.

20.7 Implement Touch-Based Controls for Mobile Devices

Bodega's Revenge runs on mobile devices, as you can see in Figure 20.16.

Figure 20.16 Bodega's Revenge on mobile devices

Bodega's Revenge uses the techniques discussed in Chapter 15 to run on mobile devices. The implementation details are nearly identical to Snail Bait's support for mobile devices, so those discussions are not repeated in this chapter.

The biggest difference between Bodega's Revenge and Snail Bait on mobile devices is the manner in which players control the game. In Bodega's Revenge, players rotate the turret by sliding a finger or thumb up or down to rotate the turret counterclockwise or clockwise, respectively. To shoot bullets from the turret, players tap the screen. In this section, we discuss the implementation of those controls.

The game's touch start event handler is listed in Example 20.29.

Example 20.29 The touch start event handler

```
game.canvas.addEventListener(
   'touchstart',

   function (e) {
      game.turret.touchStartTime = game.timeSystem.calculateGameTime();

      game.turret.lastFingerLocation = {
         x: e.changedTouches[0].pageX,
         y: e.changedTouches[0].pageY
      };

      game.turret.armed = true;

      e.preventDefault();
   }
);
```

When the player touches the game's canvas, the preceding event handler records the time of the touch and the touch's location. Additionally, the event handler arms the turret and prevents the browser from reacting to the touch event in its default manner.

When the player subsequently moves a finger or thumb, the browser invokes the event handler listed in Example 20.30.

Example 20.30 The touch move event handler

```
game.canvas.addEventListener(
    'touchmove',

    function (e) {
        var MOVEMENT_THRESHOLD = 3;

        if (game.turret.armed && !game.turret.rotating) {
            game.turret.armed = false;
            game.turret.rotating = true;
        }

        if (game.turret.lastFingerLocation.y >
            e.changedTouches[0].pageY) {

            if (game.turret.lastFingerLocation.y -
                e.changedTouches[0].pageY > MOVEMENT_THRESHOLD) {
                game.turret.direction = game.CLOCKWISE;
            }
        }
        else if (e.changedTouches[0].pageY -
                game.turret.lastFingerLocation.y > MOVEMENT_THRESHOLD) {
            game.turret.direction = game.COUNTER_CLOCKWISE;
        }

        game.turret.lastFingerLocation = {
            x: e.changedTouches[0].pageX,
            y: e.changedTouches[0].pageY
        };
    }
);
```

When a touch move event occurs, the turret starts rotating if it was armed. The direction the turret rotates depends on the finger's movement. If the finger is moving down and it has moved more than three pixels since the last touch move event, the preceding event handler sets the turret's rotation to clockwise. Conversely, if the finger is moving up and it has moved more than three pixels since the last touch move event, the preceding event handler sets the turret's rotation to counterclockwise.

Finally, when the touch ends, the browser invokes the event handler listed in Example 20.31.

Example 20.31 The touch end event handler

```
game.canvas.addEventListener(
    'touchend',

    function (e) {
        var TAP_THRESHOLD = 200, // milliseconds
            now = game.timeSystem.calculateGameTime();

        game.turret.rotating = false;

        if (now - game.turret.touchStartTime < TAP_THRESHOLD) {
            game.turret.shooting = true;
        }

        e.preventDefault();
    }
);
```

The preceding event handler stops the turret's rotation. It also checks to see if less than 200 ms has elapsed since the time of the touch start event. If it has, the event handler sets the turret's `shooting` property to `true`, which triggers its shooting event.

20.8 Conclusion

Most of this book is concerned with the implementation of Snail Bait, which is a platform video game of moderate complexity. Throughout this book we've examined various aspects of that game from its graphics and animation to its developer backdoor.

This chapter illustrated how to use what you've learned in the rest of the book to implement the simpler, but still nontrivial Bodega's Revenge. At this point, you understand the fine details of implementing 2D video games in addition to the bigger picture of putting those details together to implement your own game. Good luck!

20.9 Exercises

1. Play Bodega's Revenge on the desktop and hold down either the d or k keys to rotate the turret. While holding the key down, press and hold the spacebar.

As you hold both keys down, the turret will spin and fire bullets continuously, which makes it much easier to mow down birds. Look closely at the game's code and make sure you understand exactly what's happening when the turret is continuously spinning and firing bullets.

2. In `createTurret()`, remove the cycle behavior from the turret and play the game. What's the result?

3. In the turret artist's `draw()` method, comment out the call to `context.translate()` and play the game. Explain the result.

4. Use the code for the frame rate (fps) indicator in the early versions of Snail Bait to add a frame rate indicator to Bodega's Revenge. Put the fps indicator above the canvas on the right side of the game. How well does the game perform?

5. In `createBirdCollideBehavior()`, comment out the lines that adjust the sprite's left and top properties and replay the game. Explosions should occur underneath and to the right of the sprite that's exploding.

Glossary

animation frame   A snapshot of what the game looks like at a particular point in time. Games rapidly display animation frames. Each frame differs slightly from the preceding frame to simulate motion. An animation frame is much like a page in a flip book.

animation timer   A stopwatch with two added features: It can run for a specified duration; an easing function can be added to it. Timers encapsulate the ability to modify the flow of time for a given activity.

API   Application Programming Interface.

arena   An HTML DIV element, specific to Snail Bait, that contains all of the game's elements, and hence the game's action takes place here.

aspect ratio   The width of a device's screen divided by its height.

asset   In Snail Bait, a coin, ruby, or sapphire. When the runner collides with an asset, the game increases the player's score.

Audacity   A freely available, open source sound editing application that runs on several operating systems including Windows and Mac OS X.

audio channel   A JavaScript object that keeps track of an audio element and its status: currently playing or not.

audio sprite sheet   A single file that contains all the sound effects for a game. Audio sprite sheets may or may not contain the game's soundtrack.

backdoor   A feature that gives developers access to special powers unavailable to players, such as slowing time or making collision rectangles visible. A backdoor makes it easier for developers to playtest and debug the game.

behavior   A JavaScript object that makes a sprite do something, such as jump, fall, run, and so on. Every animation frame, the game invokes the execute() method for every behavior associated with each of the game's visible sprites. That execute() method manipulates the sprite in some fashion to give the sprite a behavior.

behavior-based game   A game that implements sprite behaviors with behavior objects. Once the underlying infrastructure is in place, nearly all of a game's development involves implementing new behaviors and attaching them to sprites.

bounce behavior   A game-independent, stateful behavior that causes a sprite to bounce up and down.

bounding area   A collision detection technique for detecting intersections between circles or polygons.

bounding box   A rectangle enclosing an object. Sprites have a bounding box that games use for collision detection.

callback function   A function that you register with some software. That software invokes your function at a particular point in time; for example, you can register a callback function that the browser invokes when an image is fully loaded.

canvas element   An HTML element in which developers can create sophisticated graphics. Each canvas element has an associated graphics context that affords a powerful API for drawing and manipulating graphics.

Cartesian coordinate   An (x, y) location in a two-dimensional plane.

cell   A rectangle in a sprite sheet that exactly encloses a pose for a particular sprite.

cell switch behavior   A sprite behavior that changes the images drawn by a sprite's artist. Useful for temporarily animating a sprite through a sequence of images, such as an explosion.

chrome   A game's HTML elements that let players manipulate game settings such as sound and music.

collision margin   A margin on the inside of a sprite's bounding box. The margin is used to shrink the sprite's collision rectangle to increase collision detection accuracy.

constructor function   A function that creates a JavaScript object.

cross-site scripting   See **XSS**.

CSS   Cascading Style Sheets. Markup that determines the look of HTML elements.

CSS pixels   The number of pixels a developer specifies in CSS for the sizes of HTML elements.

CSV   Comma-separated value.

current game time   The elapsed time since a game started.

cycle behavior   A game-independent, stateful behavior that cycles through a sprite's images in a sprite sheet.

data driven   Creating sprites from objects that define their data.

device pixels   The actual pixels on a physical display. Device pixels are fixed for a given device.

DIV   An HTML element that defines a logical division or section within a document.

double buffering   A technique by which the image a developer draws is first drawn to an off-screen canvas, then copied to the on-screen canvas. That technique can smooth jittery animations, but developers need not implement it, however, because all HTML5 canvas elements perform double buffering by default.

duck typing   A technique by which an object is not forced to conform to an interface but can just act as if it does conform.

ease-in function   A function that modifies the flow of time for a specific duration of time, so that time initially flows slowly and speeds up (or eases in) through the specified duration. At the end of the specified duration, time returns to normal.

easing functions   Functions that modify the completion percentage of a finite behavior. Compare with **transducer functions**.

ease-out function   A function that modifies the flow of time for a specific duration of time, so that time initially flows quickly and slows down (or eases out) through the specified duration. At the end of the specified duration, time returns to normal.

emitter   An object in a particle system that emits particles.

event handler   A function that the browser invokes at a particular point in time; for example, when the user clicks the mouse.

favicon   Favorite icons. A small icon that browsers display either in the address bar or in a tab.

flip book   A book whose individual pages represent a snapshot in time of an animation, where each snapshot differs slightly from the last. You create an animation by flipping the pages rapidly.

flyweight   A JavaScript object that can be used by many other objects simultaneously. Flyweights can drastically reduce memory consumption in games.

fps   Frames per second.

frame rate   The speed at which a series of animation frames games display, typically 30 to 60 times a second, to create the illusion of movement.

fuzzy object   A representation of a natural phenomenon that lacks well-defined edges and does not conform to man-made geometric shapes. Examples are smoke, fire, and water.

game-independent behavior   A behavior that works with any sprite.

gray scale   A scale of achromatic colors, usually ten, ranging in equal gradations from white to black.

Gzip   A data compression program.

HUD   Heads-up display.

image artist   A sprite artist that draws an individual image. Not used by Snail Bait.

immediate-mode graphics   A graphics system that does not retain a list of the objects it draws. An object, once drawn by the system, cannot be manipulated. Canvas is an immediate-mode graphics system. Compare with **retained-mode graphics**.

JSON   JavaScript Object Notation.

layout viewport   An off-screen viewport where a browser lays out a webpage for viewing on a mobile device. See **visible viewport**.

live-edit   The ability to change code directly in the browser's developer tools without having to change that code in a text editor. When this book went to press, only Chrome supported live-editing of JavaScript code. The functionality is available in other browsers as add-ons.

Node.js   A JavaScript framework built on Chrome's JavaScript runtime that runs JavaScript outside of the browser. Has a system of pluggable pieces (modules). Snail Bait uses http, socket.io, fs (file system), and validator Node.js modules.

nonlinear motion   Movement that is affected by a natural force such as gravity (acceleration, deceleration).

npm   Package manager of Node.js.

Ogg   A free, open container format, maintained by the Xiph.Org Foundation, that provides for efficient streaming and manipulation of high-quality digital multimedia. The Ogg container format can multiplex a number of independent streams for audio, video, text (such as subtitles), and metadata (*Wikipedia*).

opacity   A sprite property (opacity) that determines whether a sprite is opaque, transparent, or in between.

parallax effect   An effect that adds depth to 2D games by moving objects close to the player faster than objects that are further away.

particle system   A combination of small particles (sprites or other graphic objects) that simulate natural phenomena that do not have well-defined boundaries and edges.

path-based graphics   A graphics system whose graphics primitives are drawn in a canvas by creation of a path that is then stroked or filled.

platformer   A game where players navigate platforms.

PNG   Portable Network Graphics, a.k.a. PNG's Not GIF. A raster graphics file format that supports lossless data compression (*Wikipedia*).

polar coordinate   A member of a two-dimensional coordinate system in which each point on a plane is determined by a distance from a fixed point and an angle from a fixed direction (*Wikipedia*).

polyfill   A technique that determines a browser's level of support for a particular feature. If the browser supports the feature, the developer is given direct access; if the feature is not supported, the polyfill gives the developer access to a workaround that attempts to mimic the standard functionality.

profiler   A development tool that measures exactly where a game spends its time. Used to locate performance bottlenecks.

prototype object   An object that contains another JavaScript object's methods.

pulse   A flash of color that subsequently fades away.

pulse behavior   A game-independent, stateful behavior that manipulates a sprite's opacity to make the sprite appear to pulsate.

ray casting   A collision detection technique that detects collisions by monitoring the intersection of two sprites' velocity vectors. Not used in Snail Bait.

Replica Island   An open source Android game. The game's graphics, sound, and music are all covered by the Apache 2 license, which permits developers to use them in their games. Nearly all the graphics, sound, and music in Snail Bait come from Replica Island.

retained-mode graphics   A graphics system that retains a list of graphical objects; more suited to drawing programs than is immediate-mode. See **SVG**.

seek   To move to a particular position in a sound file.

Separating Axis Theorem   A mathematically intense collision detection algorithm that detects collisions between arbitrarily shaped polygons. Not used in Snail Bait. Covered in *Core HTML5 Canvas*.

shim or shive   See **polyfill**.

side-scroller   Descriptive of a game that can be scrolled horizontally.

smoking hole   A particle system that contains fire particles and that emits smoke bubbles. Over time, fire particles flicker and smoke bubles dissipate.

SnailBait object   A JavaScript object that encapsulates in a single object all Snail Bait functions and variables, to obviate the possibility of their being inadvertently overwritten. Consists of two parts: **constructor function** and **prototype object**.

socket.io   A Node.js module that furthers communication between clients, for example, between a player's computer and a game's server.

spatial partitioning   Dividing a game's space into cells, so that only sprites in the same cell can collide. Usually results in increased performance.

sprite   A graphical representation of an object, endowed with behaviors, that a game developer draws on a game's canvas.

sprite artist   A JavaScript object with a draw() method that draws a sprite.

sprite behavior   See **behavior**.

sprite container   A general object that contains other sprites. May or may not be itself a sprite.

sprite sheet   A single image of all of a game's images (sprites). Putting all the images in a single image can greatly reduce the number of HTTP requests a game has to make at startup. That reduction in HTTP requests often results in much faster load times.

sprite sheet artist   A sprite artist that draws its sprite by copying rectangles from a sprite sheet into the game's canvas.

sprite-specific behavior   A behavior that can be used only with a specific sprite.

SQL injection   A code injection technique, used to attack data-driven applications, in which malicious SQL statements are inserted into an entry field for execution (for example, to dump the database contents to the attacker) (*Wikipedia*).

stroke and fill artist   A sprite artist that draws graphics primitives, such as lines, arcs, and curves. Snail Bait uses a stroke and fill artist to draw the game's platforms.

style change event   A point in time where the browser applies all changes made to CSS attributes.

SVG   Scalable Vector Graphics. A graphics system that maintains a list of objects to draw. See **retained-mode graphics**.

this reference   A reference to an object in one of the object's methods or its constructor. In JavaScript, unlike other languages, the this reference can change depending on who invoked an object's method.

time-based motion   Movement that is strictly based on time and independent of the current frame rate.

timeline   A developer tool with which you can monitor events, frame rates, and memory usage in realtime.

timestamp   A recording of the time at a particular moment.

toast   Information that a game displays to a player for a short time.

transducer functions   Functions that modify modify a game's overall elapsed time by converting time from one value to another. The transducer property takes the current time as a parameter and returns a presumably different value for the current time.

trigger   A condition that causes a behavior to take action; typically, a Boolean variable attached to a sprite.

time system   Software that calculates the current game time. Time systems can modify the flow of time throughout an entire game, which is useful for special effects and gameplay elements.

UI   User Interface.

USB   Universal Serial Bus.

validator module   A Node.js module that validates inputs, to prevent security breaches, for example, in Snail Bait, a player's name or score.

visible viewport   A mobile device screen on which a browser copies a scaled-to-fit contents of the **layout viewport**.

WASD   The w, a, s, and d keys. A convention used to control game play by letting right-handed players use the mouse and keyboard simultaneously. Not used in Snail Bait.

XSS   Cross-type scripting. A type of computer security vulnerability typically found in Web applications. XSS enables attackers to inject client-side script into Web pages viewed by other users (*Wikipedia*).

Index

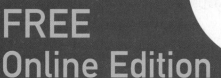
FREE
Online Edition

Safari
Books Online

Your purchase of **Core HTML5 2D Game Programming** includes access to a free online edition for 45 days through the **Safari Books Online** subscription service. Nearly every Prentice Hall book is available online through **Safari Books Online**, along with thousands of books and videos from publishers such as Addison-Wesley Professional, Cisco Press, Exam Cram, IBM Press, O'Reilly Media, Que, Sams, and VMware Press.

Safari Books Online is a digital library providing searchable, on-demand access to thousands of technology, digital media, and professional development books and videos from leading publishers. With one monthly or yearly subscription price, you get unlimited access to learning tools and information on topics including mobile app and software development, tips and tricks on using your favorite gadgets, networking, project management, graphic design, and much more.

Activate your FREE Online Edition at
informit.com/safarifree

STEP 1: Enter the coupon code: JYKUOXA.

STEP 2: New Safari users, complete the brief registration form.
Safari subscribers, just log in.

If you have difficulty registering on Safari or accessing the online edition,
please e-mail customer-service@safaribooksonline.com